Order! Order!

ORDER! ORDER!

60 YEARS OF

TODAY IN PARLIAMENT

Edited by

MARK D'ARCY

POLITICO'S

By arrangement with the BBC
BBC logo © BBC 1996
The BBC logo is a registered trade mark of the
British Broadcasting Corporation and is used under licence

First published in 2005 by
Politico's Publishing, an imprint of
Methuen Publishing Limited
11–12 Buckingham Gate
London
SW1E 6LB

10 9 8 7 6 5 4 3 2 1

Printed and bound in Great Britain by
St Edmundsbury Press, Bury St Edmunds, Suffolk

Methuen Publishing Limited Reg. No. 3543167

A CIP catalogue record for this book is available from the British Library.

ISBN 1 84275 139 5

Contents

Acknowledgements

FOR THE BEST part of eighteen months, I have pestered colleagues, MPs, peers and more or less anyone who came within range for their thoughts on and recollections of *Today in Parliament* and post-war parliamentary speeches. Members of Parliament, of either House, tend to be busy people, but many found the time to discuss these issues with me. In particular, I am grateful to the former Speakers Lord Weatherill and Lady Boothroyd, to Tam Dalyell, Sir Peter Tapsell, Richard Shepherd, Tony Benn and John Bercow for sharing their thoughts and their memories. Staff at *Today in Parliament*, past and present, have been interrogated ruthlessly, and I am thankful for their indulgence. Special thanks are due to Peter Hill, one of my illustrious predecessors as a BBC parliamentary correspondent, for allowing me to rummage through his considerable archive and draw on his extensive scholarship on the history of political broadcasting. Sean Magee of Methuen and Politico's Publishing provided invaluable guidance along the way. Above all, I would like to thank my wife, Anne, for her stoicism in enduring many months of excitable ranting about the latest speech to be disinterred from some musty volume of Hansard.

Foreword
BY TAM DALYELL

PARLIAMENT HAS ITS own idiom. Much can be learned from the language and arguments by which MPs and ministers make their case, defend their position or attack their opponents. This is the very essence of a democratic Parliament: the process by which policies and individuals are weighed and sometimes found wanting.

The House of Commons is an arena in which formidable debaters have come to grief and MPs with towering reputations outside Parliament have failed to make their mark. Success there requires a special blend of qualities.

This volume contains some of the most memorable speeches delivered during the 60-year life of BBC Radio Four's *Today in Parliament*. Here can be found Nye Bevan's compelling, lucid justification for creating the NHS, Edward Heath's arguments for joining the European Community, Denis Healey's denunciation of the Suez invasion and the furious debates around the Iraq war.

And beyond the great moments of national decision or crisis, there are the speeches of the inconvenient campaigners – Sydney Silverman battling against capital punishment, George Wigg's apparently reckless exposure of the Profumo scandal, or Humphrey Berkeley sacrificing his career in an attempt to legalise homosexuality.

Not all of them were great orators. But debate in the Commons requires much more than the ability to deliver a few ringing phrases in a powerful voice. The real masters of the chamber had the ability to marshal an argument and persuade colleagues – often on issues which aroused enormous emotion. And more than that, they needed the conviction and determination not to pursue the line of least resistance.

In the modern House of Commons, the very qualities that make the most effective parliamentarians – independence of judgement and originality of argument – often put them in direct conflict with the demands of party discipline. *Today in Parliament* will cover many conflicts in the years to come, but this will be the most important.

Introduction
AN INSTITUTION IS BORN –
OCTOBER 1945

IT SAYS SOMETHING for the way in which we are governed, that in July 1944, at the height of the Second World War, a month after D-Day, with flying bombs raining down on London and British troops locked in battle across the world, a Cabinet committee including senior ministers like Clement Attlee, the Deputy Prime Minister; Lord Woolton; Brendan Bracken; and Harry Crookshank met somewhere in Whitehall to consider the ramifications of the 1947 renewal of the BBC's charter.

The agenda that day included the possibility of broadcasting Parliament, a development enthusiastically supported, years ahead of its time, by the senior Conservative MP Leo Amery, who sent a detailed memo on the subject to the committee. Before the war, most MPs and certainly most ministers had tended to dismiss radio as a frivolous medium, more likely to mislead than to inform. Labour MPs, including the future Prime Minister Clement Attlee, distrusted the BBC because of its role during Ramsay MacDonald's National Government. The BBC had no reporter working in the Palace of Westminster – attempts to install one had been resisted by both politicians and newspaper correspondents – and its modest coverage of parliamentary news was based on the work of a Reuters journalist. When the BBC wanted to send an observer to the Commons, the Director General had to send a written request to the Speaker – and it was not always granted. On some occasions the Speaker consulted the party leaders, and access was refused if they thought the presence of broadcasters was 'inadvisable'.

The war changed attitudes, but slowly. In April 1940 two seats were reserved for the BBC, so long as the Serjeant at Arms was informed every morning whether they would be needed. The seats did not afford a good view of the Commons chamber, it was difficult to hear proceedings, and in any case the reporters were not permitted to take notes. After more lobbying, a special gallery was provided – but it was stressed that the arrangements were a specifically wartime measure, and would not necessarily continue in peacetime. And, even then, BBC correspondents did not have the same privileges as the lobby correspondents employed by the print media; they could not lurk in the lobby outside the chamber or seek contact with MPs.

But if the politicians were wary of broadcasters giving their own accounts of events in Parliament, some were becoming increasingly keen on the idea of allowing their own words to go on the air. There had been sporadic attempts to win permission to record great events before – the 1938 Budget speech, and Winston Churchill's early addresses as Prime Minister, but these had been dismissed almost out of hand. By early 1942, though, a Gallup poll had found that 65 per cent of the voters supported the recording and later broadcast of important Commons speeches by the BBC, so long as Parliament agreed. Churchill wanted a recording to be made of a statement on the war situation which he proposed to give after returning from consultations with President Roosevelt in the White House, after Pearl Harbor. The aim was partly to spare the great man – who had suffered a minor heart attack in Washington, although this was hushed up at the time – the strain of delivering the same speech twice, once in the Commons and once for the BBC, shortly after an arduous transatlantic journey. The idea was considered by the War Cabinet – under Attlee's chairmanship – and it was rejected with a fastidious shudder. 'The broadcast of Parliament generally was strongly deprecated,' the Cabinet minute concluded.[1] But on his return Churchill revived the proposal, on the advice of his Chief Whip that the Commons would almost certainly agree. That turned out to be over-optimistic. A question about the possible recording was asked by a Conservative MP, the appropriately named Captain Plugge, but the apparent parliamentary support for the idea faded, and Churchill was reluctant to press the point, eventually telling MPs he would not 'take it amiss in any way' if they refused to allow a recording.

But the extent of parliamentary coverage on the BBC news bulletins was now considerable. This was partly because there was a great deal to report – the progress of the war and the intrusion of wartime government into every facet of life meant there was plenty of direct and immediate public interest – and partly because of a conscious desire to provide a living reminder to the public that they were part of a democracy. The 6 p.m. bulletin on 10 June 1941, for example, included a detailed report on the debate on the fall of Crete, which ran to four pages of closely typed foolscap, quoting ten speakers, with a page and a half devoted to Mr Churchill.[2] All of this had to be read out in a single indigestible chunk by some hapless, if highly professional, newsreader.

A memo to the governors in 1941 described the process by which the parliamentary reports were compiled: 'A member of Reuters staff works exclusively for the BBC. He is an experienced parliamentary reporter who gives a full précis of questions and speeches. We speak to him on the telephone before lunch in case some item of news has been announced in the House, which might be used in the One O' Clock bulletin ... Our special Reuter report begins to come in early in the afternoon and ends about a quarter of an hour after the house has risen. This report is thoroughly reliable, but it does not go beyond summarising what has been said. No attempt is made to give the atmosphere of the House or to introduce any descriptive touches ...

'Every word we broadcast is part of a headline. The whole bulletin is in high light. We cannot bury part of the report which we neither want to put in the headlines nor to omit, in the comparative and decent obscurity of the *Times* parliamentary page. We work in the knowledge that what we choose for broadcasting gets immensely more publicity . . .'

The politicians had noticed too. A good indicator of the importance that was beginning to be attached to the broadcast reports was the volume of their complaints. Some were charming. R. A. Butler, then President of the Board of Education, remonstrated at the failure to report a speech from his (Labour) junior minister Chuter Ede: 'I am a little distressed . . . and cannot help feeling you would not have wished this to happen any more than I would . . .' Others were brutal. Quintin Hogg, the future Lord Hailsham, concluded his complaint about the reporting of a debate in 1943 saying: 'I do not know whether this was done from malice or incompetence, but I do think the time has come for you to take a more decided interest in impartiality.' On that particular complaint the governors were advised by the controller (news), A. P. Ryan, that 'Hogg is as inaccurate in his points of detail as he is sweeping in his conclusions. If our reporters are as light hearted in treatment of facts ... as Mr Hogg, I wonder what words Mr Hogg would find to describe their malice and competence.'[3]

Sixty years on, such exchanges continue, if not always with the same quality of syntax.

The BBC itself was eager to improve its coverage and in particular to place one of its correspondents in the Palace of Westminster itself. To those familiar with the vast extent of the BBC's Westminster operations in the early twenty-first century, the idea of a single, harassed reporter attempting to grapple with the proceedings of Lords and Commons and all the other business of Parliament is more than a little alarming. But it did at least demonstrate that the BBC's first parliamentary correspondent, E. R. Thompson, who was appointed in 1945, was indeed the thin end of a very considerable wedge. After the Commons chamber was destroyed by the Luftwaffe in 1941, MPs took over the Lords chamber, where they sat until 1950, with Thompson perched in a narrow gallery at the far end, often with knees of visitors to the public gallery jabbing into his back, and phoning in reports from a booth in the central lobby.[4] When the Commons returned to their rebuilt chamber, Thompson discovered the BBC had been allocated two seats in the front row of the new, enlarged press gallery, in line with the government front bench, a few feet above the Speaker's chair. Some press gallery traditionalists were outraged at the favour shown to the upstart broadcasters, but a meeting called to protest at the seat allocation degenerated into a fiasco. To this day, the same seats are occupied by BBC reporters, with Hansard on one side and the *Daily Telegraph* on the other.

A report on the BBC's parliamentary operations, put to the governors in March 1944, charted the growing pressure for a dedicated parliamentary report – so that proceedings in Westminster did not always have to compete for space in the news bulletins with the tumultuous events of the world war. And the new Director General, William Haley, supported the idea, although the vigour with which he pursued it suggested he did not want politicians specifying the form of any BBC programme, and wished to pre-empt them.

Like the Cabinet committee on the BBC's charter, Haley concluded that direct broadcasting of parliamentary proceedings would be difficult for ordinary listeners to understand, and sometimes downright misleading. He feared a sketch would simply open the way for endless complaints from irate parliamentarians, and instead opted for the idea of a daily fifteen-minute summary, instructing his officials to prepare plans as 'a matter of urgency'. The timing of this summary provoked considerable debate – a mid evening slot at 9 or 9.15 would be accessible to listeners, but there were anxieties about broadcasting a report before the main debate of the day had concluded. The recommended time was 11 p.m., but the Director General thought this would simply create 'pressure for a better time from the moment of its inception'. Finally a time of 10.45 p.m. was agreed.

So *Today in Parliament – TIP* – was born. Like the news bulletins, it was compiled at Broadcasting House, based on a straight précis of the day's debates and questions from an agency, now the Press Association, but was informed by a daily phone call to E. R. Thompson, who advised 'on the mood of the House'. The PA material was edited and the final script was read out by a newsreader – with a last-minute panic to include the results of late votes. The first edition was broadcast on 9 October 1945, the day Parliament reassembled after the long summer recess. This was the era of the great reforming Labour government, elected in the landslide of 1945, but that first edition began with the simple statement that: 'The House of Commons reassembled in strength this afternoon, to get down to the serious business of the session.' It described the unfamiliar scene of Churchill sitting on the opposition bench, facing the new Prime Minister, Attlee. It reported on Emmanuel Shinwell receiving a rough ride over petrol supplies, then a debate on price controls, and questions about giving British nationality to Polish citizens who were unwilling to return to their Russian-controlled homeland.

That very first edition ended by describing the debut of a young Labour politician who was to dominate politics for much of the next 30 years. Mr J. H. Wilson, junior minister at the Ministry of Works, plodded through a rather pedestrian answer to a debate on MPs' facilities. Harold Wilson (for it was he) became a much more exciting parliamentarian in later years.

The content of that first programme, if not the exact format or issues, would not be unusual 60 years later.

Undeterred by the BBC's decision to broadcast a daily report of parliamentary proceedings, the Labour government did insert a requirement to report Parliament into the corporation's new charter. 'The Governors might change their mind. They might decide not to do it,' explained the Leader of the House, Herbert Morrison. To this day *TIP* is the only BBC programme directly mandated by the charter.

The new programme was clearly under close scrutiny from on high. After three days, Haley issued a firm rebuke, warning that expressions like 'tartly' and 'pointedly' should not percolate into its reports. 'They are both comment and the beginning of a sketch,' he added. A later edict prohibited the inclusion of MPs' 'undistinguished wisecracks'.

In Westminster, meanwhile, E. R. Thompson was summoned to an audience with the Leader of the Lords, Lord Addison, to explain why a speech by the Lord Chancellor, Lord Jowitt, had not been reported. Addison, who seemed rather embarrassed by the whole business, was told the speech had not added much to the debate and had been pushed out by other material.[5] There was also a sharp spat with the Board of Deputies of British Jews, when *TIP* described the Labour MP Sydney Silverman as a 'Jewish MP'. The board, quite reasonably, pointed out that Jewish MPs 'are not elected as a Jews, they do not vote as Jews – they are elected as British citizens and they vote according to their political creed'. The point was taken.

In *Tribune*, a year after *TIP* started, MP Jennie Lee, wife of Nye Bevan, complained at the tone of its reporting: 'A housing debate that had taken just over six and a half hours, was being compressed into a quarter of an hour's summary. I would not have liked the job. Deciding what to put in and what to leave out is a highly selective affair . . . From the BBC, I got the impression of a compact, well sustained debate with the [Labour] Government coming off a bad second best. I got no impression of the empty Tory benches, of the failure of Mr Churchill or Mr Eden to turn up in the House of Commons and repeat the type of housing speeches they have been making in the country. I was surprised that some contributions to the debate which I thought quite first class were entirely ignored, and other speeches reduced to a meaningless line or two . . . I am quite certain I would be unable to do justice to a full day's debate in fifteen minutes. But I assert with equal emphasis that I know of no one else who is capable of that impossible feat. A parliamentary wavelength is the obvious answer.'

In those early years, two and a half million people listened to *TIP*, and two years after its birth, its morning sister programme, *Yesterday in Parliament* – *YIP* – took to the air. *YIP* started life as a revised *TIP*, broadcast in the morning on what was then the Light Programme, updated with any votes or other developments since *TIP* the night before, and with the word 'today' changed to 'yesterday'. Broadcast at a more accessible hour, its audience came to outstrip that of its parent programme – whose audience had dropped to a more modest level – and it became a part of many people's morning routine, a daily update on the activities of MPs and peers over the breakfast table or in the commuter's car. One of the newest additions to the armoury is the 'short *YIP*', a five-minute package broadcast at 6.45 a.m. on Radio Four's *Today* programme, where an audience of 2.7 million can hear an extract of the previous day's parliamentary business. This may be some vital debate of the day, or perhaps something quirky from the reliably eccentric Lords' Question Time. The trick is to offer something that has not been all over news bulletins for the previous eight hours – so, for example, when some great debate has commanded national attention, the short *YIP* might focus on the contributions of backbenchers, or might shift to some entirely different subject.

Of course, the style of the programmes has evolved, especially since 1978, when Parliament agreed to sound broadcasting, allowing clips of speeches – 'actuality' in broadcasters' jargon – to be used to illustrate *TIP* and *YIP*, and of course news programmes.

For *TIP* and *YIP* the effect was revolutionary. The programme now starts with the Speaker intoning his immemorial call of 'Order, order' – which is updated at the accession of each new Speaker. That first programme of the new broadcasting era began with the Welsh accents of Mr Speaker Thomas, to be succeeded by the different tones of Bernard Weatherill, Betty Boothroyd and Michael Martin.

Even within the requirements of the deliberately neutral scripting that *TIP* retains to this day, the inclusion of clips of speeches gave a far more atmospheric quality to the reporting. But there were limitations. MPs were just as cautious about the menace of editorialising journalists as they had been in Attlee's day, and one of the rules for handling Commons sound was that no excerpt could be internally edited. It is normal radio practice to clean up recorded material to make it as clear and crisp as possible. Normally a recording which said something like 'The right hon. gentleman is, if I may say so, er, in this instance, um, without beating about the bush, er, failing in his er, duty, um, to the nation,' could be edited into 'The right hon. gentleman is failing in his duty to the nation.' It's known in the trade as 'de-umming'. But for parliamentary material this process is forbidden.

This at least ensures that *TIP* staff are not confronted with the problem of misleading the public by making parliamentarians sound more fluent that they actually are. And some MPs would be, frankly, unrecognisable if divested of their trademark speech patterns – the author once attempted, as an editing exercise, to remove the 'ers' from a speech by the late Donald Dewar, who ummed and erred between almost every word. The result sounded bizarre – and nothing like Mr Dewar. The rules do mean that it is editorially much harder to include important contributions from the less fluent speakers – an important point delivered in a wearisome way is unlikely to make much impact with the listeners.

The inclusion of recorded excerpts of Commons and Lords business weakened the case for *TIP* and *YIP* to be 'voiced' by newsreaders. *TIP* had ceased to be a demanding half-hour read, but it was nearly 20 years before the newsreaders were replaced as presenters by the parliamentary correspondents who actually wrote their scripts and compiled the reports on individual parts of the day's business. That change was made at the end of 1996. At the same time the house style became a little less formal. *TIP*'s closing incantation 'and that concludes our report on today's proceedings in Parliament', became the rather less stuffy-sounding 'and that was today in Parliament'. The style of *YIP* had already changed to become a parliamentary sketch, ranging across the business of the Commons, the Lords and the increasingly important select committees. MPs are perhaps less keen on a more sardonic look at their activities – but it is worth pointing out that, while every national newspaper has ditched its daily parliamentary pages, with their straight reports of routine debates, many retain a sketch-writer. The readers may not wish to wade through long accounts of debates, but they enjoy a bit of deft irony sprinkled on the heads of their representatives.

But the key factor for *TIP* and *YIP* remains the reliance on expert parliamentary reporters. E. R. Thompson was just the first in an apostolic succession of BBC political staff – which included such luminaries as Conrad Voss Bark, who would take a perfect shorthand note on one side of his notebook while designing fishing flies on the other. He would then deliver lucid accounts of events – often direct from his shorthand pad – from a tiny cubbyhole in a cellar, known as 'the Tardis'. Now the BBC has an army of political correspondents, and a phalanx of more specialised parliamentary correspondents, whose main function is to compile *TIP* and *YIP*.

For them, a close study of Parliament and the Westminster subculture is essential. Simply identifying speakers can be a challenge. *TIP* reporters monitoring debates on the TV feed will often shout out to colleagues to identify some unfamiliar MP – it might be someone who seldom speaks or someone who has shaved off a beard, lost a lot of weight, or changed their hairstyle. In the Lords press gallery the public, who sit close by, can surely hear the *sotto voce* mutters of 'Pearson of Rannoch' or 'Wallace of Saltaire' as the more experienced hands in the Lords put names to unfamiliar faces for their less erudite colleagues.

Then there are issues of procedure and context. The bare words spoken in a debate seldom convey the complete picture. Parliamentary oratory is often in code, and the meaning needs elaboration for those not initiated into the mysteries of political discourse or familiar with the individual histories of hundreds of MPs and peers. Considerable technical skills are equally important – to boost the sound of a shouted intervention only just picked up by the network of microphones which hang above MPs, or to delicately edge into a clip of an MP who makes some important point in a gabble of indistinct syllables.

Reporting Parliament combines the functions of a theatre critic, a sports reporter and a political nerd. And for all the regular loose talk about the declining relevance of Parliament in an increasingly presidential political system, the Commons can still break ministers and defy governments. The traumatic Labour rebellions over Iraq, university top-up Fees, NHS trusts in the 2001–05 Parliament are not aberrations but events in the classic tradition of Parliament – murky concoctions of awkward principle, tribal loyalties, procedural manoeuvre and high drama.

This book covers some of these moments. It does not attempt a systematic survey of the great speeches of the *TIP* era. It does not purport to include every significant speech from the last 60 years, or even every notable speaker. That would take a much bigger tome. This is my own idiosyncratic selection: an attempt to give a flavour of parliamentary – and mostly Commons – speaking. The moments when MPs run into trouble, expose the truth, take mighty decisions or make fools of themselves.

The House of Commons, as the Labour firebrand John Maxton observed, is a sentient place. It is a community, full of enmities, friendships, rivalries, undercurrents and ambitions. Perhaps it is a touch too fond of its immemorial traditions, but maybe it is right to beware of dispelling its own special magic. And it can be revelatory.

Note on Sources

The speeches which appear in this book are drawn from Hansard, the official parliamentary report. Hansard does not give a completely verbatim report of what is said in the Commons or Lords – a certain amount of tidying up takes place to ensure that its account is intelligible. A straight transcription of a tape recording of proceedings would not read anything like as clearly as the Hansard version. MPs do sometimes dispute its reports, and corrections are occasionally made, but for the most part, it is accepted as an accurate but not quite verbatim account of what is said. Interruptions and noises off are normally only reported where the MP speaking or the Speaker responds to them. Great moments of disorder, like the moment when an infuriated Michael Heseltine waved the mace, the symbol of the Commons' authority, at Labour MPs, are reported rather antiseptically as 'interruptions'.

One

SCANDAL AND CRISIS

WHEN SCANDAL STRIKES or a policy rebounds on a government, the Commons can make or break the minister – or Prime Minister – responsible. But parliamentary big-game hunters, those seeking the head of a premier or a Cabinet minister to adorn their trophy cabinet, need to stalk their prey carefully and aim their shot precisely. Otherwise they may end up being trampled.

This chapter runs the gamut from moments of grave national crisis, like the announcement of the three-day week, to issues which question the competence and honesty of a government, like the arms to Iraq affair. The art of the parliamentarian responding to such circumstances is to get the tone right. The career of John Nott, Margaret Thatcher's Defence Secretary at the time of the Falklands War, never recovered from a nervy flash of partisanship against Labour during the tense debate which followed the Argentine invasion.

The real greats know when restraint is deadlier than attack, statesmanship more wounding than mockery. The speeches surrounding the Profumo case illustrate the point. This was a parliamentary scandal where each major act, the provocation, the fatal sin and the deadly blows to Harold Macmillan and ultimately to the Conservative Party all took place on the floor of the Commons. The accusers did not rush into a denunciation, they provoked Profumo into charging into a trap, and then used his fall to mortally wound a Prime Minister.

Perhaps the greatest challenge of all comes when the threat is from one's own side. Offending the opposition is all in a day's work; giving an opening to enemies within can be disastrous. For all the cunning of George Wigg and the subtlety of Harold Wilson, the killer blow against Macmillan over Profumo came from an enemy on the Conservative benches, who wielded the stiletto with exquisite cruelty.

At the other end of the scale, Tony Benn's appeal to Mr Speaker Weatherill to reverse a ruling was a masterpiece of niceness, bringing murmurs of approval from across the House. He invoked proud parliamentary traditions and suggested a face-saving way out, rather than committing the gaucherie of challenging a Speaker head on.

Of course, sometimes the target bites back. Roy Jenkins's rebuttal of a personal motion of censure following the escape from prison of the Soviet spy George Blake did wonders for his stature in the Labour Party and embarrassed his Tory critics – and in particular Edward Heath.

And occasionally great crises produce not a forensic speech or an impassioned denunciation, but simply a cry of pain. Gerry Fitt deserves to be ranked as one of the great political heroes of the postwar era for his unswerving opposition to terrorism in Northern Ireland. He was a convinced socialist, and his agony at having to cast his crucial vote against James Callaghan's Labour government, in the great no confidence debate of 1979, drips from the pages of Hansard.

'There is not an hon. member in the House, nor a journalist in the Press Gallery, nor do I believe there is a person in the Public Gallery who, in the last few days has not heard rumour upon rumour involving a member of the Government front bench.'

George Wigg goads the Secretary of of State for War into a fatal lie: 21 March 1963

As part of Harold Wilson's kitchen cabinet – his coterie of advisers, court-iers and odd-job men – George Wigg helped Labour exploit the series of murky sexual and spying scandals which dogged the final years of Harold Macmillan's premiership. As Wilson's Home Secretary, Roy Jenkins thought Wigg a 'half comic, half sinister' figure.[1] 'A licensed rifler in Whitehall dustbins and interferer in security matters', but he had his moments of real influence.

Wigg had first made his name as an awkward squad backbencher in the 1950s, exploiting Commons procedure to harass the Conservative government when an exhausted Labour leadership could not muster the energy to take it on. Irate Conservatives called his manoeuvres 'Wiggery-pokery'. He also emerged as a formidable inquisitor, particularly on defence matters, and the current system of annual Army Acts, authorising the continuation of the armed forces, owes much to his determination to reform an archaic legal framework.

This speech was perhaps his most important single Commons intervention, when, with a fine grasp of parliamentary procedure and legal niceties, he contrived to bring the Profumo affair into the public domain. John Profumo, the Secretary of State for War, was involved in a sexual relationship with a 'model', Christine Keeler. Worse, he shared her favours with a Soviet naval attaché, Captain Ivanov. This tangled set of relationships was beginning to emerge into public view because of a trial involving another of Keeler's boyfriends, a West Indian called John Edgecombe, who had shot at her in a row over her preference for yet another boyfriend, another West Indian, 'Lucky' Gordon. Keeler herself was in hiding, and negotiating to sell her story to the press.

All this was taking place against the background of the Vassal affair – in which a gay junior Admiralty clerk had been exposed as a Soviet spy, and questions had been raised about his relationship with a junior minister at the Admiralty – and a more general atmosphere of scandal. London seethed with rumours of high society orgies and dinners where masked naked Cabinet ministers bore placards inviting guests to beat them. But despite the spicy combination of sex, drugs, society scandal and top-level espionage, the rumours about Profumo had not yet been published in the mainstream press, although some of the details had appeared in a small private-circulation newsletter, *Westminster Confidential*. The case lent itself to Wigg's particular investigative talents. He tabulated the facts and sent a detailed memorandum to Wilson. But as Wigg recorded in his memoirs,[2] the leader of the opposition wanted 'to play it cool' and suggested Wigg pursued matters on his own responsibility.

By Thursday, 21 March, Wigg believed the moment had come. A Labour MP, Ben Parkin, had made an oblique reference to the Profumo rumours in a standing committee, in the course of a discussion of London's sewers. His cryptic remarks about missing models being obtained for the convenience of a minister of the Crown merely bewildered the chairman. Meanwhile, the *Daily Express* ran a story suggesting that Profumo had offered his resignation 'for personal reasons', and coincidentally placed next to it a picture of Keeler, with the headline 'Vanished'. Clearly, the full story was about to bubble to the surface.

Wigg had prepared for this eventuality by seeking detailed legal advice from his friend and fellow Wilson adviser Arnold Goodman on a form of words that would be neither libellous nor unfair. He seized his chance during a debate on the imprisonment of two journalists who had refused to disclose their sources to the tribunal investigating the Vassal case. Most of his discussion of that case is omitted. This extract begins when he turns, rather awkwardly, from the danger of injustice in the Vassal proceedings to the rumours swirling around Profumo.

I WENT TO THE Vassall Tribunal with some prejudice, for I was in favour of a Select Committee as against this particular form of inquiry. I listened to the proceedings, and I must say that the fact that the Tribunal did the job it did was due to a peculiarly English set of circumstances. In my opinion, the instrument was a bad one, but Lord Radcliffe and his two colleagues are wise and good men. They leant over backwards in their treatment of men who were in a very difficult position. They treated those men as kindly as was possible – and, of course – it goes without saying that they treated them courteously. But they had a job to do. They were not there in order to bring the mailed fist of totalitarianism into it, but to do a job that the House of Commons had by unanimous resolution authorised them to do. If hon. members now grumble about the results, I ask them where they were on 14 November, when we were raising our voices against this particular form of tribunal.

So far, so good. Here was a set of rumours that gained and gained in strength, consumed men's reputations might, in fact, have destroyed them and which here infringed on the security of the State. But are we quite sure that the same thing is not happening again? There is not an hon. member in the House, nor a journalist in the Press Gallery, nor do I believe there is a person in the Public Gallery who, in the last few days has not heard rumour upon rumour involving a member of the Government front bench. The press has got as near as it could – it has shown itself willing to wound but afraid to strike. This all comes about because of the Vassall Tribunal. In actual fact these great press Lords, these men who control great instruments of public opinion and of power, do not have the guts to discharge the duty that they are now claiming for themselves.

That being the case, I rightly use the privilege of the House of Commons – that is what it is given to me for – to ask the Home Secretary, who is the senior member of the Government on the Treasury Bench now, to go to the Dispatch Box – he knows that the rumour to which I refer relates to Miss Christine Keeler and Miss Davies and a shooting by a West Indian – and, on behalf of the Government, categorically deny the truth of these rumours. On the other hand, if there is anything in them, I urge him to ask the Prime Minister to do what was not done in the Vassall case – set up a Select Committee so that these things can be dissipated, and the honour of the Minister concerned freed from the imputations and innuendoes that are being spread at the present time.

It is no good for a democratic state that rumours of this kind should spread and be inflated, and go on. Everyone knows what I am referring to, but up to now nobody has brought the matter into the open. I believe that the Vassall Tribunal need never have been set up had the nettle been firmly grasped much earlier on. We have lost some time, and I plead with the Home Secretary to use that Dispatch Box to clear up all the mystery and speculation over this particular case.

'There was no impropriety whatsoever in my acquaintanceship with Miss Keeler.'

John Profumo lies to the Commons: 22 March 1963

After the speeches by George Wigg and others the day before, an alarmed government decided to squash the rumours around Profumo once and for all. He and his solicitor were summoned to a late-night conclave with the Law Officers; the Leader of the House, Iain Macleod; and Bill Deedes, the Minister without Portfolio, who was in charge of the government's press relations. He denied any relationship – although he had already admitted to the Chief Whip, Martin Redmayne, that he had been alone with Keeler in Ward's flat. He also denied that the word 'darling', with which he began an affectionate letter to Keeler, which was then in circulation, amounted to a confession of adultery. Macleod later told a journalist friend at the *Spectator* that he had posed the question in the most blunt terms: 'Look Jack, the basic question is, did you fuck her?' Startlingly, they believed him .[3]

The meeting agreed the statement Profumo delivered later that morning, including the fatal sentence denying any 'impropriety'.

WITH PERMISSION, SIR, I wish to make a personal statement. I understand that in the debate on the Consolidated Fund Bill last night, under protection of Parliamentary Privilege, the hon. gentlemen the members for Dudley [George Wigg] and for Coventry East [Richard Crossman] and the hon. lady the member for Blackburn [Barbara Castle], opposite, spoke of rumours connecting a Minister with a Miss Keeler and a recent trial at the Central Criminal court. It was alleged that people in high places might have been responsible for concealing information concerning the disappearance of a witness and the perversion of justice.

I understand that my name has been connected with the rumours about the disappearance of Miss Keeler.

I would like to take this opportunity of making a personal statement about these matters.

I last saw Miss Keeler in December, 1961, and I have not seen her since. I have no idea where she is now. Any suggestion that I was in any way connected with or responsible for her absence from the trial at the Old Bailey is wholly and completely untrue.

My wife and I first met Miss Keeler at a house party in July 1961, at Cliveden.

Among a number of people there was Dr Stephen Ward, whom we already knew slightly, and a Mr Ivanov, who was an attaché at the Russian Embassy.

The only other occasion that my wife or I met Mr Ivanov was for a moment at the official reception for Major Gagarin[4] at the Soviet Embassy.

My wife and I had a standing invitation to visit Dr Ward.

Between July and December 1961, I met Miss Keeler on about half a dozen occasions at Dr Ward's flat, when I called to see him and his friends. Miss Keeler and I were on friendly terms. There was no impropriety whatsoever in my acquaintanceship with Miss Keeler.

Mr Speaker, I have made this personal statement because of what was said in the House last evening by the three hon. members, and which, of course, was protected by privilege. I shall not hesitate to issue writs for libel and slander if scandalous allegations are made or repeated outside the House.

George Wigg immediately realised it was 'a barefaced lie'.[5] He soon accumulated evidence to prove it.

'The indolent nonchalance of the Prime Minister's attitude . . .'

Harold Wilson blames Macmillan for the Profumo scandal: 17 June 1963

Profumo's resignation and admission that he had lied to the House in his personal statement brought the witches' brew of rumour and innuendo around the government to a boil. Superficially, this might have seemed to make Macmillan and his ministers an easy target, but as he prepared for a debate on the implications of the resignation, Harold Wilson was mindful that the public mood might change. He did not want to be caught stirring the cauldron or gloating over its contents.

There were other problems too. Although the government's embarrassment was acute, no one really believed there had been any leak of sensitive information via the Profumo–Keeler–Ivanov axis. And for all the rumours that other Cabinet ministers were somehow implicated, nothing had emerged that even began to substantiate such tales.

Wilson therefore had to be extremely precise in his attack. He dealt fleetingly with the moral issues of lying to the House and the Ward–Keeler circle, and focused on the narrow issue where Macmillan was most vulnerable: that he should have known that Profumo lied when he denied having a sexual relationship with Keeler; and that he had failed to come to grips with the scandal when the warning signs emerged. The comparison with Attlee's efficient dispatch of the Belcher affair was particularly deadly.

His peroration, describing a decadent aristocratic caste casually exploiting working-class girls and covering up the risks its conduct posed to national security, encapsulated the appeal he was trying to build for Labour as a democratic, modernising party. (Although history never quite presented him with a similar scandal, Tony Blair did something similar in opposition, 35 years later.)

T HIS IS A DEBATE without precedent in the annals of this House. It arises from disclosures which have shocked the moral conscience of the nation. There is clear evidence of a sordid underworld network, the extent of which cannot yet be measured and which we cannot debate today because of proceedings elsewhere.

I believe that the feelings that have been aroused throughout the nation are similarly echoed in this House and that there are many hon. and right hon. gentlemen opposite who are as sick at heart by what has been disclosed as those on this side of the House. There is the personal and family tragedy of a man lately our colleague here. However much we condemn him – and we must condemn him – that is not the issue today.

What concerns us directly is that the former Secretary of State for War, faced with rumours and innuendoes that could not be ignored, chose deliberately to lie to this House, and in circumstances in which this House allows freedom of personal statement without question or debate on the premise that what is said is said in good faith.

What does concern us, too, is the question whether any other Minister in any sense connived at this action through foreknowledge or, being in a position to ascertain the truth, failed to take the steps that were necessary to fulfil the duty that he owed to the House.

What concerns us, also, is whether a man in a position of high trust, privy to the most secret information available to a Government, through a continuing association with this squalid network, imperilled our national security or created conditions in which a continuing risk to our security was allowed to remain.

We are not here as a court of morals, though the nation as a whole cannot escape the responsibility so to act. But questions affecting national security, questions affecting the duty of Ministers to this House, must be pressed and probed today, and this debate, in one form or another, must continue until the truth is known so far as it can ever be known.

Much has been known to hon. members and to the press for many months. Many of us have witnessed the ceaseless interweaving of innuendo and rumour. We on this side of the House knew what was being said.

I feel that I must begin by recounting to the House the facts about the information which reached us, the conception we held of the duty of an Opposition in such matters, and the action we took. We did not canvass or propagate rumours about personal conduct, but where security questions were raised, and, later, where there was a question of the inaccuracy of statements made in this House, we felt that we had a clear duty, and any other Opposition would have had that same duty.

Here Wilson gave a detailed account of the chain of events which led Stephen Ward, the 'society osteopath' at the centre of the allegations, to contact George Wigg, the Labour MP for Dudley and a close Wilson ally, who had close connections with the security services.

I had received from my hon. friend the member for Dudley a note about his very long conversation with Ward. I shall not weary the House with this. It is a nauseating document, taking the lid off a corner of the London underworld of vice, dope, marijuana, blackmail and counter-blackmail, violence, petty crime, together with references to Mr Profumo and the Soviet attaché. Quite frankly, I felt when I read it that if it were published as a fiction paperback in America hon. members would have thrown it away, not only for what it contained, but as being overdrawn and beyond belief even as credible fiction.

As I was myself going to Washington I asked my right hon. and learned friend the member for Newport [Sir Frank Soskice, soon to be Home Secretary in Wilson's first Cabinet] as a former Attorney-General, to examine the document and, if necessary, question my hon. friend the member for Dudley to see if, *prima facie*, it should be sent to the Prime Minister. When I got back from Washington some days later my right hon. and learned friend reported that it should certainly be sent to the Prime Minister and it was duly transmitted to the right hon. gentleman through the respective Chief Whips.

Again, knowledge of this was kept to the four of us concerned on this side of the House, and not a word reached the press then or subsequently until the most recent events. I think that the House must realise this: one word from us on this side in this House and we should have released an explosion as great as we have seen in the last fortnight. But we decided that, although the documents in our possession were, in a sense, dynamite, and would have touched off such an explosion, it was our duty, as a responsible Opposition, to hand over all this information to the Prime Minister, who has first responsibility for security, and not to make public use of them.

The implication of this was, of course, that the Prime Minister would handle his side of the matter with a corresponding sense of responsibility. He replied to me on 17 April. I have wondered whether I should quote these letters, but I think that it is all right because, indeed, some have already been printed in the public press. I do not complain, because this matter is one of public concern, and I know that the Prime Minister does not object to my quoting from them. Not all of them, in any case, were marked confidential.

The right hon. gentleman wrote:

'My Chief Whip has given to me the letter and enclosure from you dated April 9 and dealing with George Wigg's conversation with a Mr Stephen Ward.

I will ask the appropriate authorities to have an examination made of this information and will get in touch with you later on if this seems necessary.'

I think that the House will note a somewhat casual approach to a very serious allegation. Above all, there is the reference to 'a' Mr Stephen Ward, as though Ward were an unknown person.

After all, five Ministers had spent half the night just before that with the then Secretary of State and Ward had been quoted as the chief witness to them of the respectability of the Secretary of State's proceedings. Yet we have this reference to 'a' Mr Stephen Ward, as though he were an unknown person in whom neither the Government nor the security services could take any possible interest.

This one word – indeed, the letter as a whole – was symptomatic of the indolent nonchalance of the Prime Minister's attitude to this: the attitude of 'what has this to do with me?' That is an attitude which we have seen since, as well. Some weeks later, having heard nothing from him, I tried again, and on 14 May he wrote to me: 'There seems to be nothing in the papers you sent which requires me to take any action.'

Nine days later, on 23 May, I received a further letter from Ward, who wrote also to the Home Secretary complaining of police inquiries directed towards his patients and saying that, because of these inquiries, he now felt it no longer necessary to conceal the fact that Mr Profumo had lied to the House. I immediately sent this letter, also, to the Prime Minister and learnt, at the same time, that Ward had sent a summary of the letter he sent to the Home Secretary to the entire British press. From this moment it was a matter of common knowledge, though even so, for the reasons I have mentioned, the press did not publish that summary.

The following Monday I asked to see the Prime Minister to discuss not this letter from Ward, but the right hon. gentleman's own letter of 14 May, in which he said that no further action would be taken on the original material. The right hon. gentleman and I were accompanied at this conversation by the Patronage Secretary[6] and by the Opposition Chief Whip. The right hon. gentleman maintained the attitude expressed in his letter. Nor did Ward's letter to the Home Secretary seem to make any impression on him in this respect. I say frankly to the House that I was completely dissatisfied with the reply I had from the Prime Minister and with the position and I drew a very sharp contrast with the Prime Minister I had served under, Earl Attlee.

I told the Prime Minister that John Belcher had been crucified, his career broken, for no other crime than his unwise choice of social contacts, though at no time in the case had there been any suggestion of any risk or breach of security.

Belcher was a junior minister in the Attlee government. He had accepted gifts including sherry, burgundy and whisky – precious commodities in postwar

Britain – from various business interests. Wilson, President of the Board of Trade at the time, went to the police with allegations about Belcher's conduct, and a tribunal of inquiry was set up. Belcher had to resign as a minister and MP and returned to his former job as a railway clerk.

No one complained about that. But in this case all we got from the Prime Minister was that no action seemed to be called for.

As a result of this interview, the Prime Minister, on 30 May, wrote a further letter to me in which he said:

'I have been thinking about our talk on Monday. I am sure in my own mind that the security aspect of the Ward case has been fully and efficiently watched, but I think it important that you should be in no doubt about it.'

The right hon. gentleman told me of his decision to invite the Lord Chancellor to make an inquiry and require the information necessary from the police and the security authorities, and to report back to him.

I repeat what he said in his letter.

'I am sure in my own mind that the security aspect of the Ward case has been fully and efficiently watched, but I think it important that you should be in no doubt about it.'

So Lord Dilhorne[7] was set to work right through the Recess in order to satisfy the Leader of the Opposition who, inconveniently, was not so easy to satisfy as the Prime Minister, who was in charge of the nation's security.

This was the Thursday before the Recess. In the afternoon, I saw the Prime Minister across the Floor of the House in his place for Questions. I pushed across to him a hastily scribbled note saying that in my view he should immediately announce the commission with which he had entrusted the Lord Chancellor, in order to allay public anxiety, which was very great, because he knew that the press had already received the Ward statement. I received an acknowledgment from the Prime Minister's secretary later that evening – the Prime Minister, of course, was going away.

In fact, it was only last Monday, ten days later, when the storm had broken, that the Prime Minister, by this time very much on the defensive, did announce that the Lord Chancellor had been asked to make these inquiries. I ask why did he not announce it at the time he wrote to me about it. *The Times*, last Tuesday, had the answer, because the Prime Minister was gambling on the issue never seeing the light of day.

This has been the right hon. gentleman's attitude right through. After the Vassall case he felt that he could not stand another serious security case involving a ministerial resignation and he gambled desperately and hoped that nothing would ever come out. For political reasons he was gambling with national security. I think that this is why he was at such pains to demonstrate to me his unflappability and his unconcern.

Now I will tell the House exactly what our attitude was on the basis of the material that had reached us. Our attitude was not that there was any evidence of a leak of secret information. Let us be clear on this: whether there was a breach of security at any time, whether there was a leak of information, is something we shall never know. There cannot be any assurance on this point and I shall later explain why. There is no means now of finding out.

From that point of view, the inquiries of both the security authorities and the Lord Chancellor were bound to be fruitless, because the Prime Minister does not know whether there was any leak at all. He cannot know. What we were concerned with was clear evidence that, leaks or no leaks, there was a standing condition of a security risk as long as the Secretary of State for War was part of this quadrilateral made up of Miss Keeler, Ward, the self-confessed Soviet intermediary, and Ivanov, the Soviet attaché.

I did not myself think Ward to be a spy. He was too unstable for the Soviet authorities, who usually make use of better material; but he was undoubtedly a tool, an instrument, and his unique access to people in high places made him useful to them. But for a Secretary of State, a member of the Defence Committee of the Cabinet, with full access to all military secrets and to the military secrets of our allies, to be part of this dingy quadrilateral reveals a degree of security risk that no Prime Minister could tolerate for one moment after the facts were conveyed to him. I hope, at any rate, that there will be general agreement on that question throughout the House – that no Prime Minister could tolerate this condition of security risk for one moment after the facts were conveyed to him.

It was on 27 March that I gave the Prime Minister the information to which I have referred, eleven weeks before my insistence on an inquiry eventually forced the matter into the open – I think that there is common agreement that this matter was forced into the open as a result of the Lord Chancellor sending for the former Secretary of State for War. There were eleven weeks between then and the Prime Minister's receiving even my material – and I would hope that he was receiving material before I handed in any on this question.

Nor was it the first material that he had had. What I have to ask him is – and I hope that the Prime Minister or his Parliamentary Private Secretary will take full note of the questions being put to him, because we shall want a straight answer to every one of these questions before the debate ends – first, why did he not accept the Secretary of State's resignation when he knew the degree of security risk? Was it offered by the Secretary of State and refused by the Prime Minister? If it was not offered, why did the Prime Minister not demand that resignation? We cannot escape the conclusion that the answer to this question is that politics, and not security, came first, and because a born gambler does not operate that way.

I must now ask the Prime Minister how often he met the Secretary of State to discuss any of these questions during the past two years. Perhaps he will tell us the dates and what transpired. I am sure that he must realise that his was the responsibility in this matter and that this particular responsibility cannot be delegated to other Ministers. He had the responsibility, both as head of the security services and as the Prime Minister who appoints, and, indeed, sacks, Ministers who do not prove satisfactory. But for eleven weeks, to my certain knowledge – and this is clear from the letters I have quoted and it must have been for longer than that – the Prime Minister refused to accept that there was a security risk.

Does he now accept that there was a security risk during that period? I hope that he will tell us this, because on television on Thursday night Lord Hailsham said to Mr McKenzie:

'Well, of course there's a security problem. Don't be so silly. A Secretary of State cannot have a woman shared with a spy – if he was a spy – without giving rise to a security risk. The question is not whether there was a security risk, but whether there was an actual breach of security – be sensible.'

Lord Poole, on Saturday, said:

'As we now know, there was from the start a security risk – a serious security risk.'

Does the Prime Minister accept that now because he did not do so the last time I met him?

This risk had been there for more than two years and no amount of the press briefing which we have had in the last two or three days, no amount of Cabinet manoeuvring, no committee meetings upstairs, will disguise the fact that there opposite me is the man responsible for this continuing risk.

We shall be told. We have been told, and we may expect this to be the central theme of the Prime Minister's speech, that, of course, there was a risk, but there was no leak. That is what the Press has been assiduously briefed to say in the last 24 hours. How do we know that there was no leak? We cannot know; we shall never know. Unless the security forces knew about the relationship with this foursome – Ward, Ivanov, the Secretary of State for War and Miss Keeler –

unless they tapped every telephone call to any of the four, unless they monitored every conversation between them or any pair of them, no one can know what information was handed over from one person to another. No one can know this. Yet the Prime Minister told me in his letter of 30 May, only a few days ago:

'I am sure in my own mind that the security aspect of the Ward case has been fully and efficiently watched.'

Were they watched? He has to tell us this. The Prime Minister knows that it is a standing instruction in the security services that no Minister can be followed without the Prime Minister's express permission. Was it given in this case and, if so, will the Prime Minister tell us on what date permission was given to follow the Secretary of State for War? If the House accepts, as Lord Hailsham accepts and as Lord Poole accepts, that there was a continuing security risk as long as these two were meeting, the Prime Minister's statement that they were being efficiently watched cannot apply unless he gave his assent to the Secretary of State being watched.

When we say that there was a security risk we mean that through a personal defect of character, or a perverted political or other loyalty, or through the possibility of intolerable pressure, or through cupidity or financial need, or through a personal or family relationship, an individual is more liable than his fellows to disclose information. That is what we mean by a security risk. To diagnose such cases is the whole basis of security work. Civil servants, War Office clerks, engineers in Admiralty establishments, or workers in Ministry of Aviation contractors' works, are frequently moved on the initiative of the security authorities if any security risk condition such as I have defined is found.

There is another question which I want to put to the Prime Minister here. Even if there were no leak – and it is clear, I think, that none of us can ever know whether there was, although the Government are clinging desperately to the argument that they do not think that there was – one issue is, as I have said, this long continuing security risk from another point of view: because Soviet espionage in this country is not directed only to the transmission of secrets. Perhaps of even greater importance to them is the effort which they make to sow in the United States deep doubts about the efficiency of the British security services.

I wonder whether any hon. member for one moment can doubt that in the episode which we are debating today the Soviet espionage authorities have been handed a triumphant success, not least by the failure of the Prime Minister to take action when the facts were made available to him. This is a question which the Prime Minister must answer: does he or does he not think that there was a continuing security risk, and what effect does he think that this has had on our relations with our allies?

I come to one further quite direct question to the Prime Minister and to the House – because I think that all the House, and certainly hon. members opposite, equally with us, will demand a full answer from the Prime Minister. I want to put it to him that we must have a full disclosure in the debate today of what is going on. We want to know whether there are any more revelations to come. Have we had all that the Government now know? Or is there more still being held back in the hope, the desperate gamble, that it will not come out in some other way? Is this the whole story that we have now, or is it only that part of the iceberg which is visible above the surface of the water?

I say directly to the Prime Minister that if he purports today to give the House a full statement of everything that is known to him, and if, during the course of the next week or two, or the next month or two, there are more revelations, the House will hold him guilty, too, of misleading the House about the true facts in this situation.

First, as to Ivanov. His activities, we are told by the Prime Minister, were fully and efficiently watched. His contacts were wide. He took full advantage of this sector of London society. Why, then, was he not declared *persona non grata* by the Government?

Secondly, I want to ask the Prime Minister on what date was a full security watch placed on Ward's flat? The Prime Minister told us that Ward's side of this was fully and efficiently watched. He said that in a letter to me. Thus, he will not mind telling us on what date the watch on Ward's flat began and on what date, if any, it ended. If it were fully and efficiently watched, there must have been a watch. Will he tell us the date on which it began? He knows that I know the answer to that question.

Thirdly, when did the Prime Minister himself – I think that this is central to the whole issue – first hear these rumours about the Secretary of State and the girl? On what date? I hope that he will tell us this, because it is fundamental. The House must be told the precise date.

Fourthly, who told the right hon. gentleman? The information which I have had is that it was not, in fact, the security services, that it was a top executive of a newspaper group who had just bought one of the sets of the Keeler memoirs and who came to Admiralty House specifically on the security issue and informed the Prime Minister's staff of Miss Keeler's association with Mr Profumo; and, of course, with Edgecombe and with Gordon and with Ivanov. Will the right hon. gentleman confirm this and will he give the date?

Next, will the right hon. gentleman tell us this? On receipt of this information what did he do? Did he send for the Secretary of State for War and confront him with it? What checks did he make on receiving this information? Any hon. member opposite, in whatever capacity – in business; in the Army – on receiving information of a comparable character to this would have immediately sent for his junior and confronted him with the charge. Did the Prime Minister do this?

Fifthly, did the right hon. gentleman instruct the security services to check the accuracy of the statement by reference to Miss Keeler herself? When did the real security checks on Miss Keeler begin and how thorough were they? I think that the right hon. gentleman will realise the importance of these questions and the need to give a straight answer to them. If, in fact, the security services knew all about the Keeler relationship in 1961, it was their duty to tell the Prime Minister then, not only because he is their chief, because he is the only Minister responsible for security, but because he alone had the power to act.

The right hon. gentleman alone had the power to sack the Secretary of State for War. If they knew in 1961, when the danger was greatest, and if they did not tell the Prime Minister, there is a clear case for a ruthless inquiry into those responsible. I think that some heads would roll in the security services if this turned out to be the truth.

If they did tell the Prime Minister, then his failure over two years to sack the Secretary of State, to end the situation, would represent an inconceivable lack of responsibility on his part. But this is not all. If they did know and if they did tell him, it would mean that he connived, that he was an accessory before the fact to the gross contempt of the House involved in the personal statement on 22 March last, when the Prime Minister so clearly identified himself with the statement of the Secretary of State for War.

Frankly, I find it quite impossible to believe that the right hon. gentleman could be guilty of that. I do not believe for one minute that that was the situation. So if it is true, if I am right, then either the security services knew and deliberately withheld that information from him, in which case heads have to roll, or they did not know. If they did not know – it is a fair question to ask why they did not know, whether they should not have been on to it something follows from that. It follows that they could not have been monitoring, they could not have been watching, the effects of the Profumo–Keeler relationship.

The Prime Minister doubts this: the whole matter has been fully covered. He cannot have it both ways, because either the Keeler–Profumo relationship was known, and the security services were following it and there was no security risk, in which case the Prime Minister is very guilty for not having taken action over that period. Or the security services knew nothing about it, in which case they could not have followed it and, therefore, the Prime Minister has no warrant whatsoever for saying that there was no breach of security, because he simply does not know.

Whether the security services are blameworthy or not – the House will take a lot of satisfying on this point – they simply were not in a position to detect any possible breach of security. Therefore, I say to the Prime Minister – I think that the whole House must say to him – that, if the security services did not know, two years ago, about this relationship, then his letter to me of 30 May was totally misleading when he said:

'I am sure in my own mind that the security aspect of the Ward case has been fully and efficiently watched.'

So, on that assumption, all the complacent statements which have been fed out to the press in the past 48 hours, that there were no security leaks, are completely dishonest. The Government have no means of knowing whether there were security leaks or not. Therefore, the Prime Minister must answer these questions about the date frankly and clearly. We shall not easily allow him out of the Chamber until he does.

I will hazard my own view of the answer. The only one that I think fits the facts, except on a basis which would convict the Prime Minister and his colleagues both of scandalous unconcern for security and of being a party to misleading the House, is this. I believe that the first the security services knew or even guessed about this very big security risk was when a Sunday newspaper told them a few months ago. If this is true – the Prime Minister must be frank about this – this would imply that the £60 million spent on these services under the right hon. gentleman's premiership have been less productive in this vitally important case than the security services of the *News of the World*. He must tell us this.

It would mean, too, as I have said, that no one has any idea of the possible security breaches, because on my information the first intimation of the Profumo–Keeler relationship did not reach the Prime Minister or the security services until after Ivanov had left the country this year. So how can he say that he knows what went on?

It would mean something else. If my suggestion is correct about the Sunday newspapers, something else is involved. On the information that I have, this first allegation about the Profumo–Keeler relationship and the Profumo–Keeler–Ward triangle was made to the Government four and a half months ago. The Prime Minister is to give us the date in a minute. It was, therefore, two months before the Secretary of State's personal statement. There was plenty of time to check up with Miss Keeler. There was plenty of time to check up with the Ward set-up and with the other witnesses, who seem only too ready now to talk, especially if there is money involved.

So, though I personally acquit the right hon. gentleman of foreknowledge or complicity in this matter – of course I do, of course we all do; I mean complicity in the misleading of the House – he cannot be acquitted of a grave dereliction of duty in failing to find out. The House was grossly misled and abused, not by his complicity, but by his inadequacy.

I come now to the meeting of the five Ministers[8] late at night, till five o'clock in the morning, with the former Secretary of State for War. Did they have this MI5 material before them, the material which MI5 presumably had been investigating for two months from the day it first received it from the Sunday newspaper? Was the head of MI5 invited to this confrontation with the Secretary of State for War? If not, why not? We have been given by Lord Poole, who seems to know all about these things, an account of who was at this meeting – the Ministers, the Law Officers, the Leader of the House, the Chief Whip, and, for some reason I cannot understand, the Minister without Portfolio, the head of the Government's information services. What in heaven's name was he doing there?

Here, Iain Macleod, Chancellor of the Duchy of Lancaster and one of the five ministers involved in the meeting (the others were Martin Redmayne, the Chief Whip; the Attorney General, Sir John Hobson; the Solicitor-General, Peter Rawlinson; and the Minister without Portfolio, Bill Deedes, who had been brought into Macmillan's government to help on presentation – an early precursor to the 1990s practice of appointing a 'minister for the *Today* programme'), intervened to explain that point.

Deedes, he said, had been in the House for the debate on the two journalists and was the only other Cabinet minister present in the chamber; his presence was nothing to do with his media responsibilities. This was immediately disputed by the indefatigable George Wigg, who noted that the Home Secretary, Henry Brooke, was also there, and wondered why he had not, therefore, attended the late-night conclave with Profumo. Macleod retorted that Brooke had been involved in an earlier debate and had left the House some hours earlier. Wilson was not so sure.

As I myself was present, I cannot confirm the right hon. gentleman's recollection. He had better check the times again, because the Home Secretary and I were crossing swords with one another at about 1.30 that morning and the right hon. gentleman knows that Profumo had been sent for before that. In any case, the right hon. gentleman knows, does he not, that the Home Secretary, at that time, was in possession of vital information from police inquiries about Miss Keeler in which the Secretary of State for War's name had been mentioned? If he had gone home, why was he not brought back for so important a meeting? After all, the result of the meeting, which lasted for several hours, was a statement which misled the House.

For some reason – I should like to know why – Mr Profumo's solicitor was present. This is most extraordinary. I have never heard, and I am sure that the Patronage Secretary has not, of an hon. member seeing his Chief Whip and asking for his solicitor to be present. This is a very serious point, because I should like to know on whose initiative the solicitor was brought along. After all, if the Secretary of State for War said, 'I am not going to see the Chief Whip without having my solicitor present', this is the sort of thing which any petty crook says when he is arrested. It ought to have aroused the suspicions of the Leader of the House.

Or did the Leader of the House say, 'We have a very grave charge to put to you. You had better send for your solicitor'? I hope that we shall get a clear answer about that from the Prime Minister. If there was time to get his solicitor out of bed and bring him here, why was not there time to bring both the Home Secretary, if he had gone home, and the head of the security services? We, and, I am sure, hon. gentlemen opposite, too, will take a lot of satisfying about this meeting that took place late at night.

There is one other matter of great importance to the House. I said that the deception of the House was a grave contempt of Parliament. It is important that this should be recorded in a formal decision of the House, otherwise there is a danger, through default, of eroding the principle that any calculated deception is an abuse and a contempt. I gather that there may be difficulty about tabling a Motion on the Order Paper before we leave today, but the Government must announce that they intend to table a Motion so that it can be debated, and we must ask them to put the matter right at once. If they fail, I give notice that we shall ourselves table a Motion and demand that time be given for adequate debate.

I have dealt today with the problem of the security risk and the clear failure of the Prime Minister to fulfil his duty to this House and to the nation. I have given the Prime Minister some direct questions to which the House will insist we must have answers.

For reasons which I have given, I have not dealt with the moral challenge with which the nation is faced. The uncovering of this sleazy sector of society in London and elsewhere is a matter to be pursued elsewhere. But the papers day by day add to the odious record. Saturday's papers told of an opportunist night club proprietor who had offered Miss Christine Keeler – or should I refer to her as Miss Christine Keeler Ltd – a night club job at a salary of £5,000 a week, and I say to the Prime Minister that there is something utterly nauseating about a system of society which pays a harlot 25 times as much as it pays its Prime Minister, 250 times as much as it pays its Members of Parliament, and 500 times as much as it pays some of its ministers of religion.

But they are wrong at home and abroad who see this as a canker at the heart of our society. I believe that the heart of this nation is sound. What we are seeing is a diseased excrescence, a corrupted and poisoned appendix of a small and unrepresentative section of society that makes no contribution to what Britain is, still less to what Britain can be. There are, of course, lessons to be drawn for us all in terms of social policy, but perhaps most of all in terms of the social philosophy and values and objectives of our society – the replacement of materialism and the worship of the golden calf by values which exalt the spirit of service and the spirit of national dedication.

I once heard the Archbishop of York say that we were in danger of creating a system of society where the verb 'to have' means so much more than the verb 'to be', and now we are seeing the pay-off for that system of society. But our friends abroad are wrong if they draw the hasty conclusion that this country is entering the era of corruption which has heralded the decline of the great civilisations of the past. The sickness of an unrepresentative sector of our society should not detract from the robust ability of our people as a whole to face the challenge of the future. And in preparing to face that challenge, let us frankly recognise that the inspiration and the leadership must come first here in this House.

'Harold made an absolutely magnificent speech, the best I've ever heard him make, better than I thought possible,' wrote Richard Crossman.[9] 'It was really annihilating, a classical prosecution speech, with weight and self control.' The *Guardian*'s legendary sketch-writer Norman Shrapnel admired his perform- ance for the same reason: 'Nothing, to my mind, ever showed his sheer professionalism, his coolness and intelligence, more than his handling of this dangerous affair. Never hit a man if a push will do. Never push him if he is going to fall down anyway. That was the Wilson technique and the restraint was deadly. The Prime Minister was left to flounder and drown.'[10]

"Never glad confident morning again!"

Nigel Birch wields the dagger against Harold Macmillan: 17 March 1963

More devastating to Macmillan even than Wilson's carefully angled assault was this attack from his own ranks. Many Prime Ministers or party leaders have had cause to fear former colleagues nursing grievances on the backbenches – think of Heseltine and Thatcher, Bevan and Attlee, Lamont and Major. Nigel Birch was never as senior a figure as these, but his assassination of his leader is a classic instance of revenge, coldly savoured. He had long been one of Macmillan's most bitter opponents on the Tory benches, having resigned as Economic Secretary to the Treasury in 1957, along with the Financial Secretary, Enoch Powell, and the Chancellor, Peter Thorneycroft, over Macmillan's refusal to countenance public spending cuts. Macmillan dismissed their departure as 'a little local difficulty'. But when a second Chancellor, Selwyn Lloyd, was dispatched in the 'Night of the Long Knives' cull of senior government ministers in 1962, Birch wrote a venomous three-line letter to *The Times*, noting that this was the second time a Chancellor who tried to get spending under control had been dismissed. 'Once is more than enough,' he added.

Birch, then, had form. When he rose in the debate on John Profumo's departure, Macmillan must have known what to expect. 'He was an assassin,' wrote Julian Critchley, who bracketed him with Michael Foot as the best two speakers in the House. 'He had the kind of sardonic wit which could delight like a fine white Burgundy, and which at the same time was like acid which could strip the skin from the backs of his enemies.'[11] Drawing on his ministerial experience, Birch laid the whole responsibility for the fiasco at the Prime Minister's door, accusing him of an absurd level of credulity towards his disgraced minister.

As always, such words are far more damaging when they come from within the party, rather than from the opposition. And Birch's peroration was a superb example of the use of the stiletto.

IN MANY ORGANS of the press and, to a certain extent, during the latter part of the speech of the Leader of the Opposition, there has been a suggestion that the whole moral health of the nation is at stake and is concerned in this debate. I do not believe that that is true. As far as the moral health of the nation can be affected by any human agency, it is affected by prophets and priests and not by politicians. But this certainly has been one of the best field days that the self-righteous have had since Parnell was cited as co-respondent in O'Shea's divorce case.[12] In all these miseries, the fact that so many people have found some genuine happiness is something to which, in all charity, we have no right to object.

I must say that I view the activities of the editor of *The Times* with some distaste.[13]

This sentiment clearly appealed to an MP with Fleet Street connections – Edward Mallalieu, Labour MP for Brigg and brother of the Tribunite journalist J. P. W. 'Curley' Mallalieu, was moved to call out 'First-class stuff.'
Birch warmed to his theme.

He is a man about whom it could have been predicted from his early youth that he was bound to end up sooner or later on the staff of one of the Astor papers.

Nor do I think that this debate is primarily concerned with the security aspect although that, of course, is important. It was fully dealt with by my right hon. friend the Prime Minister and, for my part, I am perfectly prepared to accept everything that the Prime Minister said about security. I believe that what he said was right and true and I am not prepared to criticise my right hon. friend in any way, concerning the question of security.

What seems to me to be the real issue is something much simpler and much narrower. The real issue seems to be whether it was right to accept Profumo's personal statement. There are two aspects here. There is, first, the moral aspect of accepting that part of the statement which Profumo himself subsequently denied and there is a second issue of whether the Prime Minister in this case acted with good sense and with competence.

I will deal with these two issues in order. First, there is the question of accepting Profumo's statement. We know a deal more now about Profumo than we did at the time of the statement, but we have all known him pretty well for a number of years in this House. I must say that he never struck me as a man at all like a cloistered monk; and Miss Keeler was a professional prostitute.[14]

We have had a legal disquisition from my right hon. and learned friend the member for Chertsey [Sir Lionel Heald] about the legal etiquette in all this matter, but as someone who does not understand the law, I simply approach it from the basis of what an ordinary person could or would believe. Here one had an active, busy man and a professional prostitute. On his own admission, Profumo had a number of meetings with her, and, if we are to judge by the published statements, she is not a woman who would be intellectually stimulating. Is it really credible that the association had no sexual content? There seems to me to be a certain basic improbability about the proposition that their relationship was purely platonic. What are whores about? Yet Profumo's word was accepted. It was accepted from a colleague. Would that word have been accepted if Profumo had not been a colleague or even if he had been a political opponent? Everyone must, I think, make his own judgment about that.

We were told that special consideration ought to have been given to Profumo because he was a colleague. It is certainly true that a Prime Minister owes to his subordinates all the help, comfort and protection that he can give them. But surely that help, that comfort and that protection must stop short of condoning a lie in a personal statement to this House.

Then we are told, in many organs of the press and in many speeches, that special weight ought to have been given to Profumo's words because he was a Privy Councillor and a Secretary of State. I am a Privy Councillor and I have been a Secretary of State, but when I sustained the burden of both offices I did not feel that any sea change had taken place in my personality. I remained what I was, what I had always been and what I am today, and I do not believe it reasonable to suppose that any sea change took place in Mr Profumo's personality.

He was not a man who was ever likely to tell the absolute truth in a tight corner, and at the time the statement was made he was in a very tight corner indeed. There are people – and it is to the credit of our poor, suffering humanity that it is so – who will tell the whole truth about themselves whatever the consequences may be. Of such are saints and martyrs, but most of us are not like that. Most people in a tight corner either prevaricate – if anyone is interested in prevarication they will find the *locus classicus* in the evidence given before the Bank Rate Tribunal[15] by the Leader of the Opposition – or, as in this case, they lie.

This lie was accepted. I have meditated very deeply on this, and though I have given some rather tough reasons for not accepting that Profumo's statement was credible, I have after deep consideration come to the conclusion that my right hon. friend did absolutely genuinely believe it. I will give my reasons now for taking that view, and these reasons concern the competence and the good sense with which the affair was handled.

Profumo on his own admission had been guilty of a very considerable indiscretion, for a Minister at any rate. He was not a particularly successful

Minister. He had no great place in this House or in the country. I cannot really see that the Prime Minister was under any obligation whatever to retain his services, nor do I think that getting rid of Mr Profumo would, in fact, have made the political situation any worse than it then was. On the other hand, to retain him entailed a colossal risk and a colossal gamble. The difficulties and dangers were obvious enough. The press were in full cry. They were in possession of letters. They were hardly likely to have bought letters unless they had something of interest in them. Miss Keeler was pretty certain to turn up again, and if she did, editors were sure to make use of her literary talent. The dangers were enormous, and yet this colossal gamble was taken, and in this gamble, as it seems to me, the possible gain was negligible and the possible loss devastating.

The conclusion that I draw from that is that the course adopted by my right hon. friend the Prime Minister could have been adopted only by someone who genuinely and completely believed the statements of Profumo, and therefore, I absolutely acquit my right hon. friend of any sort of dishonour. On the other hand, on the question of competence and good sense I cannot think that the verdict can be favourable.

What is to happen now? I cannot myself see at all that we can go on acting as if nothing had happened. We cannot just have business as usual. I myself feel that the time will come very soon when my right hon. friend ought to make way for a much younger colleague. I feel that that ought to happen. I certainly will not quote at him the savage words of Cromwell, but perhaps some of the words of Browning might be appropriate in his poem on 'The Lost Leader', in which he wrote:

> Let him never come back to us!
> There would be doubt, hesitation and pain.
> Forced praise on our part – the glimmer of twilight,
> Never glad confident morning again!
> Never glad confident morning again!

– so I hope that the change will not be too long delayed.

Birch ended with a mocking lash at Quintin Hogg, Lord Hailsham, then in his first period in the House of Lords – he was shortly to return to the Commons in order to join the post-Macmillan leadership race. Hailsham had appeared on the BBC political programme *Gallery*. Amongst a number of controversial statements during his interview, he told the presenter Robert McKenzie that the government's three-line whip did not bind Conservative MPs to support it. In his speech in the debate, which followed Birch, George Wigg denounced Hailsham as a 'lying humbug'.

Ahead of us we have a Division. We have the statement of my right hon. and noble friend Lord Hailsham, in a personal assurance on television, that a Whip is not a summons to vote but a summons to attend. I call the Whips to witness that I at any rate have attended.

The young Peter Tapsell, sitting behind the Prime Minister, could see him tense as he recognised Browning's lines and realised what was to come. When the words were uttered, he recoiled as if slapped in the face.[16] Julian Critchley saw Macmillan's face 'contorted with pain and anger'. In the division at the end of the debate, 27 Tory MPs abstained, rather than support the government. (Ironically, their number included Lord Lambton, whose career as a junior defence minister would be ended by revelations of a relationship with a call-girl.)

Press comment on the debate and Macmillan's performance was scathing. 'Mac: The End,' 'The Stag at Bay,' 'The Lost Leader,' 'A Broken Man Close to Tears.' In his *Diaries*, Tony Benn noted: 'It is now only a matter of time.'[17]

'This Motion which, in so far as it means anything at all, is about as much of a vote of censure on his own Shadow Home Secretary as it is upon me: for it complains of my having done exactly what the right hon. and learned gentleman asked me to do.'

Roy Jenkins demolishes a Conservative censure motion over the escape of a Soviet spy: 31 October 1966

The escape of the Soviet master-spy George Blake from Wormwood Scrubs in October 1966 was a grave test for Labour's reforming Home Secretary, Roy Jenkins. Blake, who had been serving 42 years for espionage, had betrayed a number of British agents. Jenkins's immediate reaction was a statement to the Commons, announcing that Lord Mountbatten had been appointed to conduct an independent inquiry into the escape, and the wider issue of prison security in general.

This announcement did not satisfy the leader of the opposition, Edward Heath, who wrote out a motion for the immediate adjournment of the House, which, embarrassingly, the Speaker rejected – a point Jenkins taunted him on in this speech. Heath then put down a personal motion of censure against Jenkins, which was moved a week later by his shadow Home Secretary, Quintin Hogg (then in his mid-career reappearance in the Commons, having renounced his peerage to contest the succession to Harold Macmillan).

The Conservative case was that Jenkins had failed to take the decisions necessary to ensure Blake's security, but there were also wider allegations about his liberal agenda, which had included the abolition of hanging and the birch. No minister opened for the government, and so Jenkins was staking a great deal on this reply to the debate. The record of the debate does not wholly capture one of his greatest assets during this period of his career, a kind of counter-intuitive class appeal. He was simply grander than his critics, and Labour MPs delighted in his lofty dismissal of exalted Tory grandees.

THIS MOTION HAS been described by *The Times* as 'somewhat trumped up,' and by the *Spectator* as 'not very sensible' and has been treated even by the *Daily Telegraph* with a good degree of scepticism. After listening to the debate tonight I can add another comment, namely, that the Motion is extraordinarily badly drafted – a typical product of the parliamentary

ineptitude of the right hon. member for Bexhill [Edward Heath] – so badly
drafted that the right hon. and learned member for St Marylebone [Quentin
Hogg] was forced to make almost the whole of his extremely long speech well
outside its terms.

I propose to deal first with those points which are a little outside the direct
terms of the Motion, and then go to the direct issue of the Motion. The right
hon. and learned member for St Marylebone excelled himself when he said
that my right hon. friend the Prime Minister had exposed this country in a way
which was without comparison under the previous Administration. I have in
my hand a list of security scandals so long that it would take me most of the
rest of the debate to read them.

'What about Blake?' shouted Conservative MPs.

If the hon. members opposite will give up their tribal bleating I will
immediately come to Blake. I come to the question of whether Blake should
have been kept at Wormwood Scrubs, a central though not directly relevant
issue to the Motion. I do not approach the House with any desire to argue that
everything has been perfectly ordered in the past, either in my time or during
the terms of office of my predecessors. Clearly, with the benefit of hindsight
every one of us would wish that Blake had been kept in another prison.

If that were not my view I would not have taken the steps which I thought
necessary this week; to reallocate the other spies we have in custody. Nor
would I have undertaken an urgent review of all security prisoners, and that
review is nearly complete. I am bound to say, however, that if I am to listen to
lectures on this subject, the last source from which they should come is from
representatives of the Conservative Party.

What is the history of this matter? On 3 May, 1961, Blake was received into
Wormwood Scrubs and, in accordance with the normal practice for prisoners
serving long sentences, was at first located in the hospital. On 29 June he was
allocated to Wormwood Scrubs as a star prisoner – that is, a prisoner with a
long sentence but without a previous criminal record – and was moved to the
local wing and placed on the escape list. On 3 October of the same year he was
taken off the escape list and moved to D Wing, where he remained until nine
days ago.

Those decisions were all taken at a time when, for reasons which will be
obvious to the House, the loss of Blake would have been considerably more
damaging from the security point of view than can be the case today. They

were all taken when Lord Butler was Home Secretary. Were it not for the violently partisan terms of several of this evening's speeches, I would not have thought it necessary or desirable to underline that point but, in the circumstances, I most certainly do.

Further, I saw last week that Lord Butler had announced from Cambridge[18] that Blake ought to have been in Parkhurst. I always read Lord Butler's reflections in retirement with great interest, and often with admiration, but I must say on this occasion that if Lord Butler thought that Blake should have been in Parkhurst it is a great pity he did not put Blake there.

I now go on a little from Lord Butler's time to the time of his successor, Lord Brooke, as he now is. In the autumn of 1963, the question of Blake's possible transfer was raised by the security service, but it was decided, after full consultation, that it was better to leave him where he was. I should say that, contrary to certain allegations that have been widely made, there has throughout been the fullest contact between the prison department and the security service about Blake's location.

Then, in April 1964, a possible plot to rescue Blake was disclosed to the Governor of Wormwood Scrubs by another prisoner. That plot was invest-igated and was held to be without foundation but, as a result, Blake's location was again discussed with the security service, and at that stage came to the personal attention of the Home Secretary of the day.

The question was then raised whether Blake should be moved, but it was decided, after full consultation, that he should be left where he was. The decision was taken in June 1964. He was left where he was. He was not put back on the escape list – and to suggest in view of that clear history, as the right hon. and learned gentleman did, that because Mr Brooke subsequently wrote it would be a pity if Blake escaped, he had thereby made bold decisions for the future seems to me to be a most extraordinary proposition.

Quintin Hogg intervened to repeat his claim that the Conservative Home Secretary, Henry Brooke, had put Blake under constant surveillance. When, he asked, had that been relaxed, and why had Jenkins not considered relocating him? Jenkins retorted that he could not say when the special restrictions were relaxed, for the simple reason that they had never been imposed. Hogg intervened again, saying that Brooke had confirmed that he had imposed restrictions on Blake. That alone proved that an inquiry was necessary, he added. Jenkins did not budge.

I am glad that the right hon. and learned gentleman has at last been able to deliver one sentence even directly relevant to the Motion. I am coming to this point. There were no special restrictions imposed in 1964, even when the escape plot was investigated, and when the question of Blake's further location was discussed and brought up to the Home Secretary personally, but when no move took place.

Blake accordingly remained at Wormwood Scrubs and continued to gain the reputation of a model prisoner. No further allegations relating to a Blake escape were discovered by the authorities. However, it would be quite wrong to assume that this led to any slackening of the restrictions. There was no tightening in 1964 and no slackening afterwards.

That is the history, but there is one further aspect of the case with which I should perhaps deal. It is the suggestion that the escapes from Wormwood Scrubs in June created a new situation so far as Blake was concerned and that these in themselves made the need for a move obvious. But these were not the first escapes from Wormwood Scrubs. There were six in 1961 the year when Lord Butler allowed Blake to be sent there, and there had been no fewer than twelve from Wormwood Scrubs in 1959. There was another escape in 1962, three in 1963 and two in the early part of 1964. These last escapes applied over the exact period when Blake's case was being reviewed by a previous Home Secretary in the last Government who decided not to move him. The June escapes therefore were not a new factor.

I come to the exact issue posed in the Motion which, for somewhat understandable reasons in view of the way in which it was drafted, has figured singularly little in the debate. The Leader of the Opposition and his right hon. friends have used the somewhat portentous weapon of a personal Motion of censure because, as they say, I have refused to set up a specific inquiry to report as a matter of urgency on the escape of George Blake. That is the complaint in the Motion. I am not at the moment concerned with the other reasons which the Opposition have trumped up in the last week, although it is interesting to see their constant change of ground as reported in the press. The complaint in the Motion is that the inquiry is not specific and not urgent. There is no truth in either limb of that attack. The Mountbatten Inquiry is specifically, although not exclusively, charged with investigating the Blake escape. That is made as clear as it can be in the terms of reference.

As for urgency, the Mountbatten Inquiry has already begun work and is dealing first and specifically with the Blake escape. Lord Mountbatten and his assessors are already considering the preliminary reports. They will be at

Wormwood Scrubs on Wednesday of this week and they will follow up with complete determination to uncover everything that can be uncovered, and they will not hesitate to apportion blame to any system or person, whether they be Ministers or officials. If they think a separate and earlier report is called for, they will produce one; and it will be published. But in any event, they plan to complete their whole task by the end of the year, and it will be one of the most urgent independent investigations on record.

As my right hon. friend the Prime Minister said in his statement this afternoon, Blake's escape should not result in further damage to national security, but should any point touching national security be uncovered in the course of Lord Mountbatten's work, the issue would be dealt with separately.

On grounds of both urgency and specificness, therefore, this Motion is one of the thinnest ever to come before the House. So thin is it, indeed, that we are bound to ask some questions about its genesis.

At approximately 3.55 last Monday afternoon, the right hon. and learned Member for St Marylebone asked me for an assurance that Blake's escape could be made an integral part of the Mountbatten Inquiry. I told him I thought that could be done. Within a little more than two hours, at the earliest moment at which Lord Mountbatten could reach London, I agreed the terms of reference with him. They fully met the point of the right hon. and learned gentleman. Without waiting for the end of my meeting with Lord Mountbatten, I had those terms of reference published. They went out from the Press Association at 5.56 and were on the tapes at 7.12. They were presumably available to the Opposition within a few minutes.

But the Leader of the Opposition was determined to press a niggling party point. At the end of the exchanges in the afternoon, he had suffered a complete parliamentary humiliation. He had drafted in his own hand a most egregious Adjournment Motion. He then sent his right hon. and learned friend to Mr Speaker as the messenger of his folly. He might at least have gone himself. Two hours later he was still smarting under this humiliation, so much so that he either could not or would not understand that his right hon. and learned friend's point had in fact been fully met. So he insisted on tabling this Motion which, in so far as it means anything at all, is about as much of a vote of censure on his own Shadow Home Secretary as it is upon me: for it complains of my having done exactly what the right hon. and learned gentleman asked me to do.

I therefore ask the House to reject this trumped up Motion. The Blake case is of course a most serious matter. Nobody can know that better than I do. We certainly have on our hands a real problem of prison security. I believe that this problem will be met by the constructive measures we are taking, and taking quickly; but it will not be met by that combination of procedural incompetence and petty partisanship which is the constant characteristic of the right hon. gentleman's parliamentary style.

Jenkins had spent the best part of eight hours preparing his speech, and the result was, he noted in his memoirs, 'by far the greatest parliamentary triumph that I ever achieved . . . I who had been against the ropes, was rampant. Heath and Hogg were on their backs. Yet nothing of substance had happened. I had merely effectively deployed the art of tu quoque; everything I had done, Henry Brooke had done worse.'[19] His final passage attacking Edward Heath, his contemporary at Balliol, drew blood; Heath did not speak to him for nearly a year.

It was performances of this kind, which continued when he took over the Treasury in difficult circumstances, that established Jenkins as a serious challenger to the Prime Minister, Harold Wilson.

'Electricity supplies for other industry and for commercial premises will, in general, be limited to ... three specified days each week.'

Faced with a coal strike, Edward Heath introduces the three-day week: 13 December 1973

The economic crisis which shattered Edward Heath's Conservative government was the result of Britain's long-term economic problems and sheer bad luck. Heath had been attempting to curb inflation with an incomes policy, imposing annual limits on pay increase, when Arab countries more than doubled the price of oil. This kicked off a new round of price increases. At the same time, pay talks with the miners' union, the National Union of Mineworkers broke down, threatening domestic fuel and electricity supplies. The NUM wanted a deal which would have increased the wages of some of their members by 50 per cent, shattering stage three of Heath's pay policy. When their claim was refused, an overtime ban followed, and since much of Britain's coal production depended on overtime work, fuel reserves at power stations began to dwindle alarmingly.

The government had already begun preparations for petrol rationing and imposed a speed limit of 50 miles an hour, but the situation continued to deteriorate. In mid-November Heath declared a state of emergency

On 12 December, the day before Heath made this statement to the Commons, the Chancellor, Anthony Barber, told the Cabinet that Britain faced its gravest economic crisis since the Second World War. Under pressure from his party to stand firm, Heath announced a draconian package of emergency measures to a shocked House of Commons. Viewed from the prosperity of the early twenty-first century, its contents – electricity rationing, a call for householders to heat only one room, TV to end at 10.30 every night – are a shocking reminder of the sense of crisis and decline which permeated the 1970s.

WITH PERMISSION, MR SPEAKER, I will make a statement on the energy situation. The ban on overtime working by the coal miners has led to a sharp fall in coal supplies to the power stations which are now running at nearly 40 per cent below the expected level and are well below normal levels of consumption. Though the electricity supply industry started the winter with good stocks of coal, those stocks are now having to be run down at the rate of about one million tons a week at the present rate of electricity use, even after the restrictions already imposed.

To conserve coal stocks my right hon. friend the Secretary of State for Trade and Industry instructed the oil companies, on 5 December, to increase supplies of fuel oil to the power stations. But fuel oil supplies are also under pressure, and a still larger allocation to the electricity industry could be only at the expense of severe further cuts to other users of fuel oil.

Deliveries of coal and of oil to the power stations are seriously threatened by the industrial action of train drivers started yesterday by ASLEF.

The ability of the electricity industry to deal with the consequences of these disruptions of supply has been further constrained by the action of the power engineers to restrict out-of-hours working.

It is clear that, so long as the industrial action by the coal miners and the train drivers continues, stocks of fuel at the power stations will continue to be run down at a rate which could, before many weeks had passed, reach a point when large-scale interruption and disruption of electricity supply became unavoidable.

In this situation the Government have a responsibility to take the measures necessary to safeguard the electricity system from major disruption, to prevent essential services from being placed in jeopardy, and to ensure the maintenance of a reasonable level of industrial activity.

The Government judge that this requires further savings amounting to 20 per cent of electricity consumption, in addition to the measures already announced by my right hon. friend the Secretary of State for Trade and Industry. This will inevitably require reductions in consumption in homes, in industry and in commerce.

First, in homes. The Government are asking all domestic consumers to restrict the use of electricity for space heating in the home to one room, and then only if the householder has no other form of heating available.

Secondly, in industry and commerce. From next Monday 17 December, large, continuous process users will be limited to 65 per cent of their normal electricity consumption each week. Electricity supplies for other industry and for commercial premises will, in general, be limited to a total of any five days over the next two weeks ending 30 December. After that, from 31 December, they will be limited to three specified days each week, which will be consecutive, and the days will be selected on the basis of schedules drawn up for each Electricity Board area. On the days when firms are free to use electricity, they will not be able to work longer hours than usual. Maintenance or other work not involving the use of electricity could continue on other days and most shops and offices would also be able to open on those days, though they would not be able to use electricity.

Orders to give effect to the restrictions on industry and commerce will be made over the next few days. The orders will name certain essential businesses which will be exempt from these restrictions, and specify other special purposes for which the use of electricity would be permitted at all times, for example, the operation of fire-fighting equipment, computers, cheque-sorting machinery and office machinery.

From next Monday, BBC Television and Independent Television services will close down not later than 10.30 p.m. each evening, save over Christmas and on New Year's Eve.

In addition the Government ask that everyone should economise in the use of all fuels and save all the electricity they can. There are innumerable ways in which all of us can do this: by keeping rooms at lower temperatures and heating them for shorter periods; by switching off lights and by not using electrical appliances unless absolutely necessary; by setting thermostats contr-olling water-heaters, refrigerators and deep-freezers at the most economical levels; by reducing lighting levels in theatres and other places of entertainment. These are only examples: unless we can save electricity – and indeed all fuels – in every aspect of our daily lives, we shall have to impose yet further restrictions on business.

You will have noted, Mr Speaker, that the measures we propose do not include rota cuts or periods of electricity disconnection. The Government have thought it right to avoid such cuts as long as possible, particularly in view of the fact that the ban on out-of-hours working by the power engineers would mean that any cuts would have to be highly unselective and would be bound to affect essential services. But I must warn the House and the country. If we failed to achieve the necessary savings in electricity consumption as a result of the reduction in domestic consumption for which we are asking and the other measures I have announced, frequent periods of electricity disconnection would become unavoidable. Essential industries and vital services would be cut indiscriminately. Young and old alike, at home, at work, or in hospitals, would all be hit.

I should also like to say a few words to the House about the oil situation. The restrictions on oil exports by the Arab oil-producing countries affect the whole world; the developed countries of North America, Europe and Japan and the developing countries in Africa, Asia, and Central and South America.

We have been less hard hit than some other European countries, partly because – given normal levels of supply for other fuels – we are less dependent than they are on oil, and partly because the Arab producers have applied their reductions less severely to us. But, when the whole world is short of oil, we cannot escape entirely.

This month we shall probably get about 85 tons of oil for every 100 tons we expected. The figure may be lower in January. That is why we have had to ask everyone to economise in the use of oil in the home, in the office, in the factory, in the shops, on the road. But I can confirm that, on the basis of the level of supplies we now expect, the allocations of petrol and diesel to garages will continue at their present levels throughout January.

The situation has been greatly helped by the savings which drivers have made. I should like to take this opportunity to thank the public for their cooperation. It is vital that these efforts should continue. The savings in the demand for petrol over the last few days have amounted to about 15 per cent. As a result I can announce today that, although plans for rationing will proceed so that it could be introduced at short notice, it will not be introduced this side of the New Year.

The improvement of the supply position clearly depends upon progress towards a peace settlement in the Middle East. The peace conference is due to open in Geneva on 16 December. We are doing and will continue to do all we can, by diplomatic means, to promote the success of the conference and to make the Arab oil-producing countries aware of the hardship and the damage which the restrictions inflict.

We must hope that the shortage of supplies will be reversed before long. We cannot expect the sharp rise in oil prices to be reversed. This is bound to have a very damaging effect upon our balance of payments, which is in any case running in substantial deficit at present.

Until a few weeks ago we could foresee a progressive diminution in the balance of payments deficit during the course of next year. But that prospect has now disappeared. We shall have to find – and therefore to earn – much more foreign exchange to pay for the same amount of oil.

In the long run some of the money will, we hope, come back to us in payment for increased exports to the oil-producing countries, who will need the goods and services we can provide for their own development. Here again, we in Britain are more fortunate than most. Within five to seven years we can look forward to bringing two-thirds of the amount of oil we need in from the North Sea. That will in due course make an enormous improvement in our balance-of-payments position.

But that does not help in the immediate future. In the short run, if we have to have oil, as we do, and we have to pay more for it, as we shall, the country will have less to spend on other things from abroad. The Chancellor of the Exchequer will be making a statement in the House on Monday about fresh measures to achieve these purposes. For the time being as long as the shortages last we shall have to postpone some of the hopes and aims we have set ourselves for expansion and for our standard of living.

Other countries will be similarly affected by the rise in oil prices, and will be having to consider the implications for their balance of payments. In this situation there is an acute danger that, if we all independently resort to deflationary measures for the sake of our individual balances of payments, we shall set off a disastrous slump in the level of world trade. It will require all the effort and all the farsightedness of which the international community is capable to escape that consequence.

I leave for Copenhagen this evening for the Community summit meeting tomorrow. We shall be discussing the energy situation in all its aspects; but this particular aspect will be very much in mind.

The House will have seen that in his speech in London last night Dr Kissinger announced a proposal for an Energy Action Group, which would have as its goal the assurance of required energy supplies at reasonable cost. Under this proposal the nations of North America, Europe and Japan would cooperate in a programme to rationalise and conserve the use of energy, develop alternative sources of supply, and give existing producers an incentive to increase supply. I shall be discussing that matter with the other Community Heads of Government at Copenhagen: but I can say here and now that the British Government warmly welcome this imaginative proposal, which is in the great tradition of the Marshall Plan after the war.

I must apologise to the House for so long a statement; but it seemed to me that the House should be given as full a statement of the position as possible, as a basis for our debate next week.

Production fell by less than 2 per cent during the period of the three-day week and the crisis never really went away, despite increasingly frenzied efforts to resolve it. In January 1974 the miners voted for an all-out strike, forcing Heath to go to the country, posing the question 'Who governs Britain?' The voters concluded it wasn't him, and Labour formed a minority government, winning a narrow overall majority in a second election in October.

'Because of what the Government have done in the past five years – disregarded the minority and appeased the blackmailers of the Northern Ireland Unionist majority – I cannot go into the lobby with them tonight.'

Gerry Fitt votes to throw the Callaghan government out of office: 28 March 1979

Gerry Fitt is one of the heroic figures of Northern Irish politics. For years he was almost the lone parliamentary voice of the Catholic minority, and, while bitterly critical of the behaviour of the Ulster Unionists and of successive British governments, he also defied violent intimidation to denounce IRA terrorism. Michael Foot, the then Leader of the House, thought he was the bravest MP he had ever known.

Fitt had always seen himself as a Labour man, and he had worked with Callaghan before, accompanying the then Home Secretary in a perilous walkabout around the violence-torn Bogside area of Londonderry in 1969. But he had found himself increasingly at odds with Callaghan's government. Lacking a Commons majority, it had found itself bargaining for support with Fitt's Ulster Unionist opponents and making concessions to them – including granting five extra parliamentary seats for the province – which he could not stomach. In early 1979, with the government facing the prospect of defeat on a motion of confidence, Fitt could not bring himself to continue with his traditional allegiance to Labour. He was lobbied at the highest level. James Callaghan deployed his full persuasive powers to try to lure Fitt back into the government fold, even producing a bottle of gin to lubricate discussion. Fitt told him he would have no difficulty in supporting the government if the Northern Ireland Secretary, Roy Mason, was removed, but Callaghan refused. His direct warning to the independent Nationalist MP Frank Maguire – which generated much laughter in the chamber – was a key part of his speech.

Maguire was a pub owner and only occasionally left his bar to vote in the Commons. Fitt believed it would be a complete betrayal of Northern Ireland Nationalists for any of their MPs to support the government. He had little time for Maguire, having once urged him to speak out against the terrorists, only to be told that if he did, his pub would be burned down. Maguire's was potentially the decisive vote and he had been persuaded to support the government in tight spots before. The Labour whips had an established drill which required a relay of MPs to sit drinking with the Fermanagh publican until their capacity was exhausted, at which point a replacement would appear. On this occasion Northern Ireland Minister Don Concannon had accompanied Maguire to Westminster but in vain – Maguire's wife was watching Fitt in the public gallery and is said to have told her husband that he could not possibly vote for the government. (Labour's Deputy Chief Whip at the time, Walter Harrison, tells a different story; he believed Maguire was accompanied by two 'men in raincoats' – IRA minders – who had instructions to make sure he voted against the government.)

The swipe at Maguire was perhaps light relief in what was otherwise a very painful speech.

THIS WILL BE THE unhappiest speech I have ever made in this House. When I was elected in 1966, I sat on the Labour benches. I was under no compulsion to do so, but I had been a committed socialist all my life. Therefore, when I came to this House I felt proud and honoured to associate myself with the Labour cause.

When the Labour Government were defeated, I took my place among Labour members on the Opposition benches. Throughout a fourteen-year period in Parliament I have never once voted in the Conservative Lobby. I have at all times committed myself to support the policies which I honestly believed were for the good of the United Kingdom.

Even in the years when we were in Opposition and when the Conservative Government were courageously trying to grapple – and to some extent succeeding – with the problems of Northern Ireland, I voted on every other issue with the then Labour Opposition. I repeat that the Conservative Government of 1970–74 tried courageously to reach a settlement in Northern Ireland. However, all that we had built up so laboriously was wrecked by the election in February 1974. We then in May of that year experienced the UWC strike. That strike terrified the Labour Government. Since then the Labour Government have been running away. They have not stood up to Unionist and Loyalist extremists as they should have done.

When we look back in history, we see clearly that Labour Governments are not the best Governments to grapple with the Irish problem. That does not apply to Labour Oppositions. When Labour is in Opposition, one sees the real conscience of the Labour Party. Labour Members are not then restricted by the reins of office.

This evening I find myself in a most difficult position, both personally and otherwise. I heard the speech of the Prime Minister and I agreed with every word of it. I hope that when there is an election a Labour Government will be returned again. I have also heard the speeches so far from the Opposition

Benches. They do not particularly fill me with enthusiasm when one envisages an incoming Conservative Government. But I believe that the policy on Northern Ireland adopted by the Labour Government since 1974 has been disastrous for the communities in Northern Ireland. The Conservatives tried to bring people in Northern Ireland together, but the communities are now more divided than they have been since the onset of the present troubles in 1969–70.

Some journalists and others have said that there is a personality conflict between the present Secretary of State for Northern Ireland and me. That is totally untrue. The right hon. gentleman is only implementing Labour Government policies in Northern Ireland. If I criticise him, I criticise this Government. In late 1966 or early 1967 the Government went into a minority and began to make arrangements with the Ulster Unionists.

Every deal that they made so antagonised the minority community in Northern Ireland, that any denunciation of this Government gets a standing ovation from it. It is sad and heartbreaking that with my record I can stand here and say that. One must consider what the Government have achieved by these deals with the Unionists. First, there was the deal to increase the number of seats. I tried as hard as I could to explain to the Government, in public and private, at Mr Speaker's Conference and on the Floor of this House, how dangerous that was to community relations in Northern Ireland. No one believed me. It was thought that the mood would pass, that I was committed and would always be with the Government. I have not got over it and neither have the people that I represent. They see that action as consolidating Unionist supremacy in Northern Ireland.

The first Secretary of State for Northern Ireland, the right hon. member for Penrith and The Borders [Willie Whitelaw], and the Home Secretary when he was Secretary of State for Northern Ireland [Merlyn Rees] were considered in Northern Ireland to be impartial trying to do what they could to bring the communities together. The present Secretary of State [Roy Mason] is believed to be a Unionist Secretary of State. That is not personal. He is implementing Government policy, but if that is Government policy we are on the road to disaster in Northern Ireland.

The psychological effect of the increase in seats has divided the communities in Northern Ireland, and could lead to an even more dangerous situation. The minority community may say that it no longer has any faith in politics and does not believe that the Labour Government or any Government are interested in bringing about a settlement. What there is of the SDLP electorate will not split up and go to parties at one or other end of the political spectrum but will withdraw from politics altogether. In that situation there will be only one winner, the men who are using the bomb to vote, the men of violence who have consistently said that politics do not work and that the only way to achieve their ends is by terrorism and violence. Some people in Northern Ireland think that they may be right. Even at this late hour, I say to those who are so disenchanted that it is not too late and something yet might he done.

I have great respect for the Leader of the House. I have tried to put myself in his place and think of the problem facing him when the Government went into a minority after a series of by-election defeats and resignations, and presumably the right hon. member for Down South [Enoch Powell] offered to sustain the Government if a Bill was brought in to increase the number of seats.

The last thing that the right hon. member for Down South wants is a Government of any description with a big enough majority to legislate. He loves his present position, where he can hold the balance. He can go to little villages and towns in Down South and tell everyone how important he is, and he does that every weekend. I have not met another hon. member who suffers from such delusions of grandeur. Only three weeks ago in a little village in Down South the right hon. gentleman called attention to his great achievement of a promise of five more seats, and that there would be seventeen seats to represent Northern Ireland. The Unionists, of whatever description, will have thirteen or fourteen and become the third major force in British politics, and that is terrible to contemplate. My right hon. friend the Secretary of State may believe that the Unionists will not win all those seats, that the Opposition will win them and some will go to representatives such as myself. He knows more about it than I do, but I do not believe that. It would be terrible to return with a hung Parliament that depended on the votes of the Ulster Unionists.

After these deals that antagonised the minority community and created ill feeling and resentment, what thanks do the Ulster Unionists give? Do they thank the Leader of the House and say that they will vote for the Government tonight? No, they are voting tonight with the Tories. The sheer ingratitude of that crowd knows no bounds. The Northern Ireland Unionists have used the Labour Government for their ends, and tonight they will try to bring about their downfall. Seats in Northern Ireland do not change all that often. The Ulster Unionists know that they will come back with the same number. One or two may be called into question, but the possibility is that they will be back. They are not concerned about what happens in other parts of the United Kingdom.

I believe that the Labour Party will win the next election, and my speech is an attempt to point out the Government's tragic mistakes over the past five years. I did not make up my mind about how to vote tonight because of devolution in Scotland and Wales. I made up my mind the Friday before last when I read the Bennett Report on police brutality in Northern Ireland.[20] That has not received sufficient attention in this House or in the country. The report clearly states that men were brutalised and ill treated in the holding centres in Northern Ireland. Restrictions were placed on debating that report when we were discussing the Northern Ireland (Emergency Provisions) Act, and we have not been promised a debate. That report was only the tip of the iceberg. We have heard of Watergate and Muldergate,[21] and there will be a 'Bennett-gate'. When the true story emerges of what has been happening in the interrogation centres, the people in the United Kingdom will receive it with shock, horror and resentment. That is why I take this stand.

Throughout the years Hansard will tell the story of the votes that have taken place and the way in which I have voted on matters such as the House of Commons (Redistribution of Seats) Bill, the Emergency Powers Bill, the Prevention of Terrorism (Temporary Provisions) Bill, and so on. Those hon. members who are true Socialists voted with me on these matters – they were men who had nothing to gain from coming into the Lobby with me but who were activated by concern about Northern Ireland. It has been hard for me to take the fact that the Government front bench has taken a diametrically opposed view to me over Northern Ireland.

It has been said that if I do not vote for the Government tonight and there is an election, the alternative is just as bad. I do not think that that is so. I want to see a continuation of the Labour Government. But if there is a Conservative Government, I warn them not to get carried away with the belief that somewhere around the corner there is a military solution to the Northern Ireland problem. Unfortunately, that is the tune that we have heard from the Secretary of State for Northern Ireland. Every Monday morning at 10 o'clock he sees the Chief Constable. Every Monday at 1 p.m. we hear on the news that so many IRA men have been caught and so many have been sent to gaol. Every Monday the Secretary of State looks for a military solution. But there will be Mondays and Mondays and more Mondays when there will be no military solution, and there will be no solution at all until we start to grapple with the political problem of Northern Ireland.

My grievances are very clear and readily understood. Although not too many of my hon. friends will stand up and say this in the House, many of them have told me that they recognise what has been going on over Northern Ireland and that they are sorry. Many regret bitterly ever having done a deal with the devil in the person of the Northern Ireland Unionist Party. But it is too late now. In all conscience, and understanding the real needs of Northern Ireland, I would be a liar and a traitor to the people who sent me here if I were to go into the Lobby tonight with the Labour Government to express confidence in their handling of the affairs of Northern Ireland. I want to see an election as soon as possible. I want to see the Labour Government win with such a majority that never again will they have to rely on the votes of the Unionists in Northern Ireland.

Rumours are circulating in the House and throughout Northern Ireland about the levels to which this Government will stoop to maintain themselves in office for a few weeks more. I rarely agree with the Leader of the Opposition, but today she said that this Government should maintain their dignity. I believe that too. It is heartbreaking to see a Labour Government without dignity.

The hon. member for Fermanagh and South Tyrone [Frank Maguire][22] – I cannot really call him my hon. friend – is very rarely in this House and he has yet to make his maiden speech. On all the Northern Ireland issues that we have had in recent months – the Bennett report, the prevention of terrorism, the Bill on the redistribution of seats – we would have liked to have had the benefit of the hon member's opinions. We would have liked to hear whether he accepted or rejected the Government's views on such matters. But he did not appear when such issues were discussed.

There is a rumour circulating today, and if it is true it is despicable, that the hon. member is somewhere within the building, talking to someone from the Government whips' office. He cannot talk to me in case I persuade him to do as I am doing tonight. I shall be watching very carefully and if the hon. member goes through the Government Lobby tonight it will be in opposition to everything that his constituents sent him here to do. Such an action would be completely dishonest, and he has not given us the benefit of his opinion or his vote on any of the issues that affect Northern Ireland. If this Government have to depend on such a representative to get support tonight, it is a very sad day for the Labour Party and the Labour Government. It is terrible to think that they have to descend to such a level.

I have supported the Labour Government loyally in every possible way. When the election comes I shall still fight and clamour for a Labour victory in the hope that the Labour Government will have learned from their mistakes in

Northern Ireland. I hope that even now the Government will say that there was something wrong in the interrogation centres in Northern Ireland and that the Bennett report may be debated on the Floor of the House. I hope that they will establish a sworn inquiry on this matter. We do not want a committee on which everyone sits with handcuffs, or a committee with terms of reference so restricted as to make it useless. We want nothing less than a sworn inquiry – that is all that will satisfy the people of Northern Ireland.

I have a loyalty to this Government, to my own working class and trade union background, and to the whole working class movement in the United Kingdom and further afield. But I have a greater loyalty to the people of Northern Ireland who have suffered so tragically over the past ten years. I am speaking with their voice tonight. It is their voice saying that because of what the Government have done in the past five years – disregarded the minority and appeased the blackmailers of the Northern Ireland Unionist majority – I cannot go into the lobby with them tonight.

Apart from the section about Maguire, which did raise a modest titter, Fitt's speech was heard in absolute silence: the Tories, who could not have liked his arguments, did not want to heckle him and drive him into the government camp. Labour did not want to do anything which might prevent him from changing his mind. After he had spoken, the Leader of the House, Michael Foot, beckoned him to the Labour front bench and told him he sympathised with what he had said, hoped he would think again, but would always respect him, even if he could not change his vote.

'What the right hon. lady has done today is to lead her troops into battle snugly concealed behind a Scottish nationalist shield, with the boy David holding her hand.'

Michael Foot leads the Callaghan government's last stand: 28 March 1979

Almost everyone who was in the chamber to hear it believes Michael Foot's last-ditch defence of the Labour government against a Tory motion of no confidence was the greatest parliamentary performance they had ever experienced. Foot has a true orator's vocal range, and in this speech he went from silken irony, in the passages mocking David Steel and the Liberals, to thunderous denunciation, and back again. It was delivered without notes, and even his opponents laughed at the jokes, except perhaps Mrs Thatcher, although he tried hard to extract a smile from her.

For two years the government had clung to power despite being out-numbered in the House by the opposition parties. It had been sustained by extreme whipping, and astute bargaining with the Liberals, the Nationalists and the Northern Ireland parties. But part of the price for their support had been the delivery of Scottish and Welsh devolution, and when neither was endorsed in referendums, the writing was on the wall. But Foot offered a second chance at Scottish devolution (which was not to be revisited for nearly 20 years), signalled his regard for Labour's disillusioned ally Gerry Fitt, pledged continued goodwill to the Ulster Unionists and (accurately) warned the Scottish Nationalists of the electoral doom that awaited them in the ensuing election. He began after William Whitelaw, the Conservative deputy leader, had completed a deliberately dull and emollient speech intended to avoid offending the smaller parties and sending them back into the Labour camp. But Whitelaw had made a few jibes at Foot's expense, offering ironic thanks for persuading the Prime Minister not to hold an election in September 1978, before the disastrous industrial unrest of the 'winter of discontent', and recalling Foot's speech at the Moss Side by-election when he told voters: 'we offer you ten to fifteen years of exciting politics in Britain, if you have the nerve and courage to stay with us'.

THE RIGHT HON. MEMBER for Penrith and The Border [Willie Whitelaw[was good enough at the beginning of his speech to make a few kindly references to myself. Therefore, it would be churlish if I did not comment upon them. I had intended to start my speech by making a few remarks on the speeches of the representatives of the smaller parties. However, let me say at once to the right hon. gentleman that I was especially gratified that he quoted – accurately for a change – my words at the Moss Side by-election. So effective were my words on that occasion, and so overwhelming was the force of my argument, that a good Labour member was returned to the House of Commons. I am not saying that it was entirely due to my words on that occasion, but it shows that the right hon. gentleman has not picked on the most damning of all indictments against me for what I might have said.

I refer first to the speech of my hon. friend the member for Belfast West [Gerry Fitt]. I am glad that there were a considerable number of hon. members in the Chamber for my hon. friend's speech. All those who heard it, whatever their views, would have been deeply moved.

My hon. friend proved again what we on this side of the House have always recognised – that he is a man of great courage and great honour. The House is wise to heed what he says.

I did not agree with everything that my hon. friend said about the Government and our conduct in Northern Ireland. My hon. friend is one of my oldest friends in the House, and I believe that when he comes to review everything that he said he will recognise that there were some unjust comments on what has been done by my right hon. friends. Nevertheless, I respect his speech. Of course, I would have preferred that my hon. friend could have made a peroration in which he said that he would come into the Lobby with us, but even though that peroration was absent it does not detract from the admiration felt by every hon. member who heard his speech.

The hon. member for Antrim South [Jim Molyneaux – then the leader of the official Unionists, who had urged the Prime Minister to restore devolved government in Northern Ireland] also speaks for Northern Ireland. He is well aware that my right hon. friend the Secretary of State for Northern Ireland made a statement just under a year ago on many of the matters that the hon. gentleman touched on. We are pursuing those policies faithfully and properly. Anyone who reviews what the Government have done in that area cannot doubt the straightforwardness and honesty with which we have approached the problems. I do not believe that the hon. members who represent Northern Ireland, on both sides of the House, can question what I am saying.

I believe that the right hon. member for Western Isles and his party have made an error in the way that they propose to vote.

Donald Stewart was the leader of the Scottish Nationalists. They had tabled their own motion of no confidence in the government, after the failure to win a sufficient majority in a referendum on the creation of a Scottish Parliament.

The polls at the time looked grim for the SNP, and the ensuing election was a severe setback for them.

However misguided the right hon. gentleman may be, if he adheres to his apparent resolution to vote in the Lobby with those who are most bitterly opposed to the establishment of a Scottish Assembly, hon. members who heard his speech must acknowledge the remarkable allegiance that the right hon. gentleman commands from his followers. It is one of the wonders of the world. There has been nothing quite like it since the armies of ancient Rome used to march into battle. It is only now that we see the right hon. gentleman in his full imperial guise.

'Hail Emperor, those about to die salute you.'

Which brings me to the Leader of the Liberal Party [David Steel]. He knows that I would not like to miss him out. I am sure that I shall elicit the support and sympathy of the right hon. lady when I say that she and I have always shared a common interest in the development of this young man. If the right hon. lady has anything to say about the matter, I shall be happy to give way to her. I should very much like to know, as I am sure would everybody else, what exactly happened last Thursday night.

I do not want to misconstrue anything, but did she send for him or did he send for her – or did they just do it by *billet-doux*? Cupid has already been unmasked. This is the first time I have ever seen a Chief Whip who could blush. He has every right to blush. Anybody who was responsible for arranging this most grisly of assignations has a lot to answer for.

Labour MPs suspected a deal had been done when it became clear that enough minor parties were lining up with the Conservatives to defeat the government; Steel has always denied that there were direct negotiations. Cupid was Humphrey Atkins, the Conservative Chief Whip, allegedly the conduit for the arrangement with the Liberals.

That brings me to the right hon. lady. I have never in this House or elsewhere, so far as I know, said anything discourteous to her, and I do not intend to do so. I do not believe that is the way in which politics should be conducted. That does not mean that we cannot exchange occasional pleasantries. What the right hon. lady has done today is to lead her troops into battle snugly concealed behind a Scottish nationalist shield, with the boy David holding her hand.

I must say to the right hon. lady – and I should like to see her smile – that I am even more concerned about the fate of the right hon. gentleman than I am about her. She can look after herself. But the Leader of the Liberal Party, and I say this with the utmost affection, has passed from rising hope to elder statesman without any intervening period whatsoever.

Let me turn to the central theme of the right hon. lady's speech. She quoted a book which was written by Anthony Crosland, who was a good friend of hon. members who sit on the Labour benches. I hope that she will not mind if I quote from a book, published not so long ago, by Reginald Maudling.[23] I do not do this as a taunt, but I believe that it is of major significance to the House in deciding the vote and to the country at large in the more general debate over the coming weeks and months. It concerns a matter of major significance to our country over the past seven or eight years. Mr Maudling wrote of his experience in the Shadow Cabinet:

> From the start, there was a tendency in the Shadow Cabinet to move away from the Heath line of policy further to the Right: to this I was totally opposed. In particular, I could not support the arguments of Keith Joseph, who was inclined to say that all we had done in the Government of 1970–74 was wrong and not true Conservatism. I totally disagreed with this, because it seemed to me that Keith was fully entitled to measure himself for a hair shirt it he wanted to, but I was blowed if I could see why he should measure me and Ted at the same time.

I am sorry that we do not have the assistance of the right hon. member for Sidcup [Edward Heath]. That was just a prelude. And Mr Maudling continued:

> I could not help recalling Selsdon Park,[24] and the swing to the right in our policies which occurred then. And how long it had taken in Government to get back to the realities of life. I feared that the same thing was beginning to happen again.

I believe that that is an authentic account of what happened in the Shadow Cabinet when the right hon. lady, out of passionate conviction, led her party back to the Selsdon Park policies. That is the reality of the matter and the reason why the right hon. lady has never succeeded in securing full political cooperation with the right hon. member for Sidcup. There is still a great gulf between Selsdon Park Conservatives and those who learnt, in the words of Mr Maudling, 'the realities of life'. That comes from someone with great experience in the 1970–74 Government.

The Leader of the Opposition has not been able to explain very successfully to the House her special policy for dealing with devolution. We have made a proposal, but the Leader of the Opposition said in reply to my hon. friend the member for West Lothian [Tam Dalyell] that she proposed – and I think that this is a fair summary of what she said – talks about talks about talks about talks. That is her proposal for devolution. In fact, I think that my summary of her reply is rather complimentary because what she really proposes is to do nothing at all.

'Good,' shouted the robust Tory right-winger John Stokes – once described as Parliament's last link with the Middle Ages.

Conservative backbenchers shout 'Good' and the hon. member for Halesowen and Stourbridge [Stokes] shouts louder than anyone. But the Leader of the Opposition has, on the devolution question, torn up all the original policies of her party – the ones on which they fought the last general election – and now she proposes to do nothing. She has no proposals for a Scottish Assembly or any form of devolution or progress in that direction.

We believe that if this House says that it will wipe the Scotland Act off the statute book without proper consideration, very serious injury could be inflicted on the United Kingdom and on the Union itself. This House of Commons should pay respect to the referendum, even if it does not comply with the full requirement of 40 per cent laid down in the Bill.[25] It was on that basis that we made our proposal to the right hon. Lady and to the other parties. If we win the vote tonight, we will renew these proposals. I hope that every section of the House, whatever its preliminary views on the matter, will be prepared to discuss these issues afresh, otherwise there will be a deep gulf and breach, which will grow in years to come, between Scotland and the rest of the United Kingdom. That would be a highly dangerous development. I hope that Conservatives will have second thoughts on the subject.

In her speech today, the right hon. lady sought to make us forget what happened in the years of the previous Conservative Government. She also sought to give a very peculiar impression of the kind of legacy the Conservatives left behind for the Labour Government who came to power in 1974. It is interesting to note the things that she did not mention at all. She did not say a word about the balance of payments. I do not know whether she regards that as a matter of any significance. The fact is that the deficit in our balance of payments in the year that she and her right hon. friends left office was the biggest in our history – even bigger than the deficit that the Tory Party left us in 1964. But of course she wants all that to be wiped away from the public memory.

She wants to have wiped away from the public memory also the real figures of the rate of inflation when the Conservatives left office – what is more, a rising rate of inflation. There was a rate of inflation of 14 per cent in February, with 15 per cent and more in the pipeline, and a prophecy then of 20 per cent.

The Conservative MP Peter Rost reminded Foot of the then inflation rate of 8.4 per cent.

We have heard the old parrot cry from all the right hon. and hon. parrots before, and I dare say that they will utter it again. We shall hear it all through the general election campaign, but it will not alter the fact that the Conservatives left us a rising rate of inflation, zooming upwards, with threshold payments inbuilt to make the rate of inflation continue upwards. That is what they left us, and what we have done is to bring the rate down to less than half what it was when the right hon. lady and her right hon. and hon. friends were put out of office. That is another of the major aspects of what has occurred that the Conservatives wish to leave out of the reckoning.

So what will happen? What will once again be the choice at the next election? It will not be so dissimilar from the choice that the country had to make in 1945, or even in 1940 when the Labour Party had to come to the rescue of the country.

This provoked gasps from the Conservative benches.

It was on a motion of the Labour Party that the House of Commons threw out the Chamberlain Government in 1940. It was thanks to the Labour Party that Churchill had the chance to serve the country in the war years. Two-thirds of the Conservative Party at that time voted for the same reactionary policies as they will vote for tonight. It is sometimes in the most difficult and painful moments of our history that the country has turned to the Labour Party for salvation, and it has never turned in vain. We saved the country in 1940 and we did it again in 1945. We set out to rescue the country – or what was left of it – in 1974. Here again in 1979 we shall do the same. [Interruption.]

As voices rose across the chamber, the Speaker intervened to call for silence, but Foot continued to provoke them.

They are trying to stop me from getting your vote as well, Mr Speaker.

'Shame,' yelled the Conservatives.

I do not know why Conservative members are saying that this is shameful. I think that it is high time that the Tory Party recovered some sense of humour, even if it has lost everything else. Conservative members really ought to have had plenty of practice at laughing at themselves over these recent years, and they should make a better effort on this occasion.

We are quite prepared to have an election, but the Conservative Party has always had the idea that it was born to rule, although I should have thought that the country had been cured of that impression long since. It has always thought that everything must be decided according to the desires and whims of Conservative Central Office, that everything else is unpatriotic. Well, we say that this House of Commons should decide when an election takes place, and that the people will decide which Government they will have to follow this one.

We believe that once the record is fully put to the country we shall come back here with the real majority that the Labour Government require to govern for the next five years.

The result of the vote was ayes, 311 and noes, 310. So finely poised was the parliamentary arithmetic that night that, even in the final moments of the debate, it had seemed conceivable that Foot's words might swing some maverick member of one of the smaller parties and win the day for the government. Indeed, one Scottish Nationalist did run back to try to cancel out his vote against them when he realised that the motion might succeed, but in vain.

The *Daily Telegraph*'s sketch-writer Frank Johnson described the denouement: 'The final scenes of the debate and vote were the most exciting anyone could remember. Mr Michael Foot, the Leader of the House, whooped and bawled his way through a magnificent, outlandish winding up. He was in full Footage. If Mrs Thatcher is as much a threat to socialism as he made out, the country is saved.

'After denouncing her every policy, he found himself with ten minutes to go. So, in a marvellously gaga passage, he started raving about how it was always Labour who had to save the country, for example in 1940 . . . The Tories became rather angry at his failure to mention that Churchill was a member of their party at the time . . . He sat down to a vast ovation.'

When the vote was done, and the government was defeated by 311 votes to 310, a vast cheer rang out. James Callaghan defiantly promised to 'take our case to the country'. Tory MPs congaed through the central lobby, while Mr Speaker Thomas tried to quell Labour members, led by Neil Kinnock, who sang a doleful chorus of 'The Red Flag'. 'Which must,' commented Johnson, 'have been worth a few votes to the Tories in the marginals.'

'Who is the Mephistopheles behind this shabby Faust?'

Denis Healey denounces the decision to strip staff at a government intelligence agency of the right to membership of a trade union: 27 February 1984

In January 1984 the Foreign Secretary, Geoffrey Howe, caused uproar when he announced that trade unions would no longer be permitted at one of Britain's key intelligence agencies, GCHQ, the Government Communications Headquarters. In future, no employee there would be allowed to belong to a union.

GCHQ is the listening post through which Britain eavesdrops on communications across the world – the descendant of the code-breaking operations which made such a crucial contribution to victory in the Second World War. Its operations had been the target of selective action in civil service strikes, notably in a day of action, in 1981, and even though ministers had admitted that operational work had not been affected, the government – or at any rate the Prime Minister, Margaret Thatcher – had concluded that even the threat of disruption of vital intelligence work was intolerable. There were also worries about the effect on GCHQ's close partnership with American intelligence agencies. Staff were offered a payment of £1,000 if they agreed to surrender their right to union membership, or redeployment if they insisted on keeping it.

Denis Healey, then shadow Foreign Secretary, led Labour's condemnation of the decision when it came to be debated in the Commons. It was generally accepted that Howe had been forced into the ban by Thatcher, and Healey zeroed in on this fault line. He had long wanted to take on Mrs Thatcher, and this was one of the few chances he had to make a direct attack on her in the Commons. He began by describing the reaction against the ban from moderate trade union leaders, Conservative MPs and even the *Daily Telegraph*.

IN THE PAST MONTH everyone has been asking why on earth the Foreign Secretary took the decision. It was not because he believed that trade unions were likely to be spies, because he knows, as we do, that most spies since the war have been public schoolboys, masons, scientists or service men. I have no doubt that the Government have in hand measures for dealing with that particular threat to our security. The Foreign Secretary told the House this afternoon that he took the decision because the disruption at GCHQ on certain occasions between 1979 and 1981 broke the continuity of work there and might have endangered lives. He concluded – he told us again this afternoon – that membership of the trade union produces an unacceptable conflict of loyalties.

Some hon. members may have been impressed by some of the quotations that the Foreign Secretary read out in his speech from trade union leaders during those periods of industrial action. However, the trade unions have shown that there was no prejudice to the essential operations of GCHQ at the time, and the Foreign Secretary told the Select Committee that there was no evidence that any damage was done.

The most important statement by a Minister was made on 14 April 1981, after all those interruptions had taken place. Sir John Nott, the then Secretary of State for Defence, said in the House: 'I do not wish to discuss the difficulties surrounding the dispute, but up to now they have not in any way affected operational capability in any area . . . I have the highest praise for the great loyalty shown by the Civil Service to Governments of all kinds.'

It is difficult to find any convincing reason for this sudden decision by the Government – eight months after the publication of the Security Commission report on Prime[26] – except for their fear of staff reaction to the introduction of the polygraph, or lie detector, which is due to begin on an experimental basis in a few weeks' time. The lie detector has been described by a scientist who studied it as wrong on two thirds of the occasions on which it was used, and it was condemned by the Royal Commission on Criminal Procedure as unsuitable for use in court proceedings in Britain for that reason.

We all agree that there is a powerful case for guaranteeing continuity of operation at GCHQ, but the unions have now offered that in terms of a contract which is legally binding on individual employees.

If the Government had a spark of common sense, they would have jumped at the offer made by the trade unions, and the next Labour Government will do so when the opportunity arrives. But the Prime Minister has behaved in this affair, uncharacteristically, like General Galtieri,[27] who rejected her offer on the Falklands – a very favourable offer – preferred to fight, and lost. She is now gambling with people's lives. Sir Brian Tovey[28] told us that if only 10 per cent of the members of GCHQ in key areas refused to stay there, the operation would collapse. I put it to the Foreign Secretary that it is certain that many more than that will refuse, especially the radio operators at the outstations, which are the most important area of GCHQ operations. The Foreign

Secretary told us, without giving figures, that two thirds of employees had already signed, but we know that 40 per cent of employees are not trade union members, so they are taking the £1,000 and running. Some trade union members might also have signed, but there is no doubt that a very large number of dedicated men and women in key posts at GCHQ have not signed and will not sign.

The Foreign Secretary and the Prime Minister talk of conflicts of loyalty. They have forced on the staff in GCHQ the most damaging conflict of loyalty known to man – loyalty to principle as against loyalty to family. The staff know that in many cases, if they give up work at GCHQ, it will be impossible for them to find work anywhere else without breaking their family life.

One of the results of the Government's action has been to give more publicity to GCHQ in the last three weeks than it has had over the past 40 years. The Government's action is risking the disruption of the work of GCHQ at one of the most dangerous periods in the post-war world, when the Lebanon is in chaos, when the Gulf war is threatening oil supplies to the Western world, when the United States is warning of military intervention very close to the Soviet frontier, and when there is a new leadership in the Kremlin. What a wonderful moment for the Government to choose to put this vital operation in jeopardy.

The Tory MP John Browne suggested a no-strike agreement was not the only issue. He complained that the unions were resisting security precautions such as the searching of briefcases as staff left the GCHQ building. As Labour MPs shouted their annoyance, he said the unions should guarantee to support such security operations in future. Healey, to angry shouts from Conservative MPs, hit back at what he saw as a slur on working-class patriotism.

I made the point before that the threat to security in that sense, through espionage, in all Government establishments comes from former public school boys such as the hon. gentleman. The Government have never told us that they have raised these issues at any time in their discussions with the trade unions. The issue raised by the hon. gentleman is a wholly false one.

Every trade unionist in Britain feels threatened by what the Government have done. The anger felt by trade unionists was felt deeply by everyone, not least Mr Murray, who attended the meeting with the Prime Minister last week, because she was felt to be accusing trade unions of lack of patriotism, of being prepared to risk people's lives and to break their promises. The Foreign

Secretary made it crystal clear in his speech that that, in his view, is what trade union membership at GCHQ must imply. I ask the Government to recognise that they really cannot talk in those terms to people such as Terry Duffy[29] and Kate Losinska, who are now leading the campaign against the Government. What a miracle the Government have achieved in the trade union movement.

I have not wasted time on the Foreign Secretary this afternoon, although I am bound to say that I feel that some of his colleagues must be a bit tired by now of his hobbling around from one of the doorsteps to another, with a bleeding hole in his foot and a smoking gun in his hand, telling them that he did not know it was loaded.

The Foreign Secretary, however, is not the real villain in this case; he is the fall guy.

Those of us with long memories will feel that he is rather like poor van der Lubbe in the Reichstag fire trial.

This is a rather odd comparison for an ex-communist to invoke in defence of trade unionists: Marianus van der Lubbe was the young Dutch communist found in the Reichstag (Parliament) building as the fire which destroyed it in February 1933 began. Hitler's Nazi government portrayed him as the tool of the German communist leadership in the subsequent show trial, allowing it to launch a violent pogrom against them and other opponents. It is worth remembering that the man who was really behind van der Lubbe was in fact the Nazi propaganda genius, Joseph Goebbels. If this was some subtle insult to Mrs Thatcher, Healey then showered some rather more overt ones upon her – quoting some of the nicknames coined by the dissident Tory backbencher Julian Critchley.

We are asking ourselves the question that was asked at the trial: who is the Mephistopheles behind this shabby Faust? The answer to that is clear. The handling of this decision by – I quote her own backbenchers – the great she-elephant, she who must be obeyed, the Catherine the Great of Finchley, the Prime Minister herself, has drawn sympathetic trade unionists, such as Len Murray, into open revolt. Her pigheaded bigotry has prevented her closest colleagues and Sir Robert Armstrong[30] from offering and accepting a compromise.

The right hon. lady, for whom I have a great personal affection, has formidable qualities, a powerful intelligence and immense courage, but those qualities can turn into horrendous vices, unless they are moderated by colleagues who have more experience, understanding and sensitivity. As she has got rid of all those colleagues, no one is left in the Cabinet with both the courage and the ability to argue with her.

I put it to all Conservative members, but mainly to the Government front bench, that to allow the right hon. lady to commit Britain to another four years of capricious autocracy would be to do fearful damage not just to the Conservative Party but to the state. She has faced them with the most damaging of all conflicts of loyalty. They must choose between the interests of their country, our nation's security and our cohesion as a people and the obstinacy of an individual. I hope that they resolve this conflict in the interests of the nation. If not, they will carry a heavy responsibility for the tragedies that are bound to follow.

Healey thought his attack a success. In his memoirs he recorded that 'there was plenty of laughter on the Government benches at my words. Her Cabinet colleagues joined in and even the Prime Minister permitted herself a wan smile.'[31] The laughter had begun with Julian Critchley on the backbenches, and spread to the front bench when the Leader of the House, John Biffen, began to titter. But the ban stayed in place. Its removal, thirteen years later, was one of the first acts of Tony Blair's incoming Labour government.

'Truthfulness in the House is the fulcrum of our system.'

Tam Dalyell is ordered from the chamber for calling Margaret Thatcher 'a bounder, a liar, a deceiver, a cheat and a crook': 26 October 1986

In 1985 an apparently minor dispute about the future of a medium-sized but strategically important manufacturing company escalated into a serious political crisis for Margaret Thatcher. The Westland helicopter company, based in Yeovil, was facing bankruptcy. Normally, the Thatcher government, guided by its free-market philosophy, would not have intervened to save it. But Westland was an important defence manufacturer, and its demise would have damaged defence policy.

There was a political problem too. The Defence Secretary at the time was Michael Heseltine, who – against Thatcherite orthodoxy – believed in industrial intervention. He began to encroach on the departmental territory of the Trade and Industry Secretary, Leon Brittan, to promote a deal under which Westland would be taken over by a European consortium, rather than by the US helicopter giant Sikorsky, which was Mrs Thatcher's preferred solution. They were on different sides of a classic European versus Atlanticist dilemma: American ownership of the company would preclude its involvement in certain collaborative European defence projects which would compete with US helicopters; European ownership would exclude Westland from collaboration with US projects. Heseltine was openly flouting the norms of Cabinet behaviour, but what made the increasingly public dispute so toxic was his unconcealed ambition to lead his party. Thatcher faced not just a policy disagreement, but a challenge to her authority.

Much of the battle was conducted through the release of letters supporting one side or other of the argument. It culminated in the leaking of a letter from one of the Law Officers – the government's top legal advisers – the Solicitor-General, Sir Patrick Mayhew. Mayhew's letter warned Heseltine that a letter from him on the Westland question, which had found its way into the press, contained 'material inaccuracies' which he should correct. Such an authoritative rebuke from such an unimpeachable figure dealt a devastating blow to Heseltine. But the shock waves were also felt in Downing Street, where the outraged Mayhew demanded an investigation. By Whitehall convention an aura of sanctity surrounds the Law Officers, whose advice is virtually never published. This crude leak, to pursue a mere political dispute, affronted one of the most sacred commandments of British government. What made it worse was the implication that the culprit was another minister.

Not only Brittan was under the spotlight, but also two of the Prime Minister's closest aides – her press secretary Bernard Ingham and her private secretary Charles Powell. The stakes were raised in spectacular style by the most senior Law Officer, the Attorney General, Sir Michael Havers, who rose from his sickbed to warn that unless the matter was cleared up to his satisfaction, he would send the police into Downing Street to investigate the leak. So the Cabinet Secretary, Sir Robert Armstrong, was instructed to report on the matter.

Soon afterwards, Heseltine stalked out of a Cabinet meeting and out of government, claiming he had been denied his constitutional right to put his proposal for the future of Westland to the full Cabinet. Heseltine delivered a well-prepared resignation statement and later skewered Brittan in the House, when he delivered a statement on the whole Westland question.

The by now badly wounded Trade Secretary was blamed for the leak when Armstrong reported, and in due course he resigned. But his resignation was not couched in terms of a guilty culprit being scourged from the temple. The traditional exchange of letters even included the Prime Minister's hope that he would soon return to office. The suspicion persisted that he had taken the rap for the Prime Minister, and that the ultimate responsibility for the leak lay with her.

This was precisely the kind of issue which attracted the talents of Tam Dalyell. His determined deconstruction of the circumstances surrounding the sinking of the Argentine warship, the *General Belgrano*, during the Falklands War had generated considerable embarrassment for Thatcher and, ironically, Heseltine. Now he focused on the tangled circumstances of the leaking of the Solicitor-General's advice, and delivered a peroration in terms that only an Old Etonian could, by the 1980s, employ with a straight face.

O N THE 18 NOVEMBER 1985, I visited Westland at Yeoville. Taken round by Bill Gueterbock and shop stewards, I was told of the company's plight and its need for orders and of the lack of interest from Ministers. Therefore, I shall be acquitted of lack of concern about the British helicopter industry and the charge of simply making political mischief. When I was in Yeovil in November last year, the company was desperate to get Ministers to look at its problems.

If I concentrate on the law officer's letter, it is not, to borrow Brian Redhead's[32] dismissive phrase this morning, about 'Westminster shenanigans'; it is about the integrity of the British Government.

Like the rest of us, I am a party politician. But, above that in certain matters, I am a child of the House of Commons and party can come second. I care about how the House is treated by Ministers, however exalted they are. My front bench knows that I was critical of the Shadow Cabinet for not asking the Shadow Attorney General [John Morris QC] to open the debate and requiring the presence of one of the *dramatis personae* to answer – the Attorney General himself.

I begin with a direct question which I hope will be answered when the Minister replies or in response to the first oral question on Monday.

Under the byline of that careful, well-informed and trustworthy political correspondent, John Lewis, known and held in respect over the years by many of us, on the front page of the *Sunday Telegraph* on 27 July 1986 there appeared the words: 'Havers threat to call police to No. 10.'

The Attorney General was compelled to warn Sir Robert Armstrong, the Cabinet Secretary, at the height of the Westland affair that he would have the police on the doorstep of No. 10 Downing Street next morning unless he agreed to an immediate leaks inquiry. Is Mr Lewis writing the truth, or is it without foundation? I believe it to be true. If so, what is the explanation of the senior law officer of the Crown threatening to bring the constabulary to No. 10?

On 14 July 1986, I asked the Attorney General: 'Surely the usual practice is that Law Officers' letters are treated with extreme discretion and most gingerly by the Downing Street machine. Why did the Solicitor General's letter ever go near Mr Ingham and the press office, unless there was a prime ministerial instruction that it was to be leaked?'

The answer was: 'I am quite certain that there was no such instruction.'

I believe that the Attorney General was telling the truth in his own mind when he gave that answer. Does he still believe that to be true? On 25 July, I had the lucky opportunity in an Adjournment debate to set out for 30 minutes my detailed concern about the Law Officer's letter. In reply, the Minister's answer was bland and anodyne. But in three months, no attempt has been made to answer my questions.

For more than 24 years as a Member of the House I have seen Ministers of Governments of both major parties go. Some of the resignation correspondence has been sad and pained as between old party colleagues, some has been curt, bordering on the acrimonious; but never, during a quarter of a century in the House, have I read of such correspondence as that between the Prime Minister and her departing Secretary of State for Trade and

Industry. The *Daily Telegraph* of 25 January 1986 printed a letter from the
Prime Minister to the former Secretary of State for Trade and Industry, which
ended: 'I hope that it will not be long before you return to high office to
continue your ministerial career.'

How could the Prime Minister say that, if the complete picture was of a
Secretary of State for Trade and Industry who had deceived his senior civil
servants, his Cabinet colleagues and his Prime Minister for fourteen days? She
said that because it was a negotiated correspondence. Had such a letter not
been forthcoming, the right hon. and learned Member for Richmond, Yorks
[Leon Brittan] might have refused to carry the can and act as a prime
ministerial scapegoat. He could negotiate. He could spill the prime ministerial
beans. He held the ace, king, and queen of trumps.

I make no apology for quoting from Mr Peter Hennessy's article in the *New
Statesman* because I have some sympathy for the right hon. and learned
member for Richmond, Yorks. It states: 'Pressure from Conservative backbenchers forced Leon Brittan to follow Heseltine out of the Government, not
the requirements of ministerial responsibility. The need to preserve the
position of the Prime Minister, and not constitutional doctrine led the
Conservative majority on the Commons Defence Committee to "clear"
Thatcher.'

Simon Jenkins' article stated that passages had to be negotiated with Leon
Brittan, lest he step out of line in the debate.

Parliament should not be content with being given a line. Hon. members
are entitled to the truth. If we are content simply to be spun a line, we are not
doing our jobs properly.

I set out the narrative on 25 July. The right hon. and learned member
Richmond, Yorks could show that before 6 January – before an unsuspecting
Solicitor General was prompted by No. 10 to write the letter – the Prime
Minister had set down the guidelines for the strategy. Perhaps there was no
need for consultation. Mr Ingham and Mr Powell knew exactly what they had
to do before the innocent Solicitor General ever put pen to paper. If the civil
servants were not carrying out the Prime Minister's orders, they should be
punished. If she is not prepared to punish them, the Prime Minister should
admit that they were carrying out her orders.

Sir Robert Armstrong's subsequent refusal to discipline any of the civil
servants directly involved must be wholly unsatisfactory. The only reason for
not disciplining them was that the Cabinet Secretary knew full well that it
was not the more junior civil servants but the politicians that were guilty.

Mr Ingham refused, under orders, to give evidence to the Select Committee, and he is criticised for his central role in masterminding the leak of the Solicitor General's letter. If he masterminded the leak of a law officer's letter, he should be sacked; he should not bask, as he is doing, in prime ministerial favour.

The Prime Minister has always claimed that her officials acted without her knowledge and that she did not know the full circumstances of how the leak occurred until nearly a fortnight after the event. Anyone reading the report of the Select Committee on Defence must regard that as a fairy tale. The *raison d'etre* of the letter was to leak it to discredit the former Secretary of State for Defence. The only reason for persuading the Solicitor General to write the letter was to leak it.

Adam Raphael,[33] quoting a former Conservative Cabinet Minister, said: 'It is a perfectly simple story of straightforward dishonesty.' I do not know Mr Raphael's source, but I give the House my word of honour that three Conservative Privy Councillors – I shall not betray their names – who are political opponents but friends and colleagues of mine for more than 20 years, have separately said much the same thing.

When pressed, the Prime Minister blames the professional competence – 'misunderstandings' of civil servants. But paragraph fifteen of Cmnd. 9841, the Government's response to the seventh report of the Treasury and Civil Service Select Committee, states: 'The principle is clear: Ministers are accountable to Parliament for the policies and actions of their Departments.'

Pressed further, the Prime Minister authorises an inquiry, but it is an inquiry into that which she herself has set up. Simon Jenkins states that the Prime Minister is protected by adopting the doctrine of proportionality; that whatever blame might attach to her for the leak, a prime ministerial resignation would be out of proportion. But the truth is the truth is the truth and lies are lies are lies. If the Secretaries of State for Trade and Industry and for Defence laid down their political careers, why is it disproportionate that the Prime Minister should lay down hers?

Paragraph 198 shows that on 23 January I asked: 'When did the Prime Minister's press office first tell her what it had done?' The Prime Minister replied: 'I have said that I was not consulted at the time.'

She said that she had given a full account. That is not true. On Friday 25 July the narrative of how the Prime Minister organised the Law Officer's letter is spelt out. There was no full account. To say that the Prime Minister did not take part in the leak is a sustained, brazen deception. It is straightforward dishonesty. The House of Commons cannot continue to operate on that basis. Truthfulness in the House is the fulcrum of our system. The Prime Minister is a sustained, brazen deceiver now hiding behind cynical performances.

It is probably the best-known convention of the Commons that MPs do not accuse each other of lying. Dalyell had now called Mrs Thatcher a liar three times in 50 words. Deputy Speaker Harold Walker had no choice but to intervene and order him to withdraw his remarks. But Dalyell went further.

I say that she is a bounder, a liar, a deceiver, a cheat and a crook.

Walker tried again. 'Order. The hon. gentleman knows perfectly well that he cannot say that. He must either withdraw his remarks or I must invoke the powers invested in me and my responsibilities to the House. I hope that the hon. gentleman, who is a very experienced parliamentarian, will withdraw those remarks.'
    But Dalyell was absolutely unrepentant and well aware what would happen next.

I do not wish to take up my colleagues' time. Let us carry the matter no further. I stick to my remarks and I know what you must do, Mr Deputy Speaker.

Hansard then records: 'The hon. member, having used a grossly disorderly expression, was ordered by MR DEPUTY SPEAKER to withdraw the same, but he declined to comply with that direction, whereupon MR DEPUTY SPEAKER, pursuant to Standing Order No. 24 (Disorderly conduct), ordered him to withdraw immediately from the House during the remainder of this day's Sitting, and he withdrew accordingly.'
    As Dalyell doubtless anticipated, his expulsion from the chamber ensured that the allegations against Thatcher remained in the public eye.
    Leon Brittan left Parliament in 1989 to become one of Britain's two European commissioners. His seat was taken by William Hague. In 1990 Heseltine challenged Thatcher for the party leadership, dislodging but not replacing her. He returned to the Cabinet under John Major.

'Those are not meaningless rituals. They are reminders of monumental struggles to build democracy against tyranny. It is important that we should not treat them simply as tourist attractions.'

Tony Benn invokes the ancient liberties of the Commons to defend members' rights: 27 January 1987

As the GCHQ affair confirmed, the whole business of Britain's massive signals intelligence operations, intercepting communications across the globe, was painfully sensitive to the government. At the beginning of 1987, police raided the BBC offices in Scotland on suspicion that secret details of the £500 million Zircon spy satellite had been leaked to journalists making a documentary, *Secret Society*. BBC managers had already decided to postpone screening the programme, and an injunction was taken out to prevent it being shown privately.

On the basis of that injunction, Mr Speaker Weatherill banned the programme from being shown to MPs in the Palace of Westminster – a ruling which Tony Benn believed would undermine one of the most treasured rights of Parliament: that the courts could not interfere with its proceedings. When the Speaker's ruling came before the Commons, Benn, in a virtuoso procedural manoeuvre, first requested that the Speaker allow him to put down an amendment, and then persuaded MPs to accept his alternative proposal that the matter be referred to the Committee of Privileges, where the whole issue could be quietly buried. Any challenge, however tentative, to the ruling of a Speaker is fraught with danger. But Benn's speech was a masterpiece of tact, as well as argument.

IF THE MOTION PROPOSED by the Leader of the House [John Biffen, to confirm the ruling] were passed today, even the Committee of Privileges would not be allowed to see the film upon which Mr Speaker gave his ruling.

I think it is obvious to the House that the issues we are discussing go far beyond the immediate matters of controversy between the Government and the Opposition, the related question of the Campbell[34] article in the *New Statesman* on the film or the project. I do not wish to go back over the issues of last week when you took a decision, Mr Speaker, at very short notice, because it is today that we face the big decision.

Those of us who have anxieties about the implication of the decision that you took last week, Mr Speaker, wish to make it clear that those anxieties are in no sense personally related to you. Nevertheless, those anxieties are clear and specific and can be set out in the following way. If the Government are asking that we should 'confirm' your ruling, or if, as the amendment put down by my right hon. friend the member for Islwyn [Neil Kinnock, then leader of the opposition] states, we should 'accept' that decision, the difficulties go far beyond the Opposition and extend to the Chairmen and members of the Select Committees. That is why I am moving that the matter should go to the Committee of Privileges, which was set up by the House many years ago to examine matters that require complex examination. We should not reach a decision until the Committee of Privileges has reported.

The issue that we are discussing is a fundamental constitutional one of the relationship of the Commons, Members of Parliament and the electors on the one hand; and the Executive and the judiciary on the other. Although you quite properly said, Mr Speaker, that you did not wish your ruling of last Thursday to be treated as a precedent, if we confirm or accept it tonight it will appear in *Erskine May*[35] and will be quoted in future Parliaments and have a profound effect upon Parliament.

I do not believe that there is any precedent for the ruling that you gave, Mr Speaker. I have searched carefully through *Erskine May* and I can find no precedent, nor, I imagine that when the Committee on Accommodation was set up it was ever intended that the organisation of Committee Rooms of the House should be used to prevent the showing of a film on the provision of information that might assist hon. members in the course of their work.

It is right that we should look at your role, Mr Speaker, in this connection, because it is the highest office that we can bestow and you speak for us and defend us from the Executive. I have cited before, and will cite again, the words of Mr Speaker Lenthall. On 4 January 1642 the King came to the Commons to seize the five members. Mr Speaker Lenthall, described as 'a man of timorous nature', knelt and said: 'May it please your Majesty, I have neither eyes to see nor tongue to speak in this place but as the House is pleased to direct me, whose servant I am here.'

This was one of the great set pieces of parliamentary history: Charles I, accompanied by 300 swordsmen, came to the Commons to arrest the five MPs who were his principal opponents there – Pym, Hampden, Holles, Haselrig and Strode. The five had been tipped off, and had already fled by the time the monarch arrived, prompting Charles's famous observation: 'I see that the birds are flown.' This was the first and only occasion when a sovereign has set foot in the chamber. And as Charles left, outraged MPs murmured 'privilege' at his departing back. This was one of the key incidents in the build-up to the Civil War.

That was the precedent. It could be argued that if it was not in relation to five hon. members and the King, that precedent would not apply. However, we have taken it, ever since, as a statement of your role. Now when a new Speaker is elected he goes to the other place to claim the ancient privileges of the House.

I am sorry to go back to the texts, but people may not always appreciate their importance. In 1688 the 9th article of the Bill of Rights stated: 'That the freedom of speech, and debates or proceedings in Parliament, ought not to be impeached or questioned in any Court or place out of Parliament.'

Hon. members may ask whether a film shown somewhere else in the Chamber can be described as a proceeding in Parliament. Fortunately, we have a precedent for that as well. In 1938 Duncan Sandys, a member of the House and also a member of the Territorial Army,[36] received from a colleague in the Territorial Army information that there were defects in the air defence of London. He tabled a question and the person from whom he got the information was charged under the Official Secrets Act 1911. Duncan Sandys came to the House to appeal to the House to protect him by way of privilege and the person who gave the information.

I know about this matter because my father was on the Committee of Privileges or the Select Committee which reported on the case. I remember most vividly the debate in the House. The House upheld the view – I shall refer to it because it refers directly to the question as to what is a proceeding in Parliament and did so in a case involving the Official Secrets Act. I shall quote from *Erskine May*, page 93, commenting on the Committee that examined the Sandys case: 'cases may easily be imagined of communications between one member and another or between a member and a Minister, so closely related to some matter pending in, or expected to be brought before the House, that, although they do not take place in the Chamber or a committee room, they form part of the business of the House.'

That was one of the most important judgments reached by the House, especially when one considers, to its credit, that it was in the middle of war. As far as I recall, the matter was discussed in the House in May 1940, when it may well have had other matters to consider. Nevertheless, it entrenched the right of its members to receive information from someone who is not a member of the House even when that information is in respect of the security of the country.

I give that historical and legal background only to underline the enormity of the decision that it is proposed we should take without any further examination of the issues at stake. My amendment does not prejudge any of those issues, but invites the House to put the matter to the Committee that is best qualified to judge.

It is an issue that is not just of historical and legal importance, but one which will have immediate, practical importance to the future workings of parliamentary democracy. I ask the House to ask itself these important questions before hon. members go into the Lobby to vote on any of the amendments, other than the one referring to the Committee of Privileges.

First, is it right for the Government to engage in major military projects without telling Parliament? This question, as my hon. friends will know, points a finger of criticism at both Labour and Tory Governments. I think I am one of the few surviving members who sat in this House when Mr Attlee was Prime Minister and Mr Attlee developed the atom bomb without telling Parliament. At the time, that may have been considered acceptable, but I do not believe that any hon. member would accept that it would be right to do that today.

The House does not want technical details about the defence of secrets when the question of security arises. I have not read the article in the *New Statesman* and I do not particularly want to read what Duncan Campbell may say about a particular satellite. However, Parliament must know the general nature of major defence projects, their purpose and their cost. If Parliament does not know that it is abdicating its responsibilities.

The second question is whether it is right that Ministers should be able to go to any court and use the magic words 'national security' as the basis for a court injunction. In a democracy it is for the House and electors to decide what is in the national interest. And when there is a general election, it is the people's judgment as to what is in the national interest that counts. It is not for civil servants, generals, scientists or Ministers to determine what is national security. The judges of the Cheltenham case have said that if the magic words 'national security' are used they will not allow the matter to be raised.

The third question that I would like the House to consider is whether it is right that any Speaker – so as not to personalise it – hearing news of an injunction that has been issued should be able, without the explicit and specific authority of the House, to prevent hon. members from seeking available information that would assist Parliament in its work of holding Governments to account. As the court in question declined to grant an injunction against some hon. members, it is clear that it recognised the limits of its powers. Page 204 of *Erskine May* states: 'the courts admit: That the control of each House over its internal proceedings is absolute and cannot be interfered with by the courts.'

I do not know, and it is not my concern, to what extent that aspect was in your mind, Mr Speaker, when you took what you feel to have been interim action, but that is the question that we have to ask today, because we are reaching permanent decisions. The next question is whether we should accept and confirm a limit on our freedom as Members of Parliament that would assist the concealment of any matter by any Government of any Parliament – this is not just in relation to this matter – by the use of national security and injunctions. I worry greatly over the other implications of your ruling, Mr Speaker. What if the police had gone to a magistrate and asked for a warrant to search the papers of my hon. friend the member for Livingston [Robin Cook][37] at the time they were going to the home of Duncan Campbell? What would have been the position? Is it the case that the House could ever allow the courts or a magistrate to send policemen into the Palace, where already a film may not be shown, to discover the sources of information of a member who might be contemplating a parliamentary question?

If we accept the motion or the amendment, we would be placing the House of Commons and Members of Parliament for ever under the effective control of the Government, in that Ministers could bring an injunction, the court could accede to the injunction and – nobody would wish this less than you, Mr Speaker – Mr Speaker would become an agent of the Minister and his injunction and the court that upheld it, to enforce upon members the denial of the rights for which we were elected. I cannot believe, knowing you, Mr Speaker, that it would be your wish to be remembered as a 'Counter-Lenthall' whose protection did not extend to hon. members in this position.

I should like to make a final comment as an old member of the House. We all take children and visitors round the House. I do and have done for many years. We tell them that we keep Black Rod out. We tell them about the Outlawries Bill, we tell them that the House decides on its own business before it gives attention to the Gracious Speech. We tell them about the Army and Air Force (Annual) Act and the order to prevent a standing Army being maintained and we tell them about the five members. Those are not meaningless rituals. They are reminders of monumental struggles to build democracy against tyranny. It is important that we should not treat them simply as tourist attractions.

For all those reasons, I appeal to hon. members of all parties to pass the amendment that refers the matter to the place where these implications can be fully considered. I appeal to the Leader of the House to recognise the importance of his role in granting a free vote to Conservative members on the question of reference to the Committee of Privileges. If that is rejected, the matter will have to be dealt with by the motion on the Order Paper. In 36 years in the House I cannot recall a debate as important as this and I am grateful to you, Mr Speaker, for allowing my manuscript amendment to be put on the Order Paper tonight along with the motion and the other amendments before us.

Benn believes Weatherill allowed his amendment because he had realised that he had made a mistake in his original ruling.[38] Weatherill thought this speech one of the best he had ever heard, one of the rare instances where a single member swung the Commons through sheer power of argument.

Bootleg copies of the *Secret Society* documentaries were soon circulating across the country. They were eventually broadcast more than a year later.

'Ministers changed the guidelines, but were more worried that Members of Parliament and the public might find out than they were about what Saddam Hussein might do with the weapons.'

Robin Cook on the findings of the arms to Iraq inquiry: 15 February 1996

In a dazzling parliamentary career, this speech probably ranks as Robin Cook's greatest triumph, not least because of the technical difficulties placed in his way. He was responding to the long-delayed publication of Sir Richard Scott's inquiry into the arms to Iraq affair, in which the government stood accused of secretly abandoning its arms embargo against Saddam Hussein's regime to allow the Matrix Churchill company to make a lucrative export deal, supplying parts for a giant cannon or 'super-gun'. Two senior ministers were accused of failing to inform Parliament – William Waldegrave, the Chief Secretary to the Treasury, who had been involved in his previous incarnation as a Foreign Office minister and Sir Nicholas Lyell, the Attorney General, the government's chief legal adviser. The scandal had detonated when the trial of Matrix Churchill's directors for breaking the embargo collapsed on evidence from the former minister Alan Clark that the government had given tacit approval. It later emerged that ministers had signed public interest immunity certificates to deny the defence access to documents which could have exonerated them.

While ministers had been given eight days to study the five-volume, 2000-page report, Cook had just two hours, alone in a guarded room, with no assistants, no documents and just a pen and paper. And that much was granted only after the Speaker had intervened to say that the half-hour the government proposed to allow him was insufficient. Without total mastery of the facts of this intricate scandal, it would have been impossible to make much out of such limited contact with the report.

Cook eviscerated the government defence. His voice and bearing were perfect for expressing derision, and after a Commons statement by the President of the Board of Trade, Ian Lang, who blithely asserted that Scott had cleared both his colleagues, he had plenty of opportunity to employ them.

Procedurally, this was a response to a statement, and therefore had to be phrased as questions about its content.

T HE PRESIDENT [of the Board of Trade, Ian Lang] has just made a statement in which he laid blame on the Opposition, official advisers and the system, but accepted no blame for Ministers. The public outside will not find that a credible or dignified response to such a serious report.

I have spent the past three hours studying the report. It fully vindicates our two central charges – that Ministers changed the guidelines on defence sales to Saddam Hussein and that they repeatedly refused to admit that, either to Parliament or to the courts.

I did not recognise the report that I read from the statement that the House has just heard. The right hon. gentleman tells us that the Government accept many of the report's recommendations. Those recommendations arise from Sir Richard's conclusions. If the Government are going to accept his recommendations—

Conservative MPs began to shout demands that Cook stop making assertions and put a question.

Here is the question: does that mean that the Government will accept the conclusions on which the recommendations were based?

The right hon. gentleman has just accepted what witness after witness from the Government at the Scott inquiry tried to deny: that the guidelines on defence sales were changed and that the Government failed to inform Parliament of the change. Now that he has accepted that conclusion, will he also accept Sir Richard's conclusion that that failure was, in his words, deliberate and the result of three Ministers agreeing to give that no publicity? It is in the report. Will he also accept the conclusion that the reason that they gave it no publicity was that they did not want the public outrage that would greet it?

The President described the statement by the Chief Secretary as inaccurate. Does he accept the conclusion of Sir Richard Scott that the Chief Secretary signed letters to Members of Parliament denying that the guidelines had been changed, which were misleading and that, in the words of Sir Richard Scott, 'he was in a position to know that was so'?

Does the President accept – he did not mention it in his statement – that Sir Richard's conclusion is that Government statements on defence exports to Iraq, in his words, 'consistently failed' to comply with *Questions of Procedure for Ministers*[39] and thereby failed to discharge the principle of ministerial accountability?

The President's statement contained no mention of the super-gun. I presume that he is aware that the longest chapter in the report is on the super-gun. Does he accept the conclusion in that chapter that there is, in Sir Richard's words, 'clear evidence' that the Government knew about the super-gun a full year before its seizure by Customs and Excise? Does he accept that, in Sir Richard's opinion, Parliament could and should have been told, and that the failure to tell Parliament constituted, in his words, 'a further example of a failure to discharge the obligations of accountability'?

Does the President accept Sir Richard's conclusion that the intelligence information that the machine tools from Matrix Churchill went into the Iraqi arms programme was, in Sir Richard's words, 'so strong' that for Ministers to maintain that they were possibly for civilian use was 'the equivalent to the . . . use of a blind eye'?

Does the President accept the conclusion that public interest immunity certificates, denying the defence in the Matrix Churchill trial an entire class of documents, had never before been used in any criminal trial and Sir Richard recommends that they should never be used again? Will the Government at least give an assurance that they will never repeat the practice that led to that prosecution of Matrix Churchill?

Does the President accept that Sir Richard Scott found 'risible' the defence claim by the then Minister of State, Foreign and Commonwealth Office, the right hon. member for Watford [Tristan Garel-Jones], that the release of the documents would cause 'unquantifiable damage' to the public interest? If the right hon. gentleman does not think that being called risible is a criticism, when will he recognise a criticism?

Does the right hon. gentleman accept that the Attorney General was personally at fault in terms of the failure of the Government's Law Officers to instruct the prosecution to tell the trial judge that the current Deputy Prime Minister signed his certificate with reservations? Will he say whether the Government accept those conclusions – it takes only one word to say it: yes or no? He has had plenty of time to work it out: he has had eight days to study a report that Members of Parliament have had eight minutes to read.

The Commons had suspended its sitting for ten minutes to allow MPs a glimpse of the report, before Lang's statement.

His difficulty in answering the question is not that he has not had the time to make up his mind, but that his colleagues could not survive his acceptance of those conclusions.

Are the Government really going to ask us to accept a report that says that the current Chief Secretary signed 27 letters to Members of Parliament that were misleading, and which he was in a position to know were misleading, then tell us that he can remain in office as if the report had never been published? Is the President really going to ask the House to accept a report that shows that the Attorney General wrongly advised Ministers and failed to tell the court that at least one Minister signed under protest, then tell us that the Attorney General can also stay in office? Is the President really going to ask the House to accept a report which, over five volumes, demonstrates how this Government misjudged Saddam Hussein, misled Members of Parliament and misdirected the prosecution, then tell us that no one in the Government will accept responsibility for getting it wrong?

Will the President, before he passes the buck any further, confirm that yesterday, civil servants named in the report were told that any public comments they made must be cleared with their head of department, must be consistent with Government policy and must not criticise Ministers? How dare Ministers blame civil servants while ordering civil servants not to blame Ministers.

The report goes beyond the career of individual Ministers or the reputation of some officials. It reveals the price that Britain pays for a culture of secrecy in government. The report documents how Ministers changed the guidelines, but were more worried that Members of Parliament and the public might find out than they were about what Saddam Hussein might do with the weapons.

The President now has a second opportunity to rise to the occasion. Will he now tell us which Ministers accept responsibility for what went wrong while they were in office? Will he tell us whether the Government will dismiss those Ministers who, in the opinion of Sir Richard, failed to discharge the obligation of ministerial accountability to the House? Will he take the steps that are now essential if the Government are to be trusted in office? I warn the President that if he fails to answer those questions, the Government will forfeit any right to remain in office.

The ministers involved survived, but the reputation of the government had taken another battering. The cumulative effect of a series of sexual and political scandals was to become devastatingly clear in the election the following May. Tony Blair, then leader of the opposition, told Cook his speech was 'one of the highlights of my time in Parliament. You were not merely brilliant, you lifted the whole morale of our troops.'[40]

Two

VIRTUOSOS

THE VIRTUOSOS ARE the real parliamentarians – the ones members will dash into the chamber to hear. They will have something important to say, and they will say it in wonderful, luminous language, beautifully delivered and perfectly attuned to that elusive Snark-like construct, the 'mood of the House'. The *TIP* era began with two real masters – Winston Churchill and Nye Bevan. Few parliamentarians can hope to approach the magnificence of their speeches. But virtuosity does not always require the highest oratorical ability. Enoch Powell would mesmerise opponents through sheer intellectual quality. Brian Walden and Conrad Russell delivered genuinely original thoughts. Bernadette Devlin stunned the House with a debut of passionate eloquence, made all the more impressive by a first-hand account of the frightening events in Northern Ireland – although she never made quite the same impact again. The speeches in this chapter range from brilliant knockabout to lucid policy discussion. And there must be a special place for those who articulate the national mood in a moment of grief. It is impossible not to be moved by Harold Wilson's tribute to Churchill – or by John Major's valediction for his immediate political rival, John Smith.

For a daily programme on parliamentary proceedings, the virtuosos can cause problems. You cannot broadcast everything, so should an oration from a former minister, full of wit and insight, and preferably a few good jokes, take precedence over some hard-working backbencher who might well be in the chamber more often, and who, for once, has not been crowded out by the ex-ministers and vastly senior members who normally take precedence? This is a very real dilemma and one that is not easily solved – and *TIP* editors strive to avoid giving the impression that all Commons debates are dominated by the usual suspects.

But real virtuosity demands inclusion, not least because the very best parliamentarians can 'make the weather', and change the terms of a debate. The impact of Nye Bevan's brilliant exposition of the need for a national health service is with us 60 years later, when many of the achievements of the Attlee government have been reversed. The great tragedy of William Hague's career (at the time of writing at any rate) is that his sparkling Commons talents have mostly been deployed in opposition, rather than constructively, in arguing for some great landmark reform from the government benches.

Naturally there are dozens of parliamentarians, past and present, who might have been included in this chapter. This idiosyncratic selection is based partly on sheer historic importance, partly on quality and partly on a certain regard for those prepared to make an unpopular or inconvenient case regardless of whether the wider world is paying much attention.

'It is cardinal to a proper health organisation that a person ought not to be financially deterred from seeking medical assistance at the earliest possible stage.'

Nye Bevan creates the National Health Service: 30 April 1946

In 1941 the wartime coalition announced that as soon as possible after the war, a 'comprehensive hospital service' would be created. A year later, Beveridge included a free National Health Service among his proposals for tackling the 'five giants' of want, disease, ignorance, squalor and idleness in the better society promised at the end of the war. In 1944 a White Paper outlined the principles which would underlie a free service. But for all its coalition provenance, the bill that Aneurin Bevan placed before the Commons on 30 April 1946 did not reflect a cross-party consensus. His National Health Service would take over the patchwork of local authority and charity hospitals, rationalise the provision of general practitioners, and vastly extend dental services. It was as massive an act of nationalisation as any undertaken by the Attlee government.

Resistance was bitter. Senior figures from the British Medical Association denounced the bill in terms that evoked Churchill's prediction that a postwar Labour government would need a Gestapo. 'It looks to me like a first step, and a big one, towards National Socialism as practised in Germany,' announced the former BMA medical secretary Dr Alfred Cox, who warned that the Bill would create a British 'medical führer'.[1] Doctors would be reduced to state functionaries. There would be a mass exodus of British doctors to other parts of what was still referred to as the Empire. On Bevan's left flank, some Labour MPs were unhappy that he proposed to allow consultants to continue to take private, fee-paying patients while receiving for the first time a salary for hospital work. (This later proved to be a wise concession, because it prevented united opposition by the medical profession. Bevan was later to say of the consultants that he had 'stuffed their mouths with gold'.)

So when Bevan rose to open a three-day debate on his National Health Service Bill, he had a storm of criticism to face down. His biographer and disciple, Michael Foot, thought his greatest virtue as a parliamentarian was that he took the strongest arguments of his opponents head on. This wonderfully lucid speech is a series of justifications for a unified health service. He explained why all hospitals had to be under unified regional boards, why doctors would no longer be able to sell their practices and why some fee-paying treatment would continue to be permitted.

The *Guardian*'s parliamentary correspondent Harry Boardman thought his 75-minute speech a triumph. 'Masterful, yet conciliatory, cogent and persuasive.

'He had a manuscript, but why he had it, heaven knows. He completely ignored it. Here was a real parliamentarian acting on the House through living speech and not the meticulous reading of a manuscript. Mr Bevan is the most fluent member of the House, not excepting Mr Churchill . . . He held the close attention of the House throughout his long speech. Not for a moment did it relax.

'He had a most flattering reception from the Government benches and he sat down to salvo after salvo of cheers from the same quarter.'[2]

But despite the cheers Bevan won in the chamber, this speech was just the beginning of an epic struggle. As he spoke, the BMA were meeting in Tavistock Square to reject his bill. Even though it received the royal assent on 6 November, it was not finally accepted by the GPs until July 1948.

IN THE LAST TWO years there has been such a clamour from sectional interests in the field of national health that we are in danger of forgetting why these proposals are brought forward at all. It is, therefore, very welcome to me – and I am quite certain to hon. members in all parts of the House – that consideration should now be given, not to this or that sectional interest, but to the requirements of the British people as a whole. The scheme which anyone must draw up dealing with national health must necessarily be conditioned and limited by the evils it is intended to remove. Many of those who have drawn up paper plans for the health services appear to have followed the dictates of abstract principles and not the concrete requirements of the actual situation as it exists. They drew up all sorts of tidy schemes on paper, which would be quite inoperable in practice.

The first reason why a health scheme of this sort is necessary at all is because it has been the firm conclusion of all parties that money ought not to be permitted to stand in the way of obtaining an efficient health service. Although it is true that the national health insurance system provides a general practitioner service and caters for something like 21 million of the population, the rest of the population have to pay, whenever they desire the services of a doctor. It is cardinal to a proper health organisation that a person ought not to be financially deterred from seeking medical assistance at the earliest possible stage. It is one of the evils of having to buy medical advice that, in addition to the natural anxiety that may arise because people do not like to hear unpleasant things about themselves, and therefore tend to postpone consultation as long as possible, there is the financial anxiety caused by having to pay doctors' bills. Therefore, the first evil that we must deal with is that which exists as a consequence of the fact that the whole thing is the wrong way round. A person ought to be able to receive medical and hospital help without being involved in financial anxiety.

In the second place, the national health insurance scheme does not provide for the self-employed, nor, of course, for the families of dependants. It depends on insurance qualification, and no matter how ill you are, if you cease to be insured you cease to have free doctoring. Furthermore, it gives no backing to the doctor in the form of specialist services. The doctor has to provide himself, he has to use his own discretion and his own personal connections, in order to obtain hospital treatment for his patients and in order to get them specialists, and in very many cases, of course – in an overwhelming number of cases – the services of a specialist are not available to poor people.

Not only is this the case, but our hospital organisation has grown up with no plan, with no system; it is unevenly distributed over the country and indeed it is one of the tragedies of the situation that very often the best hospital facilities are available where they are least needed. In the older industrial districts of Great Britain hospital facilities are inadequate. Many of the hospitals are too small – very much too small. About 70 per cent have less than 100 beds, and over 30 per cent have less than 30. No one can possibly pretend that hospitals so small can provide general hospital treatment. There is a tendency in some quarters to defend the very small hospital on the ground of its localism and intimacy and for other rather imponderable reasons of that sort, but everybody knows today that if a hospital is to be efficient it must provide a number of specialised services. Although I am not myself a devotee of bigness for bigness sake, I would rather be kept alive in the efficient if cold altruism of a large hospital than expire in a gush of warm sympathy in a small one.

In addition to these defects, the health of the people of Britain is not properly looked after in one or two other respects. The condition of the teeth of the people of Britain is a national reproach. As a consequence of dental treatment having to be bought, it has not been demanded on a scale to stimulate the creation of sufficient dentists, and in consequence there is a woeful shortage of dentists at the present time. Furthermore, about 25 per cent of the people of Great Britain can obtain their spectacles and get their eyes tested and seen to by means of the assistance by the approved societies, but the general mass of the people have not such facilities. Another of the evils from which this country suffers is the fact that sufficient attention has not been given to deafness, and hardly any attention has been given so far to the provision of cheap hearing aids and their proper maintenance. I hope to be able to make very shortly a welcome announcement on this question.

Here Bevan set out the goal of universal provision in key areas of specialist medicine – opticians, psychiatric care and, in the longer term, care of adolescents.

There are, of course, three main instruments through which it is intended that the Health Bill should be worked. There are the hospitals; there are the general practitioners; and there are the health centres. The hospitals are in many ways the vertebrae of the health system, and I first examined what to do with the hospitals. The voluntary hospitals of Great Britain have done invaluable work. When hospitals could not be provided by any other means, they came along. The voluntary hospital system of this country has a long history of devotion and sacrifice behind it, and it would be a most frivolously minded man who would denigrate in any way the immense services the voluntary hospitals have rendered to this country. But they have been established often by the caprice of private charity. They bear no relationship to each other. Two hospitals close together often try to provide the same specialist services unnecessarily, while other areas have not that kind of specialist service at all. They are, as I said earlier, badly distributed throughout the country. It is unfortunate that often endowments are left to finance hospitals in those parts of the country where the well-to-do live while, in very many other of our industrial and rural districts there is inadequate hospital accommodation. These voluntary hospitals are, very many of them, far too small and, therefore, to leave them as independent units is quite impracticable.

Furthermore – I want to be quite frank with the House – I believe it is repugnant to a civilised community for hospitals to have to rely upon private charity. I believe we ought to have left hospital flag days behind. I have always felt a shudder of repulsion when I have seen nurses and sisters who ought to be at their work, and students who ought to be at their work, going about the streets collecting money for the hospitals. I do not believe there is an hon. member of this House who approves that system. It is repugnant, and we must leave it behind – entirely. But the implications of doing this are very considerable.

I have been forming some estimates of what might happen to voluntary hospital finance when the all-in insurance contributions fall to be paid by the people of Great Britain, when the Bill is passed and becomes an Act, and they are entitled to free hospital services. The estimates I have go to show that between 80 per cent and 90 per cent of the revenues of the voluntary hospitals in these circumstances will be provided by public funds, by national or rate funds.

A Labour MP shouted out: 'By workers' contributions.'

And, of course, as the hon. member reminds me, in very many parts of the country it is a travesty to call them voluntary hospitals. In the mining districts, in the textile districts, in the districts where there are heavy industries it is the industrial population who pay the weekly contributions for the maintenance of the hospitals. When I was a miner I used to find that situation, when I was on the hospital committee. We had an annual meeting and a cordial vote of thanks was moved and passed with great enthusiasm to the managing director of the colliery company for his generosity towards the hospital; and when I looked at the balance sheet, I saw that 97 per cent of the revenues were provided by the miners' own contributions; but nobody passed a vote of thanks to the miners.

But of course, it is a misuse of language to call these 'voluntary hospitals'. They are not maintained by legally enforced contributions; but, mainly, the workers pay for them because they know they will need the hospitals, and they are afraid of what they would have to pay if they did not provide them. So it is, I say, an impossible situation for the state to find something like 90 per cent of the revenues of these hospitals and still to call them 'voluntary'. So I decided, for this and other reasons that the voluntary hospitals must be taken over.

I knew very well when I decided this that it would give rise to very con-siderable resentment in many quarters, but, quite frankly, I am not concerned about the voluntary hospitals' authorities: I am concerned with the people whom the hospitals are supposed to serve. Every investigation which has been made into this problem has established that the proper hospital unit has to comprise about 1,000 beds – not in the same building but, nevertheless, the general and specialist hospital services can be provided only in a group of that size. This means that a number of hospitals have to be pooled, linked together, in order to provide a unit of that sort. This cannot be done effectively if each hospital is a separate, autonomous body. It is proposed that each of these groups should have a large general hospital, providing general hospital facilities and services, and that there should be a group round it of small feeder hospitals. Many of the cottage hospitals strive to give services that they are not able to give. It very often happens that a cottage hospital harbours ambitions to the hurt of the patients, because they strive to reach a status that they never can reach. In these circumstances, the welfare of the patients is sacrificed to the vaulting ambitions of those in charge of the hospital. If, therefore, these voluntary hospitals are to be grouped in this way; it is necessary that they should submit themselves to proper organisation, and that submission, in our experience, is impracticable if the hospitals, all of them, remain under separate management.

Now, this decision to take over the voluntary hospitals meant, that I then had to decide to whom to give them. Who was to be the receiver? So I turned to an examination of the local government hospital system. Many of the local authorities in Great Britain have never been able to exercise their hospital powers. They are too poor. They are too small. Furthermore, the local authorities of Great Britain inherited their hospitals from the Poor Law, and some of them are monstrous buildings, a cross between a workhouse and a barracks—

'And a prison,' a Labour MP interrupted.

Or a prison. The local authorities are helpless in these matters. They have not been able to afford much money. Some local authorities are first-class. Some of the best hospitals in this country are local government hospitals. But, when I considered what to do with the voluntary hospitals when they had been taken over, and who was to receive them I had to reject the local government unit, because the local authority area is no more an effective gathering ground for the patients of the hospitals than the voluntary hospitals themselves. My hon. friend said that some of them are too small, and some of them too large. London is an example of being too small and too large at the same time.

It is quite impossible, therefore, to hand over the voluntary hospitals to the local authorities. Furthermore – and this is an argument of the utmost importance – if it be our contract with the British people, if it be our intention that we should universalise the best, that we shall promise every citizen in this country the same standard of service, how can that be articulated through a rate-borne institution which means that the poor authority will not be able to carry out the same thing at all? It means that once more we shall be faced with all kinds of anomalies, just in those areas where hospital facilities are most needed, and in those very conditions where the mass of the poor people will be unable to find the finance to supply the hospitals. Therefore, for reasons which must be obvious – because the local authorities are too small, because their financial capacities are unevenly distributed – I decided that local authorities could not be effective hospital administration units. There are, of course, a large number of hospitals in addition to the general hospitals which the local authorities possess. Tuberculosis sanatoria, isolation hospitals, infirmaries of various kinds, rehabilitation, and all kinds of other hospitals are all necessary in a general hospital service. So I decided that the only thing to do was to create an entirely new hospital service, to take over the voluntary hospitals, and to take over the local government hospitals and to organise them as a single hospital service. If we are to carry out our obligation and to provide the people of Great Britain, no matter where they may be, with the same level of service, then the nation itself will have to carry the expenditure, and cannot put it upon the shoulders of any other authority.

A number of investigations have been made into this subject from time to time, and the conclusion has always been reached that the effective hospital unit should be associated with the medical school. If you grouped the hospitals in about 10 to 20 regions around the medical schools, you would then have within those regions the wide range of disease and disability which would provide the basis for your specialised hospital service. Furthermore, by grouping hospitals around the medical schools, we should be providing what is very badly wanted, and that is a means by which the general practitioners are kept in more intimate association with new medical thought and training. One of the disabilities, one of the shortcomings of our existing medical service, is the intellectual isolation of the general practitioners in many parts of the country. The general practitioner, quite often, practises in loneliness and does not come into sufficiently intimate association with his fellow craftsmen and has not the stimulus of that association, and in consequence of that the general practitioners have not got access to new medical knowledge in a proper fashion. By this association of the general practitioner with the medical schools through the regional hospital organisation, it will be possible to refresh and replenish the fund of knowledge at the disposal of the general practitioner.

Here Bevan dismissed the idea of separating the planning and executive authorities for the NHS, predicting that such a division would lead to 'paper planning' or bad execution. And he ruled out the idea of making regional health boards into 'conferences' of different interest groups as 'a recipe for chaos'.

When we come to the general practitioners we are, of course, in an entirely different field. The proposal which I have made is that the general practitioner shall not be in direct contract with the Ministry of Health, but in contract with new bodies. There exists in the medical profession a great resistance to coming under the authority of local government – a great resistance, with which I, to some extent, sympathise. There is a feeling in the medical profession that the general practitioner would be liable to come too much under the medical officer of health, who is the administrative doctor. This proposal does not put the doctor under the local authority; it puts the doctor in contract with an entirely new body – the local executive council, coterminous with the local health area, county or county borough. On that executive council, the dentists, doctors and chemists will have half the representation. In fact, the whole scheme provides a greater degree of professional representation for the medical profession than any other scheme I have seen.

I have been criticised in some quarters for doing that. I will give the answer now: I have never believed that the demands of a democracy are necessarily satisfied merely by the opportunity of putting a cross against someone's name every four or five years. I believe that democracy exists in the active participation in administration and policy. Therefore, I believe that it is a wise thing to give the doctors full participation in the administration of their own profession. They must, of course, necessarily be subordinated to lay control – we do not want the opposite danger of syndicalism. Therefore, the communal interests must always be safeguarded in this administration. The doctors will be in contract with an executive body of this sort. One of the advantages of that proposal is that the doctors do not become – as some of them have so wildly stated – civil servants. Indeed, one of the advantages of the scheme is that it does not create an additional civil servant.

It imposes no constitutional disability upon any person whatsoever. Indeed, by taking the hospitals from the local authorities and putting them under the regional boards, large numbers of people will be enfranchised who are now disfranchised from participation in local government. So far from this being a huge bureaucracy with all the doctors little civil servants – the slaves of the Minister of Health, as I have seen it described – instead of that, the doctors are under contract with bodies which are not under the local authority, and which are, at the same time, ever open to their own influence and control.

One of the chief problems that I was up against in considering this scheme was the distribution of the general practitioner service throughout the country. The distribution, at the moment, is most uneven. In South Shields before the war there were 4,100 persons per doctor; in Bath 1,590; in Dartford nearly 3,000 and in Bromley 1,620; in Swindon 3,100; in Hastings under 1,200. That distribution of general practitioners throughout the country is most hurtful to the health of our people. It is entirely unfair, and, therefore, if the health services are to be carried out, there must be brought about a redistribution of the general practitioners throughout the country.

One of the first consequences of that decision was the abolition of the sale and purchase of practices. If we are to get the doctors where we need them, we cannot possibly allow a new doctor to go in because he has bought somebody's practice. Proper distribution kills by itself the sale and purchase of practices. I know that there is some opposition to this, and I will deal with that opposition. I have always regarded the sale and purchase of medical practices as an evil in itself. It is tantamount to the sale and purchase of patients. Indeed, every argument advanced about the value of the practice is itself an argument against freedom of choice, because the assumption underlying the high value of a practice is that the patient passes from the old doctor to the new. If they did not pass there would be no value in it. I would like, therefore, to point out to the medical profession that every time they argue for high compensation for the loss of the value of their practices, it is an argument against the free choice which they claim. However, the decision to bring about the proper distribution of general practitioners throughout the country meant that the value of the practices was destroyed. We had, therefore, to consider compensation.

I have never admitted the legal claim, but I admit at once that very great hardship would be inflicted upon doctors if there were no compensation. Many of these doctors look forward to the value of their practices for their retirement. Many of them have had to borrow money to buy practices and, therefore, it would, I think, be inhuman, and certainly most unjust, if no compensation were paid for the value of the practices destroyed. The sum of £66,000,000 is very large. In fact, I think that everyone will admit that the doctors are being treated very generously. However, it is not all loss, because if we had, in providing superannuation, given credit for back service, as we should have had to do, it would have cost £35 million. Furthermore, the compensation will fall to be paid to the dependants when the doctor dies, or when he retires, and so it is spread over a considerable number of years. This global sum has been arrived at by the actuaries, and over the figure, I am afraid, we have not had very much control, because the actuaries have agreed it. But the profession itself will be asked to advise as to its distribution among the claimants, because we are interested in the global sum, and the profession, of course, is interested in the equitable distribution of the fund to the claimants.

The doctors claim that the proposals of the Bill amount to direction – not all the doctors say this but some of them do. There is no direction involved at all. When the Measure starts to operate, the doctors in a particular area will be able to enter the public service in that area. A doctor newly coming along would apply to the local executive council for permission to practise in a particular area. His application would then be re-referred to the Medical Practices Committee. The Medical Practices Committee, which is mainly a professional body, would have before it the question of whether there were sufficient general practitioners in that area. If there were enough, the committee would refuse to permit the appointment. No one can really argue that that is direction, because no profession should be allowed to enter the public service in a place where it is not needed. By that method of negative control over a number of years, we hope to bring about over the country a positive redistribution of the general practitioner service. It will not affect the existing situation, because doctors will be able to practise under the new service in the areas to which they belong, but a new doctor, as he comes on, will have to find his practice in a place inadequately served.

Here Bevan discussed the new payment system proposed for GPs – combining a basic salary with a capitation fee for each patient, while continuing to allow fees to be charged for private consultations.

The third instrument to which the health services are to be articulated is the health centre, to which we attach very great importance indeed. It has been described in some places as an experimental idea, but we want it to be more than that, because to the extent that general practitioners can operate through health centres in their own practice, to that extent will be raised the general standard of the medical profession as a whole. Furthermore, the general practitioner cannot afford the apparatus necessary for a proper diagnosis in his own surgery. This will be available at the health centre.

The health centre may well be the maternity and child welfare clinic of the local authority also. The provision of the health centre is, therefore, imposed as a duty on the local authority. There has been criticism that this creates a trichotomy in the services. It is not a trichotomy at all. If you have complete unification it would bring you back to paper planning. You cannot get all services through the regional authority, because there are many immediate and personal services which the local authority can carry out better than anybody else. So, it is proposed to leave those personal services to the local authority, and some will be carried out at the health centre. The centres will vary; there will be large centres at which there will be dental clinics, maternity and child welfare services, and general practitioners' consultative facilities, and there will also be smaller centres – surgeries – where practitioners can see their patients.

There you have the three main instruments through which it is proposed that the health services of the future should be articulated.

There has been some criticism. Some have said that the preventive services should be under the same authority as the curative services. I wonder whether Members who advance that criticism really envisage the situation which will arise. What are the preventive services? Housing, water, sewerage, river pollution prevention, food inspection – are all these to be under a regional board? If so, a regional board of that sort would want the Albert Hall in which to meet. This, again, is paper planning. It is unification for unification's sake. There must be a frontier at which the local joins the national health service. You can fix it here or there, but it must be fixed somewhere. It is said that there is some contradiction in the health scheme because some services are left to the local authority, and the rest to the national scheme. Well, day is joined to night by twilight, but nobody has suggested that it is a contradiction in nature. The argument that this is a contradiction in health services is purely pedantic, and has no relation to the facts.

I apologise for detaining the House so long, but there are other matters to which I must make some reference. The two Amendments on the Order Paper rather astonish me. The hon. member for Denbigh [Sir Henry Morris-Jones] informs me, in his Amendment, that I have not sufficiently consulted the medical profession—

Morris-Jones, the Liberal National MP for Denbigh – effectively a Conservative – interrupted to say that his criticism was that there had been no consultations.

I intend to read the Amendment to show how extravagant the hon. member has been. He says that he and his friends are

> . . . unable to agree to a measure containing such far-reaching proposals involving the entire population without any consultations having taken place between the Minister and the organisations and bodies representing those who will be responsible for carrying out its provisions . . .

I have had prepared a list of conferences I have attended. I have met the medical profession, the dental profession, the pharmacists, nurses and midwives, voluntary hospitals, local authorities, eye services, medical aid services, herbalists, insurance committees, and various other organisations. I have had 20 conferences. The consultations have been very wide. In addition, my officials have had thirteen conferences, so that altogether there have been 33 conferences with the different branches of the profession about the proposals. Can anybody argue that that is not adequate consultation? Of course, the real criticism is that I have not conducted negotiations. I am astonished that such a charge should lie in the mouth of any member of the House. If there is one thing that will spell the death of the House of Commons it is for a Minister to negotiate Bills before they are presented to the House. I had no negotiations, because once you negotiate with outside bodies two things happen. They are made aware of the nature of the proposals before the House of Commons itself; and furthermore the Minister puts himself into an impossible position, because, if he has agreed things with somebody outside, he is bound to resist Amendments from members in the House. Otherwise he does not play fair with them. I protested against this myself when I was a private member. I protested bitterly, and I am not prepared, strange though it may seem, to do something as a Minister which as a private member I thought was wrong. So there has not been negotiation, and there will not be negotiation in this matter. The House of Commons is supreme, the House of Commons must assert its supremacy, and not allow itself to be dictated to by anybody, no matter how powerful and how strong he may be.

Morris-Jones interrupted again to ask if Bevan would take the same line with the Miners' Federation. This was a reference to the talks held by the wartime coalition Secretary of Labour, Ernest Bevin, who did negotiate with the Miners' Federation over the issue of the 'Bevin Boys', who were in effect conscripted to work in the mines. But as Bevan was quick to point out, he attacked his near namesake for negotiating.

Certainly. That is exactly what I did. The hon. member was a member of the House at the time, and he should remember it. These consultations have taken place over a very wide field, and, as a matter of fact, have produced quite a considerable amount of agreement. The opposition to the Bill is not as strong as it was thought it would be. On the contrary, there is very considerable support for this Measure among the doctors themselves. I myself have been rather aggrieved by some of the statements which have been made. They have misrepresented the proposals to a very large extent, but as these proposals become known to the medical profession, they will appreciate them, because nothing should please a good doctor more than to realise that, in future, neither he nor his patient will have any financial anxiety arising out of illness.

The leaders of the Opposition have on the Order Paper an Amendment which expresses indignation at the extent to which we are interfering with charitable foundations. The Amendment states that the Bill

> ... gravely menaces all charitable foundations by diverting to purposes other than those intended by the donors the trust funds of the voluntary hospitals.

I must say that when I read that Amendment I was amused. I have been looking up some precedents. I would like to say, in passing, that a great many of these endowments and foundations have been diversions from the Chancellor of the Exchequer. The main contributor was the Chancellor of the Exchequer. But I seem to remember that, in 1941, hon. members opposite were very much vexed by what might happen to the public schools, and they came to the House and asked for the permission of the House to lay sacrilegious hands upon educational endowments centuries old. I remember protesting against it at the time – not, however, on the grounds of sacrilege. These endowments had been left to the public schools, many of them for the maintenance of the buildings, but hon. members opposite, being concerned lest the war might affect their favourite schools, came to the House and allowed the diversion of money from that purpose to the payment of the salaries of the teachers and the masters. There have been other interferences with endowments. Wales has been one of the criminals. Disestablishment interfered with an enormous number of endowments. Scotland also is invo- lved. Scotland has been behaving in a most sacrilegious manner; a whole lot of endowments have been waived by Scottish Acts. I could read out a large number of them, but I shall not do so.

Do hon. members opposite suggest that the intelligent planning of the modern world must be prevented by the endowments of the dead? Are we to consider the dead more than the living? Are the patients of our hospitals to be sacrificed to a consideration of that sort?

A Labour MP suggested a precedent: Henry VIII did it. This brought a flash of Welsh national pride from Bevan.

He was a good king, too; he had many good points. We are not, in fact, diverting these endowments from charitable purposes. It would have been perfectly proper for the Chancellor of the Exchequer to have taken over these funds, because they were willed for hospital purposes, and he could use them for hospital purposes; but we are doing no such thing. The teaching hospitals will be left with all their liquid endowments and more power. We are not interfering with the teaching hospitals' endowments. Academic medical education will be more free in the future than it has been in the past. Furthermore, something like £32 million belonging to the voluntary hospitals as a whole is not going to be taken from them. On the contrary, we are going to use it, and a very valuable thing it will be; we are going to use it as a shock absorber between the Treasury, the central Government, and the hospital administration. They will be given it as free money which they can spend over and above the funds provided by the state.

I welcome the opportunity of doing that, because I appreciate, as much as hon. members in any part of the House, the absolute necessity for having an elastic, resilient service, subject to local influence as well as to central influence; and that can be accomplished by leaving this money in their hands. I shall be prepared to consider, when the Bill comes to be examined in more detail, whether any other relaxations are possible, but certainly, by leaving this money in the hands of the regional board, by allowing the regional board an annual budget and giving them freedom of movement inside that budget, by giving power to the regional board to distribute this money to the local management committees of the hospitals, by various devices of that sort, the hospitals will be responsive to local pressure and subject to local influence as well as to central direction.

I think that on those grounds the proposals can be defended. They cover a very wide field indeed, to a great deal of which I have not been able to make reference; but I should have thought it ought to have been a pride to hon. members in all parts of the House that Great Britain is able to embark upon an ambitious scheme of this proportion. When it is carried out, it will place this country in the forefront of all countries of the world in medical services. I myself, if I may say a personal word, take very great pride and great pleasure in being able to introduce a Bill of this comprehensiveness and value. I believe it will lift the shadow from millions of homes. It will keep very many people alive who might otherwise be dead. It will relieve suffering. It will produce higher standards for the medical profession. It will be a great contribution towards the wellbeing of the common people of Great Britain. For that reason, and for the other reasons I have mentioned, I hope hon. members will give the Bill a Second Reading.

'Like ... *Hamlet,* with no one in the part of the First Gravedigger.'

Iain Macleod savages Aneurin Bevan: 27 April 1952

Few politicians make their reputation with a single Commons speech. But with this spectacular attack on one of the undisputed parliamentary greats of his era, Iain Macleod became a hero of his party and, shortly afterwards, a minister. He was to build a career out of a devastating turn of phrase and a willingness to risk the unorthodox, attracting along the way Lord Salisbury's famous complaint that he was 'too clever by half'.

The occasion was the second reading debate for a bill to introduce more charges into the National Health Service. Macleod had long planned to make an impact in the chamber, carefully selecting a spot below the gangway on the government benches, where he could both catch the Speaker's eye and easily be watched by the leadership on the front bench.[3] The Deputy Speaker, Sir Charles MacAndrew, had intended to call Macleod as the first speaker from the Conservative backbenches, but instead called on a nervous new Conservative arrival, Philip Ingress Bell, to make his maiden speech. This presented Macleod with a great opportunity, because the first Labour backbencher to be called was Aneurin Bevan, the founder of the NHS and probably Labour's most formidable debater. Macleod would follow him, his slingshot loaded to bring down a parliamentary Goliath.

Bevan gave him a considerable opportunity, with a rather overwrought peroration, suggesting that the introduction of more NHS charging represented 'the first long step in establishing in this country, the beginnings of the end of British parliamentary government'. Macleod's first sentence was a rejoinder to that claim. The Prime Minister, Churchill, who had been about to leave his seat, sat down to hear more.

Macleod had been in charge of, amongst other things, health policy, in his days at the Conservative Research Department. His speech demonstrated a complete mastery of the subject, an impressive memory and a mordant turn of phrase. He more than redeemed his opening promise, and the infuriated Bevan intervened four times without puncturing Macleod's argument.

I WANT TO DEAL CLOSELY and with relish with the vulgar, crude and intemperate speech to which the House of Commons has just listened. Before I come to the speech of the right hon. member for Ebbw Vale [Nye

Bevan] – and I acknowledge freely that he represents what I may call the real opposition to this Measure – there are one or two matters to which I should like to call the attention of the House.

Macleod dealt briefly with the reasons given by the opposition front bench for voting against new charges within the NHS. They did not dare increase the ceiling set on National Health Service spending when Sir Stafford Cripps was Chancellor during the Labour government, he said. Thus any shortfall would have to come from charges to NHS patients – and the Conservatives had supported Labour ministers in imposing such charges. Now they were in power, they found Labour spokesmen opposing similar charges, but had no realistic alternative.

The history of the charges in the National Health Service is by no means complicated. Here I want to come more closely to the right hon. member for Ebbw Vale [Bevan]. I would like before I start to say that I am delighted that he has recovered sufficiently to be at this debate today. My hon. friend the member for Bolton, East [Philip Bell], who quoted Shakespeare today will agree that to have a debate on the National Health Service without the right hon. gentleman would be like putting on *Hamlet* with no one in the part of the First Gravedigger.

Let me deal first with the problem with which the right hon. gentleman dealt, in passing, that this Measure is connected with the Chancellor's Budget. He said that in some ways it is a miserable Budget, because it makes the rich richer. It really does not lie in the mouth of a member of a party whose Budgets for successive years were the delight of the speculator and the joy of the spiv, to say that.

The first mention of charges in this connection was, as the right hon. gentleman will remember, in the 1949 Budget speech of Sir Stafford Cripps, when that right hon. gentleman said: 'There is, indeed, a very good argument for imposing some special charge or tax . . .' my right hon. friend has quoted this 'but . . . we should await the outcome of another year.'

Now we come to 24 October 1949, the beginning of the proposal of the charge for prescriptions. The Leader of the Opposition, who was Prime Minister at the time, announced in this House – no 'ifs,' no 'buts' about it – that they were going to save £10 million, with certain exemptions, from the pharmaceutical service. He added:

> The purpose is to reduce excessive and, in some cases, unnecessary resort to doctors and chemists.

The right hon. gentleman has quoted it and said he shuddered to think of the cascades of medicine that were pouring down our throats. He has been shuddering for 28 months, because it has been going on all the time. It is just not true that the cost of drugs is the major influence in the cost of the pharmaceutical service. The cost of drugs has gone up, in the period that we are discussing, from £35 million to £50 million or £51 million, and the number of prescriptions has gone up from 202 million, to 207 million, and now to 229 million. The case for the shilling charge is much stronger now than it was then.

The right hon. gentleman reminded the House of what happened on Friday, 9 December 1949, when this charge was put on in another place and was brought to this House, when there was an attempt to shuffle it through without any discussion at all. There was a vote at the end, and it was 138 to nine. The debate is worth reading. The right hon. gentleman has quoted what he said. I recommend every hon. member of this House to turn up his speeches. It is true that if we read now we can find, like raisins in a bun, arguments put forward by the right hon. gentleman why this charge was impracticable; but he knew something at the time that nobody else did. He knew that he was going behind the back of his Cabinet and his leader to defraud the House of Commons.

The implication was that Bevan had never really accepted the Labour government's policy of a one-shilling prescription charge, and had tried to frustrate it. An infuriated Bevan, backed by a supporting chorus of Labour members, denounced that as 'a most unworthy statement'. A Treasury committee had found the proposals impracticable, he said – and his colleagues shouted demands for Macleod to withdraw what he had said.

I have nothing to withdraw. The right hon. gentleman has been a long time in this House and I do not think that he objects to this form of debating at all.

I want to take up his next point. In the Budget speech of 1950, Sir Stafford Cripps said:

> It is not proposed to impose any charge immediately . . . since it is hoped that a more easily administered method of economising . . . can be introduced shortly.

He was referring to the Cohen Committee.[4] He went on:

> The power to charge will, of course, remain so that it can be used later if it is
> needed.

The Cohen Committee has now become the official alibi of the Socialist Party
for their muddle over the prescription charges. The Leader of the Opposition,
in a most extraordinary statement to the House – I gave him notice that I
would raise this point – on 31 January, 1952 gave as the most important reason
why this charge was not introduced, that the Cohen Committee was set up and
was managing to restrict from the drugs which could be prescribed a great
many things which were not drugs. He said: 'We did get a closer hand on it.'

Let us look at how they got a closer hand on it. The right hon. gentleman did
not seem to be aware – I know that the hon. member for Ebbw Vale is – that
the Cohen Committee was set up not after October, 1949, when we had this
proposal but in July, 1949, and it had been going for four months at the time
of this proposal. The Committee's first Interim Report, which has not been
published, was in December 1949, and there have been four other reports
since. The terms of reference of the Cohen Committee bore not the slightest
relationship to the main problem which was before the House at the time.

It was the right hon. member for Ebbw Vale himself who said, in the debate
of 9 December:

> It is aspirins, bandages and so forth, costing less than a 1s. which in a large
> number of cases could have been purchased by the patient . . . That is where
> the abuses lie.

The terms of reference of the Cohen Committee had nothing to do with that
sort of problem.

The Cohen Committee have not succeeded as we know, in reducing in any
way the flow of drugs or the money spent on drugs, but the Cohen Committee
have succeeded in doing admirable work in excluding from the National Health
Service such things as glucose, wholemeal bread, disinfectants, toilet
preparations and the like. That is the contribution which is being made, and if
that is what the Leader of the Opposition calls getting a closer hand on it then
no wonder the pharmaceutical service and other things are in the mess they are.

A doctor and future Minister for Health , Barnett Stross, Labour MP for Stoke-
on-Trent Central, who was medical adviser to the miners' and pottery unions,

intervened to suggest that the steady increase in prescriptions was matched by a corresponding fall in self-medication – people buying their own medicines. Macleod treated a sensible question seriously.

The fall in self-medication is not something that can be gleaned from the Estimates, but I am not dodging that point. I will come back to it in a few minutes because I appreciate the importance of dealing with that matter. The history of the dental charge is much more simple. Here I want to put an inquiry to the right hon. gentleman. I am not doing so in any hostile spirit. It is something I genuinely want to know and have always wanted to know. The Coalition White Paper in February 1944, in words similar to the ones which the right hon. gentleman used on Second Reading in 1946, said that a full dental service remained a proper objective, but that there were not enough dentists. On Second Reading the right hon. gentleman used these words:

> We have not enough dentists and it will therefore be necessary for us in the meantime to give priority treatment to certain classes, expectant and nursing mothers, children, school children in particular, and later on we hope adolescents. Finally we trust that we shall be able to build up a dental service for the whole population.

That seems to me to be about as good sense as has been talked about dentistry in this House of Commons or anywhere else, but it also seems to me to be a proposal that there should be a half in and half out service which the right hon. gentleman condemned in his speech tonight. Everything that has happened in the Dental Service stems from the failure to obey what the right hon. gentleman said on Second Reading.

It is from that that the cuts in remuneration came; it is from that the School Dental Service reduction has come; it is from that that an honoured profession has become a music-hall joke; it is from that the 1951 Act and the 1952 Bill come. I want to ask the right hon. gentleman to tell the House why it was that he failed to carry out the undertaking he gave to this House about the dental services on the Second Reading of the Act.

Again Bevan was provoked into intervening. Dentists, he said, had been leaving the school dental service long before the creation of the NHS, because private practise was much more attractive – and in the end he had found it simpler to take the whole population into the dental service. Macleod was unimpressed and his rejoinder drew more shouts of protest.

I am grateful for that explanation but it is entirely inaccurate. Oh, yes, certainly it is. First, the figures of the right hon. gentleman about the School Dental Service are inaccurate. The right hon. gentleman made a great reputation in the previous two Parliaments by always speaking at the end of the health debates and never answering any points. He is much less effective when he comes down into the arena. First, he does not know the figures. In 1939 there were 866 dentists in the School Dental Service. It is trite that the figure now is not much less, 40 or 50 were the last figures I saw. But the figure at the end of 1947, before the pull of the National Health Service drew the dentists and the potential dentists away from the School Dental Service, was about 1060, and it is from that figure down to the low one of 810 we have now that is the measure of the failure of the right hon. gentleman to carry out his guarantees.

Two Labour MPs tried to intervene – allowing Macleod to make the mocking suggestion that Bevan needed 'care and protection'. Bevan himself rose yet again to suggest that the children formerly dealt with by the school dental service were now being treated by the main NHS. Macleod's dismissive response brought shouts of 'No' from Labour MPs.

That is utterly ineffective. Of course it is. The right hon. gentleman simply does not know what he is talking about. When I deal with the effect of these charges I shall deal with that point as well. For the moment I will only say this to the right hon. gentleman: He went down about a month ago to explain his conduct in this House to his constituents – something which I gather is in the nature of an annual event. Unless *The Times* of Monday 10 March misrepresented him, he said this:

> When we come to debate the National Health Service cuts, I assure you I will not be restrained by any previous commitments made by anyone.

Nobody can complain about the enthusiasm with which the right hon. gentleman started to carry out his plans, because he made it quite clear that he was not going to be restrained even by the commitments he made himself.

Of this question of the School Dental Service and whether these proposals will be effective, which is, in my view, the main justification for these proposals if there is one, I will speak later. I want to come to the 1951 Bill. Mr Speaker, do you recall that on the occasion of that Bill the Opposition held on the Floor of the House one of what are laughably referred to as their private parliamentary meetings? This was a great convenience for hon. members because, although explanations of these meetings in the press are unusually full, they are rarely verbatim and they do not include the Division lists. But we can see exactly what happened at the end of the day a year ago when these proposals were before the House. We can see exactly how much the froth and the speeches were worth. The general tenor of hon. members who spoke against the Bill was, shortly, that they disliked the Bill a great deal but that they preferred the Bill to a Tory Government.

'Hear, hear,' shouted Ernest Fernyhough, the Bevanite Labour MP for Jarrow, but Macleod was quick with a caustic reply.

I am glad the hon. gentleman agrees, because it has obviously escaped him that he has ended with both the Bill and with a Tory Government. The Bill, as was the case last year, is to some extent dominated—

At this point the debate was suspended for three hours for a brief colonial diversion, an adjournment debate on the Bechuanaland Bamangwato tribe chieftainship. Macleod, who had seemed completely calm in the chamber, began trembling in nervous reaction. He sought advice from colleagues during this interlude and spoke for another half-hour, having decided to strike a somewhat more positive note, rather than continue his attack on Bevan. His detailed analysis of the effect of dental charges is omitted. Bevan, assuming Macleod would not resume, was not present.

When we interrupted this debate a little more than three hours ago, to discuss the succession to the Bamangwato tribe, I was in the middle of a good tempered and hard-hitting duel with the right hon. member for Ebbw Vale, but at the moment the right hon. gentleman does not appear to be in the Chamber.

I wanted briefly to raise three most important issues that seem to lie behind this Bill. I was saying at 7 o'clock that the debate a year ago was dominated by the doctrine of the ceiling, and the right hon. member the ex-Minister of Health said this a year ago. So it was and so to a lesser extent is it today.

We know how the ceiling originated in the National Health Service and how in the Budget of 1950 Sir Stafford's chopper[5] came down on the expenditure as it was then running. The right hon. member for Ebbw Vale said earlier in his speech tonight, and appeared to take pride in it, that in the first full year's experience of the scheme the Estimates were not exceeded. It is necessary to look a little behind the meaning of that. The right hon. gentleman was talking about the Estimates of 1950–51. This scheme started on the 5 July 1948. It is arguable, if the right hon. gentleman wishes so to argue, that he learned nothing from the first ten months of the scheme and very little from the succeeding year. It seems to be not a thing of which one should be proud.

Indeed, it can well be said by those deeply interested in the Health Service that the greatest service the right hon. gentleman rendered to the Health Service was to let expenditure run riot in those years because, finally, when the chopper came down there was money available for health. The point I want to make about the ceiling is that everyone will agree that the ceiling of £400 million is an irrational one. It would mean in itself nothing, just as, for example, the ceiling of £410 million on the food subsidies means nothing in itself. We have been committed to a ceiling of £8 per head. There has been no examination, assuming there must be a limit to decide whether it should be £7, £8, £10, or £11: we do not know.

It is a great pity – and let us admit it – that we have to discuss these charges in the backwash of the Budget, just as we had to discuss the charges of the Socialist Government in the backwash of last year's Budget. There is a genuine case to be made, apart from the economic one, and I have always believed in these charges. It seems to me quite absurd that, when the economic reasons reinforce the social and ethical ones, we should not support them.

My final observation is that a year ago there were some dissentients amongst the socialists about the merits of the Health Service, and there were bitter attacks on their front bench from behind and from below the Gangway. Let it be made quite clear that rejection of this Bill tonight means a surrender to the views of the right hon. member for Ebbw Vale. Many people, members of the Socialist Party, who spoke so bitterly against the right hon. gentleman a year ago may like to reflect a little more closely before they follow their bellwether into the Lobby tonight.

The quip that a debate on the NHS without Bevan was like a production of Hamlet without the First Gravedigger was a sign both of growing confidence and of his ability to improvise – he had intended to say it was like Hamlet without the Ghost, but this was deadlier. As the barb struck home, Churchill turned to his Chief Whip, Patrick Buchan-Hepburn, and asked, 'Who is this?'

'Macleod, Sir.'

'Ministerial material?'

'He's still quite young.'

'What has that got to do with it?'

Youth was not an argument to use on Churchill, who had been Home Secretary at 35, and who, alone in the Commons, could recall F. E. Smith's coruscating debut, almost half a century before. Six weeks later, he made Macleod Minister for Health. It was not then a Cabinet level post, but Macleod had been given a department of his own.

Bevan's biographer, Michael Foot, disputes the legend that grew up around Macleod's speech. He did not believe Macleod managed to sustain his accusations, particularly of 'going behind the back of his Cabinet and his Leader, to defraud the House of Commons'.[6] But the effect on Tory morale and on Macleod's own career was indisputable. And the parliamentary legend persists. Forty years on, leading politicians like Michael Howard and Robin Cook have recycled Macleod's phrases and jokes. Howard promised to 'deal closely and with relish' with allegations against him over the sacking of the head of the Prison Service, in a debate in 1996, and Cook greeted an intervention by the Euro-sceptic Bill Cash with the quip about *Hamlet* and the First Gravedigger in 1997.

Macleod, said the sketch-writer Edward Pearce, 'had an ear for poetry'.[7] Any ambitious backbencher seeking to make a name for themselves will study this speech.

'We, and all nations, stand, at this hour in human history, before the portals of supreme catastrophe and of measureless reward.'

Winston Churchill contemplates the destruction of civilisation: 3 November 1953

The prospect that the Cold War between East and West might turn into a real war, fought out with the terrible new thermonuclear weaponry the United States had just tested, haunted Winston Churchill during the final phase of his long career. He came increasingly to fear that his heroics in the Second World War had served only as a preface to a new and infinitely more devastating conflict. In May 1953, in the course of a sweeping assessment of the state of the world, in a foreign affairs debate in the Commons, Churchill had proposed a summit of the leading powers to broker a more solid and lasting peace. It was not an idea which found favour in America, where the President, his wartime colleague Dwight Eisenhower, distrusted Churchill's brand of personal diplomacy – a view probably shared by the British Foreign Office. The public reaction in Britain and the Commonwealth was encouraging, but Churchill was not able to press his idea on his sceptical partners, because in June he suffered a severe stroke.

In the absence of Anthony Eden, also ill, the government was led by Rab Butler, and it was far from clear that Churchill would ever be able to grasp the reins again. But over the summer, this astonishing man – now in his seventy-eighth year – made a miraculous recovery. In October he was able to address the Conservative Party conference for nearly an hour, concluding that he remained as Prime Minister not from the love of office, but because he thought he might have some influence on other countries in building a lasting peace.

Less than a month later he delivered this speech in the debate on the Queen's Speech. Chips Channon set the scene in his diaries.[8] 'Winston, who had not been present at the Opening of Parliament this morning, rose amidst cheers and it was immediately clear he was making one of the speeches of his lifetime. Brilliant, full of cunning and charm, of wit and thrusts, he poured out his Macaulay-like phrases to a stilled and awed House. It was an Olympian spectacle . . .'

The first half of the speech – not reproduced here – dealt with the domestic issues of the day, such as farming, housing and the state of the railways, before concluding that the end of wartime rationing was in sight. Then he turned to foreign affairs and the threat of nuclear war.

W E SHALL HAVE another debate, on foreign affairs in the near future, and I shall not attempt anything like a general survey today. Comparing the outlook now with two years ago, I think it would be true to say that it is less formidable but more baffling. The issues as they had shaped themselves in the days of our predecessors were clear-cut. The vast three-year rearmament plan was just getting into its stride. The war in Korea was still raging. General Eisenhower was organising Western Europe. A feeling of crescendo and crisis filled the air. Our Socialist Government, with the full support of the Conservative Opposition, were marching with our American allies in a vehement effort to meet the Soviet menace.

The main structure of this position is maintained, and no weakening in British purpose has resulted from the change of Government. Nevertheless, certain important events have happened which, rightly or wrongly, have somewhat veiled, and, it may be, actually modified the harshness of the scene. The fighting in Korea has shifted from the trenches to the tables. We do not know yet what will emerge from these stubborn and tangled discussions. But whatever else comes, or may come, as a result of the Korean War, one major world fact is outstanding. The United States have become again a heavily armed nation.

The second world event has been the death of Stalin and the assumption of power by a different regime in the Kremlin. It is on the second of these prodigious events that I wish to dwell for a moment. Nearly eight months have passed since it occurred and everywhere the question was, and still is asked, did the end of the Stalin epoch lead to a change in Soviet policy? Is there a new look?

The only really sure guide to the actions of mighty nations and powerful Governments is a correct estimate of what are and what they consider to be their own interests. Applying this test, I feel a sense of reassurance. Studying our own strength and that of Europe under the massive American shield, I do not find it unreasonable or dangerous to conclude that internal prosperity rather than external conquest is not only the deep desire of the Russian peoples, but also the long-term interest of their rulers.

It was in this state of mind that six months ago I thought it would be a good thing if the heads of the principal States and Governments concerned met the new leaders of Russia and established that personal acquaintance and relationship which have certainly often proved a help rather than a hindrance. I still hope that such a meeting may have a useful place in international contacts.

On the other hand, one must not overlook the risk of such a four-power conference ending in a still worse deadlock than exists at present. It certainly would be most foolish to imagine that there is any chance of making straight away a general settlement of all the cruel problems that exist in the East as well as in the West, and that exist in Germany and in all the satellite countries. We are not likely straight away to get them satisfactorily dealt with and laid to rest as great dangers and evils in the world by personal meetings, however friendly. Time will undoubtedly be needed – more time than some of us here are likely to see.

I am, of course, in very close touch with President Eisenhower, and my hope was that at Bermuda we might have had a talk about it all. I was sorry to be prevented by conditions beyond my control. We are at present looking forward to the four-power conference of Foreign Secretaries, and we earnestly hope it will take place soon. If it leads to improvements those themselves might again lead to further efforts on both sides. We trust we shall soon have a favourable answer to our conciliatory invitation to the Soviets.

I have mentioned two dominant events that have happened in the last two years. But there is a third which, though it happened before, has developed so prodigiously in this period that I can treat it as if it were a novel apparition which has overshadowed both those I have mentioned. I mean the rapid and ceaseless developments of atomic warfare and the hydrogen bomb.

These fearful scientific discoveries cast their shadow on every thoughtful mind, but nevertheless I believe that we are justified in feeling that there has been a diminution of tension and that the probabilities of another world war have diminished, or at least have become more remote. I say this in spite of the continual growth of weapons of destruction such as have never fallen before into the hands of human beings. Indeed, I have sometimes the odd thought that the annihilating character of these agencies may bring an utterly unforeseeable security to mankind.

When I was a schoolboy I was not good at arithmetic, but I have since heard it said that certain mathematical quantities when they pass through infinity change their signs from plus to minus – or the other way round. I do not venture to plunge too much into detail of what are called the asymptotes of hyperbolae, but any hon. gentleman who is interested can find an opportunity for an interesting study of these matters. It may be that this rule may have a novel application and that when the advance of destructive weapons enables everyone to kill everybody else nobody will want to kill anyone at all. At any rate, it seems pretty safe to say that a war which begins by both sides suffering what they dread most – and that is undoubtedly the case at present – is less likely to occur than one which dangles the lurid prizes of former ages before ambitious eyes.

I offer this comforting idea to the House, taking care to make it clear at the same time that our only hope can spring from untiring vigilance. There is no doubt that if the human race are to have their dearest wish and be free from the dread of mass destruction, they could have, as an alternative, what many of them might prefer, namely, the swiftest expansion of material well-being that has ever been within their reach, or even within their dreams.

By material well-being I mean not only abundance but a degree of leisure for the masses such as has never before been possible in our mortal struggle for life. These majestic possibilities ought to gleam, and be made to gleam, before the eyes of the toilers in every land, and they ought to inspire the actions of all who bear responsibility for their guidance. We, and all nations, stand, at this hour in human history, before the portals of supreme catastrophe and of measureless reward. My faith is that in God's mercy we shall choose aright.

Churchill had reasserted his mastery over the House and the government. Harold Macmillan, who had visited the invalid Prime Minister during his convalescence, was awed. 'It seems incredible that this man was struck down by a second stroke at the beginning of July. I wd not have believed it possible at any time during the summer or even the early autumn.'[9]

Channon described the aftermath: 'He sought refuge in the Smoking Room and, flushed with pride, pleasure and triumph, sat there for two hours sipping brandies and acknowledging compliments. He beamed like a schoolboy.'

A summit with the French and Americans followed, but Churchill's hopes of full peace and disarmament talks with the Soviets were brusquely dismissed by Eisenhower. Dejected by this failure, he finally left Downing Street in 1955.

'The seat which by . . . general wish of the House should be left vacant this afternoon.'

Harold Wilson pays tribute to 'a good House of Commons man': 25 January 1965

With the death of Sir Winston Churchill, the Commons mourned arguably its greatest ever member. Seemingly determined to die as an MP, he had only retired from the Commons, under pressure from his constituency party a few months earlier, at the 1964 general election. The *Guardian*'s eminent sketch-writer Norman Shrapnel described the great man's Commons twilight in the early sixties: 'this war-winner and sole survivor of Queen Victoria's Parliament would lurch inch by precarious inch to his place, sometimes impatiently rejecting helping hands that sought to steer him. Would he make it? He always did, though there were agonising moments. He would sit for an hour or two, hunched like a premature statue of himself, just occasionally exchanging greetings, or at least on his own part, some sign of recognition with some old colleague. He even went through the polite and dutiful convention of pretending to care when someone pointed out to him where they had got to on the order paper; though more than once towards the end, he would be holding it upside down.'[10]

His final appearance in the House was on 27 July 1964. Less than six months later, the legend was dead. Harold Wilson led the recollections of his extraordinary personality, magnificent language and heroic achievements with this elegiac speech. Formally, he was moving a vote of thanks to the Queen for having ordered a state funeral.

I N ACCEPTING THIS Motion, this House, and, by virtue of its representation in this House, the nation, collectively and reverently will be paying its tribute to a great statesman, a great parliamentarian, a great leader of this country.

The world today is ringing with tributes to a man who, in those fateful years, bestrode the life of nations, tributes from the Commonwealth, from our wartime allies, from our present partners in Europe and the wider alliance, from all those who value the freedom for which he fought, who still share the desire for the just peace to which all his endeavours were turned. Winston Churchill, and the legend Winston Churchill had become long before his death, and which now lives on, are the possession not of England, or Britain, but of the world, not of our time only but of the ages.

But we, sir, in this House, have a special reason for the tribute for which Her Majesty has asked in her Gracious Message. For today we honour not a world statesman only, but a great parliamentarian, one of ourselves.

The colour and design of his greatest achievements became alive, on the parliamentary canvas, here in this Chamber. Sir Winston, following the steps of the most honoured of his predecessors, derived his greatness from and through this House and from and through his actions here. And by those actions; and those imperishable phrases which will last as long as the English language is read or spoken, he in turn added his unique contribution to the greatness of our centuries-old parliamentary institution.

He was in a very real sense a child of this House and a product of it, and equally, in every sense, its father. He took from it and he gave to it.

The span of 64 years from his first entry as its youngest member to the sad occasion of his departure last year covers the lives and memories of all but the oldest of us. In a parliamentary sense, as in a national sense, his passing from our midst is the end of an era.

He entered this House at 25 – already a national and controversial figure. He had fought in war, and he had written of war he had charged at Omdurman, he had been among one of the first to enter Ladysmith, an eye-witness of the thickest fighting in Cuba, a prisoner of a Boer commando, though not for as long as his captors intended. [He escaped.]

And he brought his own tempestuous qualities to the conduct of our Parliamentary life. Where the fighting was hottest he was in it, sparing none – nor asking for quarter. The creature and possession of no one party. He has probably been the target of more concentrated parliamentary invective from, in turn, each of the three major parties than any other member of any parliamentary age, and against each in turn he turned the full force of his own oratory. If we on this side of the House will quote as a classic, words he uttered over half a century ago about the party he later came to lead, hon. members opposite have an equally rich treasure-house for quotations about us, to say nothing of right hon. and hon. gentlemen below the Gangway. [The Liberals.]

When more than 40 years after his first entry as a young MP he was called on to move the appointment of a Select Committee about the rebuilding of this Chamber,[11] he proclaimed and gloried in the effect of our parliamentary architecture on the clarity and decisiveness of party conflict; he recalled, with that impish quality which never deserted him, the memories of battles long past, of his own actions in crossing the floor of this House, not once in fact but twice.

For those who think that bitter party controversy is a recent invention and one to be deplored, he could have had nothing but pitying contempt. And as he sat there, in the seat which I think by general wish of the House should be left vacant this afternoon, in those last years of the last Parliament, silently surveying battles which may have seemed lively to us, could we not sense the old man's mind going back to the great conflicts of a great career and thinking perhaps how tame and puny our efforts have become?

A great parliamentarian, but never a tame one – they misjudge him who could even begin to think of him as a party operator, or a manipulator, or a trimmer, or a party hack. He was a warrior, and party debate was war; it mattered, and he brought to that war the conquering weapon of words fashioned for their purpose, to wound, never to kill; to influence, never to destroy.

As Parliament succeeded Parliament he stood at this Box, at one time or another holding almost every one of the great Offices of State. He stood at the Box opposite thundering his denunciation of Government after Government. He sat on the bench opposite below the Gangway, disregarded, seemingly impotent, finished. His first Cabinet post – the Board of Trade – made him one of the architects of the revolution in humane administration of this country. He piloted through the labour exchanges; he led the first faltering steps in social insurance.

The Home Office and then the more congenial tenure of the Admiralty, Ministerial triumph and Ministerial disaster in the First War. Colonies, War, the Treasury: the pinnacle of power, and then years in the wilderness. The urgent years, warning the nation and the world, as the shadow of the jackboot spread across an unheeding Europe. And then came his finest hour. Truly the history of Parliament over a tempestuous half-century could be written around the triumphs and frustrations of Winston Churchill.

But, sir, it will be for those war years that his name will be remembered for as long as history is written and history is read. A man who could make the past live in *Marlborough*, in his dutiful biography of Lord Randolph,[12] who could bring new colour to the oft-told tale of the history of the English-speaking peoples, for five of the most fateful years in world history, was himself called on to make history. And he made history because he could see the events he was shaping through the eye of history. He has told us of his deep emotions when, from the disaster of the Battle of France, he was called on to lead this nation.

'I felt,' he said, 'as if I were walking with destiny, and that all my past life had been but a preparation for this hour and for this trial. Ten years in the political wilderness had freed me from ordinary party antagonisms. My warnings over the last six years had been so numerous, so detailed, and were now so terribly vindicated, that no one could gainsay me. I could not be reproached either for making, the war or with want of preparation for it.

'I thought I knew a good deal about it all, and I was sure I should not fail. Therefore, although impatient for the morning, I slept soundly and had no need for cheering dreams. Facts are better than dreams.'

His record of leadership in those five years speaks for itself beyond the power of any words of any of us to enhance or even to assess. This was his finest hour, Britain's finest hour. He had the united and unswerving support of the leaders of all parties, of the fighting services, of the men and women in munitions and in the nation's industries, without regard to faction or self-interest. In whatever role, men and women felt themselves inspired to assert qualities they themselves did not know they possessed. Everyone became just those inches taller, every back just that much broader, as his own was.

To this task he brought the inspiration of his superlative courage, at the hour of greatest peril, personal courage such as he had always shown, and indeed which needed a direct order from his Sovereign to cause him to desist from landing on the Normandy beaches on D-Day; moral courage, the courage he had shown in warning the nation when he stood alone, now inspired the nation when Britain and the Commonwealth stood alone. There was his eloquence and inspiration, his passionate desire for freedom and his ability to inspire others with that same desire. There was his humanity. There was his humour. But above all, he brought that power which, whenever Britain has faced supreme mortal danger, has been asserted to awaken a nation which others were prepared to write off as decadent and impotent, and to make every man, every woman, a part of that national purpose.

To achieve that purpose, he drew on all that was greatest in our national heritage. He turned to Byron – 'blood, tears and sweat.' The words which he immortalised from Tennyson's 'Ode on the Death of the Duke of Wellington' might well be a nation's epitaph on Sir Winston himself.

> Not once or twice in our rough island story,
> The path of duty was the way to glory;
> He that walks it, only thirsting
> For the right, and learns to deaden
> Love of self, before his journey closes,
> He shall find the stubborn thistle bursting
> Into glossy purples, which outredden
> All voluptuous garden-roses.

The greatest biographer of Abraham Lincoln said in one of his concluding chapters: 'A tree is best measured when it is down.'

So it will prove of Winston Churchill, and there can be no doubt of the massive, oaken stature that history will accord to him. But this is not the time.

We meet today in this moment of tribute, of spontaneous sympathy this House feels for Lady Churchill and all the members of his family. We are conscious only that the tempestuous years are over; the years of appraisal are yet to come. It is a moment for the heartfelt tribute that this House, of all places, desires to pay in an atmosphere of quiet.

For now the noise of hooves thundering across the *veldt*, the clamour of the hustings in a score of contests; the shots in Sidney Street, the angry guns of Gallipoli, Flanders, Coronel and the Falkland Islands, the sullen feet of marching men in Tonypandy; the urgent warnings of the Nazi threat; the whine of the sirens and the dawn bombardment of the Normandy beaches – all these now are silent. There is a stillness. And in that stillness, echoes and memories. To each whose life has been touched by Winston Churchill, to each his memory. And as those memories are told and retold, as the world pours in its tributes, as world leaders announce their intention, in this jet age, of coming to join in this vast assembly to pay honour and respect to his memory, we in this House treasure one thought, and it was a thought some of us felt it right to express in the parliamentary tributes on his retirement. Each one of us recalls some little incident – many of us, as in my own case, a kind action, graced with the courtesy of a past generation and going far beyond the normal calls of parliamentary comradeship. Each of us has his own memory, for in the tumultuous diapason of a world's tributes, all of us here at least know the epitaph he would have chosen for himself. 'He was a good House of Commons man.'

'**I saw with my own eyes 1000 policemen come in military formation into an oppressed, and socially and economically depressed area like wild Indians, screaming their heads off to terrorise the inhabitants.**'

Bernadette Devlin reports to the Commons about the violence on the barricades of the Bogside in a stunning maiden speech: 22 April 1969

In 1967, the long-dormant problems of Northern Ireland began to encroach on the national political agenda, with the emergence of the civil rights movement, which pressed for an end to discrimination against the Catholic population in areas like policing, employment and housing, and an end to the gerrymandering which stifled their political voice. The movement was peaceful at first, but violence erupted in the Catholic Bogside area of Londonderry in 1968. The moribund IRA revived and there was also terrorism from the protestant Ulster Volunteer Force.

Bernadette Devlin's arrival in the Commons after a surprise by-election victory allowed MPs to hear first-hand about the violence and the under-lying problems. The weekend after her election, rioting had erupted in Londonderry. James Callaghan, the Home Secretary, announced in the House that he had agreed to send troops to guard essential installations in Northern Ireland. Paul Rose, a Labour MP who chaired the Campaign for Democracy in Ulster, successfully demanded a full debate and Devlin seized the opportunity. 'Just like Joan of Arc,' shouted the BBC's parliamentary correspondent Conrad Voss Bark as he emerged from the press gallery.

After being introduced to the House by Rose and the future SDLP leader Gerry Fitt, Devlin delivered her maiden speech almost immediately. She had made a few notes during a hectic flight to London but, having heard the previous speaker, the Ulster Unionist Robin Chichester-Clark, she didn't really need them. He had blamed the recent violence in the Bogside on rioters and gangs of youths who had attacked the police with petrol bombs – 'not the types of people who necessarily spend a long evening on the intellectual contemplation of the evils of the local government franchise in Northern Ireland'.

'Everything I detested about the system was written in his Tory face,' she wrote later.[13] 'It was a bitter speech, but it wasn't in my own analysis of it a good speech. It merely stated that the situation was medieval, and that there was no longer anything to be gained from Westminster discussing it: the time for Westminster's discussion and Westminster's action had almost passed, and all they could do was decide which side of the House was going to take the blame for Northern Ireland.'

Brian Walden, then a Labour MP, remembers vividly the tiny figure and the huge impression she made with her passionate oratory.

I UNDERSTAND THAT IN making my maiden speech on the day of my arrival in Parliament and in making it on a controversial issue I flaunt the unwritten traditions of the House, but I think that the situation of my people merits the flaunting of such traditions.

I remind the hon. member for Londonderry [Robin Chichester-Clark, a Protestant landowner, who become an Employment Minister in Edward Heath's government after the 1970 election; his brother James became Prime Minister of the devolved Stormont government, succeeding Captain O'Neill, shortly after this speech] that I too was in the Bogside area on the night that he was there. As the hon. gentleman rightly said, there never was born an Englishman who understands the Irish people. Thus a man who is alien to the ordinary working Irish people cannot understand them and I therefore respectfully suggest that the hon. gentleman has no understanding of my people, because Catholics and Protestants are the ordinary people, the oppressed people from whom I come and whom I represent. I stand here as the youngest woman in Parliament, in the same tradition as the first woman ever to be elected to this Parliament, Constance Markievicz, who was elected on behalf of the Irish people.

This was not a modest comparison. Constance Markievicz, the 'Rebel Countess' (she was married to a Polish count), was a Republican heroine, the first woman to be elected to Parliament. She won the Dublin St Patrick's seat in 1918, as a Sinn Fein candidate, while in jail in Holloway Prison for her role in the Easter Rising. In line with Sinn Fein policy, she refused to take up her seat in Westminster.

This debate comes much too late for the people of Ireland, since it concerns itself particularly with the action in Derry last weekend. I will do my best to dwell on the action in Derry last weekend. However, it is impossible to consider the activity of one weekend in a city such as Derry without considering the reasons why these things happen.

The hon. member for Londonderry said that he stood in Bogside. I wonder whether he could name the streets through which he walked in the Bogside so that we might establish just how well acquainted he became with the area. I had never hoped to see the day when I might agree with someone who represents the bigoted and sectarian Unionist Party, which uses a deliberate policy of dividing the people in order to keep the ruling minority in power and to keep the oppressed people of Ulster oppressed. I never thought that I should see the day when I should agree with any phrase uttered by the representative of such a party, but the hon. gentleman summed up the situation to a 't'. He referred to stark, human misery. That is what I saw in Bogside. It has not been there just for one night. It has been there for 50 years – and that same stark human misery is to be found in the Protestant Fountain area, which the hon. gentleman would claim to represent.

These are the people the hon. gentleman would claim do want to join society. Because they are equally poverty-stricken they are equally excluded from the society which the Unionist Party represents – the society of landlords who, by ancient charter of Charles II, still hold the rights of the ordinary people of Northern Ireland over such things as fishing and as paying the most ridiculous and exorbitant rents, although families have lived for generations on their land. But this is the ruling minority of landlords who, for generations, have claimed to represent one section of the people and, in order to maintain their claim, divide the people into two sections and stand up in this House and say that there are those who do not wish to join the society.

The people in my country who do not wish to join the society which is represented by the hon. member for Londonderry are by far the majority. There is no place in society for us, the ordinary 'peasants' of Northern Ireland. There is no place for us in the society of landlords because we are the 'have-nots' and they are the 'haves'.

We came to the situation in Derry when the people had had enough. Since 5 October, it has been the unashamed and deliberate policy of the Unionist Government to try to force an image on the civil rights movement that it was nothing more than a Catholic uprising.

How can we say that we are a non-sectarian movement and are for the rights of both Catholics and Protestants when, clearly, we are beaten into the Catholic areas? Never have we been beaten into the Protestant areas. When the students marched from Belfast to Derry, there was a predominant number of Protestants. The number of non-Catholics was greater than the number of Catholics. Nevertheless, we were still beaten into the Catholic area because it was in the interests of the minority and the Unionist Party to establish that we were nothing more than a Catholic uprising – just as it is in the interest of the hon. member for Londonderry to come up with all this tripe about the IRA.

I assure the hon. member that his was quite an interesting interpretation of the facts, but I should like to put an equally interesting interpretation. There is a fine gentleman known among ordinary Irish people as the Squire of Ahoghill. He happens to be the Prime Minister, Captain Terence O'Neill. He is the 'white liberal' of Northern Ireland. He is the man who went on television and said to his people, 'There are a lot of nasty people going around and if you are not careful you will all end up in the IRA. What kind of Ulster do you want? Come with me and I will give you an Ulster you can be proud to live in'.

Captain O'Neill listed a number of reforms which came nowhere near satisfying the needs of the people. Had he even had the courage of his convictions – had he even convictions – to carry out the so-called reforms he promised, we might have got somewhere. But none of his so-called reforms was carried out.

Terence O'Neill was removed as Prime Minister at Stormont later that month, because of his willingness, under pressure from Harold Wilson, to make some concessions to the civil rights movement.

We come to the question of what can be done about incidents like that in Derry at the weekend. Captain O'Neill has thought of a bright idea – that tomorrow we shall be given one man, one vote. Does he think that, from 5 October until today, events have not driven it into the minds of the people that there are two ideals which are incompatible – the ideal of social justice and the ideal and existence of the Unionist Party? Both cannot exist in the same society. This has been proved time and again throughout Northern Ireland by the actions of the Unionist Party.

In the general election, Captain O'Neill had the big idea of dividing and conquering. Captain O'Neill, the 'liberal' Unionist, said, 'Do not vote for Protestant Unionists because they are nasty Fascist people.' When the election was over, he had no qualms about taking the number of so-called 'Fascist' Unionist votes and the 'liberal' Unionist votes together, adding them up and saying, 'Look how many people voted Unionist.'

We, the people of Ulster, are no longer to be fooled, because there are always those of us who can see no difference between the Paisleyite faction and the O'Neill faction, except that the unfortunate Paisleyite faction do not have hyphenated surnames. So we are faced with the situation that Captain O'Neill may, in the morning, say, 'You now have one man, one vote.' What will it mean to the people? Why do the people ask for one man, one vote, with each vote of equal value to the next?

The Unionist policy has always been to divide the people who are dependent upon them. The question of voting is tied up mainly with the question of housing, and this is something which the House has failed to understand. The people of Northern Ireland want votes not for the sake of voting but for the sake of being able to exercise democratic rights over the controlling powers of their own areas. The present system operates in such a way that Unionist-controlled councils and even Nationalist-controlled councils discriminate against those in their areas who are in the minority. The policy of segregated housing is to be clearly seen in the smallest villages of Ulster. The people of Ulster want the right to vote and for each vote to be of equal value so that, when it comes to the question of building more houses, we do not have the situation which we already have in Derry and in Dungannon.

In Dungannon, the Catholic ward already has too many houses in it. There is no room to build any more in that ward. It would appear logical that houses should be built, therefore, in what is traditionally known as the Protestant ward. But this would give rise to the nasty situation of building new houses in the Unionist or Protestant ward and thus letting in a lot of Fenians who might outvote the others.

I was in the Bogside on the same evening as the hon. member for Londonderry. I assure you, Mr Speaker – and I make no apology for the fact – that I was not strutting around with my hands behind my back examining the area and saying 'tut-tut' every time a policeman had his head scratched. I was going around building barricades because I knew that it was not safe for the police to come in.

I saw with my own eyes 1000 policemen come in military formation into an oppressed, and socially and economically depressed area – in formation of six abreast, joining up to form twelve abreast like wild Indians, screaming their heads off to terrorise the inhabitants of that area so that they could beat them off the streets and into their houses.

An unfortunate policeman with whom I came into contact did not know who was in charge in a particular area. I wanted to get children out of the area and I asked the policeman who was in charge. He said, 'I don't know who is running this lot.' I well understand this kind of situation at individual level, but when a police force are acting under orders – presumably from the top, and the top invariably is the Unionist Party – and form themselves into military formation with the deliberate intention of terrorising the inhabitants of an area, I can have no sympathy for them as a body. So I organised the civilians in that area to make sure that they wasted not one solitary stone in anger. [Laughter.]

Hon. members may find this amusing and in the comfortable surroundings of this honourable House it may seem amusing, but at two o'clock in the morning on the Bogside there was something horrifying about the fact that someone such as I, who believes in non-violence, had to settle for the least violent method, which was to build barricades and to say to the police, 'We can threaten you.'

The hon. member for Londonderry said that the situation has got out of hand under the 'so-called civil rights people'. The one thing which saved Derry from possibly going up in flames was the fact that they had John Hume, Member of Parliament for Foyle,[14] Eamonn McCann,[15] and Ivan Cooper,[16] Member of Parliament for Mid-Derry, there. They went to the Bogside and said, 'Fair enough; the police have occupied your area, not in the interests of law and order but for revenge, not by the police themselves but because the Unionist Party have lost a few square yards of Derry and people have put up a sign on the wall saying 'Free Derry'. The Unionist Party was wounded because nothing can be morally or spiritually free under a Unionist Government. They were determined that there should be no second Free Derry. That is why the police invaded that area. The people had the confidence of those living in that area to cause a mass evacuation and to leave it to the police alone, and then to say, 'We are marching back in and you have two hours to get out.' The police got out.

The situation with which we are faced in Northern Ireland is one in which I feel I can no longer say to the people 'Don't worry about it. Westminster is looking after you'. Westminster cannot condone the existence of this situation. It has on its benches members of that party who by deliberate policy keep down the ordinary people. The fact that I sit on the Labour benches and am likely to make myself unpopular with everyone on these benches—

'No!' shouted Labour MPs.

Any Socialist Government worth its guts would have got rid of them long ago.

There is no denying that the problem and the reason for this situation in Northern Ireland is social and economic, because the people of Northern Ireland are being oppressed not only by a Tory Government, a misruling Tory Government and an absolutely corrupt, bigoted and self-interested Tory Government, but by a Tory Government of whom even the Tories in this House ought to be ashamed and from which they should dissociate themselves. I should like in conclusion to take a brief look at the future. This is where the question of British troops arises. The question before this House, in view of the apathy, neglect and lack of understanding which this House has shown to these people in Ulster which it claims to represent, is how in the shortest space it can make up for 50 years of neglect, apathy and lack of understanding. Short of producing miracles such as factories overnight in Derry and homes overnight in practically every area in the North of Ireland, what can we do? If British troops are sent in I should not like to be either the mother or sister of an unfortunate soldier stationed there. The hon. member for Antrim North [Henry Clark] may talk till Doomsday about 'Our boys in khaki', but it has to be recognised that the one point in common among Ulstermen is that they are not very fond of Englishmen who tell them what to do.

Possibly the most extreme solution, since there can be no justice while there is a Unionist Party, because while there is a Unionist Party they will by their gerrymandering control Northern Ireland and be the Government of Northern Ireland, is to consider the possibility of abolishing Stormont and ruling from Westminster. Then we should have the ironical situation in which the people who once shouted 'Home rule is Rome rule' were screaming their heads off for home rule, so dare anyone take Stormont away?

Another solution which the Government may decide to adopt is to do nothing but serve notice on the Unionist Government that they will impose economic sanctions on them if true reforms are not carried out. The interesting point is that the Unionist Government cannot carry out reforms. If they introduce the human rights Bill and outlaw sectarianism and discrimination, what will the party which is based on, and survives on, discrimination do? By introducing the human rights Bill, it signs its own death warrant. Therefore, the Government can impose economic sanctions but the Unionist Party will not yield. I assure you, Mr Speaker, that one cannot impose economic sanctions on the dead.

'The House thought it was delightful. Great stuff! Great sincerity! Which showed the House up for what it was,' Devlin recalled. 'Somebody said something they really meant, without clothing it in non-offensive language, without the formality of neatly typing it out and underlining the bits that were to be emphasised, and everyone said, "hear, hear!" The press were just the same. The press had built me up so much on the baby of Parliament, swinging MP, guess-whose-birthday-it-is-today angle that they couldn't in consideration of their own sales turn round and condemn the speech. I made a scathing attack on Unionism and the whole British landlord invasion of Ireland, but even the Tory papers carried it.'

Despite her own verdict, she made a tremendous impression. Women MPs were a rarity in those days, and the sight of the tiny but impassioned newcomer making such a furious denunciation of the Ulster Unionists had an electrifying effect. When she sat down, the next speaker, Jeremy Thorpe, compared her to some of the great Irish nationalist MPs of the past – Charles Parnell, Tim Healy, John Redmond, adding that the whole House respected her courage.

The next Commons intervention by Devlin to hit the headlines came in 1972, in the wake of the Bloody Sunday killings by British troops. She physically attacked the then Home Secretary, Reginald Maudling, as he announced an inquiry by the Lord Chief Justice, clawing his face with her fingernails.

'I want the closed shop enshrined in national law.'

Brian Walden analyses different class perceptions of the law: 27 January 1971

The departure of Brian Walden from the House of Commons to present LWT's *Weekend World* deprived Parliament of one of its most original minds. Walden probably became a more prominent public figure over the ensuing ten years, as he vivisected a generation of politicians in long interviews on live television, but debate in Westminster was the poorer for it.

This speech was made during the committee stage of the Industrial Relations Bill, Edward Heath's attempt to regulate trade unions and industrial disputes. The measure had been the centrepiece of the 1970 Conservative manifesto and it was not dissimilar to proposals in the previous government, when Barbara Castle's White Paper *In Place of Strife* (1969) produced an open split in Harold Wilson's Cabinet.

The committee stage – the detailed line-by-line consideration – of the bill was taken on the floor of the Commons. Walden intervened when discussion moved on to amendments guaranteeing the right not to join a union, even where a closed shop was operated. He warned against importing American-style right-to-work laws into Britain. To a British ear their name might suggest legislation to provide jobs for the unemployed, but in fact these were anti-closed shop laws which meant that workers did not have to join a union or pay regular union dues to win or keep jobs. They could also resign union membership without losing their job. Under the 1947 Taft Hartley Labour Act, individual states could enact their own right-to-work laws, and most states in the 'old South' did. Walden argued that the Heath government's bill represented the individualist world view of middle-class professionals and failed to grasp the more collectivist mindset of working-class trade unionists.

It was a speech which made a considerable impression on the future Tory Chancellor Geoffrey Howe, who as Solicitor-General under Heath had been one of the main architects of the bill. Asked by the author which speeches had impressed him most in his parliamentary career, he immediately named this one.

I HAD ALREADY SAID to some of my hon. friends that I wanted desperately to speak on this Amendment. Let me be clear, because the House wants no weasel words, I mean that I am standing up to defend the operation of the closed shop. I know that there is a difficulty, as my hon. friends do, about the use of the words 'closed shop' and '100 per cent union membership,' but I am taking it fairly freely. Of course I am not saying – hon. gentlemen opposite will understand this – that I want the closed shop enshrined in national law. What I am saying is that I do not want anything that prohibits it enshrined in law.

The reason that I am making this speech is that this is something of which I have practical experience. I went to the United States and saw – indeed, if I had stayed in honest employment I would have written about – the operation of the closed shop and the right-to-work laws of the United States. My old friend and pair the Solicitor General [Geoffrey Howe] peregrinated around that country and came back not only with this but with many of the other fancy franchises which we find in the Bill.

Though, as my hon. friends know, I love the United States dearly, I want to know why it is that we choose to take examples like this from a country which is notorious for its rate of strikes, its union corruption, the viciousness of its labour wars and the general malpractices which exist in its industry. As this principle is the whole pith of right-to-work legislation in America, and hon. gentlemen opposite are always busily telling us that we do not do things which other countries do and that we should learn from them, it is important to know why the Secretary of State has picked on this principle.

I wish to comment not on the principle of the closed shop – though I shall have something to say about that later – but about the closed shop in practice. What is this right-to-work legislation? It is precisely what the right hon. gentleman has decided is going on under the provision in subsection (1)(b). Although there is a good deal that we could say about the agency shop and the fragmentary effect which will result, the fact remains that subsection (1)(b) allows a man not to join a union.

The A. F. of L.-C.I.O. [the American Federation of Labor and Congress of Industrial Organizations – the US equivalent of the TUC] has spent more millions of dollars than my hon. friends will ever see getting over the concept of the right-to-work legislation in industrial states in America. It has been doing this because the operation of right-to-work laws has been observed in other states: broadly those states in the East and mid-West. They have been applied in the West, except, of course, in California, and these laws have also gone through in the South, which is perhaps ominous.

We know how people south of the Mason-Dixon line feel about individual liberty and the freedom of the subject. We also know why these are the states with right-to-work laws. The right hon. gentleman was wrong when he said in reply to an intervention from one of my hon. friends that there was no evidence one way or the other about this. There is, and if he had looked into this matter he would have found it. From the first time that figures were available about states in America where right-to-work laws were operating, it was found that after those laws were passed, union membership fell and did not recover proportionately in those states.

Much of the trouble is that the world about which we hear from the right hon. gentleman does not approximate to the real world in which we live. If one goes to, for example, Alabama, one sees how they go about introducing right-to-work laws. Those in command say, 'We can bring in some money, and a new factory, but the trouble is that they do not want to bring the factory down from Philadelphia. But we know you could do with the factory and the extra money which it would bring here in Alabama. If we go to a lot of trouble, we think we could get that factory for you. Under the right-to-work law, you will have the right not to belong to a trade union. We feel that if you want this little town in Alabama to boom and prosper, the best thing you can do, for the sake of all concerned, is to accept this law because those we represent do not want any union trouble.'

I suppose that before this week most hon. gentlemen opposite would have said that that sort of thing could never happen here in Britain. It can. They would probably have said that the double wage packet – the 'kick-back payment' to prevent people joining the union – could never arise here. It is happening on construction sites in Britain.

Moreover, if non-unionism of this kind is allowed – this is a point which my hon. friends have kept putting to the Government but which we cannot seem to get through to hon. gentlemen opposite, primarily because my hon. friends talk of practice while the Secretary of State [for Employment, Robert Carr] talks only of so-called principle – all sorts of other difficulties arise. They are not worried about Jehovah's Witnesses or the son of the local Conservative agent who feels that, for political reasons, he cannot join the union. They are worried about the 'freeloaders' and the general climate of opinion which will exist if one equates non-unionism with trade unionism.

It is difficult for people who work in professional jobs, as I have always done, to understand people like my father, who always worked in manual jobs. The real differences are psychological. A large number of working-class people are held to their opinions by psychological environment.

What the right hon. gentleman will do – I am sure unwittingly – by this provision in the name of principle, and by giving to a man who has sincere religious convictions the right to stand out from union membership, is to encourage the very worst British employers to create in their firms the sort of climate which makes it difficult for one to exercise one's rights. That is what the hon. gentleman never talks about.

Of course, if a man is black in Alabama he can join a union. There is no state law that says he cannot; there is no Federal law that says he cannot. Why is it, then, that many do not? First of all, to be an A.F. of L.-C.I.O. organiser in the South is to put one's life in danger. A Negro in Mississippi just does not exercise that right to join a trade union. I am not worried about Metrovickers or Longbridge, Birmingham, but I am worried about some of the small factories where this Clause will create a climate of opinion which prohibits people from joining.

Moreover – and this comes from American experience, too – one of the facts about trade unionism in every Western country is that a great deal of the membership – and by 'a great deal' I mean anything up to 15 per cent or 20 per cent – is of a passive type. It exists because of a climate of opinion. In every Western country the most passive section of the membership – and I do not criticise them as such – are women. If this Bill is passed in its present form, trade union organisers will talk themselves blue in the face, but a very large number of women will become 'nons' and will simply go out of the union. We only have to look at the Post Office now to see that situation.

It is all very well for hon. members opposite, who would welcome such a situation. We understand them very well. What we do not understand are the hon. member for Paddington South [Nicholas Scott, a rising One Nation Conservative, later PPS to Robert Carr and a minister under Margaret Thatcher] and the right hon. gentleman the Secretary of State, who tell us quite sincerely that they want stronger unions. If they want stronger unions they cannot keep subsection (5)(b) in the Bill. That paragraph is a recipe for extending the right of the freeloader, of all the people who do not wish to join a union, to stay out, because it creates a climate in which they can do so.

I have listened to these debates, and I have read them. I have tried to understand why it is that people of good will do not seem able to have a meaningful dialogue. I think that it has a good deal to do with class. I do not say that because I want to stir up – that is the very thing I do not want to do, though this Bill will do it. This Measure has touched pools of class consciousness which will become obvious to hon. members opposite in the next few years.

It is very difficult for people with a certain background, with a certain temperamental inclination, with a certain view, for instance, of patriotism and of the courts, who have a certain view of responsibility and of duty, people with a background that has been not only in their own lives but in their training basically individualistic, to grasp how much so many of us on this side are shaped by a different set of values; no better, no worse – just different.

They are collective values. They are values very well understood. Indeed, the whole reason why the Labour Party exists is that we were able to stand together as a group when we were anonymous. There are very few of us here today with any name or reputation who would be here were it not for the fact that millions of anonymous people stood together.

I do not want the right hon. gentleman to have any doubt at all that in any judgment this is a part of the Bill which the trade unions will never accept. Any chance he has of moderation from the other side will be dead if he attacks what the unions regard as their most fundamental and sacred right, and the eventual end of all that will be what I fear most; that by the time we have gone through this whole performance there will be no moderates left.

Walden's prophecies proved accurate. The Industrial Relations Act was never accepted by the trade unions and never allowed to operate as the government intended. It provoked mass demonstrations and the Heath government was forced into contortions to avoid jailing trade unionists who defied its requirements. In the end it was one of the major factors behind the epidemic of strikes which brought the government down.

'As I see the right hon. gentleman walking around the country, looking puzzled, forlorn and wondering what has happened, I try to remember what he reminds me of.'

Michael Foot mocks Sir Keith Joseph: 29 October 1980

After Labour's defeat in 1979, James Callaghan held on for more than a year before announcing his departure from the party leadership. His aim was 'to take the shine off the ball' and absorb the inevitable criticisms in order to protect his favoured successor, the former Chancellor Denis Healey.[17] As it turned out, the delay had the reverse effect, allowing the anti-Healey forces to organise. At that time Labour leaders were still elected by MPs alone, although the party was in the process of devising a new electoral college system for future contests.

This opposition day debate held with Labour ahead in the polls and the leadership election under way, was something of a beauty contest between the two leading candidates: the veteran right-winger Denis Healey and the equally veteran left-winger Michael Foot. Foot, winding up, produced a memorable performance, his voice dropping effortlessly from thundering condemnation to the most delicate irony, and soaring back. His target was a Labour hate figure, the cerebral ideologue of the government's monetarist economic policy, Sir Keith Joseph, at whose door he laid the blame for a deep and painful recession – the worst since the war.

Would the older generation of Conservative 'Wets' in Mrs Thatcher's Cabinet have the gumption to reverse her policies, he wondered?

W E READ IN THE NEWSPAPERS that the Cabinet is to discuss these matters and possibly some aspects of public expenditure cuts tomorrow. I should like to intrude into that meeting, if I may, and offer my assistance to those sections of the Cabinet that deserve it.

The Secretary of State for Employment [James Prior, one of Mrs Thatcher's leading 'Wet' critics] is sometimes represented as a good man who fell among monetarists. I would not go as far as that. I shall come back to him in a moment. At any rate, I am chalking him up on my slate as one of the good ones.

Here Foot gave a long list of Cabinet ministers who, he said, did not really believe in the Prime Minister's 'monetarist malarkey'.

The only people who seriously believe in the policy that the Government are pursuing is the diminishing little band headed by the right hon. lady. I sometimes feel that, when the right hon. lady stands on the burning deck all alone at the end, the only person who will be supporting her will be the Minister for Social Security [Patrick Jenkin]. I have warned the right hon. lady before. Does she not realise that we have put him here as an agent provocateur in order to test what damn fool statements can be made in Tory Governments? I warn the right hon. lady that she needs a few better companions around her if she wants to deal with unemployment.

I realise that I have discriminated in favour of the wets. I have revealed to the House quite openly, as I would normally do, who are my favourites, but I should not like to miss out the Secretary of State for Industry [Sir Keith Joseph, one of the key free-market thinkers behind government policy] who has had a tremendous effect on the Government and our politics generally. As I see the right hon. gentleman walking around the country, looking puzzled, forlorn and wondering what has happened, I try to remember what he reminds me of. The other day I hit on it.

In my youth, quite a time ago, when I lived in Plymouth, every Saturday night I used to go to the Palace theatre. My favourite act was a magician-conjuror who used to have sitting at the back of the audience a man dressed as a prominent alderman. The magician-conjuror used to say that he wanted a beautiful watch from a member of the audience. He would go up to the alderman and eventually take from him a marvellous gold watch. He would bring it back to the stage, enfold it in a beautiful red handkerchief, place it on the table in front of us, take out his mallet, hit the watch and smash it to smithereens.

Here, Foot smashed his fist down on the Dispatch Box in a mighty and resounding blow – something, he admitted later, he had always wanted to do. At the same point his voice dropped from booming anecdote to vitriolic irony.

Then on his countenance would come exactly the puzzled look of the Secretary of State for Industry. He would step to the front of the stage and say 'I'm very sorry. I have forgotten the rest of the trick.' That is the situation of the Government. They have forgotten the rest of the trick. It does not work. Lest any objector should suggest that the act at the Palace theatre was only a trick, I should assure the House that the magician-conjuror used to come along at the end and say 'I am sorry. I have still forgotten the trick.'

We face a serious situation which, in some respects, is even worse than the 1930s and we have a Government who have learnt none of the lessons of the 1930s. We have to teach them. The way that our politics are to develop will depend first on what happens within the Cabinet and the Conservative Party. The troubled mind in the Conservative Party is widespread. Everyone who has listened to the speeches of Conservative members can see that it is becoming very widespread. I am so generous that I will not even ask those Conservative members who agree with the Government's policies to put up their hands. I do not believe that we would get even the few who enthusiastically obeyed on the previous occasion.

The disbelief does not exist only among trade unionists, Labour supporters and those in the sort of constituency that I represent. Throughout the country there is a rising disbelief in the policy that the Government are pursuing. If the right hon. members that I have mentioned could capture a few more allies, it would be possible for them to change the situation, though that would not transform the whole industrial situation. The damage has gone so deep that it will be difficult to reverse it.

In addition, the cuts in public expenditure have not yet had their full effects by any means. We all learn from our own constituencies and I was horrified last week not only to hear what is happening in the steel industry, where most of those who are still at work are kept there by the compensation scheme and are on short time, but to discover that those working in new factories are having to face short-time working and the prospect that their industries may also have to close. If Conservative members go to any industrial area they will discover that the disbelief in their policies is widespread among managements, workers and everybody else.

What will happen if the Cabinet manage to say that the lady must turn?[18] That will not solve everything; I agree with my right hon. friend the member for Leeds East [Denis Healey], who said that earlier in the debate. However, it will assist, and the sooner we can get it, the better. If they do not succeed in that, they will all go down, because in the meantime we shall organise the biggest protest campaign that this country has seen since the 1930s. We shall have a campaign from one end of the country to the other.

We shall fight the Government here in the House and outside. Shall we call it a Midlothian campaign? It will be against the atrocities of unemployment this time instead of the other atrocities against which Mr Gladstone campaigned.[19] I remind the House that when he embarked upon his Midlothian campaign Mr Gladstone was 68 years old. I must inform Conservative hon.

members, who may not be aware of the facts, that Mr Gladstone lived thereafter to form three – or was it four? – separate Administrations. So there is hope for all my hon. friends, including my right hon. friend the member for Leeds East.

I hope that in that campaign we can combine other great themes. I believe that in the course of the campaign we shall be able to restore hope to our people, because there is no future for our country in the gospels of despair, in the doctrines of mass unemployment, in the idea that the way in which people can be made to work is by being whipped to work, whether by whips or scorpions.

What we must restore to the country is the proper sense of community in dealing with this great crisis. Just as in the greatest crises of our country in this century it was the Labour movement that came to the rescue, so it will be on this occasion too. We give due notice to the Conservative Party that we intend from this moment on to rouse the country from one end to the other and to ensure that as soon as the opportunity comes we get not merely what we had for five years – a tender, difficult situation with a majority one day and no majority the next – but the full majority to carry through the democratic, Socialist reforms that this country requires.

It is unlikely that this speech was in any way decisive in the Labour leadership election – although a good parliamentary performance always raises morale. Shortly afterwards, Foot won the leadership by 139 votes to Healey's 129, on a second ballot.

'What a crusade the Secretary of State is leading, to be sure.'

Gerald Kaufman explains how Michael Heseltine had enabled council house tenants to buy their rented properties: 15 January 1980

Few pieces of legislation from Margaret Thatcher's first term aroused such visceral opposition from the Labour benches as the requirement placed on local councils to allow their tenants to buy council houses. The measure was an undoubted vote winner for the Conservatives and transferred valuable assets to tenants, often at knock-down prices. But Labour objected on the grounds that it would undermine public housing provision for those in most need, and would cream off the best of the council housing stock.

Leading their defence was Gerald Kaufman, Labour's razor-tongued shadow Environment Secretary. Kaufman had been Harold Wilson's political secretary in Downing Street and a minister in the 1974–79 Labour governments. Here he demonstrated the talent for extended political ridicule which made him one of the more feared debaters in the Commons, heaping derision on the Environment Secretary, Michael Heseltine.

T HIS SECOND READING debate has inevitably centred on the provision in the Bill for compulsory sales of council houses. But the House should pay attention to the many other pernicious provisions in the Bill. The most fundamental change is in clause 80 – the removal of the Housing Act 1957 duty on local authorities regularly to prepare plans for the provision of new homes in their areas. This is a statutory duty that local authorities have had imposed on them for many years under Governments of both parties. Its removal strikes at the heart of publicly provided housing in this country.

This is accompanied by other proposals that illustrate the Government's detestation of local authority housing and their vendetta against council tenants. Clause 116 means the return to the provision in the Housing Finance Act 1972, repealed by the Labour Government in 1975, that councils should be allowed to make a profit out of the rents they charge their tenants. In clause 41, there is the specific and deliberate removal from the Labour Government's tenants' charter of the right of tenants to be consulted about the rents that they pay.

Here Kaufman warned that the bill would mean higher housing costs for tenants who bought their homes, and scoffed at a recent decline in the number of council houses that had been sold.

What a disappointment the poor figures must be to the Secretary of State. We all remember his rousing rhetoric at the Conservative Party conference in the autumn. He told the cheering throngs at Blackpool that the sale of council houses would be seen as 'a great social revolution'. He proclaimed: 'I can think of no act of social policy more likely to change the attitude of countless thousands of our people than the enfranchisement of council tenants.'

He promised a 'great crusade' against Labour-controlled councils that opposed his policy. He described them as the feudal barons denying the peasants their land. The right hon. gentleman issued this stern warning: 'If it is a fight they want we shall lead our party across their heartlands, carrying our message door to door.'

The right hon. gentleman had his chance, because in one of the greatest Socialist heartlands of all, the constituency of Manchester Central, we had a by-election in the autumn. The overwhelming majority of electors in that constituency live in council property and they waited behind their doors in suspense and anticipation, ready for the Secretary of State's promised knock.

We all know that it usually takes brute force to keep the right hon. gentleman away from the political stump, but the doors of Manchester Central remained unthumped. In fact, Manchester did not even see the Secretary of State during the by-election campaign. As for the Tory candidate, he did not even mention the sale of council houses in his election address, and when the votes were counted it turned out that the peasants had voted for the feudal barons. The Tory candidate got 1,275 votes, and *Magna Carta* lost its deposit.

The problem is that the Secretary of State is a great fighter when words are his weapon. But, sadly, in his crusade he seems to be leading an army of conscientious objectors. Let us be fair to the Secretary of State. He is fighting so many crusades at once that he cannot win them all immediately. As we know, another of his battles is against bureaucracy. He spelt out his views vividly in a speech that he made in Cheltenham in July. It was a major oration and at times his language reached Demosthenic heights. Take this extract, which I quote in its entirety: 'Sale of council houses. Get on with it.'

But it was on the subject of bureaucracy that the Secretary of State was at his most eloquent. He said: 'We are now at a point where the web of bureaucracy is too dense, too pervasive, and entangles far more than it ought . . . Local councils . . . do not need, they do not want, the fussy supervision of detail which now exists.'

Let us look at the Housing Bill and see how in it the Secretary of State gets rid of the web of bureaucracy and the fussy supervision of detail. Let us consider, in particular, how a council tenant goes about exercising his right to buy a house. It is a simple straightforward procedure. First, the tenant serves a written notice on the council under clause 5(1). The council responds by serving a notice on the tenant under clause 5(1). For good measure, the council then serves a further notice on the tenant under clause 10(1). Then, not resting on its laurels, the council sends the tenant a form under clause 10(3). The tenant has been left out of things a bit, so he counters smartly by serving another written notice on the council under clause 11(1).

A new participant now makes his appearance – the District Valuer. He makes a determination or a redetermination under clause 11(2). The council cannot let that go by, so it makes a representation to the District Valuer under clause 11(3). The tenant is not going to let that pass, so he makes a representation to the District Valuer under clause 11(3). In response, the council serves a notice on the tenant under clause 11(4). The council then follows this up by sending the tenant a form under clause 11(5).

It is now the tenant's turn again. He serves a notice in writing on the council under clause 12(1). Back to the council, which serves a notice in writing on the tenant under clause 12(3). Various moves now become possible. The council can serve a notice on the tenant under clause 15(2). The tenant can serve an injunction on the council under clause 15(8). The council, getting desperate, may make a covenant under clause 18(1). The council may serve a notice on the tenant under clause 18(2), or it may give a consent to the tenant under clause 18(2).

Yet another character now appears – the Chief Land Registrar. He can enter a restriction under clause 18(5). Back to the council, which must give the tenant a certificate under clause 19(2). Enter now the Secretary of State. He may give the council notice in writing under clause 22(1), and he may repeat the process under clause 22(2). Then, in a masterstroke, the Secretary of State may withdraw his notice in writing to the council under clause 22(1) by giving the council further notice in writing under clause 22(5). The pace then quickens. The Secretary of State may execute a document under clause 23(1). The Chief Land Registrar can register the tenants under clause 23(3). He shall then supply the Secretary of State with a document under clause 23(4).

Along the way, the House will be relieved to hear, the Secretary of State has all sorts of little jobs to do. He may make an order under clause 7(3), or regulations under clause 9(4), or orders under clause 17(1) and clause 20(2), or regulations under clause 21(1), or a determination under clause 22(7), or an order under clause 25(1). That is how the Bill makes it easy for the council tenant to buy his house and how the Secretary of State fulfils his promise to get rid of fussy supervision of detail and to destroy the web of bureaucracy.

What a crusade the Secretary of State is leading, to be sure. His straggling troops are groping their way down a murky labyrinth, accompanied by a qualified solicitor and a filing clerk. Instead of a glorious war-cry such as 'God for Michael, England and St Margaret,' the slogan on his pennant reads 'Please complete this form in triplicate.'

Kaufman quoted a series of criticisms of the bill from authoritative bodies including the National Farmers' Union, the Association of District Councils and the National Housing and Town Planning Council. He also cited comments from the Tory Reform Group – headed by an impressive array of heavyweight 'Wet' grandees – the National Council of Building Material Producers and the National Economic Development Council.

The Secretary of State, who has the effrontery to talk about enough new house building to meet demand, is certain to leave office with the unenviable record of having not only presided over but deliberately brought about the worst housing programme since the war. That is the grim truth behind this despicable Bill, and that is why we shall vote against it tonight.

Of course, the opposition did not stop the bill – and the right to buy had an enormous impact, helping extend home ownership in England and from 57 per cent of housing stock to 68 per cent. Margaret Thatcher considered it one of her most successful – and electorally rewarding – policies.

"'You will learn if you need a new hair style – and where to get it – and the type of glasses to suit your face.'"

Ian Gow makes the first televised parliamentary speech: 21 November, 1989

As parliamentary private secretary to Mrs Thatcher in her first term – which in his case meant a great deal more than bag carrier – Ian Gow was sometimes thought the most powerful man in her government. He became a minister after the 1983 election and might have aimed for Cabinet office, but resigned in 1985, in protest at the signing of the Anglo-Irish Agreement, the precursor to the Northern Ireland peace process. In most respects, though, he remained a close ally of Mrs Thatcher, who must have enjoyed his jibes at the expense of Euro-federalists and her internal critics. This speech moving the vote of thanks for the 1989 Queen's Speech was also notable because it was the first in the Commons to be televised – the cameras having been installed during the long summer recess.

I AM MINDFUL OF THE honour done by my constituents through my being invited to make this speech. A year ago, the Leader of the Opposition, quoting the admirable Mr Colin Welch of the *Daily Mail*, described my hon. friend the member for Pudsey [Sir Giles Shaw] – who had just moved the motion – as a 'roly-poly version of Dr Bodkin Adams'.

A sinister comparison: Dr John Bodkin Adams, a rather gnomic Eastbourne GP, was acquitted of the murder of an elderly patient after a sensational trial in 1957. It was later revealed he had been the beneficiary of 132 wills. Since his death, evidence has emerged to suggest he helped 25 patients to their graves.

The House, and certainly my hon. friend the member for Aldershot [Julian Critchley], may think that that description applies rather better to me. I am sad to have to confirm that the good doctor is no longer with us – sad, because at each dissolution of Parliament he used to send a £5 note for my fighting fund.

I have always voted against the televising of the proceedings of this House, and I expect that I always will. Despite my strongly held opinions, a letter that I received – three weeks ago – I believe that a copy was sent to each of us and possibly even to you, Mr Speaker – made the following preposterous assertion:

> The impression you make on television depends mainly on your image (55 per cent) with your voice and body language accounting for 38 per cent of

your impact. Only 7 per cent depends on what you are actually saying.

This prompted an ironic 'hear, hear' from Labour MPs, for which Gow was prepared.

I thought that I should enlist the sympathy of the Opposition with that last proposition.

The letter went on – and hon. members may think that this is an extravagant claim so far as I am concerned:

> We can guarantee to improve your appearance through a personal and confidential image consultation. You will learn if you need a new hair style – and where to get it[20] – and the type of glasses to suit your face.

The House will understand why I considered that I was beyond redemption on both counts.

Eastbourne has been a separate parliamentary constituency since 1885. Then the electorate was 8,000; today it is 80,000. I am glad to report that for 100 out of those 104 years Eastbourne has been represented in the Conservative interest. The solitary lapse took place in 1906, but four years of Liberal representation were more than enough and provoked the highest turnout ever recorded – 90.3 per cent – at the following general election. Since then, Eastbourne has been true blue, and, since 1974, dry as well. East Sussex has long attracted the retired and semi-retired. Lord Shawcross[21] lives at Friston, the right hon. member for Leeds East [Denis Healey], whose decision not to seek re-election to this place we all deplore, is the squire of Alfriston and Lord Callaghan has his estate nearby. It will be a source of satisfaction to the Opposition, particularly to those who sit below the Gangway, as it is to me, to learn that those three comrades have been able to share in the growing prosperity of the nation created during the premiership of my right hon. friend the Prime Minister.

Others have shared in that prosperity. Over these past years, 1,657 former tenants of our borough council have bought their houses or flats. They remember that the right-to-buy legislation was fiercely opposed by the Labour Party. I was proud to have had a hand in extending the opportunities for home ownership in the Housing Act 1985.

Last month, phase two of our district general hospital was opened. All the medical wards have been transferred from St Mary's hospital, which was built in Napoleonic days, to our new hospital. I am pleased to be able to tell the House that our hospital has informed my right hon. and learned friend the

Secretary of State for Health of its intention to seek approval to become a self-governing hospital trust within the National Health Service.

In August 1980, the House gave a Third Reading to the Eastbourne Harbour Bill. Indeed, 180 of my right hon. and hon. friends stayed up until 6.10 a.m. to vote for it. The House will want to know that construction work on the harbour project is well under way. Jobs are being created in the short and long term. The new harbour will keep Eastbourne in the vanguard – no, ahead of the vanguard – of Britain's increasingly important and increasingly successful tourist industry. When the harbour is completed, our fishermen will no longer have to drag their craft on to the beach. There will be berths for 1,800 small boats. Miners from Bolsover, entrepreneurs from Newham North-West, refugees from Brent East, grocers from Old Bexley, intellectuals, real or imagined, from Chesham and Amersham and the hon. baronet the Member for Clwyd North-West [Sir Anthony Meyer], whose reported aspirations to become the Queen's First Minister I am unable to endorse – all these and many more besides – will be able to moor their boat or seek refuge from the storm in the new Eastbourne harbour.

This was a list of some of Mrs Thatcher's Commons critics, including Dennis Skinner (Bolsover), Tony Banks (Newham North West), Ken Livingstone (Brent East), the Tory 'Wet' Sir Ian Gilmour (Chesham and Amersham), and Sir Edward Heath (Old Bexley and Sidcup), whom *Private Eye* had nicknamed 'the Grocer'. Sir Anthony Meyer was later to challenge Margaret Thatcher for the leadership of the Conservative Party as a stalking horse, hoping to win enough votes to weaken her position and perhaps attract a more heavyweight challenger.

Perhaps provoked, the Liberal Democrat Simon Hughes attempted to intervene.

There is absolutely no way in which I shall give way to a member of the Liberal Party.

I must leave the virtues of Eastbourne and turn to the merits of the Gracious Speech. I welcome the commitment to support the remarkable changes taking place in Eastern Europe. Speaking in Poland last month, the German Chancellor said that Moscow, Warsaw, Prague, Budapest and Vienna – he made no mention of Leipzig – were as much a part of Europe as London, Brussels, Paris, Rome or Berlin. Dr Kohl was echoing General de Gaulle's famous concept of a *Europe des patries* stretching from the Atlantic to the Urals. It is a concept which I share. I am strongly in favour of the free movement of people, goods and capital within the twelve countries that make up the Community, but I have no confidence in the presumed superior wisdom of the Commission in Brussels as compared with the judgment, fallible though it is, of this elected House of Commons. Recent events in Eastern Europe have reinforced that view. If we look forward to the day – as I do – when the whole European family can share in that freedom and democracy which we enjoy, the long-term enlargement of the Community is more likely to come about if the nation states of the twelve do not succumb to the vaulting ambitions of the supranationalists.

I also welcome the commitment in the Gracious Speech to defeating terrorism in Northern Ireland, Great Britain and Europe. We should send a message from this place, to friend and foe alike, that our resolve will never weaken, that those who choose the bullet and the bomb will gain no concessions from Her Majesty's Government, and that their campaign of terror is as odious as it is futile. Terrorism flourishes where those who perpetrate it believe that one day terror will triumph. That is why all of us need to give no hint that it ever will.

The Gracious Speech reaffirms the Government's commitment to pursue firm financial policies, designed to reduce inflation. It is of deep regret to me that inflation is now more than 7 per cent. High interest rates are not the only weapon to defeat inflation, but they are an essential weapon. I hope that the abatement of inflation until we secure our declared aim of stable prices will characterise the stewardship of my right hon. friend the Chancellor of the Exchequer. Yesterday the President of Romania made a speech in Bucharest which lasted for six hours and which was punctuated by 67 standing ovations. I am thankful that I was not asked to move a vote of thanks to him, but it has been an honour to have been asked to make this speech. It will be a matter of relief to the House to know that there is no precedent for the mover of the Loyal Address being asked to do so on a subsequent occasion.

Gow's welcome for the commitment to defeat terrorism in Northern Ireland was consistent with the staunch Unionist principles which had led him to resign from the government. They – and his personal closeness to Mrs Thatcher – were presumably the reasons which led the IRA to murder him, by car bomb, eight months after this speech. In the ensuing by-election the seat was won by the Liberal Democrats.

'When I think of John Smith, I think of an opponent, not an enemy.'

John Major pays tribute to John Smith: 12 May 1994

The heart attack which killed John Smith, the leader of the opposition, on a May morning in the mid 1990s, came at a time when, more than any Labour leader for fifteen years, he had looked like a premier-in-waiting. His party was basking in triumph from the local elections held just a few days earlier. The humiliation of Black Wednesday and the continuing Tory splits over Europe – both of which he had exploited to great effect at the Dispatch Box – had made the assumption almost universal that Smith would soon preside over a Labour government.

But the grief that swept the Commons when his death was announced was more than an elegiac sadness for a lost leader. Smith was beloved in a way that few political leaders of the twentieth century could ever hope to be. When Madam Speaker Boothroyd announced his death to the House, there was a catch in her normally steady voice. On the Labour benches some MPs were quietly weeping.

This tribute by John Major, to a man who had proved a formidable rival, was a masterpiece of grace and generosity, giving a rare glimpse of their behind-the-scenes meetings over tea, or something stronger. 'If Major managed anything else with so sure a touch, he'd be unchallenged as leader,' wrote the *Guardian*'s parliamentary sketch-writer, Simon Hoggart.

WHEN I HEARD THE tragic news of John Smith this morning, I thought it right that the House should meet this afternoon to pay tribute to a distinguished parliamentarian and then adjourn. I do not believe that there would have been the stomach for any other business in the House today.

I know that the whole House would wish me first to express my deep and warm sympathy for Mrs Smith and for John Smith's family, his wife and his daughters. In the House, we have lost a formidable senior member of very rare ability.

To the Labour Party also, I offer my deep sympathy. After some serious hammer blows that they have faced among their colleagues in recent months, they have lost a leader and, I know, for many of them a deep and close friend of many years' standing. But above all, Elizabeth Smith, Sarah, Jane and Catherine have lost a husband, a father and a part of their lives which can never be replaced. John Smith was one of the outstanding parliamentarians of modern politics. He was skilled in the procedures of this House, skilled in upholding its traditions, a fair-minded but, I can say as well as any member in the House, tough fighter for what he believed in and, above all, he was outstanding in parliamentary debate. As one would expect of a barrister and Queen's Counsel, he was always master of his brief, however complex and however detailed it might be. But beyond being master of his brief, on good days – and for him there were many good days – his speeches could shape and move the will of the House in the way that few members are able to do.

Over recent years, both as Prime Minister and as Chancellor of the Exchequer, I had the pleasure and the privilege of facing John Smith across this Dispatch Box. I learned on those occasions to acknowledge the skill and the wit with which he mastered his arguments. He had that rare ability to switch with speed from irony to sarcasm to invective and to fact, and sometimes, in the heat of parliamentary debate, to half fact, on every occasion knowing exactly how and when to move from one mood to the other for maximum parliamentary and political effect. Those are formidable skills, they are rare skills and, even for those against whom those skills were deployed, it is hard to bear that we will never see or hear those skills in this House again.

He had no malice. There were things that he cared for passionately. He lived for them; he fought for them; he cared for them. But he carried his fight fairly, without malice, without nastiness. The bruises that existed soon faded after a dispute with John Smith. In our parliamentary democracy, it is the fate of party leaders to dispute, to scorn, to disagree. We have an adversarial system of politics – the best in the world, I believe, but adversarial. So it was in the nature of my political relationship with John Smith that we frequently clashed in public and in the House, yet afterwards, in private, we met often and amiably – again, no bruises.

Inevitably, the Prime Minister and the Leader of the Opposition have to conduct business in private and on confidential matters. Whenever we did, I always found him courteous, fair minded and constructive, but also tough for what he was seeking and what he believed in. We would share a drink – sometimes tea, sometimes not tea – and our discussions on those occasions ranged far beyond the formal business that we were transacting. To the despair of my private office and, I suspect, sometimes of his, the meetings extended far beyond the time that was immediately scheduled for them.

Under our constitution, the role of the Leader of the Opposition is unique. It is a vital role – not in government, but vital to the determination of the way in which we conduct our affairs and to the protection of people who oppose the Government on a range of issues. The Leader of the Opposition is in the anteroom of power, yet not in the seat of power itself. In that position – perhaps for a short time, perhaps for a long time – he must maintain his party's hunger for government and never let that appetite diminish. He must remain confident and never let the years of waiting sour or embitter him or the nature of public life. He must keep alive hope and ambition and must keep sharp the cutting edge of his own party's beliefs. If I may judge him from this side of the House, it seemed to me that John Smith trod that path for his party and its supporters in the country with skill and assurance that few have matched.

Political differences are not the be-all and end-all of relationships for members of the House. When I think of John Smith, I think of an opponent, not an enemy; and when I remember him, I shall do so with respect and affection. When I think of his premature death, I shall think of the waste that it has brought to our public life – the waste of a remarkable political talent ; the waste of a high and honourable ambition to lead our country; the waste of a man in public life who, in all his actions, retained a human touch; and, in some ways above all, the waste of the tranquillity and happiness that his past endeavours would have so richly deserved in the years to come.

Let me end where I began. In the weeks that lie immediately ahead, John's family will need all their courage. Let us show by what we say and do today that, while we cannot bear for them their pain, we can offer them the comfort of shared respect and shared grief.

'John was no sobersides.'

Margaret Beckett, as acting leader of her party, leads Labour's mourning for John Smith: 12 May 1994

From May to July 1994, Margaret Beckett was the leader of her party, taking it through a European election campaign with dignity and efficiency – qualities that also emerge in this brief eulogy to her fallen leader.

I THANK THE PRIME MINISTER in all sincerity for what he has said, and the spirit in which he has spoken. Opposition members also mourn our country's loss, but we grieve for our own. There are few people the announcement of whose death would bring tears to the eyes of everyone who knew them; John Smith was such a man. He was, as the Prime Minister said, a man of formidable intellect, of the highest ethics and of staunch integrity. Part of the conventional wisdom of British politics was that he looked like a bank manager – something that caused him amusement, and some bank managers some resentment. Perhaps in consequence, he was often labelled unduly sober or excessively cautious – especially by those who judge readily – and judged on the facade. But, although he certainly had a safe pair of hands, appearances were deceptive. John was no sobersides. He had a wicked sense of humour, often displayed – as the Prime Minister said – in the House. He loved a good gossip, and he liked nothing better than a convivial drink with friends, when he was excellent company.

One of his favourite sayings was that to succeed in politics, you have to be prepared to take a risk. In fact, I used to joke with him that he was an ideal combination in a political leader: someone who looked the acme of sober judgment, but was perfectly prepared to take a flier when he thought the occasion called for it.

Some months ago, I saw a political profile of John which featured a photograph of him as a young boy. He had a wicked grin from ear to ear, his tie was around his ear and the text mentioned that his shirt tails were always hanging out. It was a kind of *Just William* of a picture. Those who saw John Smith every day had no difficulty in detecting that boy in the statesman and the leader.

Not long ago, I observed to a colleague that I had never known a man like John. He had such calm certainty, such natural strength and self-confidence; but, while he had supreme confidence, he lacked any trace of cockiness or conceit. He just knew what he could do. I have never known a man so at ease with himself.

He adored his family, and our hearts go out to Elizabeth and to the girls. He was at his most lovable when he was talking about his daughters – for the love and support that John offered to, and received from, his family was not only the core of his personal life; it was central to his political life and beliefs. He wanted for others the richness he enjoyed.

He said to me recently, 'Why would anyone bother to go into politics, unless it was to speak up for people who cannot speak up for themselves?' That feeling for others, along with his hatred of injustice, was the force which drove him – the service to which he gave his life.

Last night, he spoke at a gala dinner in London. He was in fine fettle and in high spirits. He spoke not from a text but from notes, and when he sat down I congratulated him especially on his final sentence – spoken, as it was, off the cuff and from the heart. They were almost the last words I heard him say. He looked at the assembled gathering, and he said:

'The opportunity to serve our country – that is all we ask.' Let it stand as his epitaph.

'That must be the first instance of something being put into the Queen's Speech entirely as a joke.'

William Hague dismisses the Queen's Speech: 17 November 1999

William Hague's term as Conservative leader is an object lesson in the limits of parliamentary oratory. He was a brilliant performer at the Dispatch Box, regularly trouncing Tony Blair. He dispensed memorable jokes, biting satire and pointed phrases for four years, but when he led his party into the 2001 general election the Conservatives barely dented Labour's huge majority, and Hague resigned.

His critics suggest that although the jokes were brilliant, the underlying political strategy was inconsistent and ineffective. Too often his alternative policies seemed overly populist and paper-thin. And too often he targeted government embarrassments which, although relished by the Westminster Village, had little resonance to voters outside.

In this speech, responding to the 1999 Queen's Speech, Labour's self-destructive infighting over the nomination for Mayor of London provided rich entertainment for Conservative (and, more discreetly, Labour) backbenchers. Hague also sought to damage Tony Blair's personal credibility, with a hilarious recital of the improbable personal revelations he had made in various interviews.

A S USUAL, THERE ARE some things that we can welcome in today's Queen's Speech, and we will look closely at the detail of Bills dealing with mandatory drug testing, reform of the Child Support Agency, wildlife protection and other measures in the programme. We will also look with great interest at the Government's proposed reform of the system for children in care. Because of my time as Welsh Secretary, when I set up the north Wales child abuse inquiry, I am distressingly familiar with the scandal of the treatment of children in care. We owe these vulnerable children everything, but, too often, we give them worse than nothing despite the dedication and commitment of so many staff. I hope that the Government can tackle this national disgrace.

Hague then turned his fire on the Liberal Democrats, who had just switched leaders from Paddy Ashdown to Charles Kennedy. Ashdown had, it emerged, been considering rather more than cooperation on electoral and consti-tutional reform; he had been hoping for a close partnership or even coalition with Labour – which proved undeliverable from both sides. His successor appeared as a panellist on the BBC 2 comedy quiz *Have I Got News For You.*

We also welcome the absence of some things from the Queen's Speech – for instance, any measure to meet the Prime Minister's manifesto commitment to hold a referendum on proportional representation in this Parliament. The poor old Liberal Democrats have behaved themselves all year, not saying boo to a goose, and they look cheerfully expectant on days such as this. What do they get in return? Nothing. What a shame that the Liberal Democrat leader has gone in a few short months from *Have I Got News for You* to *I'm Sorry I Haven't a Clue*.

Of course, the Liberal Democrats are not the only ones having problems with electoral systems at the moment. After the shambles we have seen in London in the past few days, I do not know how the Prime Minister could, with a straight face, write these words into the Queen's Speech:

My Government . . . will make it easier for people to participate in elections.

Tony Blair and the Labour leadership were going through procedural contortions to prevent Ken Livingstone from becoming Labour's candidate for Mayor of London. Eventually their favoured candidate, the former Health Secretary Frank Dobson, did win the Labour nomination, only to be defeated by Livingstone, who ran as an independent.

That must be the first instance of something being put into the Queen's Speech entirely as a joke. If the Prime Minister is finding the problem so difficult, I have a solution for him. Why does he not split the job of Mayor of London? The former Health Secretary can run as his 'day-mayor' and the hon. member for Brent East [Ken Livingstone] can run as his 'night-mayor'. The Prime Minister is thinking about it, I can tell.

We cannot be so charitable about much of the rest of the Queen's Speech. Of course we welcome the state visit by the Queen of Denmark,[22] and I understand that future state visitors may soon be able to enjoy London's newest tourist attraction. We read in the newspapers that the Prime Minister now employs so many spin doctors that he is thinking of moving somewhere bigger and turning Downing Street into a museum. It could be even more exciting than the dome: followers of the mayoral election can walk through the zone of indecision; take a ride on the gravy train, and see the chamber of broken promises.

Unfortunately, however, the 'year of delivery'[23] zone will not be ready for the millennium. Do hon. members remember the Prime Minister's year of delivery? He promised that he would cut class sizes, and a year later class sizes have risen. Where is the action in the Queen's Speech to improve schools? He promised lower waiting lists, and a year later the waiting lists for the waiting lists are double what they were. Where is the action to speed up treatment for heart bypasses and other serious operations? He promised to be tough on crime, and a year later police numbers have fallen. Where are the measures to reverse the fall in police numbers?

This Queen's Speech will do nothing to reverse the Prime Minister's broken pledges. This is supposed to be the programme that will take Britain into the new century and it is probably the last full programme of this Parliament, but it contains nothing for families, nothing for savers, nothing for schools, nothing for the NHS and nothing for business. There is nothing in this Queen's Speech to make next year anything other than another year of no delivery.

The Prime Minister has produced a Queen's Speech in which, unbelievably, those departments that have made the greatest mess of things this year get the most legislation next year. It is as though he had devised a competition to make sure that the most incompetent Cabinet Ministers spend as much time as possible in the one place where he will never clap eyes on them – here in the House.[24]

Who has won the competition? Perhaps it is the Deputy Prime Minister. No, even in the league of incompetence he has not quite made it to the top. Step forward the Home Secretary [Jack Straw] this year's winner of the league for departmental foul-ups, ineffective legislation, ministerial bungling and misrepresentation of his own policies. He deserves his victory.

Labour MP James Plaskitt intervened to ask how scrapping the national minimum wage would help families. Hague responded by repeating Tory warnings that the newly-enacted national minimum wage would increase unemployment.

There is nothing in this Queen's Speech to help families. The effect of the minimum wage on the level of wages and employment remains to be seen, and every sensible person should consider those effects.

The Home Secretary faces a situation in which crime is set to rise after years of falling; each month shows record numbers of bogus asylum seekers; terrorist suspects have been released because the Government left out key parts of legislation; Soviet spies are uncovered but not charged; injunctions are taken out against newspaper leaks by Ministers who live by leaks; and there was a complete distortion of police numbers in the Home Secretary's conference speech, which was then exposed by a letter from another member of the Cabinet. It is enough to make people want to leave the country, but under this Home Secretary people cannot even get a passport.

A series of current scandals: the Soviet spy was 87-year-old Melita Norwood, who passed British nuclear secrets to the Soviet Union. This emerged in the archive of stolen Soviet intelligence documents smuggled into Britain by the defector Vasili Mitrokhin. She was not prosecuted because the copied documents did not constitute sufficient evidence. The injunction was taken out by the Attorney General, John Morris, to stop newspapers from revealing that William Straw, the 17-year-old son of Home Secretary Jack Straw had been cautioned for possession of cannabis, after a newspaper sting operation. The injunction did not apply in Scotland and the name soon emerged. On police numbers, Straw had promised to recruit 5,000 extra police officers in his speech to the 1999 Labour conference, but it emerged that he had no control over the numbers recruited by individual police forces, and that any impression that police numbers would rise was inaccurate; in fact, because of retirements and so forth, the number might actually fall. A leaked letter from the Chief Secretary to the Treasury, Alan Milburn, revealed his view that the extra 5,000 would only 'stabilise' numbers. And at the time there were serious problems in the Passport Agency.

With at least ten Home Office Bills to come, we might think that at least one would be tough on crime or tough on the causes of crime.[25] Now we know that that was part of the great Labour lie. Where is the common-sense legislation to ensure tougher and more honest sentencing? Where is the common-sense legislation that would put victims first? Where is the common-sense legislation to reverse the cut in police numbers and get the police on to the streets?[26] Instead, we have a Bill to abolish trial by jury.[27]

> Surely, cutting down the right to jury trial, making the system less fair, is not only wrong but short-sighted, and likely to prove ineffective.

That is what the Home Secretary himself said just two years ago.

The Government are doing not what they promised to do, but what they promised not to do. They say one thing and do another. They said before the election that they would protect jury trials and increase police numbers. Now jury trials are being abolished, while police numbers have fallen by 1000.

Who came second in the league of incompetence? This time no one can deny the Deputy Prime Minister his due, for who could doubt that he has had a vintage year? He started it with his immortal statement about the green belt:

> The Green Belt is a Labour achievement and now we're going to build on it.

The right hon. gentleman was standing in at Prime Minister's Question Time so much that Wednesday is now the only day that the Prime Minister spends in this country. As Lady Richard[28] revealed recently, the Deputy Prime Minister has even been chairing Cabinet meetings. She says in her diary for a Cabinet meeting on 19 June:

> Blair said he was in favour of the Millennium Dome and then disappeared, leaving John Prescott in charge. The meeting fell apart.

The Deputy Prime Minister reminds me a little of an ageing Soviet leader in the old days. [Jeers from Labour MPs.] I know that Labour members do not like hearing about the Deputy Prime Minister. The right hon. gentleman's power is taken from him, but he is still brought out to wave to the crowds at the party conference. Everyone pretends that he only has a cold, but it is rather worrying that he seems confused by simple questions and has to take a car to go even a couple of hundred yards. All around him his friends are quietly disappearing: Lord Macdonald is taking over his Department and Lord Falconer is taking over his role – purely for his own protection, of course.

John Prescott was a rich target for mockery: he had pledged to reduce the number of car journeys – but was soon criticised for using an official car to take him a few hundred yards from his hotel to the party conference. Gus Macdonald, a Labour peer, was made Transport Secretary. Prescott had been overlord of the Department of the Environment, Transport and the Regions. The change was seen as ending his control in this area. And Lord Falconer, the Prime Minister's former flatmate, who later became Lord Chancellor, had been put in charge of the Millennium Dome project.

From the way in which the Transport Bill will hit middle Britain, it seems that the Deputy Prime Minister, who has been excluded from the Prime Minister's election team, has joined our election team. The Bill proposes congestion taxes, motorway taxes and car-parking taxes, on top of more rises in fuel taxes and road taxes. We welcome effective measures to improve rail safety, but most of the transport Bill is a declaration of war against everyone who drives a car.

It is a vicious stealth-tax assault on car drivers. To Mondeo man,[29] once so cherished by new Labour's spin doctors, it is another kick in the teeth. People work hard and save hard to own a car. They do not want to be told that they cannot drive it by a Deputy Prime Minister whose idea of a park-and-ride scheme is to park one Jaguar so that he can ride away in the other.[30]

The transport Bill is not only about cars. To try to fool their own backbenchers, the Government have stuck the privatisation of air traffic control on the end in the hope that no one will notice. The Deputy Prime Minister will present a Bill that is rambling, over-inflated, illogical and ridiculously cumbersome – funny coincidence, that.

Everyone is asking where the Minister of Agriculture, Fisheries and Food [Nick Brown, a former Labour Chief Whip] is in the league of incompetence. Indeed, where is he today? The Prime Minister has encouraged him to be like Manchester United, abandoning domestic competition and going inter-national. The Minister is in the super-league for running the worst Department of Government in the whole of Europe. Indeed, we can con-gratulate him on winning that league. He has totally failed to defend Britain's interests; he has caved in to French demands after launching a boycott of all French food and spending a hectic three weeks trying to avoid camembert; and he has done what no one could have believed possible by turning our T-bone steak into an accessory to a crime.

It had been banned as a precaution against transmission of BSE – mad cow disease – to humans. Hague accused Blair of repeated capitulation in European negotiations, and tamely acquiescing to the creation of a highly taxed and highly regulated European superstate, while pretending it would never happen.

The Prime Minister finds it difficult to tell the truth about many matters, however trivial. Three years ago, he confided to Des O'Connor that when he was fourteen, he stowed away on a plane from Newcastle to the Bahamas. In Newcastle airport's 61-year history, there has never been a flight to the Bahamas. In 1969, the only exotic destinations served by Newcastle were Jersey and the Isle of Man.

In an interview with a local radio station in 1997, the Prime Minister spoke of his passion for football and reminisced about watching his favourite Newcastle player, centre forward Jackie Milburn, from a seat behind one of the goals at St James' Park. There are two problems with that statement: seats were not installed behind the goals until the 1990s and Jackie Milburn left the club when the Prime Minister was four years old.

The Prime Minister was at it again last week when he told listeners of the rock station Heart FM that his favourite tune was 'Where the Streets Have No Name' by U2; when he appeared on *Desert Island Discs*, it was Samuel Barber's 'Adagio for Strings' and Francisco Tarrega's 'Recuerdos de la Alhambra'.

When the Prime Minister stands at the Dispatch Box and says that pensioners will not be hit by a new £500 tax, or that waiting lists are coming down, or that there will be 5,000 extra police, we have to bear in mind that nothing that he says about anything can be relied on. That might be funny when he is talking about tunes, food and childhood memories, but when he is talking about taxes, waiting lists, class sizes and police numbers he is seeking to debase and destroy the currency of political discourse in this country. Given the Prime Minister's example, it is no wonder that the Government's whole existence is based on selective leaks, twisted statistics, distorted facts, half truths and a total determination to prevent people from finding out what is really going on.

People across the country know what should have been in the Queen's Speech. Schools should be at its heart. There should be a Bill to guarantee parents real power and to create free schools run by head teachers and governors, not Whitehall bureaucrats. There should be a Bill to give patients in the NHS a guaranteed maximum waiting time, based not on party political targets but on actual medical need.

There should be Bills to bring about a revolution in crime fighting to prevent the rise in crime. There should be a Bill to protect the homes and assets of people who have saved for their long-term care. There should be help for working women to take career breaks to look after their children, with family scholarships to help them if they want to get back to work. [Interruption.] Labour members ask for proposals, and then do not like them when they get them.

There should be moves to reduce the size and cost of government. Those costs have grown by £1 billion a year since this Government took office. There should be a Budget that would put an end to Labour's stealth taxes with an open and honest guarantee to cut the overall burden of tax in the lifetime of a Parliament.

The Queen's Speech should have spelled out to everyone that Britain will not be a pushover in Europe or anywhere else. It should have made it clear that we will be in Europe and not run by Europe and that we can make a success of our own currency, if we so wish.

The Labour Government pursue their own political priorities instead of rising to the challenge of preparing Britain for the new century. Future Queen's Speeches should not duck that challenge. They should turn the common sense of the British people into common-sense policies for the country. That is what the Opposition have to deliver – the common-sense revolution.

The truth that people will never hear from this Prime Minister is that this Queen's Speech does too little to prepare for the future, to widen our advantages over our competitors or to release the potential of our people. It does nothing that relates to the common-sense instincts of the British people.

'Although socialism is widely held by the establishment to be outdated, the things that are most popular in British society today are little pockets of socialism.'

Tony Benn gives the Commons some old-time religion: 16 May 2000

Tony Benn came within a whisker of winning the Labour Party over to his vision of socialism in the early 1980s. But three successive party leaders had erased the policy commitments to nationalisation, unilateral nuclear disarmament and withdrawal from the EU which he had written into Labour's 1983 manifesto. But Benn had continued, defiantly, to use the S-word, long out of fashion in Tony Blair's New Labour. In this speech in the Commons parallel chamber, Westminster Hall, where 'non-contentious' debates are held, he did something very unusual; he discussed ideology in Parliament.

'I felt that socialists were no longer on the defensive,' he wrote.[31] 'The case is reasonable, the arguments are sensible, the support for those ideas widespread.'

O N 23 APRIL 1901, Keir Hardie,[32] the then Member for Merthyr Tydfil, moved the following motion:

That, considering the increasing burden which the private ownership of land and capital is imposing upon the industrious and useful classes of the community, the poverty and destitution and general moral and physical deterioration resulting from a competitive system of wealth production which aims primarily at profit making, the alarming growth of trusts and syndicates able by reason of their great wealth to influence Governments and plunge peaceful Nations into war to serve their interests, this House is of the opinion that such a condition of affairs constitute a menace to the well-being of the Realm, and calls for legislation designed to remedy the same by inaugurating a Socialist Commonwealth founded upon the common ownership of land and capital, production for use and not for profit, and equality of opportunity for every citizen. [*Official Report*, 23 April 1901; Vol. 92, c. 1175.] I had asked for a debate on socialism, but I was summoned to the Table Office and told that as no one had ministerial responsibility for socialism, it would have to be about wealth and poverty in the economic system. A Treasury Minister has obligingly attended.

Here Benn traced the evolution of socialist ideas through their biblical roots to the first trade unions, the Chartists and the suffragettes. socialism, he said, was about moral values, democracy and internationalism. Common ownership was only part of it, and not an essential part. The nationalisation of the Post Office by Charles II, or of BP by Winston Churchill, were not inspired by socialist ideology.

Although socialism is widely held by the establishment to be outdated, the things that are most popular in British society today are little pockets of socialism, where areas of life have been excluded from the crude operation of market forces and are protected for the benefit of the community.

One of the great impetuses in the postwar years for the advance towards the welfare state – with its socialist inspiration – was the argument, which I remember well because I made it myself, that if the nation could plan for war, it could plan for peace. We had full employment during the war. If we could plan to have full employment to kill people, why could we not plan to have full employment in peacetime, and so be able to build the houses and provide all the nurses and teachers that we needed? This idea was strongly entrenched and was in some ways non-controversial.

If one looks at the people who have described themselves as socialists in the last century, one finds two different types. I have mentioned what we were able to achieve in this country guided by the ideas that I have outlined. The Soviet Union had no democratic basis whatever for its socialism. It was born in revolution and suffered greatly in the war. In the end, the Soviet Union crumbled because, although the Soviet Communist Party, which called itself socialist, was overwhelmingly the largest party, it did not have the consent of the people.

The other type are the Social Democrats, who abandoned socialism altogether. The most powerful advocates of capitalism today are to be found among the Social Democrats. I do not want to be controversial, but it is a fact that there are no more powerful advocates of market forces and globalisation than those in the party that describes itself as new Labour.

Although globalisation has brought a great deal of industrialisation, it has also produced acute poverty in the third world. The gap between rich and poor is wider now than a hundred years ago. There is the grossest exploitation of people in third world countries. People here can invest their capital in the third world, where wages are lower, and then lay off people in Britain – who then go on to unemployment benefit – and make their profits in much poorer countries.

We made great advances towards democracy from 1832 to the end of the European empires and the creation of the welfare state, but the power in a globalised economy is unaccountable. Major multinational companies are not accountable to the people whom they employ or to the nations in which they work. I spent my life as a Minister negotiating with oil companies and large multinationals that were more powerful than nation states. Indeed, they operated in this country like a colonial power.

Such activities have severe implications for our political system. The idea of representation has been replaced with the idea of management. I represent the interests of the people of Chesterfield as best I can and I also represent my convictions. People know what my convictions are when they vote and can get rid of me if they do not agree with them. But now we are all being managed on behalf of a global economy. Someone once said that, if we do not control the economy in the interests of the people, we have to control the people in the interests of the economy. That process is going on at a great pace.

We are told about our international competitors as if competition were at the core of a peaceful world; that is not a view that I share. The lack of accountability has a profound effect on the emerging democracies in the third world. They are often denied the benefit of the hundreds of years of parliamentary experience from which we gained. However, even in this country, the power of the multinationals is increasingly becoming such that Governments tremble before them. I was in the Cabinet in 1976 when we crumbled before the International Monetary Fund, which had serious consequences for the party and the Government.

We are now moving into another aspect of the political consequences of globalisation – the Third Way.[33] The idea is that it would be better for all the good people at the top to get together. The project is a coalition of people who believe that there is a common view at the top and that that is the only way in which to manage the economy. It is a one-party state. As a Minister, I visited Moscow and met the central committee of the Communist Party and the commissars. They had not been elected. I then went to Brussels and met the commissioners. They had not been elected. I met representatives of the central bank. They, too, had not been elected. The reduction of democratic control as a result of globalisation is a serious problem, and Europe is part of it.

I fear the consequences that will arise if people do not believe that they are represented. One consequence is apathy. If people do not vote because they do not believe that it makes a difference, the consequences for the legitimacy of the Government who win are profound. Low turnout is one aspect of that apathy. A low turnout, accompanied by cynicism, is a recipe for conflict and repression.

My age allows me to recall what happened in Germany before the war, where a despairing people turned to Hitler, who blamed the Jews and the trade unionists for their problems. He told the people that he would give them full employment, and by God he did – he rearmed them, and we had a war as a result.

It is necessary to say plainly and clearly that peace without social justice is impossible. We cannot have a peaceful society or a peaceful world if the principles of social justice are secondary to the search for profit. A society that is built around people and not profit is what lies at the heart of the socialist idea.

In the debate to which I referred at the outset of my remarks, Keir Hardie concluded:

> We are called upon at the beginning of the twentieth century to decide the question propounded in the Sermon on the Mount as to whether or not we will worship God or Mammon. The present day is a mammon-worshipping age. Socialism proposes to dethrone the brutal god Mammon and to lift humanity into its place.

That is a very religious way of putting it, but it explains the idea that has moved people to do things. All real change comes from underneath. The idea of cooperation rather than competition appeals to most people in their own lives. Competition creates insecurity and anxiety, while cooperation is always dominant when people look after their disabled children or their old parents. I think that that idea is of value.

I want to leave time for what will be a full debate, so I shall conclude on the policies that may follow from the ideas that I have advanced. First, we must expand the public services and ensure that they are publicly funded. In the immediately postwar years, the idea of national insurance was based on that of universal benefits. I do not believe that it is right for people to be means-tested before they are entitled to benefits for which they have paid, either through national insurance contributions or taxation. That is especially true of the need to link pensions with earnings. I am proud to have been in the Cabinet that made that link and I am distressed that it was reversed, at a cost of about £30 a week to pensioners. [Under Margaret Thatcher, but not reversed by Tony Blair – a source of considerable complaint within the Labour movement.]

We should have expanded public services for the provision of health care and education, which should be open, so as to allow every child access to the full range of knowledge in schools that are comprehensive in what they offer. Also, there should be access to the media, which does not usually cover the concerns of those who do not have wealth and power. I should add to that list the legal services, which are very expensive but absolutely necessary.

The second item on my list is the revitalisation of local government. I referred to the great Liberal achievements of the nineteenth century, and there are many examples of such achievements in the twentieth century. Local government should have the funding that it requires, the right to raise its own money – if it can persuade its electors to give it that money – and general powers that are not tied up by specific grants that local authorities administer but do not decide.

Thirdly, if we are genuinely interested in the idea of full employment, it is essential that we support manufacturing industry. For most of my life as a Minister, I tried as best as I could – sometimes successfully, but generally not – to reverse deindustrialisation. In 1948, Britain launched 48 per cent of all the ships launched in the world. In 1970, we had the largest motorbike industry in the world. In 1974, we had the largest machine tool industry and the largest car industry in Europe. That has all gone.

It is in the national interest to protect ourselves from invasion from abroad. We would resist anyone who tried to bomb our car factories, but if somebody buys and closes those factories, it is regarded as an inevitable consequence of globalisation. I do not think that that is a sustainable position. The same is true of privatisation. I hesitate to quote Harold Macmillan, but he said that privatisation was selling the family silver. That is not an example that would come immediately to mind for most families, but it was a vivid description of the sale of our natural assets.

We must have civil liberties. I refer not just to legal liberties and an end to discrimination, but to the acceptance of trade union rights. It is amazing that we talk about a global economy but that we do not legislate to implement the rights given to trade unions in the International Labour Organisation. I have introduced a Bill on the matter – the House may want to consider it – as such legislation is necessary.

We need a fairer tax system. I cannot understand why any Government should ring fence the rich and say, 'Whatever we do, we will not ask you to pay more', when people on benefits are continually being faced with demands to open the books and be examined in an attempt to deal with benefit fraud.

It is often argued that no one has any power over multinationals, but I do not believe that. Multinational companies spend millions of pounds on trying to win popular support through advertising campaigns because they know that it is necessary to retain the goodwill of host Governments. I believe that it is necessary to treat multinationals as international agents and to negotiate with them as if they were countries.

We must have stronger environmental laws. Keir Hardie was a passionate environmentalist, who complained about the rain forests in the United States being cut down. He was also a great believer in animal rights. On one occasion, Hardie was followed home from the House of Commons by a journalist from the *Daily Mail*, who hoped to find out to whom he talked in the street – no doubt, in an attempt to uncover some scandal. The journalist said that he patted all the horses that he saw in the street. Being a miner, Hardie appreciated the value of the pit pony.

We need to end the arms trade, which is far more serious than the drugs trade that receives so much attention. The arms trade allows arms manufacturers to arm both sides in a conflict. Then, when those arms are used, the world demands a ceasefire. I sometimes wonder whether the idea is to discover which arms work best so that more can be sold afterwards, as we saw in the case of the Exocet[34] that sank HMS *Sheffield* during the Falklands war.

Finally, we should try to build the United Nations as an embryonic, democratic institution, in accordance with the aspirations of the Chartists, who wanted to establish democratic government in Britain. If we are to have a global system, it must be a worldwide system, but it must be based on democratic accountability. My conviction is that the UN is being bypassed by NATO, whereas the UN should have responsibility, through the General Assembly, for controlling multinationals, which cannot be disciplined in any other way. The World Trade Organisation and the IMF should also be accountable to the United Nations General Assembly. That would be true internationalism rather than globalisation.

Those are my convictions. I am a socialist and I became a socialist through experience. After 50 years in the House and many years as a Minister, I realise the way in which power is exercised to shape our society. As I leave the House of Commons and approach a new political life at the end of this Parliament, I shall want to put those arguments to the electors as a non-candidate when the election comes, because I honestly believe that the ideas have much more support than the British establishment, any Government or the House yet realises.

All progressive change has come from underneath, and it might be worth remembering that there is a different tradition from those ideas with which we are presented every day. If we remember that, we might make more progress in winning public support for what needs to be done.

Benn left the Commons in 2001, 'to devote more time to politics'. Given his long struggle, 40 years before, not to succeed to his father's seat in the Lords, he was not offered a peerage. He remains a familiar figure at Westminster – and was kind enough to speak to the author for this book over a mug of tea in the canteen.

'That is an abdication of responsibility which invites retaliation.'

Conrad Russell dissects the government's approach to social security benefits: 25 June 2001

The son of a great philosopher and the descendant of a Whig Prime Minister, Conrad Russell might have been the product of a selective breeding programme designed to produce the perfect Liberal Democrat peer. He was a political radical with an utterly traditional appearance – a bent figure in an old suit with the waistband of his trousers held by braces somewhere in the vicinity of his ribcage. But it was a foolish minister who dismissed him because of his appearance. His dry, clipped voice could flay a thin argument with the precision of a surgeon's scalpel, always with impeccable syntax. Hansard editors normally have to tidy up the grammar of those whose words they report. It is hard to imagine they ever needed to with Lord Russell.

In this speech, made during the debate on the Queen's Speech which followed the 2001 election, he considered the thinking behind the creation of the new Department for Work and Pensions, which administered both the social security system and the 'New Deal' programme, which offered training and support to help people off benefits and into work. He detected a streak of authoritarianism beneath the surface.

I WANT TO SAY A LITTLE about public services. I declare an interest – mercifully, I do so in this Session for the last time – as a serving university teacher. At Question Time today, the noble Lord, Lord Walton of Detchant, drew our attention to a major problem in the public services and the fact that increasingly people are developing a reluctance to work. Before the Government talk too much about reform, they should think about why such reluctance is becoming so strong. Most people who go into the public services do so out of a sense of vocation; they certainly do not do so for the money. That sense of vocation and Treasury public service agreements sit rather uneasily together, especially when those agreements – which are back, somewhat to my regret, at the Treasury – are driven by the pursuit of efficiency, which is always concerned with getting people to do more rather than with how well the job is being done.

I remember extremely vividly a conversation with an intensive care nurse – probably the best nurse I have ever seen in action. After the patient had drifted off into a healing sleep, the nurse, observing that no one else was at that moment awake, paused a moment and said, 'I am about to go back to speak to the sixth form at my old school and I am going to tell them, "Whatever you do, never go into nursing. There is more expected of you than you can possibly do. You are set up to fail and you can therefore choose only between demotivation and burn-out."' Every public servant to whom I have repeated that story, and members of my profession, recognised it instantly. In fact, as I see it, for the past 25 years all government pressure has been to make me do my job worse and worse each year. I have got very tired of that, and I am not alone in my view. Governments, after all, should recognise that their expertise in such matters is limited.

Mr Richard Caborn[35] has given rise to a certain amount of merriment by not being able to answer questions in a sports quiz. I want to attack not Mr Caborn, but his critics, who did not recognise the difference between a Minister of Sport and a sportsman. It is like expecting the commander of a battleship to understand fiddly details about how to get better value for money from the ship's engines; that is not his department. I remember the late Baroness Macleod of Borve[36] saying that when her husband was Minister of Health, he would never have had a doctor in the ministry; different jobs were involved. When governments talk about, for example, improvements in education, they are outside their element; they are not competent to recognise an improvement in education. Unless governments are prepared to let those who work in the public services have their own values, they might find that they have to pay market rates to attract such people, which would be very expensive.

We have had a lot of argument recently about the role of the public or private sectors in the delivery of public services. We on these Benches do not make an ideological issue in that regard. We have never gone in for the attitude that involves saying, 'Four legs good, two legs bad'. That attitude comes from the twentieth century's politics of class conflict, against which we set our face at the beginning of that century; we are very glad that we did so. For us, that is more of a matter of horses for courses. The public and private sectors both have excellences. The question is: which excellence belongs to this particular job? The answer involves identifying the function that is required.

The great discipline of the private sector is competition. When there is no competition, the excellence of the private sector cannot be brought to bear. That applies especially when there is a single monopoly purchaser, against whom there can be no competition. Also, it is the nature of the market to have losers as well as winners; if it does not, it is not a market. One sees that in the supply of school places. After he had been at the ministry responsible for education for a few years, Lord Joseph[37] realised that it was impossible to combine a market in school places with a universal supply of places.

We need to think about what we want to do. That has not been done nearly enough. When it happens, we might have a slightly more worthwhile debate. The bulk of what we have to deal with concerns the Minister's brief; namely, all of the various issues involving welfare reform. I say in passing that I agree with my noble friend Lady Williams of Crosby[38] in her regret that the Government have adopted the slightly pejorative American use of the word 'welfare' and do not continue to talk, as we always have, of social security. It is clear that all that we do in this context happens in a global market and that the playing field in that market is not level. Capital can move at a few seconds' notice across the world. Labour, even if there were no restrictions on its movement, is much less easily uprooted. That creates a big advantage to capital and tends to downgrade the price of labour. Too far in that direction and we could see a serious drop in the general level of world demand, which would not be good for the world's economy. When we discuss the cost of social security, we should bear in mind those questions along with narrower questions.

The relationship between the state and the market is a seesaw, and a seesaw should never become immobile. The Government have reached a seriously mistaken diagnosis of what they think is wrong with the social security system. The White Paper, *Towards Full Employment*, published earlier this year, states:

> Rather than being a solution to these problems, the welfare system had become part of the problem itself.

The Government have asserted that many times but it has not yet been proved or even seriously argued for. If the Minister can put me right in that regard I shall be grateful. The Government think – this illusion is centuries old – that the problem is having to make people want to work. It is not usually a problem to make people want to work; after all, work is to many people their only social life as well as their only means of earning money. When people do not want to work, that is usually a matter of physical or mental illness or it involves the thinking behind the old proverb that, 'hope deferred maketh the heart sick'.

There are of course many categories of people – they are determined by geography, race, gender or disability – for whom work is difficult. The Minister and I know all about that. We have had exchanges on such matters many times. I shall not detain her now. But a great many of the people who do not get work have some disadvantage.

I raise in passing the question whether in some areas, like the ward next door to mine, there is a covert postcode discrimination by employers so that it is much more difficult to obtain work if one comes from those areas. If we could address that – I do not immediately see how – it would be nice.

Beyond that, a lot of the Government's policies on welfare reform have sprung out of the mind of Mr Michael Portillo[39] and the Jobseekers Act. The key innovation in that legislation was not the 'actively seeking work' requirement. That is not particularly controversial. What was crucial in that Act was the assumption that the state and its organs are the supreme judges of the work people should seek – for which jobs they should apply and which jobs they should not leave – and that the state's judgment takes priority over that of the people concerned.

Of course, the state is at a major disadvantage in relation to information. So there is at least a rebuttable presumption that the state might get some of these things wrong. If it has got them wrong and disqualification from benefit is inflicted as a result, that is a particularly severe penalty.

There is one case which particularly tickled me. It happened under the previous government but it could easily have happened under this Government. A man in Cardiff, a lifelong supporter of the Labour Party, was offered a job pulling pints at the Cardiff Conservative Club. He refused it and was told that he was voluntarily unemployed and could have no benefit. I believe that that discomposes me a great deal more than it discomposes new Labour Ministers. I do not think that that should have happened. There is, after all, such a thing as an individual conscience. If you deny that, you will not get a conscientious workforce and the losses out of that may be more than are realised.

Another sphere where private judgment matters, because it has the information, is as regards partners. I heard what the Minister said about interviews for partners. It could be argued that that is the down-side of equality. The argument has substance. But the requirement of interviews and, even more, if they are to come in, the existence of targets can create a rebuttable presumption and the existence of targets backed by the power to disentitle benefits may be a very severe pressure indeed.

The Minister may remember the noble Lord, Lord Evans of Parkside, speaking in our debates on single parents in 1997. He described the occasion when he was six, when his father said goodbye after breakfast, went down the pit and never came back. He said that for a year afterwards, he and his younger sister would never let their mother out of their sight. He said it would have been absolutely useless to encourage her to seek work.

Where there is an inflexible bureaucratic rule, it is impossible to respond to a case like that and a Government who cannot respond to such a case are not living in the real world. The Government should think about their targets for getting single parents into work because they involve a really serious intrusion into the sphere of private judgment. They should watch, too, how many of the people disentitled to benefit are removed from the claimant count. I accept the point made by the noble Baroness, Lady Blackstone,[40] in her Written Answer to me of 8 May last that not all of them are removed from the claimant count. But when the Prime Minister, in the House of Commons on the 20th of this month, boasted of the reduction in the claimant count, he should have been able to say how much of that reduction was achieved simply by taking people off the count by disentitlement. 'She left my employment', as Goldfinger put it. It is worrying.

There have been, since 1997, 701,000 people sanctioned under the Jobseekers Act. That is an awful lot of people. We do not know anything about what happened to them and we should do.

As regards housing benefit, the Minister knows my views. I ask her to stick to the commitment of the 1986 Act that income support is not meant to cover rent. Before she speaks, as the Government do, about work incentives, I ask her to look again at the DETR and the DSS research on housing benefit. I know she knows it well. I should like to think that anything that the Government do will be compatible with that research. If it is not, it will take up a good deal of time in this Chamber.

Finally, we should not lose sight of the purpose of benefits. The purpose of benefits is not to cure poverty. That they have not done so is no reproach to the Government. The purpose of benefits is to alleviate poverty until something better can be done. That is a very necessary purpose.

I have a pupil at the moment who has just finished his exams. He is still in those intervening days between the end of the exams and the beginning of the right to social security, which is quite a long time on an empty stomach. He has absolutely nothing to live on. He spent his last penny ringing me up and ran out of money before he could tell me where he was and before I was able to do anything about it.

We talk about rights and responsibilities. They are interlocked. They are not necessarily contingent. If you do not believe in the death penalty, you do not believe that the right to life is contingent on good behaviour. I do not, in fact. But if we want people to exercise their responsibilities rather better – and I must confess that I do – then how we exercise our responsibilities to them is a matter to which we should not be indifferent. If we tell people, 'We do not care whether you have anything to eat. You are nothing to do with us. Go away. We have forgotten about you', that is an abdication of responsibility which invites retaliation. I do not think it is wise.

Three
THE AWKWARD SQUAD.

ONE RECOGNISABLE SUBSPECIES in the Commons is the crusading MP, who latches onto an inconvenient issue and refuses to be fobbed off. The recently retired Tam Dalyell's 40-year career of asking unwelcome questions is the classic example – but he stands in a long and continuing parliamentary tradition, which runs through all parties.

Sometimes the awkward squad are animated by an injustice or impropriety and demand that it should be addressed. Sometimes they pursue a wider – but usually unfashionable – cause. Sometimes, as in the case of Richard Crossman below, they are willing to fly in the face of their own government's policy and even of patriotic opinion. A full-dress parliamentary campaign will not normally consist of a single speech – there will be questions, interventions, early day motions (which MPs sign, but which are never debated; the early day at which this is supposed to happen, by mystifying parliamentary convention, never actually arrives), the mobilisation of all-party groups as well as quiet conversations with ministers in the division lobbies, letters to the press, appearances on the *Today* programme, if possible, and every other device a resourceful politician can muster.

These are examples of speeches challenging ministers (and in one case an aspirant opposition leader) on issues they would rather not talk about. Scores of MPs could have been included in this section, and for the most part the speeches which are included are there because they required particular courage or delivered a particularly telling blow – or both.

'This dreadful unconscious drift into a blind prejudice, covered by a cloak of self-righteousness.'

Richard Crossman denounces Ernest Bevin's policy on Israel: 26 January 1949

In the postwar Labour government, it was a brave backbencher who antagonised the Foreign Secretary, the awesome Ernie Bevin. After all, Bevin's capacity for vendetta was already legendary. His epic feud with his great rival Herbert Morrison generated one of the all-time great Bevinisms – told that Morrison was his own worst enemy Bevin snarled, 'Not while I'm alive 'e aint.' But in 1946 Richard Crossman defied him. Bevin appointed him to the Anglo-American Committee of Inquiry, which reported on the future of Palestine. The issue was Jewish immigration, which had created major problems, as the British colonial authorities tried to balance Jewish aspirations for a national homeland – the future state of Israel – and the increasing resentment of the Arab population. Crossman surprised Bevin with his pro-Zionist stance. He helped engineer a recommendation for an additional 100,000 European refugees to be allowed into Palestine – an action Bevin called 'a stab in the back'.

Crossman emerged as a serious critic of Bevin's policies – and not just on Israel. When he and a group of Labour backbenchers moved an amendment to the King's Speech in the Commons, calling for a change in foreign policy, the Foreign Secretary, who was attending the UN in New York, demanded their names. As each was read out, he added,'I'll break him.' On that occasion Crossman was outmanoeuvred and ended up trying, rather humiliatingly, to prevent it being voted on.

This speech, delivered to an angry and hostile House, was made during a debate on government policy on Israel, after the newly created state had survived the first onslaught against it by Arab forces. It came after a series of press articles in which Crossman had attacked Bevin directly. One included a quote from an Israeli army major, who said: 'If we were to put up a statue to the Englishman who did most to create the state of Israel, we would have to choose Ernest Bevin. By trying to destroy us, he gave us no alternative to taking our destiny into our own hands.'[1] It was followed by another piece headlined: 'I accuse Bevin'. This was dangerous conduct from a first-term backbencher, but it was eclipsed by this performance in the chamber.

Crossman's biographer, Anthony Howard, described this speech as 'one of the great philippics of the 1945–50 parliament'. It was good enough to help persuade more than 60 Labour MPs to rebel, at least to the extent of failing to vote for the government motion. *Tribune* called it 'the speech of a lifetime'.

Crossman began by recalling how little support his earlier warnings about the government's policy had attracted.

N OW THE OPPOSITION, after three and a half years, stages a death bed repentance beside the rotting corpse of the Foreign Secretary's policy which it supported for three years – one or two individuals were exceptions I agree – but I did not hear very loud or brave voices raised when we tried to protest and warn this country where it was going . . . this House and the country as a whole have been behind the Foreign Secretary in what he did. Only a very few of us have consistently opposed him.

I want to analyse his mistakes because it is relevant, in looking into the future, to see what went wrong. I believe that we can trace in the mind of the Foreign Secretary two stages. The first was a very natural one when he came to see the Palestine problem. I think he said to himself, 'I am a very experienced negotiator. Surely, this is not beyond my power. Jews and Arabs are ordinary, reasonable human beings. After all, I have had more difficult trade union negotiations to deal with and I will have a try. I will get them round a table and persuade them to agree.' That was a worthy ideal. Some of us knew, however, that from the start it was absolutely hopeless to believe that the method of solving problems in industrial affairs in Great Britain could be applied with the faintest hope of success in the atmosphere of Palestine.

Out of the Foreign Secretary's disappointment at the failure of his negotiations grew what I describe as the second stage of his development, which can be summed up in that Irish expression: 'He grew neutral against the Jews.'

That is to say, he continued to say and, I think, to believe that we were neutral, but every action he took, whether he thought so or not, seemed in Palestine, in Lake Success and, if I may say so, in every capital of the world, to be somewhat less than neutral and to be somewhat hostile against one side. His speech this afternoon was a crowning example of that attitude, a complete unconscious disclosure of his gross partiality.

I had the privilege recently of staying with Dr. Weizmann.

Chaim Weizmann was the first President of Israel, a charismatic figure Crossman had met during his work on the Anglo-American Committee – Crossman's two articles attacking Bevin were both sent from Weizmann's home. He was later to keep a picture of Weizmann in his study; the only other photographs there were of family members.

No statesman's policy has been more deliberately ruined by this country than Weizmann's. He stood for the British connection and lived here for 42 years and served this country well. I will quote one anecdote to show the small mean things which matter so very much. When he left this country to become President, he decided to return his passport to the Home Secretary. He wrote a dignified and long letter of thanks for his 42 years in England, during which time he had contributed in no little way to the assistance of this country. He did not receive even an official acknowledgment. That is the kind of thing which bites very deep. That is what I call 'neutrality against the Jews'.

Add those little things together and we get this dreadful unconscious drift into a blind prejudice, covered by a cloak of self-righteousness. That is what we have got instead of a policy today. Here we are as a nation totally unaware that in the outside world the decision of a British Labour Government, in the middle of a baking summer, to send three shiploads of Jews back to Belsen was not called strict neutrality but was thought to show a certain feeling against one side. Those things are not forgotten in Palestine, nor in the Middle East, nor all over the world.

We have to face the fact in the Debate, as the right hon. member for Woodford [Winston Churchill] said, that our Middle Eastern policy is in ruins today. We have temporarily lost the friendship of the Jews, but it is going to be far easier to restore friendship with Israel than with the other countries of the Middle East. On that tragic 7 January, when our aeroplanes were shot down, the really important factor was the refusal of the Egyptians to ask for our assistance under the 1936 Treaty.

This is a reference to the five RAF Spitfires, stationed to defend the Suez Canal, which were shot down by Israelis over the Negev Desert.

Their armies had been utterly exterminated and considerable Jewish forces were threatening Egypt, but, so great was the animosity towards Britain that they preferred to come to what might be humiliating terms with Israel, than to accept assistance from us.

Our third and greatest loss was the loss of our own integrity, the blindness which came upon the Government as the only alternative to admitting their mistakes, their refusal to hear the real facts, and their readiness to believe sheer propaganda. I want to make a list of some of the fantastic prejudices which have gone by way of Intelligence. Here, I regret to say, Foreign Office officials in the Middle East and the Middle East High Command are gravely responsible for misleading the Government time after time with so-called Intelligence reports which were nothing but pro-Arab propaganda. The first and basic instance was referred to by the right hon. member for Woodford and it was summed up to me by David Ben-Gurion [Prime Minister of Israel] who said to me, 'When you go back to London you may think of Whitechapel and then think of us and believe we are the same, but we are not. We are the people who decided that Whitechapel was not good enough for us, who decided to be real men. Think of us as like yourselves and ask what you, a Britisher, would do in our position and you will get it right.' He also said, 'I may have to be the Jewish Churchill,' and that has come true.

Why did they fight? Heavens above, they had escaped from pogroms and ghettos. To where else could they escape? They had come either to the final dead end, or to the beginning of a new world and they were not going to lie down and have their throats cut to make a Roman holiday for our strategic convenience. How can we regard as aggressive or imperialist a little people which, by a miracle, came through this terrible war? They were not fighting with their backs to the wall, but with their backs half way through the wall, and nowhere could they be more than about ten miles from a battlefront. But they are told, 'Now you have your backs two inches from the wall, you are wicked aggressive imperialists if, in the course of trying to get at one of the people who hit you on the head, you go two feet inside his territory.' And they turn to us and say, 'We cannot understand you British. Have you not enough imagination to see what we have been through? Can you not have imagination to see what we have been through? Why should you accuse us of all these things?'

I wish to stress that it is not too late for reconciliation. There is still, I stress and repeat, a deep underlying devotion to this country. It is covered over by a bitterness all the more bitter because of the expectations that existed. As some Jew said to me, 'We would not have minded this if Hitler had done it but for you to have done it, to whom we owe everything in the world!' If, despite this bitterness, there came a new magnanimity in British policy I am completely confident that, not within months but within years we could re-establish the relations of that great period when we had vision in which we saw a splendid future, when we believed in a new civilisation, when we built the Mandate and ourselves helped the Arabs with the help of the Jews. We could go back to all this quite easily, on the one condition that some people here admit, not publicly but privately, that they have been wrong.

'Why not publicly?' an MP shouted.

It is difficult to ask them to do it publicly – that they will in their heart of hearts analyse what went wrong and draw the conclusion that we have to make a change.

What is no use is a grudging half-hearted recognition by men who still believe their own propaganda. We used to say during the war that what got the Germans down was that they believed their own propaganda. The danger here is the same that the Government believe all their propaganda about an aggressive Imperialism, and vast Jewish forces that are to overflow the whole Middle East; although there are 800,000 Jews, 40 million Arabs and quite a lot of British about. If all that prejudice and propaganda could be done away with, if people here could see the realities, it would mean a great deal. But, as an hon. member says, I am dubious if we shall get it from certain individuals on the Government front bench.

The war between Arab and Jew in Palestine was far more violent than people here seemed to realise. There were murder gangs in many Arab villages for months on end after 29 November and the Jews reacted. The Jews were not gentle; they were very ruthless. They wiped out villages where there had been violent resistance from strongpoints. They said, 'General Montgomery taught us that. That is what he did in the Arab revolt. When an Arab was difficult he blew up the house.'

There was a war on. It was a cruel war on both sides. Every civilian had a gun. If an Arab had been firing at the Jews and the Jews won, he left the gun and ran away. Only 70,000 Arabs survive in Israel today. These 70,000 are a privileged and pampered minority. They are receiving £1 18s. a day for unskilled work picking citrus. They have been given the same wage rates as Jewish labourers. They are doing well, but I do not think that we can hope for a mass return. Nor do I think that it would be wise.

I want to conclude with these words. I must say that this debate marks the end of a quite disastrous period in our Middle Eastern affairs. We have wasted not only money but British lives in a futile attempt to keep deserts deserted and to stem the tide of progress for strategic reasons. Prejudice, to my mind, has blinded the Foreign Secretary, his foreign advisers and his military advisers, and compelled this country to accept a grave diplomatic defeat and humiliation. I would say this. It is not the first time this has happened. It happened to us with the American colonies under Lord North; it happened to us in South Africa, and it happened to us in Ireland. But on each occasion before, a unique British greatness was displayed magnanimity in defeat.

It is very easy for a great power to be magnanimous when it has won, but the greatest quality is for a great power to be magnanimous when it has been defied by a small one, and the small power has pulled it off. That is the mark of greatness – whether at that point the great power shakes hands and does it openly and frankly. That is the issue. Today I waited and waited, wondering whether the Foreign Secretary could be big enough to do that. He staked his career, his personal career, on solving the Jewish problem. He could be remembered as the man who staked all, lost everything down to the last penny, and then, with the last penny, won the whole thing back again. But can we believe him? Do his words give us the justification for feeling that that change of heart has happened? If they could, I would vote for the Government today, since they cannot, I shall be unable to do so.

'We cannot, we dare not, in Africa of all places, fall below our own highest standards.'

Enoch Powell calls for heads to roll over the deaths of detainees in Kenyan prison camps: 27 July 1959

One of the most shameful episodes in the final days of British colonial rule in Africa was the killing of eleven Mau Mau terrorist detainees at the Hola prison camp in Kenya. They were beaten to death by prison warders in an exercise designed to make them take part in forced labour, then an accepted rehabilitation measure. This was part of an exercise known as the Cowan Plan, after the colonial civil servant who devised it, J. B. T. Cowan, the Acting Assistant Commissioner of Prisons for Kenya. The Cowan Plan was approved by the colonial government the day after the House of Commons had rejected a motion calling for an investigation into the prison camps in Kenya. When the deaths at Hola were announced, it was claimed at first that the prisoners had been poisoned by tainted water from a water cart, or had died in a fight over the water – excuses which attracted Enoch Powell's Olympian derision. Those responsible faced little retribution. One white officer was required to leave a few months before his due retirement date. Later in 1959, Cowan was awarded an MBE. But pressure from MPs forced the government to investigate and produce a White Paper on the incident.

When the Commons debated the contents of the White Paper, Powell, then on the backbenches following his resignation over the failure to control government spending, broke ranks to denounce the killings. He was the only Conservative to do so. He trod a perilous line but managed to avoid direct criticism of the government – and he specifically absolved the Colonial Secretary, Alan Lennox-Boyd, of responsibility. He dealt with the comments of Sir John Peel, a rather blimpish Conservative MP who had served in the Colonial Administrative Service, that the detainees who had taken the Mau Mau oath were 'desperate and sub-human individuals' with a dismissiveness that managed to convey scorching contempt. He insisted that, in the name of responsible government, blame for the whole affair should not be shuffled off onto minor bureaucrats – repeatedly citing documents from the government's White Paper to make the case that officials in the colonial government of Kenya, whose combination of callousness and muddle had led to the deaths, should be punished.

MANY ASPERSIONS HAVE been cast and many imputations made by hon. members opposite in the course of this debate with which I could not for an instant associate myself. And yet I cannot regret that even at this hour the House is once again considering the affair of Hola Camp. For the further documents relating to the deaths which were issued as a White Paper last week confirm what was already pretty clear from the earlier evidence, that it could be to the credit neither of this House nor of this country that the matter should rest where it now stands.

The affair of Hola Camp was a great administrative disaster, and to that administrative disaster there were three aspects. There was the authorisation of an operation which in its nature was likely to have fatal results; there was the failure to see that that operation, such as it was, was at least carried out with the minimum of risk; and, finally, there was the incident, which it is difficult to find a word to describe, of the water cart communiqué. The new documents show that the responsibility for all three aspects of this administrative disaster goes higher than can be discharged by the premature retirement of the officer in charge of the camp or by the retirement, accelerated by a few weeks, of the Commissioner of Prisons.

The central document in the White Paper of last week, and it has often been referred to in this debate, is the minute of 17 February addressed by the Commissioner of Prisons to the Minister of Defence. That Minute enclosed two other documents, Folios 9 and 10 on the file. Folio 9 was the Cowan Plan as drafted and intended by Cowan and put up by him as a proposal to his senior officers. Folio 10 was the extraordinary message which Sullivan [the camp commandant] had sent to Cowan on the 14th which can hardly be described otherwise than as a *cri de coeur*. It is impossible to read that document without sensing through it the state of mind of the man who wrote it or being aware of the risks which were attendant upon the situation which it reveals.

I will only remind the House of the ominous facts which it disclosed, that the Ministry of Works on the site had asked to be 'disassociated entirely from any such operation' and the request for a senior superintendent, 'with appropriate powers of summary punishment' to 'be present when the policy outlined is implemented'. It was clear evidence, among other things, that the Cowan Plan, Folio 9, was not what Sullivan, *vide* Folio 10, thought he was expected to implement. Incidentally, therefore, if there is blame for the failure to implement the Cowan Plan accurately, that responsibility must rest on all those who should have become aware, through seeing Folio 10, that Sullivan had misunderstood the Cowan Plan. With these two documents underneath, went this Minute, Folio 11, from the Commissioner of Prisons to the Minister of Defence. The Commissioner of Prisons had not yet taken a decision on the Cowan Plan. Indeed, when he saw it he gave instructions that 'no action should be taken until authority was given' by his office. When he looked at 9 and 10 together, he decided that he, on his responsibility, could not authorise any action to be taken, and submitted it to his Minister, saying – and I am sorry to quote these words again, but they are essential, 'The plans Mr Cowan worked out at (9) could be undertaken by us, but it would mean the use of a certain degree of force, in which operation someone might get hurt or even killed. I think this situation should be brought to the notice of the Security Council and a direction given on what policy should be adopted.'

He then again referred to the 'action as planned at (9), with the risk of someone getting hurt or killed.'

Those were not idle words, the reference to someone getting hurt or killed. He said in evidence to the Committee of three that the risk he had in mind that someone might get killed or hurt included 'warder staff as well as detainees.' Since the Commissioner of Prisons knew that in the Cowan Plan the numerical superiority of the warders to the detainees was to be overwhelming, the fact that he regarded the likelihood of being killed as applying to warders as well as to detainees is evidence of the degree of risk and danger which he associated in his mind with the Cowan Plan – the original, correct Cowan Plan, Folio 9. This was apart from the evidence in Folio 10 that things were going wrong, that it would not be that plan which would be put into effect, and that Sullivan had misunderstood.

He considered the responsibility for putting this into effect was not only one that he could not take, but it was one he could not advise his Minister to take alone, without reference to the Security Council.

Incidentally, the action of the Commissioner of Prisons disposes of the notion that the Cowan Plan for Hola was, as has often been said – and I quote the expression in the leading article in the *Daily Telegraph* yesterday

> the application of a long-standing and highly successful technique of rehabilitation!

The truth is that it was the application of a modification, and a very important modification, of the technique which had elsewhere yielded good results.

When my right hon. friend spoke in the debate on 16 June last, he was careful to put that correctly. He said: 'The proposals were the adaptation of a proved and successful technique to the circumstances of Hola.'

They were, in fact, as proposed now in the Cowan Plan, something which represented such a serious departure from anything attempted before, something so dangerous in themselves, that he could not envisage the responsibility to carry them out being taken otherwise than by the Security Council itself.

The Minister of Defence decided that it was not necessary, and the Minister of Defence and the Minister of African Affairs took upon themselves the responsibility for authorising an operation which they had been warned involved the risk of death, in a minute accompanied by a paper which showed to anyone who cared to read it that not even that operation, dangerous as it was, was the one which Sullivan contemplated carrying out.

The hon. lady the member for Blackburn [Barbara Castle – who had initiated the debate and also made a memorable speech] was a little too kind to the Minister for African Affairs. She overlooked the fact that he as well as the Minister of Defence had all the relevant papers in front of him. Those two men took upon themselves, with their eyes open and with full knowledge, not only the responsibility for the Cowan Plan but the responsibility for allowing the deformed version of it to go forward. It was authorised – now we come to the second phase, the execution – with the indication that it should go forward 'subject to the proviso that' the Commissioner 'should first ensure that he has a sufficient number of warders at Hola to cope with possible eventualities.'

So, warned of the danger implicit, aware from the S.O.S. that all was not well, the Ministers responsible, the Ministers who had given the decision, left the matter there and just sent it down the line.

Those two men, who knew that they had authorised – without reference, as advised by the Commissioner of Prisons, to the Security Council – an operation involving the risk of death, learnt on the afternoon of 3 March that on the day on which that operation was carried out, ten men had died at Hola Camp; and on 4 March, after – and these are the words of the publicity officer: 'a good deal of discussion as to whether violence was the cause of the deaths of these men,' in a meeting presided over by His Excellency the Governor, they were parties to the issue of the water cart communiqué.

Those documents, that evidence, prove to me conclusively that the responsibility here lies not only with Sullivan and Lewis, but at a level above them. It lies with those to whom they actually appealed for help, whom they warned of the danger, from whom they received, indeed, a decision which transferred responsibility upwards, but no other, help or guidance. That responsibility, transcending Sullivan and Lewis, has not been recognised; but it cannot be ignored, it cannot be buried, it will not just evaporate into thin air if we do nothing about it.

I am as certain of this as I am of anything, that my right hon. friend the Secretary of State from the beginning to the end of this affair is without any jot or tittle of blame for what happened in Kenya, that he could not be expected to know, that it could not be within the administrative conventions that these matters should be brought to his attention before or during the execution. When I say my right hon. friend was in this matter utterly and completely blameless, that is of a piece with his administration of his high office generally, which has been the greatest exercise of the office of Colonial Secretary in modern times. It is in the name of that record, it is in the name of his personal blamelessness, that I beg of him to ensure that the responsibility is recognised and carried where it properly belongs, and is seen to belong.

I have heard it suggested that there were circumstances surrounding this affair at Hola Camp which, it is argued, might justify the passing over of this responsibility – which might justify one in saying, 'Well, of course, strictly speaking, that is quite correct; but then here there were special circumstances.'

It has been said – and it is a fact that these eleven men were the lowest of the low; sub-human was the word which one of my hon. friends used. So be it. But that cannot be relevant to the acceptance of responsibility for their death. I know that it does not enter into my right hon. friend's mind that it could be relevant, because it would be completely inconsistent with his whole policy of rehabilitation, which is based upon the assumption that whatever the present state of these men, they can be reclaimed. No one who supports the policy of rehabilitation can argue from the character and condition of these men that responsibility for their death should be different from the responsibility for anyone else's death. In general, I would say that it is a fearful doctrine which must recoil upon the heads of those who pronounce it, to stand in judgment on a fellow human-being and to say, 'Because he was such-and-such, therefore the consequences which would otherwise flow from his death shall not flow.'

It is then said that the morale of the Prison Service, the morale of the whole Colonial Service, is above all important and that whatever we do, whatever we urge, whatever we say, should have regard to that morale. 'Amen' say I. But is it for the morale of the Prison Service that those who executed a policy should suffer – whether inadequately or not is another question – and those who authorised it, those to whom they appealed, should be passed over? I cannot believe that that supports the morale of a service.

Going on beyond that, my hon. friend the member for Leicester, South-East [John Peel] reminded the House how proud the Colonial Service is of the integrity of its administration and its record. Nothing could be more damaging to the morale of such a service than that there should be a breath or a blemish left upon it. No, sir, that argument from the morale of the Prison Service and the Colonial Service stands on its head if what we mean is that therefore the consequences of responsibility should not follow in this case as they would in any other similar case.

Finally it is argued that this is Africa, that things are different there. Of course they are. The question is whether the difference between things there and here is such that the taking of responsibility there and here should be upon different principles. We claim that it is our object – and this is something which unites both sides of the House – to leave representative institutions behind us wherever we give up our rule. I cannot imagine that it is a way to plant representative institutions, to be seen to shirk the acceptance and the assignment of responsibility, which is the very essence of responsible Government.

Nor can we ourselves pick and choose where and in what parts of the world we shall use this or that kind of standard. We cannot say, 'We will have African standards in Africa, Asian standards in Asia and perhaps British standards here at home.' We have not that choice to make. We must be consistent with ourselves everywhere. All Government, all influence of man upon man, rests upon opinion. What we can do in Africa, where we still govern and where we no longer govern, depends upon the opinion which is entertained of the way in which this country acts and the way in which Englishmen act. We cannot, we dare not, in Africa of all places, fall below our own highest standards in the acceptance of responsibility.

'As Mr Powell sat down, he put his hand across his eyes. His emotion was justified for he had made a great and sincere speech,' noted the *Daily Telegraph*.[2] He had demonstrated real passion to those who thought him a desiccated logician. Such was the effect of the speech that many expected Powell to be brought back into government at the earliest opportunity – but all the Prime Minister, Harold Macmillan, would offer him after the 1959 general election was a junior post in the Department of Education, which Powell refused. He returned to the government as Minister for Health in July 1960.

'Habitat will be destroyed. Its uniqueness will go.'

Tam Dalyell campaigns to save frigate birds, tortoises and the great booby: 25 October 1967

Searching out a particular speech by Tam Dalyell is a revealing experience. While most MPs take up a column or less in the index of Hansard, Dalyell takes up not just columns, but pages. The range of his interests and enquiries is enormous, and generations of frustrated ministers have had to field complex, well-directed and often nearly unanswerable questions on unpredictable subjects.

In the process, Dalyell has acquired a reputation for mild eccentricity as well as for dogged persistence and acute analysis. In his diaries for 1981[3] Alan Clark records a revealing exchange with Robin Cook, then a junior Treasury spokesman under Michael Foot: 'I remarked ruefully that talent was being better used in the Labour Party than in our own. He said this was due to Michael's innovations. He cited the example of Tam Dalyell [then opposition spokesman on science] saying that he was absolutely brilliant, then adding somewhat to my surprise ". . . but he is unreliable."

'"Unreliable? What do you mean?"

'"Well he sometimes goes his own way, you cannot rely on him always to speak to the ministerial brief. Which is a good thing of course," he said hurriedly, but unconvincingly.'

The press gallery veteran Edward Pearce believes Dalyell is 'a natural argufying rebel, not a stupid bore, not a failed creep working off resentment, but someone who is out by taste and preference and thus free to fight only the battles he cares for'.[4] Dalyell claims to have taken Harold Macmillan's advice only to rebel on one thing at a time.[5]

But he always seemed to have a number of irons in the fire. Party leaderships tend to be uncomfortable with independent thinking and stubborn principle, but it does have the advantage of bringing unexpected issues into the arena.

One such was Dalyell's campaign to prevent the construction of a military airbase on an obscure Indian Ocean atoll of Aldabra – where a unique ecology would be destroyed if the plan went ahead. Oceanography was one of the consistent themes in Dalyell's questioning over the decades, and he launched a major parliamentary campaign to save the island and its wildlife, catching the Defence Secretary, Denis Healey, rather by surprise.

Healey and defence planners wanted an Indian Ocean base which could be reached by air without overflying Arab nations which might close their airspace in a moment of crisis. Aldabra fitted the bill.

'Since it was inhabited only by giant tortoises, frigate birds and the great booby, we expected no political difficulties,' he wrote in his memoirs.[6] 'We reckoned without the environmental lobby, which won its first great victory against us, aided by a brilliant campaign of parliamentary questions from the assiduous Tam Dalyell.'

This speech, in an adjournment debate when the campaign was close to success, gives an idea of the level of detailed argument with which Dalyell belaboured ministers for decades.

ALTHOUGH THERE IS A sparse attendance in the House tonight I assure my hon. friend [Merlyn Rees, Under-Secretary at the Ministry of Defence responsible for the RAF, was to reply to the debate] that his answer will be very widely read by even thousands of scientists, perhaps of very many different disciplines, who are deeply concerned about this subject. I shall be discussing his reply tomorrow with the Director of the United States Marine Science Programme, who is coming to lunch with me.

First, I want to deploy the case, as I see it, of the Royal Society, which has been very helpful in briefing me and clearing up all sorts of points. The Royal Society says that, as the result of a further detailed study of the situation set out in a memorandum detailing the scientific interests in Aldabra, and the probable effects on its ecological system, the Society is convinced that any extensive development of the atoll will inevitably destroy the greater part of these biological features, the result of a long period of evolution in isolation from the great land masses which make Aldabra unique among the atolls of the world.

The Royal Society goes on to say that alone of the Indian Ocean elevated atolls, Aldabra has never been mined for guano and has never been stripped of vegetation and soils. Weeds and pests have not been introduced, so that unique forms of life ill adapted to competition with invaders have been retained.

I will not trouble the House with the details of this memorandum. It is sufficient to say that 10 per cent of the plants in Aldabra are found nowhere else in the world, that 28 per cent of the 127 species of insects are endemic, and there are extremely interesting crustaceans, molluscs, fruit bats, and fresh water fish. For geologists, most of the high limestone islands have had their ecological systems irreversibly altered by man's activities and only Aldabra and Henderson Island, in the Pacific, remain.

Briefly, that is the start of the scientists' case. It is not up to me to put words into the mouth of the Secretary of State for Defence, but, as I understand it, his argument was this in his meeting with the Royal Society. My right hon. friend said, 'I can give the undertaking that if a decision is eventually taken to go ahead with the building of an airfield or a harbour on the island, we will ensure that the scientific bodies are fully and continuously consulted. Our object is to ensure that the changes to the ecosystem of the island are kept to a minimum.'

In this matter I do not doubt for one moment the good faith of the Ministry of Defence, but, with the best will in the world, can any kind of protection, in fact, be carried out? It seems to me that there are dangers from accidental interference. There are dangers from bored personnel. Those of us who have had the good fortune to visit remote military or naval units understand the human reasons that make them bored and they want a little excitement. Naturally, they go exploring and, perhaps, hunting.

The gist of this part of the argument is that during the construction period itself inevitably, whether we like it or not, and with the maximum good will on the part of the Ministry of Defence, habitat will be destroyed. Its uniqueness will go. My understanding is – my hon. friend can confirm this – that, in deference to the views of the scientists, the Ministry of Defence has made a decision to concentrate its activities on the east part of South Island.

I would praise the Government for being flexible in this matter. They have not been rigid. I am not saying that hitherto the Government have been at all unreasonable to the scientists in their attitude. There is no criticism of the Government on this point. However, it is the view of the Royal Society, backed up by the American Academy of Scientists, possibly the two most distinguished scientific bodies in the Western world, that the decision to concentrate on South Island does not change the original view put forward by the Royal Society.

The Royal Society says that the proposition is still valid, that any installation will disturb the ecosystem. Besides, the east part of South Island, for which the installation is proposed, is the most interesting area of all. It is not the Champignon dense scrub area; it is the Platin open bush area. This question of the Platin open bush area is crucial. It is this area which contains the freshwater pools which, as I understand, would have to be filled in, with consequent destruction of the breeding grounds of the tortoises and many other animals.

Then there is the question of the frigate birds. Here, I personally do not go so far as some of the ornithologists who have written to the press. My understanding is that the frigate birds will create problems. These problems could, perhaps, be partially overcome, though I should hate them to be overcome in the same way as the Americans on Midway, disgracefully, in my view, have tried to eliminate the albatross population of the Central Pacific. The situation would very much depend on thermal conditions, but my understanding is that the habits of the frigate birds are such that they could not be relied on to be at a particular spot at a particular time of year – it would depend on weather conditions – and there would, therefore, be grave difficulty and danger to our pilots.

There is also the other difficulty, of which my hon. friend is aware, that the frigate birds go away when they are young and return as mature birds. Whatever happens in this situation, therefore, the frigate birds would be returning each year for five or six years, so that there would be aircraft danger for a very long time. If we are talking of a time span of five or six years before flying and approach flying is safe, this seems to me, in a sense, to vitiate the argument on Aldabra as a whole, because it must be seen in the context of my right hon. friend's whole defence policy and the timing of withdrawal from the Middle and Far East. We will be out of Sharjah and Bahrain before the last annual crop of frigate birds has returned.

I think that we also have time to deal with another argument of Marshal of the Royal Air Force Sir Dermot Boyle. Sir Dermot argued that, far from being a hindrance to science, the base will give access to Aldabra to scientists who have never had it before. I understand that he argues that, far from being bad from the scientists' point of view, the base is a good thing.

The answer is that during the construction period the ecosystem will be destroyed. The whole ecological system will be irretrievably harmed. For many of us it is not basically a question of preserving the rail, the tortoise or a breed of turtle. Much the most important aspect is the question of disturbing the total habitat.

Perhaps the real answer crisply put to Sir Dermot Boyle's arguments is to be found in paragraph three of the Royal Society's latest paper, which says: 'Future scientific study of Aldabra depends on its remaining undisturbed. The disturbance during construction will be so great that meaningful work in many areas will be no longer possible. By the time the RAF station is operational the ecology will have been damaged irreversibly. The RAF will certainly keep alive the tortoises as a species, and perhaps even the ibis and the rail, and it will doubtless try to live with the frigate birds; but preservation of the more obvious and larger animals is not what the Royal Society case is about. Large numbers of alien invertebrates and weeds will certainly arrive,

and the massive habitat disturbance of the construction phase will aid their
rapid spread: hence changes in the ecosystem cannot be prevented. The fact
that if the base is built then access will be easier for scientists is thus irrelevant
as an argument in its favour.'

This should be understood by the Defence Department when it makes up
its mind.

Here Dalyell posed some detailed questions about the cost of developing
Aldabra, arguing, based on issues like the configuration of the atoll and the
depth of the ocean there, that the expense would be far greater than the
£20 million estimated by the Ministry of Defence.

This subject should be debated by the whole House before a final decision is
reached. As I said at the beginning, it would be better if there were a Select
Committee of Defence to probe these detailed and difficult matters. I have had
the opportunity tonight which seldom comes to Members of Parliament –
without keeping any colleagues out of the debate, which we all hesitate to do –
to put forward in great detail some of the considerations surrounding Aldabra.

I would have hoped that there would be many opportunities for other hon.
members, in this very complicated, technical age in which we live, to be able to
make the kind of probing inquisitorial speech that I have made – not
slamming the Government before any decision has been made, but asking
some awkward questions to which there may be satisfactory answers but which
no one can say ought not to have been asked.

I thank the House for its patience.

Dalyell won his case. Healey concluded that a base on Aldabra made little
military sense, and any remaining prospect that it would be built vanished in
the spending cuts which followed the devaluation of the pound the following
month, and Britain's subsequent withdrawal from most 'East of Suez' defence
commitments.

Aldabra's four main islands, Grande Terre, Malabar, Polymnie and Picard,
are almost untouched to this day – but at the time of writing the environmental movement and Dalyell are mobilising to prevent a luxury hotel being
built there to cater for eco-tourists.

'The bleak impersonal word "disablement" is a synonym for personal and family tragedy.'

Jack Ashley's first Commons speech after going deaf: 16 July 1968

Ten-minute rule bills are the routine stuff of parliamentary business – a way of publicising an issue with a ten-minute Commons speech, but one which very seldom leads to actual legislation. What is remarkable about this speech by Jack Ashley was that he had just become almost totally deaf, and was far from certain that he could function as an MP at all.

With the hearing in his right ear failing, Ashley had undergone surgery to correct a perforation in his left eardrum. Complications set in, and the result was that he lost almost all traces of hearing. His memoirs[7] record the toil and embarrassment of learning to function without hearing and his conclusion that he would have to resign his seat. But when the news emerged, it became clear many people wanted Ashley to stay, including the Prime Minister, Harold Wilson; Iain Macleod, then shadow Chancellor and John Silkin, the Labour Chief Whip. Finally a special meeting of Ashley's local party in Stoke-on-Trent confirmed that his supporters wanted him to stay. Intensive lip-reading practice made it possible for Ashley to follow debates in the chamber at least partially, and the redoubtable matriarch of Liverpool politics, Bessie Braddock, allowed him to sit in her habitual place on the front bench below the gangway, which was the best vantage point for watching MPs as they spoke.

The final hurdle was to prove that he could deliver a speech. An opportunity was provided by Dr David Owen, who had been preparing a ten-minute rule bill on the need for a commission to investigate the problems of disabled people, when he was made Navy Minister. Knowing of Ashley's interest in the issue, Owen offered him the bill. Ashley prepared carefully – he practised in the chamber with the MP Eric Ogden and worked out a series of discreet signals to ensure he did not speak too softly or too loudly.

Normally, the chamber empties when ten-minute rule bills are moved, but on this occasion the Prime Minister and leader of the opposition, and most of the House, stayed. The speech was delivered without a hitch; Ogden's signals were unused.

The speech got off to a promising start when Ashley was welcomed back to the chamber by the Speaker, Horace King, to warm 'hear hears' from MPs.

FORTY-EIGHT HOURS AGO, in Trafalgar Square, I attended a rally of men and women whose lives are lived in pain and poverty. They represented the chronic sick and the disabled – over a million men and women who are prisoners in hospital beds, or in their own bedrooms or in wheel chairs. I regard that demonstration, marked by the silent symbols of dignity and courage, as eloquent testimony of the need of the Bill I seek to bring in.

I know that the House is rightly concerned with the grave national affairs which are its direct interest, but it is always willing to accept responsibility for the problems of minorities and of individuals. I think that I can best illustrate the problem of the disabled minority by reading a short extract from a letter which I received recently from a woman whose husband is disabled by multiple sclerosis. She wrote:

> He was a fine, hard-working athletic type, but he became redundant and we were forced back on to National Assistance. I could not begin to tell you how we live on this. Every day is a nightmare of penny pinching and scraping.

She goes on:

> We are condemned to live the life of poverty, and, considering the society in which we live, surely our hardships are enough to bear without abject poverty, too. Do you know, it has actually been suggested to him, that I must make some sacrifices – and this from a minor official. Ludicrous, is it not, when every moment of our lives is a sacrifice?

To me, that letter proves that the bleak impersonal word 'disablement' is a synonym for personal and family tragedy. It has also proved, at any rate to me, the urgent need to establish a commission which can investigate immediately the problems of the disabled, and also to look at the anomalies involved, because I can assure the House that some of the anomalies involved are quite incredible. For example, a husband who is totally disabled by multiple sclerosis gets only one-third as much as the man who is industrially injured but similarly disabled.

The size of the family can be the same, the responsibilities of the family can be the same, the disease and the pain to be endured can be the same, yet one family is entitled to receive up to just 2s. short of £24 a week, while the other family can only receive less than £8 a week. The main reason for this anomaly is that special allowances granted to one family are denied to another. I believe that this ranks as one of the most remarkable examples of discrimination of modern times, and the sad irony of that situation is that the very man who is discriminated against is, by definition, less able to fight on his own behalf.

That discrimination which is exercised against disabled men is even worse in the case of women. The disabled housewife is, believe it or not, entitled to not one penny, even though she may be totally paralysed. This is an astonishing state of affairs. The consequences for a totally disabled paralysed housewife are simple and quite direct. She can either pay for someone to come in and look after her and her husband and home, which, of course, cannot be afforded by people on a low income, or, alternatively, her husband can give up his job to look after her and the family and they live on supplementary benefit.

The only other choice left is for the family to be broken up. This entails the wife going into hospital and the children going into the care of the local authority at a minimum total cost of £50 a week. This is family tragedy, compounded by economic chaos.

As these anomalies are so indefensible and so odd, one is compelled to look around at the major countries of western Europe. Bad as we are in this respect perhaps we can find some consolation if we discover that there are even worse, but the astonishing fact is that most of the major countries of western Europe are paying disablement income to their disabled. So we have to lower our sights a little and look at the countries which have no great pretensions to be the major countries of western Europe.

In Stockholm recently, there has been a seminar on the social security statistics of Scandinavian countries. It was called *Social Security in Nordic Countries*. All these countries give generous disablement payments, not only to their industrially disabled but to their other disabled, including housewives. The countries included in that report are Norway, Sweden, Denmark, Finland and Iceland. Iceland is providing for its disabled men and women while the cripples of Great Britain have to be carried to rally in Trafalgar Square to demand not charity, but justice and to request not sympathy, but action.

I am aware of the economic difficulties confronting the Government. I have no wish to introduce a partisan note this afternoon, but I believe that, despite these economic difficulties, the Government have a very proud record of social legislation, but this is cold comfort for the disabled who are denied a disablement income.

I realise and accept that the Government are concerned with the plight of the disabled and have initiated an inquiry into the incidence of disability. This is a great step forward, but it will be at least eighteen months, possibly two years, before the results of such an inquiry can be made known. My concern is that at the end of those eighteen months or two years the Government will be faced with the task of embarking on an examination of the problems of paying a disablement benefit.

Any such payment involves highly complicated issues. For example, on what basis should a disablement income be paid? How is one to assess the degree of disablement? What is to be the definition of disablement? Should disablement payment be made for loss of earning power or loss of faculty? It may even be necessary to visit other countries, such as the pioneer Iceland. This could involve a delay of a number of years. I am asking the House to establish a commission – not a Royal Commission, but a commission – of able and energetic men who could do all the necessary preliminary work so that there is no delay in paying a disablement income.

In seeking the leave of the House to introduce my Bill, I point out that the sponsors disagree profoundly on many issues, but on this they are united. They are offering the Government a suggestion and an opportunity of contingency planning so that the thousands of disabled people who are depending on them and waiting on them will not be required to wait too long.

On the formal walk past the government front bench to present the bill to the Speaker, Ashley felt someone touch his arm. It was Harold Wilson. He lip-read the words 'Well done, Jack.' Decades of campaigning on disability issues were to follow.

'I, too, remember Tudor Watkins.'

Dennis Skinner and friends thwart Enoch Powell: 7 June 1985.

In 1985, Enoch Powell[8] rallied formidable Conservative support for his Unborn Children (Protection) Bill – a private member's bill to outlaw the new scientific technique of embryo experimentation. The bill would have made it illegal to create a human embryo by in vitro fertilisation for any purpose other than to allow a woman to have a child.

Powell told MPs he felt a 'sense of revulsion, deep and instinctive', towards the idea that a human embryo should be 'subject to experiment to its destruction for the purpose of the acquisition of knowledge'.[9]

The bill was opposed by medical specialists and ministers in the Department of Health, but Powell showed the strength of his position when he won a second reading by 238 votes to 66. Even so, private members' bills are notoriously vulnerable to procedural tricks, and Powell's opponents spun out debate on another bill so that the House ran out of time to consider Powell's. When he tried to force a vote, an ugly scene ensued as angry MPs surrounded the Deputy Speaker, even damaging the arm of his chair in the mêlée. It seemed Powell had been defeated.

But he turned the tables with a virtuoso parliamentary manoeuvre. The Conservative MP Andrew Bowden, whose own private member's bill was due to be debated on 7 June, agreed to relinquish his debating time to help the Powell bill through its remaining stages. He tabled a motion saying that the House should not adjourn at its normal time of 2.30 p.m., but should continue to sit until all the 20 amendments to the bill had been dealt with – through the weekend, if necessary. And when Mr Speaker Weatherill ruled that the motion, although unprecedented, was in order, it seemed Powell had trumped his adversaries.

Cometh the hour, cometh Dennis Skinner. The Labour MP for Bolsover was among the opponents of the bill, and he hit upon an equally cunning parliamentary device. He decided to move the writ for a by-election then pending in the Welsh seat of Brecon and Radnorshire. Again, this was unprecedented. Normally the writ for a parliamentary by-election is moved by the whips for the party which holds the seat, without debate. But a close study of the parliamentary bible *Erskine May* convinced Skinner that he could move the writ, and debate it, and that it would take precedence over other business. It was, he said, 'a flash of inspiration', going well beyond the ordinary Commons filibuster.

'The ploy was to get a debate on another issue,' Skinner said.[10] 'If his

[Bowden's] debate started, the game was up. The clerk's department told me it wasn't possible, senior people told me I couldn't do it and Jack Weatherill went spare when I went to get the piece of paper I needed to officially move the writ.' Skinner was so cagey that he didn't even tell the all-party group of MPs opposing Powell about his tactics until the night before the debate. The ploy worked, thanks partly to the Speaker's indulgence, and partly to the acquiescence of the two front benches, who wanted the Powell bill stopped, but baulked at opposing it openly. The debate was dragged out until it was impossible for Bowden's motion to be considered, although towards the end Mr Speaker Weatherill's patience was clearly beginning to fray.

'Whenever you see something on the news about stem cell research and all the new treatments it could mean, it is only possible because we stopped Powell that day,' Skinner said. 'I never spoke to Enoch very often, but to give him his due, he stood up from his usual seat on the top bench and said to me: "No one could have done it, only you." It was without doubt the most important thing I have ever done.'

Four years later history repeated itself. Skinner used the same trick again, on the writ for the Richmond by-election,[11] to disrupt a Bowden-like attempt by Ann Widdecombe to make more debating time for a bill to cut the time limit for abortions. Conservative MPs retaliated by debating the writ for another by-election, at Pontypridd, at length, and eating into the time available for opposition debates. In 1990 the Commons voted to change its standing orders to stop this particular manoeuvre.

The speech itself is not great parliamentary rhetoric. Given its humdrum subject matter, it was never likely to be. Skinner and his various allies had to be careful to stay in order and to speak about Brecon and Radnor and the issues which might emerge in the election, hence his half-serious reproofs to colleagues who might have lured him off the subject. There are moments when their glee is perceptible. The rather frosty exchange with Dale Campbell-Savours was one of the few moments when the real purpose of the debate was allowed to surface. Skinner spoke for about three quarters of an hour, before his allies continued. I have not reproduced the whole speech, just a few highlights. Skinner began with a formal Commons incantation.

I BEG TO MOVE, THAT MR Speaker do issue his Warrant to the Clerk of the Crown to make out a new Writ for the electing of a Member to serve in this present Parliament for the County Constituency of Brecon and Radnor in the room of Tom Ellis Hooson, Esq., deceased.

I mention Tom Hooson, and I think that it would be appropriate at this stage to remind hon. members of his untimely death and pay a tribute to the service that he gave to the House. I must admit that to me Brecon and Radnor does not immediately suggest Tom Hooson, because I had a great friend from that area, Caerwyn Roderick. I believe that the name of Caerwyn Roderick is synonymous with Brecon and Radnor, and that is how I managed to get to know a little bit about the place and about the magnificent service that he gave to our party, the Labour Party, and to my right hon. friend the member for Blaenau Gwent [Michael Foot], the then leader of the Labour Party, in his capacity as parliamentary private secretary.

Therefore, when I heard that there was the possibility of the writ for Brecon and Radnor being delayed, and I read the usual outpourings in the press – it must have been about a fortnight ago – I thought that it would be a good idea to get the thing hurried along. It so happened that at that time there was the suggestion that other matters would be moved this Friday. I am not sure whether I was thinking of moving the writ early, before the shock waves of the suggestion of the right hon. member for South Down [Enoch Powell] hit the House of Commons, or whether it came after that, but it was about that time. I must make that point, because I am trying to show that it is purely a coincidence that my application falls on the day when other matters might have been discussed.

Here Tam Dalyell, another eminent member of Labour's awkward squad, with a record of campaigning on scientific issues, intervened. 'Before my hon. friend leaves the question of Caerwyn Roderick, may I also mention Tudor Watkins? Only three days ago, I visited Lady Watkins in Brecon. He gave great service to the House between 1945 and 1970, and anyone who is interested in agriculture and hill farming should respect the memory of Tudor Watkins.'
Skinner drew breath and replied . . .

I, too, remember Tudor Watkins. He had left by the time I came to the House, but I used to see him at Labour Party conferences. I know that my hon. friend the member for Linlithgow [Tam Dalyell] went to see Tudor's widow the other day while on his tour of the Falklands, the *General Belgrano* and Miss Murrell.[12] He goes all over the country on a solo campaign which is gaining ground, and I am pleased to say that the *General Belgrano* and all those other matters will become an issue in the by-election.
A less convivial intervention came from another – normally awkward – Labour

backbencher, Dale Campbell-Savours, who recalled that Tom Hooson was a great advocate of life issues and suggested that Skinner's procedural manoeuvre did a great disservice to his memory. Skinner was undeterred.

My hon. friend has a bit of a cheek, because he is part of a small group in the House which proposed to change the business of the day in a way which many people – not me – thought was an abuse of the procedures. Now he is trying to chide me for doing something to which I plead not guilty. In any case, Mr Speaker, I think you would agree with me – I know you would – that we should talk about the issues that will be discussed during the by-election campaign and not become involved in genetic engineering and other matters. I should say in passing that it is a bit rich that there is all this complaint about genetic engineering, yet the right hon. member for Down South is acting as the master scientist and pottering about with that young embryo, the hon. member for Brighton Kemptown [Andrew Bowden].

About 40 minutes of amiable knockabout followed, culminating in an intervention by Liberal MP Alan Beith, who wondered if the government and opposition Chief Whips had conspired to prevent the by-election writ being moved – thus delaying an important contest.

When the current leader of the Liberal Party in the House today starts talking like that, I worry about his position *vis-à-vis* you, Mr Speaker, because I do not want any unnecessary trouble and what the hon. gentleman has just suggested borders nigh on heresy. He has suggested that plans have been made when we know that everything today has been spontaneous. I must admit that I had a little help from the Clerks in the Table Office. I shall not name them because they did a good job and I do not want to hamper their promotion.

I look forward to the continuation of this debate, Mr Speaker. Having spent a few moments making the argument, I bring you this little blue form and rest my case.

Powell's bill was defeated. The Liberal Richard Livsey, famed as a breeder of speckle-faced sheep, won the Brecon and Radnorshire by-election.

'His first reaction to attack is denial and refuge in semantic prestidigitation.'

Ann Widdecombe denounces her former boss: 19 May 1997

The sacking, in the dying days of the Major government, of the head of the Prison Service, Derek Lewis, rebounded on the man who ordered it, the then Home Secretary, Michael Howard, when he ran for his party's leadership less than a year later. Ann Widdecombe was Prisons Minister at the time. Her biography[13] records that she was warned when she took office that Howard and Lewis did not get on. She got on with him rather better, reportedly receiving gifts of flowers and chocolates. She had considerable respect for Lewis's achievements and saw his sacking as an unjust response to a flawed report into a series of prison breakouts. Lewis had refused to suspend the governor of Parkhurst Prison, despite intense pressure from Howard to do so. The subsequent controversy turned on whether Howard threatened to overrule Lewis, and even sack him – which Howard denied. At the time Widdecombe did not resign, but when Howard became a candidate for the leadership she set out to stop him. In the process she coined the phrase that has haunted Howard's career ever since: 'there is something of the night about him'. Those words were not uttered in this speech – they would have been out of tune with a consciously restrained and carefully factual denunciation.

IT IS NOW GENERALLY KNOWN that what I have to say will be less than encouraging to my right hon. and learned friend the member for Folkestone and Hythe [Michael Howard]. First, I pay very great and very genuine tribute to his work at the Home Office. He put the protection of the public at the top of the agenda, and he kept it there. His term of office saw a fall in crime and a vast improvement in Her Majesty's prisons. He introduced a raft of measures to make Britain a more orderly place, and had the courage to make much-needed reforms to our widely abused asylum system.

It is therefore with genuine sadness and considerable reluctance, which I have had to overcome, that I turn to the rest of my remarks. But for my utter conviction of their rightness and of the imperative that lies behind them, I should not be making these remarks at all.

Earlier, I alluded to the fact that there had been a great improvement in Her Majesty's prisons under the former Home Secretary. That improvement was the result of the efforts of two men: my right hon. and learned friend and the former head of the Prison Service, Mr Derek Lewis.

Mr Lewis was an outstanding director-general. He inherited an appalling and troubled service, which in fourteen years we had not got right. Escapes took place daily, assaults were rife, industrial relations were chaotic and financial management poor. Under his vigorous leadership, escapes fell by a staggering 77 per cent; overcrowding was reduced, despite a sharp rise in the number of prisoners; purposeful activity was increased by hundreds of thousands of hours, despite a reduction in costs per place; industrial relations were transformed; and the private finance initiative was so successfully run that it became a model for the rest of Whitehall.

There was still a great deal to be done – that is common ground – but it would have been unreasonable to expect everything to be achieved in the first eighteen months, which is when the escape from Whitemoor occurred [a breakout of IRA prisoners, which – embarrassingly – occurred while a TV documentary crew were in attendance, on 9 September 1994]. After all – although I hesitate to point it out – we still had things to achieve after eighteen years.

The Learmont report [the report by General Sir John Learmont on a breakout from Parkhurst Prison in January 1995] – which was used by the Home Secretary to dismiss Mr Lewis – took no account of that progress; nor did it attempt to measure it, because that was not the general's brief. But, when – two months after Derek Lewis had left – the general was briefed to measure progress on implementation, this time on the Woodcock[14] recommendations, he found:

> In the space of less than a year the Prison Service has made more headway than could reasonably have been expected.

In his *Spectator* article, the former Home Secretary says that any chief executive of a private company who had received such a damning report would have been expected to resign. I say that any chief executive who had secured a 70 per cent improvement in performance would in fact have received the highest rewards.

What did we actually achieve by the dismissal of Mr Lewis? We had to pay him £220,000 in compensation, in return for which the taxpayer received nothing at all. We had to pay his costs, in the sum of £41,000, in return for which the taxpayer received nothing at all. We had to pay our own costs, in the sum of some £16,000. A most unnecessary bill of more than a quarter of a million pounds was the cost to the general public of my right hon. and learned friend's decision.

And, for all that, did we eliminate disasters from the Prison Service? No. Only a few months later, approximately 541 prisoners were released before the end of their sentences. They did not even have to break out. The fact is that there were disasters in the service before Lewis – including high-profile escapes – disasters in the service during Lewis, and disasters in the service after Lewis; but, as the current Director-General – to whom I pay considerable tribute – has told the Home Affairs Select Committee, the real progress has been made since the granting of agency status and that was due largely to the man who ran the agency at the time.

A dismissal meeting on the 15th lasted 20 minutes; a meeting on the 16th lasted twelve minutes, with, again, the former Home Secretary refusing to hear Mr Lewis's defence. Although we had had the report on 27 September, a decision was not communicated to Mr Lewis until 15 October, and he was then given six hours in which to resign. That was subsequently extended, and, in the meantime – although he had been asked to resign and to give notice and was therefore presumably still head of the service – he was not admitted to meetings, and not copied into documents then being prepared for the statement. It is not surprising that Mr Lewis did not go quietly.

I might add that it was the minutes of those meetings that convinced me that minutes of meetings may be perfectly accurate without reflecting the tone and full content of the meetings. For example, there was a question of security audit which showed that the then Home Secretary believed that Mr Lewis had set up security audits only after Whitemoor. In fact, they had been set up before Whitemoor, which suggests that Mr Lewis did not need a disaster to see the importance of security. That exchange is not recorded.

To tell Mr Lewis that the governor of Parkhurst should be suspended is completely different from instructing Mr Lewis. My right hon. and learned friend has frequently said that he did not instruct Mr Lewis – and he did not: there is common ground on that. However, he told him that the governor of Parkhurst should be suspended. The threat of instruction was distinct and was the second allegation, and we need to make sure that the two are disentangled.

Widdecombe recalled that Jack Straw, the Home Secretary in Tony Blair's new government had been trounced by Howard in a debate on Lewis's departure.

The reason why the right hon. member for Blackburn, now the Secretary of State for the Home Department, came to such grief in the debate on 19 October 1995 was that there was insufficient precision in using terms, and my right hon. and learned friend is very precise in his terms. In the debate, my right hon. and learned friend was asked by the hon. member for Sunderland

South [Chris Mullin]: 'Mr Lewis says that he was given a deadline by the right hon. and learned gentleman by which to agree to the removal of Mr Marriott, after which he would be overruled. Is that true?'

My right hon. and learned friend replied categorically: 'There was no question of overruling the Director-General.'

Oh, yes, there was. As he rather belatedly admitted last week, and as documentary evidence within the department shows, after Mr Lewis had been asked to reconsider his decision, my right hon. and learned friend took advice on whether he could instruct Derek Lewis to suspend Mr Marriott – this bearing in mind that he had told the House that he had not personally told Mr Lewis that Marriott should be suspended.

But my right hon. and learned friend was now carrying matters to the extent of seeking to instruct Mr Lewis, and, after consultation with the Cabinet Office and legal advisers in the Department, he was advised that he could not instruct him. Therefore, it cannot be said that there was no question of overruling the Director-General. The question was asked, it was pursued, and it was answered in the negative.

Hon. members will note that there has been much interest in the press this week as to whether there was a direct threat from the former Home Secretary to the former director-general that my right hon. and learned friend would have to consider overruling him if, when he had reconsidered his decision, he did not come to a different view. We know that he was sent out to reconsider his decision. We know that, during that time, advice was taken on whether he could indeed be overruled. It is very strange that my right hon. and learned friend refused to answer that question fourteen times on *Newsnight* last week, and was so uncharacteristically tongue-tied that he could not explain, as he later claimed, that he was simply unsure about that element of such a traumatic disagreement, and needed to check the papers.

Although it was not debated in the House on 19 October, questions had been raised in that week as to whether the Home Secretary had threatened not only to overrule Mr Lewis, but to sack him. This was ten months before he was sacked. I can confirm that he did talk about sacking him that day, but not to Mr Lewis himself. Mr Lewis subsequently found out from a third party, but it shows the degree of ferocity that existed in that fateful meeting.

Therefore, the questions to my right hon. and learned friend are these. Why did he say that he had not personally told Mr Lewis that Mr Marriott should be suspended immediately, when he had? Why did he say that there was no question of overruling Mr Lewis, when the question had been pursued as far as consulting the Cabinet Office and legal advisers? Why did he say that he could not recall at that distance in time why Mr Lewis had been asked to leave the meeting, when he had received only the previous day an account of that meeting, which showed that Mr Lewis had been asked to reconsider his decision?

Why did my right hon. and learned friend say that he was giving the House a full account, when he well knows that important issues that were discussed in the House were in fact omitted from the minutes that he laid before it as a full account? Will he now, to clear any doubt at all that may exist in the minds of hon. members, ask the current Home Secretary to release the full transcript of the meeting, minus of course anything that might have involved security in our prisons?

I should say that, intriguingly, when I asked the Home Office whether I could have access to the document, it was denied, on the perfectly proper basis that I had not been involved in the meeting at the time. I then said, 'Ah, but the document does then exist,' and I was told, 'Yes, but it might need some adjustment.'

My right hon. and learned friend has a problem, in that his first reaction to attack is denial and refuge in semantic prestidigitation. Why did he not simply come to the House on 19 October and say, 'So what? Yes, I did tell the Director-General that Marriott should have been suspended. Yes, I did feel about it so strongly that I put huge pressure on him. Yes, I did tell him to reconsider his decision, and, yes, I did consider overruling him'? It was just too important not to consider it. Why on earth did he not say that, to what I have no doubt would have been high cheers from the then Government benches? He could not do so because he had dug a hole for himself over policy and operations, and he would never have had to dig such a hole had he been prepared to keep the Director-General in place.

My right hon. and learned friend has made much of how he is the one to take tough decisions. Tough decisions concern a great deal more than instant law and instant dismissals. The toughest decision of all that he would have had to take was to come to the House on 16 October, told it that a damning report had been received, but that half its recommendations had already been implemented or were actively being put in hand; that the progress of the Prison Service under the Director-General was of such outstanding quality that he was continuing, with my right hon. and learned friend's personal support; and that he, the Home Secretary, also had no intention of resigning, because there was no direct connection between himself and what had happened.

That would have been tough, because the then Opposition would have howled for a head, and, if they were not given Mr Lewis's, they might have howled for that of my right hon. and learned friend, but we had a majority, so there was no reason to suppose that they would get it. However, he had been through that terrible sort of confrontation in the House in January, immediately after the Parkhurst breakout, and he was not quite tough enough to face it again in October.

Courage and toughness are both more than instant law and instant dismissal. We demean our high office if we mistreat our public servants. As hon. members, we demean ourselves if we come to the House to indulge in a play of words and make statements which, although they may not be untrue – they never are in the House – may be unsustainable.

My decision to do what I have done today was extremely difficult to reach, and I have agonised over it for months. One of the worst moments was when I decided that I would do it. I knew how shocked, hurt and upset not only my right hon. and learned friend but many of my colleagues would be, but I formed the view that I could do no other. I reached my decision in the interests of giving very belated justice to Mr Lewis, of giving some comfort to his wife Louise – who supported him faithfully while he gave us seven days a week looking after the Prison Service – partly of clearing my own conscience, although that is my problem, because I should have resigned at the time and did not.

'Hear, hear' shouted MPs,

Yes, I agree. I reached that view also to draw to the attention of the House the overwhelming necessity for the Leader of the Opposition – whoever he will be – and the new Prime Minister to clean up Parliament's image in the eyes of the British people. It is not enough to preserve our own positions at all costs. When we occupy high positions, and certainly when we occupy such positions in justice departments, justice must be our first concern.

I am aware that I probably will not be forgiven for my decision by some Conservative members until the day I leave Parliament. If I had not done what I have done today, however, I would not have forgiven myself until I left Parliament and beyond.

This brutal, footnoted denunciation of an ex-Cabinet minister by one of his subordinates was unparalleled. It provided rich entertainment for Labour MPs, causing Widdecombe to rebuke them for smugness. But for the most part, it was heard in silence. It succeeded in its main purpose, holing Howard below the waterline. His leadership campaign flopped. She told her biographer that she found the speech a painful ordeal – but that she never regretted it.

'The Bill has revealed the structures under which civil liberties will be seriously curtailed.'

Douglas Hogg attacks the terrorism bill: 14 December 1999

There is something Edwardian about Douglas Hogg. John Major's former Agriculture Minister is the kind of lawyer politician now rather rare in the Commons. He brings a QC's lucidity to his speeches, and delivers them with a rather antique parliamentary courtesy, swivelling with remarkable flexibility at the waist to project his voice into all corners of the chamber. He would not have been out of place in the age of F. E. Smith or Rufus Isaacs, when eminent barristers trod a well-worn path to Cabinet office; in an era of professional politicians he seems an anachronism. But, as befits the son and grandson of Lord Chancellors, he is a formidable advocate for traditional liberties, and against the encroachments of 'crackdown' legislation. In December 1999, well before the events of 11 September 2001 provoked the war on terror, the then Home Secretary, Jack Straw, introduced a bill giving sweeping new powers to the police and other law enforcement agencies. Mr Hogg feared that acts of civil disobedience which would have been considered criminal would now be dealt with more sternly.

INEVITABLY, I SHALL FOCUS on the aspects of the Bill with which I disagree. There are a number of those, but I recognise the merit behind the Bill's general approach. I see great advantage in having one statute that consolidates or codifies – I do not use those terms in a technical sense – the law, so that one does not have to deal with various statutes.

It is good to introduce a Bill that brings together the relevant legislation. However, I am uneasy about the Bill's definition of 'terrorism' and 'terrorist'. The definitions of terrorism in clause 1, and of a terrorist in clause 38, lie at the heart of the Bill. The reason is that the various powers, offences, duties and obligations that the Bill sets out are directed to the pursuit of terrorism and to the identity of the terrorist. I shall return to those obligations and offences, but I begin with the definitions.

The definition of terrorism goes far beyond the traditional definition. Historically and in previous enactments, we have essentially directed our attention to campaigns against the state, which have been defined in various statutory language. As was appropriately said from the Government benches, the Bill includes attacks on the corporate estate, which is an extraordinary departure in our concept of terrorism.

The definition of terrorism that appears in clause 1 includes the use of the threat of serious violence against persons or property. In my remarks, I shall focus on serious violence against property. What do we mean by that? The Home Secretary was right: he cannot give an absolute definition. However, we can be sure that the courts will attach a meaning to 'serious violence'. I shall suggest some activities which, in all probability, do constitute serious violence.

If I supported animal liberation, which I do not, I would recognise that breaking open mink cages to release mink was an act of serious violence to property. If I wanted to interfere with the laboratories of research stations and decided to smash my way in and release the animals, that would be a serious act of violence to property. Those are not speculative acts – all of them have happened frequently. For example, the hunt saboteurs – a particularly disagreeable group of people – threaten serious violence to property. Incidentally, they threaten serious violence to individuals as well.

I strongly disapprove of all those characters, and I am glad to say that existing criminal law covers, in almost every respect, their activities. However, if I ask myself whether they should be treated as terrorists, I am bound to say, no way. Why not? Let us consider some of the consequences that attach to an activity that falls within the scope of terrorism; or, for that matter, let us consider what happens to activities that are connected with individuals who fall within the definition of a terrorist.

First, there is the power of proscription. The Home Secretary can tell Greenpeace or the Animal Liberation Front, for instance, 'Because you are associated with what are clearly acts of terrorism, I am entitled to proscribe you' – and he is so entitled, according to the Bill. What is the right of appeal? We are told, in short order, that there is such a right, but that is rubbish. What there is, is a commission. Is the commission to review the merits of proscription? Oh, no – under the Bill, the commission must decide whether, in accordance with the principles of judicial review, the exercise has been carried out properly. That is entirely different. That is one of my less important objections to the Bill, but it is certainly an objection.

Anyone who pursues an activity that comes within the scope of clause 1 can be proscribed by the Home Secretary, with no effective right of appeal. However, there are much more serious objections of a more practical character. Let us suppose that one of the organisations that could come within the scope of clause 1 wants to raise some money. Let us suppose that it asks for money, as it is bound to do: Greenpeace, the Animal Liberation Front and anti-abortion activists certainly do. Asking for money in connection with an activity that is capable of being terrorism is capable of constituting an offence, according to the Bill. Moreover, contributing money is an offence under clause 14. We should be very careful if we are feeling generous.

The Home Secretary says, 'This is all artificial, because the Director of Public Prosecutions would never agree to a prosecution'. That may be true, but what is the individual citizen to reckon in advance? Does he know Mr Calvert-Smith as well as I do? Of course he does not.

This generated some protest from the Labour benches.

Does the Home Secretary wish to intervene? I shall give way if he does. He clearly does not wish to, so I think that he is making my point.

The ordinary citizen will know only that his act is capable of constituting an offence; whether he is prosecuted will depend on the wisdom of the Director of Public Prosecutions. What will that individual do? He will feel that he cannot become involved in a democratic activity. Moreover, banks and accountants who happen to be handling the affairs of such organisations will probably be under a duty to make a disclosure, and will probably be deemed to have committed an offence if they do not do so. We are told that the Director of Public Prosecutions would never be so foolish as to authorise a prosecution, but can the banks and the accountants count on that? Will they not say, 'As a result of an abundance of caution, we will make a disclosure'?

The issue goes even further. Clauses 23, 24 and 25 contain powers of seizure and forfeiture; clause 39 contains a power to arrest without warrant; clause 35 contains a power to exclude people from a designated area, and clause 41 contains a power to search premises and property. Generally speaking, all those powers are triggered by a reasonable ground for the belief that the organisation involved is embarking on acts of terrorism. Uncomfortable as this may be for Ministers, we have already established that the act of terrorism has been broadly defined by clause 1, and is capable of including many acts that no one in his right mind would consider to be acts against the state. That is thoroughly undesirable.

I want to draw attention to another power, which I think would be even more distressing for some Labour members. It lies in clause 60, which states that an individual who had, for example, maintained an armed campaign against people whom we considered undesirable, and who then came to this country, would face prosecution. Let us be clear about this. Mr Barzani and Mr Talabani – whom the former Prime Minister, my right hon. friend the member for Huntingdon [John Major], the former Home Secretary, Lord Hurd and I met, and encouraged to wage war against Saddam Hussein in northern Iraq – were clearly doing things that came within the scope of clause 60. If they came to this country, they could be prosecuted. If they came to someone like me – a practising lawyer – and asked whether they could safely come to this country, I would have to tell them that, under this legislation, they could be prosecuted. I would add that whether they would be prosecuted would depend on the good sense of the Director of Public Prosecutions. That is a bizarre state of affairs, which is entirely wrong. As I have said, I do not approve of such activities, but I do not want to make them constitute terrorism.

That takes me to my second, related point, and here I draw on my experience of the Foreign Office. Clauses 1 and 57 include in the concept or definition of terrorism acts that are committed abroad. Let us take two recent examples. The Kosovo Liberation Army was engaged in a struggle against the Serbs in Kosovo. I do not want to discuss the merits of that, but what the KLA was doing certainly involved acts of violence against persons and property. Its acts constituted, or were capable of constituting, acts of terrorism within the terms of clause 1.

I used to meet the Kurds of northern Iraq on behalf of the Prime Minister and the Foreign Secretary. We positively encouraged them to try to throw Saddam Hussein out of the area. They were using force, and therefore fell within the scope of clauses 1 and 57. If they were to raise money in this country, as they did – indeed, the Government probably gave them money – that would constitute an offence under clause 14. Those are offences. The only consolation that we can offer those people is that they would not be prosecuted because of the provisions of clause 113, under which the DPP would not give his consent. I feel that this is a serious departure from the principles that we should be implementing in this country.

I personally think that the Bill has revealed the structures under which civil liberties will be seriously curtailed. By extending the definition of terrorism, we put at risk our long tradition of giving sanctuary to people who are fighting oppressive regimes abroad. We put at risk the democratic right of people to protest. I may not approve of that protest – I frequently do not agree with protests – but I do not want protesters to be classified as terrorists.

Left to myself, I would probably divide the House on giving the Bill a Second Reading. However, there is not sufficient support for that, so I shall not do so. However, the Bill should be committed to a Special Standing Committee because it requires very careful consideration. If the Liberal Democrats move their motion, I shall support it. I hope that other hon. members who are worried about civil liberties will do likewise.

'The culture of defensive secrecy that still pervades our policing system.'

John McDonnell reveals the findings of a secret inquiry into the botched investigation of the death of his constituent Ricky Reel: 20 October 1999

John McDonnell is a charter member of Labour's backbench 'usual suspects', a regular left-wing rebel. He is a veteran of Ken Livingstone's Greater London Council, which in the 1980s pressed for oversight of the Metropolitan Police to be taken from the Home Secretary and given to a local police authority. That reform was to happen a year after this speech, with the creation of a Greater London Authority, but the case of the unexplained death of his constituent Ricky Reel and the failings of the ensuing investigation reinforced his concern about the way the Met handled cases involving people from the ethnic minorities.

McDonnell had known the Reel family and their son Ricky – he recalls him as 'a nice lad'[15] – before the tragedy which befell them. When he heard about the handling of the case and in particular the dismissive way in which the family's fears for their missing son were treated, he became involved. Home Office ministers were buttonholed in the voting lobbies, questions were asked in the House and the Chief Commissioner of the Metropolitan Police was bombarded with letters, and eventually the Police Complaints Authority conducted an inquiry.

But to McDonnell's fury the report of the inquiry was kept confidential. He obtained a copy and used this adjournment debate to read the findings into the public domain.

I WISH TO RAISE ONCE more in the House the case of the death of my constituent Lakhvinder Reel, known affectionately to his family and friends as Ricky. I applied for this debate at the request of the Reel family, and everything that I say tonight reflects their views and is said with their permission.

Sadly, this week we commemorate the second anniversary of Ricky's death, yet two years on we still do not know how he came by his death on that tragic night of 15 October 1997. He went out that evening with his friends to Kingston and was racially attacked and, a week later, his body was found in the Thames. When someone goes missing in suspicious circumstances, it can often be difficult to discover exactly what happened to them. Mr and Mrs Reel and I accept that. However, I believe that our system failed, and continues to fail, the

Reel family in their search for the truth about how their beloved son met his death two years ago. The purpose of this debate is to learn some of the lessons of the mistakes of the past two years and to seek a way forward in assisting the Reel family in finding the truth and coming to some understanding of what happened to Ricky.

There are two issues that I wish to address. Given the concerns expressed by many hon. members about this case, I appreciate their wish to intervene. The first issue is the failure of our policing system to respond to the needs of a family experiencing possibly the most traumatic event that can be visited on any family – the loss of a family member. The second is the continuing failure of our legal system to assist the family adequately in their search for the truth of what happened to their son.

Let us examine the policing failures. No matter how unpalatable it is for us to accept, I fear that we must now acknowledge that our policing system has failed the Reel family. This is not an attempt to scapegoat, single out or blame individual police officers or to dismiss the support and hard work of many police officers in the investigation of Ricky's death. I pay tribute to them. However, there were admitted failures in the original investigation of Ricky's death and in the way in which the Metropolitan police service responded to the Reel family. As important, the culture of defensive secrecy that still pervades our policing system clearly undermined, and continues to undermine, the confidence of the Reel family in the capacity of the police to appreciate and respond to their needs.

Let me explain. Over the past decade, the Metropolitan police has changed the way it describes itself from 'Metropolitan police force' to 'Metropolitan police service'. The translation from force to service is intended to symbolise the acknowledgment that our police are not some body of force set above society but a service responsive, and responsible, to our community. Police officers are employed to serve members of the public, but the refusal of the Metropolitan police to operate openly and transparently during this investigation demonstrates that secrecy is still deeply embedded in the Met and that there is an institutional reluctance to accept that the Met is the servant of the public and should therefore be accountable to the public that it is serving.

This continuing culture of secrecy also undermines the potential for building confidence in the Metropolitan police following the Lawrence case and the Macpherson inquiry. The culture of secrecy is best exemplified in this case by the refusal of the Metropolitan police to publish the report of the inquiry of the Police Complaints Authority into its initial investigation of Ricky's death. The recommendations of the Macpherson report state clearly the need for openness and transparency. Recommendation 10 stated:

> investigating officers reports resulting from public complaints should not attract Public Interest Immunity as a class. They should be disclosed to complainants, subject only to the 'substantial harm' test for withholding disclosure.

The PCA report into the Metropolitan police's early investigation of Ricky Reel's death was instigated as a result of a series of formal complaints lodged by Mrs Reel on 21 November 1997. The PCA appointed officers from the Surrey police in December 1997 to investigate the complaints. That was unusual in that the complaint was being investigated by the Surrey police while the Metropolitan police investigation was continuing. The PCA investigators examined existing and fresh evidence and reinterviewed family, friends, witnesses and police officers involved in the investigation.

From July 1998, the Reel family have sought access to the completed PCA report and its publication. The Metropolitan police are the owners of this report, and it appears that it is their decision whether and to whom it should be released. I find it extraordinary that a matter of such public interest should be left to the decision of the very service that is being investigated.

The conclusions of the PCA inquiry are multiple. I draw upon some of them. In respect of communications with the Reel family during the initial police investigation, the need for clear, careful and considerate communication with the family was critical in investigations of that kind – as was learned from the Lawrence inquiry. In the investigation, we discovered that

> Mrs Reel and other members of the family were visited or contacted by telephone by a total of ten different officers, from three different areas –

in the space of two days –

> Each of them delivering slightly different messages.

The report concluded:

> This situation led to Mrs Reel being provided with conflicting information; being unaware of who was coordinating the investigation; believing that there was a conflict

between two police divisions, and –

> being unable to gain accurate knowledge of what action was or was not being
> taken.

The report states that the identification and interviewing of witnesses was vital
to the lines of inquiry. It acknowledges that Mrs Reel herself identified and
located some of the witnesses. The inquiry also revealed that, in some
instances, no records were checked by the Metropolitan police to confirm or
support witness accounts; cross-referencing of information did not take place;
and some witnesses were not found until the PCA investigating team found
them. Witness information was sometimes not passed on from junior to
senior officers. The PCA report states that there were 'no debriefings', which
would have been

> common in investigations of this nature; as a result, potentially important
> information was lost.

Diane Abbott, an ally from the London Labour left, intervened to suggest that
the case was especially sad in light of the Lawrence case, where the Met had
mishandled the investigation into the murder of a young black man. She had
seen the report and noted that the property records at Kingston Police Station
showed that a videotape from British Rail at Kingston had been seized by a
policeman but it was never viewed and was eventually destroyed. She was
shocked that the police should treat vital evidence so lightly. McDonnell
agreed.

I can give confirmation on that matter and add to my hon. friend's remarks.
The PCA inquiry reveals that all video evidence from shops was not seized
promptly enough to provide information. The PCA states that videotapes
from two restaurants

> may have provided information to the investigation had they been seized
> promptly,

but they were not. The British Rail tape was indeed seized, not viewed and
destroyed.

Regarding photographic evidence, the three friends of Ricky Reel were
never shown any photos of known racist offenders or offenders who had

previously been involved in racial incidents in the area, in an attempt to identify the youths involved in the racial attack on the group.

Another Labour MP, Peter Bradley, asked why the police had not followed their standard practice of showing photographs – rogues' galleries – of known offenders to possible witnesses in the Reel case. That, he said, 'appears to have been a flagrant dereliction of duty'. Again McDonnell agreed.

I believe that the PCA investigators considered that that was important. The PCA found:

> The Met did not initiate this type of inquiry at a timely point in their investigation.

The police did not at any time choose to show the photos of known local racist offenders to Ricky's companions on the night. I believe that that was a dereliction of duty and lessons must be learned for future investigations.

On forensic information, the PCA inquiry revealed that no clothing or personal items retrieved from Ricky's body were subject to forensic examination. Details of his clothing were not recorded and the PCA concluded:

> given the high priority accorded to the search for Ricky, the decision to call a special post mortem and circumstances before his disappearance, the way in which forensic evidence was dealt with is difficult to justify.

Another London Labour MP, John Cryer, found this extraordinary. McDonnell thought so too.

The key issue is that the investigation was into a missing person report, but that the link between the racial attack earlier in the evening and Ricky going missing was not made soon enough. Not only was insufficient forensic evidence taken, but, as the PCA states, it is hard to justify why independent expert judgment was not sought on some issues.

On the post mortem, the report makes it clear that no one was clear about who was in control of the post mortem examination and who should have been asking the right questions. On verification at the scene, the report reveals that no forensic analysis was conducted at the area where it was assumed Ricky entered the river; no fingerprint examination was made of the railing nearby and no foliage was taken; and there was no examination of the concrete block, although photographs were taken. The report concludes that forensic examination of the bank would have been helpful: it might or might not have substantiated the claim that the incident was an accident, but it would at least have challenged that theory.

The PCA report states that a key element in the investigation was identifying the means of escape used by the earlier attackers. The inquiry highlighted the role of the No. 281 bus, which the attackers may well have boarded. The Metropolitan police did not check the records of work or tickets on the No. 281. The report states that the No. 281 was

> the most likely line of inquiry to lead to identification of the youths or other witnesses.

The failure to follow up that line of inquiry was described as 'a significant omission'.

The PCA considered that there was no evidence that the Met progressed lines of inquiry into other potential witnesses from crime reports, arrests, fixed penalty notices on the night, accident reports, or racial incidents reported since 1997. In its general inquiries, the Met made no inquiries in respect of, for example, Ricky's mobile phone usage that evening. The PCA had to investigate the medical evidence relating to Ricky itself. On the involvement of the community in Kingston, the report states the PCA's belief that active and earlier involvement of the racial equality council would have been helpful to provide lines of inquiry in the area.

Overall, the report condemns the investigation because it lacked focus, it eliminated the racial incident earlier in the evening too readily, it lacked thoroughness, and there was a failure to initiate an early reconstruction of what happened that night. There was also confusion over the ownership of the investigation of the racial incident. The investigators came to the conclusion of accidental death before there was corroboration, and there was a failure to adopt policies that would have ensured that professional standards were maintained in the detail of the investigation.

One action that stemmed from the early demands of the family was the introduction of a fresh investigation team, and I commend the Metropolitan police for bringing in that new team. However, in addition, the inquiry set out in some detail a series of recommendations for the reform of policing practices, and the problem now is that those recommendations, commendable though they seem, are part of the PCA report, which the Met keeps secret. That completely misses the point of the Macpherson report into the Lawrence case.

Public confidence can be restored and maintained in any public service only if mistakes, when they occur, are honestly admitted, and any remedial action is openly and honestly displayed. In this instance, the failure to publish the PCA report means that we cannot allow for an honest admission of mistakes. More important, it provides no opportunity for the Met to display what lessons it has learned and what improvements have been made. It thus misses completely an opportunity to regain the confidence of the community in our police service.

Such has been the anguish of Mr and Mrs Reel over those events that I appreciate why they feel that only a public inquiry can bring into the open what happened to their son, what went wrong with the investigation and how such problems can be avoided in future. I ask the Home Secretary to consider that request.

The inquest will start in November, and the Reel family are asking for financial support to secure their legal representation. I urge the Government to provide that assistance and to do all in their power to provide the family with the resources to determine the truth about what happened to their son.

I believe that we can all learn lessons from the case – lessons about respect, openness and accountability, and about the relationship of public service to the community that it serves. By highlighting the case again – this is, I believe, the eighth time that I have raised it in the House – we may not only help to discover what happened to Ricky that terrible night, but learn the lessons that will help to prevent further tragedies such as Ricky's death. I certainly hope so.

At the time of writing, the events leading up to Ricky's death are still unknown. An annual event to remember him is held at Kingston Town Hall.

Four

WAR

T HIS CHAPTER FOCUSES on parliamentary events during three conflicts: the Suez invasion of 1956, which prompted a bruising round of almost daily debates and statements, and ultimately destroyed Anthony Eden; the Falklands War of 1982, which could have ended the premiership of Margaret Thatcher, but instead was its making; and the Iraq war of 2003, in which Tony Blair had to face a huge rebellion on the Labour backbenches and persistent questions about his own candour and integrity. It also includes a stark reminder of an earlier conflict – Llin Golding's chilling account of the horrors of the Buchenwald Concentration Camp.

Wars always pose a challenge to broadcasters – objectivity can be misinterpreted as a lack of patriotism or even as outright treason (a charge made by the *Sun* during the Falklands War). The BBC faced criticism over its coverage on a variety of grounds during the Falklands and Iraq wars, but, because of the bitter parliamentary dissent, Suez was a particular test for *TIP* – with the hardline Conservative Suez Group demanding that the BBC should not report the conflicts of opinion in the House, for fear of undermining the nation's morale. This was rejected, but a BBC governor and former Conservative MP, Mrs Thelma Cazalet-Keir, was installed in Westminster to scrutinise the journalists' output; she ruled that their reporting was fair, balanced and impartial. The political climate certainly justified such extraordinary editorial supervision: Eden's fury at the BBC, which had reported statements by Nasser, and hostile foreign comment, as well as the government line, brought him to the point, in October 1956, of ordering his Lord Chancellor, Lord Kilmuir, 'to prepare an instrument which would take over the BBC altogether and subject it wholly to the will of the Government'. Kilmuir's draft was rejected as inadequate and the unfolding crisis prevented further action.

The 11 September 2001 terrorist attacks and the build-up to the Afghan and Iraq invasions produced a sharp and sustained increase in audience figures for news programmes in general, but particularly for *TIP* and the direct TV coverage of parliamentary debates, statements and question times on BBC Parliament. Perhaps the audience, bemused by the conflicting arguments, wanted more direct access to the debates in the Commons chamber. This peaked in the fourth quarter of 2001, when the number of people tuning into *TIP* every week rose to 2.9 million. There was some fall-off, but there were still 2.6 to 2.7 million people listening in the first half of 2003, as the Commons debated the invasion of Iraq.

'We may have a position tomorrow in which British tanks are shooting down women and children in the streets of Port Said.'

Denis Healey accuses Britain and France of taking international law into their own hands: 30 October 1956

Wars are normally bipartisan affairs in British politics – at least while the shooting continues. The 1956 Suez crisis, in which Britain and France invaded Egypt after President Nasser nationalised the Suez Canal, was a glaring exception to that rule. Almost uniquely, British troops engaged in a shooting war which was denounced by the opposition in Parliament. Nothing comparable happened in any other twentieth-century conflict – certainly not during the Falklands or Gulf wars. The contrast with events nearly half a century later, when Tony Blair led Britain into the invasion of Iraq, is stark and richly ironic.

The Prime Minister, Anthony Eden, had succeeded Churchill in 1955, after a long and distinguished spell in the Foreign Office. A golden age was anticipated with a seasoned and internationally admired leader presiding over the final recovery from the privations of war.

But Eden was a sick man, in considerable pain following a botched operation on his bile duct, and under constant medication. Many believe the pain and the drugs warped his judgement, and the events of Suez left his considerable reputation in tatters. Twenty years before, Eden had opposed appeasement of Hitler and Mussolini. Now he saw Nasser as another fascist dictator who had to be faced down. It was a view shared by the new Labour leader, Hugh Gaitskell, who made that exact comparison in the Commons. So at the outset, at least, there was a measure of cross-party consensus that the appropriation of the canal was a blow to British interests in the Middle East which had to be reversed.

The canal was nationalised in July 1956. When Parliament was recalled in September, attempts at a diplomatic solution had come to nothing. Eden was attempting to mobilise a Suez Canal Users' Association, while Labour wanted to rely on the UN to resolve the crisis. Gaitskell proclaimed that the use of force was not justified, and that Labour would not support military action unless it was sanctioned by the UN.

In October Eden signed a secret agreement, the Sèvres Protocol, under which Israel would launch an attack on Egypt, and British and French troops would then seize the Suez Canal on the pretext of protecting a vital international waterway. Along the way, he misled both his Cabinet and the

Commons about his collusion with Israel, insisting the action was purely to protect a vital international waterway, and ensure continued free passage for shipping.

On 29 October, Israeli troops swept across the Sinai peninsula and two days later, the Anglo-French force began bombing Egyptian targets, while paratroops seized Port Said at the head of the canal. World opinion was outraged. The Soviets (who themselves had just dispatched tanks to crush the democratic stirrings in Hungary) engaged in nuclear sabre-rattling. The Commonwealth was divided and even those nations which supported Britain had little enthusiasm. And, crucially, the American government was furious and began to put pressure on the fragile British economy by threatening a run on the pound.

The tumultuous series of Commons debates held as these events unfolded were amongst the angriest ever seen. 'The Opposition could truly be described as seething with wrath that at moments rose to a turbulence that, as the Speaker said, could if it had not been brought under control, have made the debate impossible,' wrote the *Manchester Guardian* sketch-writer, Harry Boardman.[1] What amounted to a rolling censure debate continued for some days, encompassing a Saturday sitting, and several periods of wild disorder. One such was touched off by the Labour MP Sydney Silverman, who enquired, simply, whether Britain was at war with Egypt. Another came when Eden, prematurely as it turned out, announced he had received a 'flash signal' that the Egyptian commander at Port Said was discussing surrender terms, provoking a brief explosion of Tory delirium.

One of the first MPs to denounce the Suez adventure was the young Denis Healey. In the whole of his political life, he wrote in his memoirs,[2] he had never been so angry for so long. He thought it an act of total folly, compounded by deliberate attempts to mislead the House. Anger gave his Commons interventions a force they had previously lacked. This speech was made in the short Commons debate which Gaitskell secured after being given fifteen minutes' notice of an Anglo-French ultimatum demanding a ceasefire between Egypt and Israel; the two countries that warned they would seize the canal zone if the fighting continued. Healey homed in on the crucial weakness in Eden's plans – a complete lack of international support – and made the deadly comparison with Soviet actions in Hungary. Above all, he voiced suspicions that the government was not telling the truth.

THERE ARE MANY MEMBERS, of whom I am one, who as a result of what the Prime Minister has so far said, have a feeling that this Government and the French Government are taking the law into their own hands.

I should, therefore, like to ask the Prime Minister if he will now answer certain questions. The British and French Governments are by no means the only Governments which have obligations in this area, nor are they the only Governments whose nationals and interests may be threatened if the fighting continues. The Prime Minister has said that he believes he is acting in the spirit of the Tripartite Agreement. But the United States of America is also a signatory to that Agreement. The first question I want to ask the Prime Minister is this: were the United States Government consulted when the British and French Governments took the decision which the Prime Minister has announced, and did they approve of that decision?

Secondly, some of our allies in the Middle East are vitally concerned with any action which may be taken and, while I do not in any way wish to inflame passions at this moment, I would point out that feeling among our Arab allies is extremely hostile to the French Government, particularly as a result of events during the last seven days. I should therefore like to ask the Prime Minister whether he has consulted our allies in Jordan and Iraq upon the steps which he proposes to take, and whether they approve?

Thirdly, the Commonwealth is vitally concerned, no less than we are, in the safety and security of the Canal, and I hope that this Government take seriously the view of their friends who are also members of the Common-wealth. I would therefore ask the Prime Minister whether the Commonwealth Governments have been consulted about this decision and whether they have approved of it.

One final question. The British people are also vitally concerned to prevent any step being taken which may lead to general hostilities between this country and the whole of the Arab world, with a majority of the United Nations opposed to us. I cannot feel that the Prime Minister has done his duty if he has taken this step without prior consultation with the Opposition. As a backbench member of the Opposition, I should like to know what steps the Prime Minister has taken to obtain the support of at least half the country before taking so grave a step.

The step which he has threatened to take is a military ultimatum by two Governments against two others. If the Prime Minister is correct in suggesting that unfavourable replies may be received and, therefore, that action may be taken even during the night, we may have a position tomorrow in which British tanks are shooting down women and children in the streets of Port Said. If this is not the case, how do the Government propose to implement their threat to occupy the Canal? This, after all, is the subject we are all discussing – the question of peace and war – and I think it would be both a crime and a tragedy if at the moment when freedom and national independence are being suppressed by Russian tanks in Hungary, this Government did anything without international support which led to a similar impression being given to world opinion.

Healey became a major participant in the furious debates that continued throughout the Suez crisis, delivering some memorable invective along the way. He enquired if Eden had exchanged congratulations with the Soviet Secretary-General Khrushchev, who had just sent troops into Hungary to crush its tentative democratic reforms; when the extent of the Suez debacle was clear, he proposed that Eden should receive the Nobel Peace Prize, for conclusively proving that international aggression did not work; and he tested the outermost limits of parliamentary protocol by asking the Speaker, on a point of order, 'What is the parliamentary expression that comes closest to expressing the meaning of the word liar?'

'What they have done now, by refusing to accept the United Nations Resolution, is virtually to destroy that institution, which the Prime Minister once described as the hope of mankind.'

Hugh Gaitskell begs Conservative MPs to unseat their Prime Minister: 3 November 1956

As opposition leader, Gaitskell had to be more measured than Healey, but he went far enough for the Conservatives to condemn him as a reckless opportunist. On 2 November, the opposition moved a motion of no confidence against the government. The next day he made this speech, replying to a statement from Eden rejecting a UN resolution calling for an end to hostilities. Eden told the House that the Anglo-French 'police action' was needed to protect the canal and separate the Egyptian and Israeli combatants. He set out the conditions under which he would welcome a UN force to guard the canal, once the situation had been stabilised.

Gaitskell's response was to accuse Eden of shattering the fragile authority of the UN and to issue a rallying call to Conservative doubters to overthrow their leader.

T**HE FIRST PARAGRAPH** of the Resolution carried by 64 votes to 5 in the General Assembly of the United Nations calls upon all parties now involved in hostilities to agree to an immediate cease-fire and to halt the movement of military forces and arms into the area.

It is unfortunately perfectly clear, both from the reports of the continuing and, indeed, intensification of bombing by British planes and from the Prime Minister's statement this morning, that the British Government are not carrying out the recommendation of the Assembly. We are, therefore, faced with the position that our Government are defying a Resolution of the United Nations Assembly, carried by a majority which is larger, I believe, than that on any other Resolution previously carried by the Assembly. We can only say that, for our part, we regard this as utterly deplorable.

As regards the conditions laid down by the Government, it is no part of the business of Her Majesty's Government to lay down conditions in this matter. It is their duty, as loyal members of the United Nations – if they were loyal members – to accept that majority decision.

'And sell Britain?' shouted Conservative MPs.

I must ask the Prime Minister a number of questions on his statement. First of all, is he aware that the Egyptian Government have already announced that they are prepared to agree to an immediate ceasefire if all the other parties do so as well? Therefore, one of the combatants at any rate has already agreed to this.

Secondly, is the Prime Minister aware, as he should be, because the Minister of Transport and Civil Aviation has announced it, that the Suez Canal is now blocked and that the consequence of the intervention by Her Majesty's Government, far from facilitating the passage of ships through the Canal, has had precisely the opposite effect?

Is the Prime Minister further aware that the Israeli Government have announced that the fighting in the Sinai Desert area is virtually at an end, and that, therefore, the original situation, from that point of view, has substantially changed?

The Canal is blocked, there has been no rescue operation for British ships, no British lives have been saved, and all that has happened is that the intervention of Her Majesty's Government on behalf or, rather, against Egypt has no doubt prematurely brought the operations in the Sinai Desert to a close.

'Warmonger,' Labour MPs yelled at Eden – bringing answering shouts from the government benches, which punctuated the rest of Gaitskell's speech.

In those circumstances, what is the objection . . .

What Her Majesty's Government have undoubtedly done, of course, is to intervene against Egypt, which was clearly attacked by Israel. I do not know whether they regard that as a matter of which they should be proud. I do not know whether they regard that as separating the combatants. I do not know whether they regard that as settling hostilities. What they have done is to bomb a number of civilians as well as military installations in Egypt. What they have done is to destroy all faith in collective security. What they have done now, by refusing to accept the United Nations Resolution, is virtually to destroy that institution, which the Prime Minister once described as the hope of mankind.

I must also ask the Prime Minister this. He speaks of the United Nations force, which has been proposed by Mr Lester Pearson [Canadian External Affairs Minister], being brought in.

Conservative shouts continued to disrupt Gaitskell's argument.

Never mind; it was proposed in the Assembly of the United Nations . . .

We need not really go into this. We proposed this long, long ago. The Prime Minister speaks of the United Nations deciding to constitute and maintain such a force until an Arab-Israel peace settlement is reached and until satisfactory arrangements have been agreed in regard to the Suez Canal.

So far as an Arab-Israel peace settlement is reached, there is a case – in our opinion, a strong case – for a United Nations force to police the Armistice Agreement frontiers of the Arab States and Israel. Is it the view of Her Majesty's Government that this United Nations police force should do that, and if they do that, what reason is there for such a police force to operate in the Canal Zone at all?

Secondly, I would ask why the Prime Minister has brought in the phrase about satisfactory arrangements being agreed in regard to the Suez Canal. Does he mean by that that Egypt is to be bound to accept, by force, the eighteen-power proposals, or what does he mean by it, and why indeed should the settlement of the Suez Canal issue be brought into the matter at all?

Finally, by what right is the Prime Minister now proposing that, until the United Nations force is constituted, both combatants have still to accept the original ultimatum?

All this is unquestionably in defiance of the Resolution of the General Assembly. One cannot get away from that. For our part, we regard the Government's reply today as the most tragic statement that has been made in this House since 1939.

I know that passions run very high on both sides of the House in this matter, but I do beg hon. members opposite to realise how terribly anxious we are about the implications of this action. It may be possible, and no doubt is possible and comparatively easy, for British and French forces to subdue Egypt – nobody ever doubted that – but do hon. members not reflect in their hearts that the implications of this defiance of the Resolution of the Assembly mean that in future that Assembly can never hope to cope with any international crisis again?

Do not hon. members appreciate that at this time above all, when the news of Russian aggression in Hungary is coming through, it is an immense tragedy that the moral strength of this country and of the United Nations, because of our action, is so gravely damaged? We have had a great opportunity – and even now it would have been open to the Government – despite all that has happened, to accept the Resolution of the General Assembly, to say that in the light of this and because we believe in international order and because we believe in the Charter of the United Nations, despite everything that has been said and done in the last few days, we are prepared to accept it.

The Government could, if they had done that, to some extent at least have restored our reputation and moral authority. They could, if they had done that, at once have made it a thousand times easier to deal with the Hungarian situation.

'How?' shouted furious Conservatives.

I beg hon. members – I repeat that I know how high passions rise – to listen to my words on this. We represent very many millions of British people. We represent on this issue the point of view of millions of men and women, not all Labour Party supporters, many of them of no political persuasion, and, I venture to say, many of them persons who have hitherto voted Conservative.

If only the Government had been prepared to accept the Resolution, much of the damage could have been repaired. Unfortunately, they have refused. They have not only refused but are continuing the war against Egypt, continuing the bombing and the destruction and the casualties. All that has been put forward today is a niggling, haggling kind of proposal, which is . . .

Again there was a roar of derision from the Conservative benches.

Up to this moment, I for my part had hoped for a change in Government policy. I had hoped originally that the Government would have accepted our first proposal to defer action. They refused. I hoped then that the pressure of world opinion upon them would have made them change their mind, and I hoped finally that the passing of this Resolution by such a vast majority in the United Nations Assembly would have brought them to their senses.

Alas, that is not so, and we can draw only one conclusion. That is that if this country is to be rescued from the predicament into which the Government have brought it, there is only one way out, and that is a change in the leadership of the Government. Only that now can save our reputation and re-open the possibility of maintaining the United Nations as a force for peace. We must have a new Government and a new Prime Minister. The immediate responsibility for this matter rests upon the only people who can affect the situation – hon. members opposite. I beg them to consider in their hearts to where we are being led at the moment. I beg them to consider the appalling international consequences of this grave error, and I ask them, having done so, to do their duty.

On 6 November, in response to intense American pressure, Eden announced a ceasefire. He had insisted on taking all the Suez debates himself, and the strain had taken its toll. His health collapsed, and on 23 November he retreated to Jamaica for a complete rest. On 3 December, his Foreign Secretary, the future Speaker Selwyn Lloyd, announced the withdrawal of British troops. Three days later, the government survived another confidence debate in the House, this time an epic two-day affair which culminated in a vitriolic exchange between Gaitskell and R. A. Butler, who, deputising for Eden, evaded the Labour leader's questions about the level of collusion with Israel with a disdainful swipe at his refusal to support the Government.

Eden returned to Britain a week later, and reappeared in the Commons on 17 December, where he did his best to seem his normal nonchalant self. But his healthy tan did not conceal his nervous fidgeting. Even the cheers of his supporters had a valedictory quality, and a month later, on 9 January, he resigned, to be succeeded by Harold Macmillan.

'I must tell the House that the Falkland Islands and their dependencies remain British territory.'

Margaret Thatcher pledges to regain the Falkland Islands: 3 April 1982

Margaret Thatcher believed this was the most difficult debate she had ever had to face as Prime Minister. On Friday, 2 April 1982, Argentine forces seized Britain's South Atlantic dependency, the Falkland Islands. Argentina, which had long claimed the islands as its own, had continued to negotiate over their status almost until the invasion.

The humiliation of seeing British territory seized, a British governor expelled and British troops held prisoner by invaders could well have ended Thatcher's premiership. An inadequate response would have triggered an eruption of fury from the Conservative backbenches. Thus she had two purposes when she spoke to a specially recalled House of Commons on the Saturday after the invasion: to demonstrate that the invasion could not have been predicted or prevented; and to announce the dispatch of a task force to retake the islands if efforts through UN and American mediation did not lead to an Argentine withdrawal.

With the fate of the government and the Prime Minister in the balance, the atmosphere was electric. 'Mrs T open[ed] for the Government sounding both defiant and embarrassed, as well she might,' wrote the Labour diarist Giles Radice.[3]

THE HOUSE MEETS THIS Saturday to respond to a situation of great gravity. We are here because, for the first time for many years, British sovereign territory has been invaded by a foreign power. After several days of rising tension in our relations with Argentina, that country's armed forces attacked the Falkland Islands yesterday and established military control of the islands.

Yesterday was a day of rumour and counter-rumour. Throughout the day we had no communication from the Government of the Falklands.[4] Indeed, the last message that we received was at 21.55 hours on Thursday night, 1 April. Yesterday morning at 8.33 a.m. we sent a telegram which was acknowledged.

At this point, according to Alan Clark,[5] the words 'we sent a telegram' set the whole opposition laughing and sneering. Thatcher, who had been speaking 'slowly but didactically', then 'changed gear and gabbled'.

At 8.45 a.m. all communications ceased. I shall refer to that again in a moment. By late afternoon yesterday it became clear that an Argentine invasion had taken place and that the lawful British Government of the islands had been usurped.

I am sure that the whole House will join me in condemning totally this unprovoked aggression by the Government of Argentina against British territory.

This brought a solemn 'Hear, hear.'

It has not a shred of justification and not a scrap of legality.

It was not until 8.30 this morning, our time, when I was able to speak to the governor, who had arrived in Uruguay, that I learnt precisely what had happened. He told me that the Argentines had landed at approximately 6 a.m. Falklands' time, 10 a.m. our time. One party attacked the capital from the landward side and another from the seaward side. The governor then sent a signal to us which we did not receive.

Communications had ceased at 8.45 a.m. our time. It is common for atmospheric conditions to make communications with Port Stanley [the capital] difficult. Indeed, we had been out of contact for a period the previous night.

The governor reported that the Marines, in the defence of Government House, were superb. He said that they acted in the best traditions of the Royal Marines. They inflicted casualties, but those defending Government House suffered none. He had kept the local people informed of what was happening through a small local transmitter which he had in Government House. He is relieved that the islanders heeded his advice to stay indoors. Fortunately, as far as he is aware, there were no civilian casualties. When he left the Falklands, he said that the people were in tears. They do not want to be Argentine. He said that the islanders are still tremendously loyal. I must say that I have every confidence in the governor and the action that he took.

I must tell the House that the Falkland Islands and their dependencies remain British territory. No aggression and no invasion can alter that simple fact. It is the Government's objective to see that the islands are freed from occupation and are returned to British administration at the earliest possible moment.

Argentina has, of course, long disputed British sovereignty over the islands. We have absolutely no doubt about our sovereignty, which has been continuous since 1833. Nor have we any doubt about the unequivocal wishes of the Falkland Islanders, who are British in stock and tradition, and they wish to remain British in allegiance. We cannot allow the democratic rights of the islanders to be denied by the territorial ambitions of Argentina.

There was a good deal of bellicose comment in the Argentine press in late February and early March, about which my hon. friend the Minister of State for Foreign and Commonwealth Affairs [Richard Luce, who was to resign over the invasion] expressed his concern in the House on 3 March following the Anglo-Argentine talks in New York. However, this has not been an uncommon situation in Argentina over the years. It would have been absurd to dispatch the fleet every time there was bellicose talk in Buenos Aires. There was no good reason on 3 March to think that an invasion was being planned, especially against the background of the constructive talks on which my hon. friend had just been engaged. The joint communiqué on behalf of the Argentine deputy Minister of Foreign Affairs and my hon. friend read:

> The meeting took place in a cordial and positive spirit. The two sides reaffirmed their resolve to find a solution to the sovereignty dispute and considered in detail an Argentine proposal for procedures to make better progress in this sense.

There had, of course, been previous incidents affecting sovereignty before the one in South Georgia, to which I shall refer in a moment. In December 1976 the Argentines illegally set up a scientific station on one of the dependencies within the Falklands group – Southern Thule. The Labour Government attempted to solve the matter through diplomatic exchanges, but without success. The Argentines remained there and are still there.

Two weeks ago – on 19 March – the latest in this series of incidents affecting sovereignty occurred; and the deterioration in relations between the British and Argentine Governments which culminated in yesterday's Argentine invasion began. The incident appeared at the start to be relatively minor. But we now know it was the beginning of much more.

Here Thatcher traced the series of Argentine incursions into British territories in the South Atlantic, including the landing of 60 Argentines, who claimed to be scrap metal dealers with a contract to demolish an abandoned whaling station, on South Georgia, a Falklands dependency. They were ordered to leave, but ten remained.

But it soon became clear that the Argentine Government had little interest in trying to solve the problem. On 25 March another Argentine navy ship arrived at Leith to deliver supplies to the ten men ashore. Our ambassador in Buenos Aires sought an early response from the Argentine Government to our previous requests that they should arrange for the men's departure. This request was refused. Last Sunday, on Sunday 28 March, the Argentine Foreign Minister sent a message to my right hon. and noble friend the Foreign Secretary [Lord Carrington, who later resigned] refusing outright to regularise the men's position. Instead it restated Argentina's claim to sovereignty over the Falkland Islands and their dependencies.

My right hon. and noble friend the Foreign and Commonwealth Secretary then sent a message to the United States Secretary of State asking him to intervene and to urge restraint.

By the beginning of this week it was clear that our efforts to solve the South Georgia dispute through the usual diplomatic channels were getting nowhere. Therefore, on Wednesday 31 March my right hon. and noble friend the Foreign Secretary proposed to the Argentine Foreign Minister that we should dispatch a special emissary to Buenos Aires.

Later that day we received information which led us to believe that a large number of Argentine ships, including an aircraft carrier, destroyers, landing craft, troop carriers and submarines, were heading for Port Stanley. I contacted President Reagan that evening and asked him to intervene with the Argentine President directly. We promised, in the meantime, to take no action to escalate the dispute for fear of precipitating the very event that our efforts were directed to avoid. May I remind Opposition members what happened when, during the lifetime of their Government . . .

That last point produced shouts of anger from the Labour benches – which rose pre-emptively as Mrs Thatcher moved on to the previous Labour government's handling of an earlier episode of sabre-rattling in Buenos Aires. 'We did not lose the Falklands,' interrupted the left-winger Jeff Rooker.

Southern Thule was occupied. It was occupied in 1976. The House was not even informed by the then Government until 1978, when, in response to questioning by my hon. friend the Member for Shoreham, now Minister of State, Foreign and Commonwealth Office, the hon. member for Merthyr Tydfil [Ted Rowlands, the junior Labour Foreign Office minister under Anthony Crosland] said: 'We have sought to resolve the issue through diplomatic exchanges between the two Governments. That is infinitely preferable to public denunciations and public statements when we are trying to achieve a practical result to the problem that has arisen.'

That brought Rowlands to his feet to point out that Southern Thule was 'a piece of rock in the most southerly part of the dependencies, which is completely uninhabited and which smells of large accumulations of penguin and other bird droppings'. There was a vast difference between that and the Falklands, where 1,800 were now under Argentine occupation. Mrs Thatcher, he said, should have the grace to make that distinction. She stuck to her guns.

We are talking about the sovereignty of British territory which was infringed in 1976. The House was not even informed of it until 1978. We are talking about a further incident in South Georgia which – as I have indicated – seemed to be a minor incident at the time. There is only a British Antarctic scientific survey there and there was a commercial contract to remove a whaling station. I suggest to the hon. gentleman that had I come to the House at that time and said that we had a problem on South Georgia with ten people who had landed with a contract to remove a whaling station, and had I gone on to say that we should send HMS *Invincible*, I should have been accused of war mongering and sabre rattling.

Information about the Argentine fleet did not arrive until Wednesday. Argentina is, of course, very close to the Falklands – a point that the hon. member for Merthyr Tydfil cannot and must not ignore – and its navy can sail there very quickly. On Thursday, the Argentine Foreign Minister rejected the idea of an emissary and told our ambassador that the diplomatic channel, as a means of solving this dispute, was closed. President Reagan had a very long telephone conversation, of some 50 minutes, with the Argentine President, but his strong representations fell on deaf ears. I am grateful to him and to Secretary Haig for their strenuous and persistent efforts on our behalf.

On Thursday, the United Nations Secretary-General, Mr Perez De Cuellar, summoned both British and Argentine permanent representatives to urge both countries to refrain from the use or threat of force in the South Atlantic. Later that evening we sought an emergency meeting of the Security Council. We accepted the appeal of its President for restraint. The Argentines said nothing. On Friday, as the House knows, the Argentines invaded the Falklands and I have given a precise account of everything we knew, or did not know, about that situation. There were also reports that yesterday the Argentines also attacked South Georgia, where HMS *Endurance* had left a detachment of 22 Royal Marines. Our information is that on 2 April an Argentine naval transport vessel informed the base commander at Grytviken that an important message would be passed to him after 11 o'clock today our time. It is assumed that this message will ask the base commander to surrender.

Before indicating some of the measures that the Government have taken in response to the Argentine invasion, I should like to make three points. First, even if ships had been instructed to sail the day that the Argentines landed on South Georgia to clear the whaling station, the ships could not possibly have got to Port Stanley before the invasion . . . Opposition members may not like it, but that is a fact.

Secondly, there have been several occasions in the past when an invasion has been threatened. The only way of being certain to prevent an invasion would have been to keep a very large fleet close to the Falklands, when we are some 8,000 miles away from base. No Government have ever been able to do that, and the cost would be enormous.

Thirdly, aircraft unable to land on the Falklands, because of the frequently changing weather, would have had little fuel left and, ironically, their only hope of landing safely would have been to divert to Argentina. Indeed, all of the air and most sea supplies for the Falklands come from Argentina, which is but 400 miles away compared with our 8,000 miles.

That is the background against which we have to make decisions and to consider what action we can best take. I cannot tell the House precisely what dispositions have been made – some ships are already at sea, others were put on immediate alert on Thursday evening.

The Government have now decided that a large task force will sail as soon as all preparations are complete. HMS *Invincible* will be in the lead and will leave port on Monday.

I stress that I cannot foretell what orders the task force will receive as it proceeds. That will depend on the situation at the time. Meanwhile, we hope that our continuing diplomatic efforts, helped by our many friends, will meet with success.

The Foreign Ministers of the European Community member states yesterday condemned the intervention and urged withdrawal. The NATO Council called on both sides to refrain from force and continue diplomacy.

The United Nations Security Council met again yesterday and will continue its discussions today. [Laughter.] Opposition members laugh. They would have been the first to urge a meeting of the Security Council if we had not called one. They would have been the first to urge restraint and to urge a solution to the problem by diplomatic means. They would have been the first to accuse us of sabre rattling and war mongering.

We are now reviewing all aspects of the relationship between Argentina and the United Kingdom. The Argentine *chargé d'affaires* and his staff were yesterday instructed to leave within four days.

As an appropriate precautionary and, I hope, temporary measure, the Government have taken action to freeze Argentine financial assets held in this country. An order will be laid before Parliament today under the Emergency Laws (Re-enactments and Repeals) Act 1964 blocking the movement of gold, securities or funds held in the United Kingdom by the Argentine Government or Argentine residents.

As a further precautionary measure, the ECGD has suspended new export credit cover for the Argentine. It is the Government's earnest wish that a return to good sense and the normal rules of international behaviour on the part of the Argentine Government will obviate the need for action across the full range of economic relations.

We shall be reviewing the situation and be ready to take further steps that we deem appropriate and we shall, of course, report to the House.

The people of the Falkland Islands, like the people of the United Kingdom, are an island race. Their way of life is British; their allegiance is to the Crown. They are few in number, but they have the right to live in peace, to choose their own way of life and to determine their own allegiance. Their way of life is British; their allegiance is to the Crown. It is the wish of the British people and the duty of Her Majesty's Government to do everything that we can to uphold that right. That will be our hope and our endeavour and, I believe, the resolve of every member of the House.

'As she sat down, contempt rolled down like thunder from the benches around her,' wrote Simon Jenkins and Max Hastings in their account of the ensuing war.[6] Mrs Thatcher's fate now depended on defeating the invasion, either by diplomacy or war. The weakness of her position was underlined when she was forced to promote Francis Pym, one of her most plausible challengers for the leadership if things went awry, to Foreign Secretary, in place of Lord Carrington. Pym proved to be far more keen than Thatcher on a negotiated settlement and was unceremoniously dumped at the first possible opportunity, the post-election reshuffle in 1983.

Shortly after Thatcher's speech, when Enoch Powell spoke, he reminded the House that Mrs Thatcher had been nicknamed 'the Iron Lady' by the

Soviet media. 'In the next week or two, this House, the nation and the right hon. lady herself will learn of what metal she is made.' This comment had a sequel.

The recriminations were at least postponed and diverted to targets other than the Prime Minister. The Foreign Secretary, Lord Carrington, resigned the following week, and the backbench diarist Alan Clark recalled giving ministers a hard time at a private meeting of Tory MPs.

Meanwhile ships and troops were assembled for war to defend a British possession which most of the nation had not even heard of a week before, half a planet away.

'We are grossly dissatisfied with the conduct of the Government during the past month. We shall sustain them despite that, because we recognise that our service men's lives might be put at risk.'

Dr David Owen pledges his support for military action to return the Falklands to British rule: 3 April 1982

As the parliamentary leader of the newborn Social Democrats (Roy Jenkins had been returned to the Commons at the Glasgow Hillhead by-election a few days before, but had yet to take over), the former Labour Foreign Secretary Dr David Owen had a chance to sharpen up the breakaway party's rather soft-focus identity. In this speech, he 'spoke for England' far more emphatically than Mrs Thatcher. He had one telling advantage: when he was at the Foreign Office, the discreet dispatch of naval vessels to the South Atlantic had silenced an earlier bout of Argentine bellicosity. So while Thatcher was on the defensive, Owen could point to his effective handling of an apparently similar crisis, and ask why his approach had not been repeated. 'He had a good war', his Alliance partner, the Liberal leader David Steel, remarked.[7]

THE GOVERNMENT HAVE THE right to ask both sides of the House for the fullest support in their resolve to return the Falkland Islands and the freedom of the islanders to British sovereignty. They will get that support and they deserve it in every action that they take in the Security Council and elsewhere. However, the Government must restore the confidence of the country and the House in their ability to carry out that mission.

I agree with the Leader of the Opposition that this is not the time to have an examination. There will come a time when an inquiry will be necessary and we must examine in great detail all that has happened or not happened during the past six weeks. However, it is necessary to examine a central question: why was no preparatory action taken a month ago? It cannot be said that this is a question of intelligence. Our own newspapers were carrying major stories. On 25 February the *Guardian* carried a story entitled: 'Falklands raid hint by Argentine army.' On 5 March there was the headline in *The Times*: 'Argentina steps up Falklands pressure'.

There was ample warning that the position was deteriorating. We knew of the horror of the military junta in the Argentine and we knew of its actions. Only a few days ago, 3,000 political prisoners were taken, only to be released amid the euphoria of the invasion of the Falkland Islands. We knew that the military were jockeying for position in the navy, the army and the air force. We have known that for many years. It was for that reason four years ago, when a similar position developed, that naval forces were sent.

The Secretary of State for Defence, in his press conference with the Foreign Secretary yesterday, said: 'If we had made an earlier move to prepare the task force we would have precipitated, quite possibly, a military response – the very kind of thing by the Argentinians that we tried to avoid.'

The question that the Foreign Secretary, more than the Secretary of State for Defence, must answer is why no action was taken. On the precedent of the past, it was possible to deploy a naval force and to bring it back without any publicity. It was possible to use it in negotiations with the Argentines, knowing full well that we had behind us a naval force and the capacity to stop an invasion.

I say to the Prime Minister – the Leader of the Opposition [Michael Foot] fairly mentioned this fact – that the Prime Minister of the day took complete control of that issue. On my recommendation, the Secretary of State for Defence deployed the forces, but that small Cabinet meeting discussed the rules of engagement and the possibility of having to intervene were a naval force to come on to the Falkland Islands. That is the reality that the Prime Minister must now face.

Enough of the past. This is not a moment for censure. The reality is that our naval forces will set sail, which I support. I say to the right hon. member for Down South [Enoch Powell] that I am sure that the Royal Marines conducted themselves in the Falkland Islands in the best spirit of the Royal Marines.[8]

The question that we must now ask is how we can restore confidence. There have been rumours in the newspapers that the Secretary of State for Defence [John Nott] tendered his resignation, only for it to be refused. I would have expected no less of him, because he is a man of honour. Ministers must now consider their position and the quality and strength of the Government during the next few critical weeks.

Absent from the debate have been any positive suggestions. The Prime Minister is entitled to know where the House hopes she will now guide the country. There is much to be said for declaring our right to a 200-mile limit round the Falkland Islands. It would be perfectly compatible with international law to declare that no Argentine vessel should appear within that limit and that, if it did, the British Navy would take action.

The precedent for the use of peaceful military action is the Cuban missile crisis and the use of a naval blockade. We still have a very strong Navy, but only just.[9] We have the capacity to put a naval blockade on that 200-mile limit and to enforce it as long as we have hunter-killer submarines there. I hope that the Secretary of State for Defence can breach one aspect of security and let us know that there is a hunter-killer submarine in the area. If not, the House and the Argentines should assume that it is very nearly there. The hunter-killer submarine could effectively take action, if necessary. The Argentine Government should have fair warning to remove their vessels from the area. It is necessary to back up our diplomacy with the resolution and the capacity to deploy our forces.

We all know that there will be great difficulties in a resisted offence against the Falkland Islands. There are massive forces on the islands, but nothing said in the House should exclude any possibility of repossessing them. I believe that they will be repossessed by a combination of firm diplomacy backed by the use of the Navy. They are far away and there are logistic difficulties, but we should not make too much of those. Perhaps we can call on some of our Commonwealth friends in New Zealand and Australia to help us – at least with refuelling.

The Prime Minister misjudged the atmosphere of the House most seriously. It is now necessary for the message to come from the House that we are grossly dissatisfied with the conduct of the Government during the past month. We shall sustain them despite that, because we recognise that our service men's lives might be put at risk.

There is no question of anyone in the House weakening the stance of the Government, but the Prime Minister must now examine ways of restoring the Government's authority and ask herself why Britain has been placed in such a humiliating position during the past few days.

The right hon. lady said that it would have been absurd to send forces, but I do not agree. It would have been the right decision a month ago. The absence of that decision has meant humiliation. The House must now resolve to sustain the Government in restoring the position.

Perhaps Owen's approach was a shade too bellicose for some of his SDP–Liberal Alliance colleagues, but it established him and the SDP much more firmly in the public mind, and boosted the Alliance's appeal to Conservative voters. He sounded 'like a statesman', wrote Giles Radice,[10] and established himself as an effective performer in the news studios and the country, showing a flair which kept the tiny SDP, with just six MPs after the 1983 election, in independent existence when it could easily have evaporated.

'They are reported to be flying white flags over Port Stanley.'

Margaret Thatcher declares victory: 14 June 1982

Eight weeks after her tense appearance to announce the dispatch of the task force, Thatcher was able to come to the Commons to announce that the war was over, and Britain had won. An extraordinary period in which the nation had been glued to the radio for hourly reports of air, land and sea battles, in which losses and disasters, as well as victories, had been announced by a sepulchral-voiced Ministry of Defence official, was over. Thatcher's political standing – never that great before the war – soared.

O N A POINT OF ORDER, Mr Speaker. May I give the House the latest information about the battle of the Falklands? After successful attacks last night, General Moore [the commander of the British forces] decided to press forward. The Argentines retreated. Our forces reached the outskirts of Port Stanley. Large numbers of Argentine soldiers threw down their weapons. They are reported to be flying white flags over Port Stanley. Our troops have been ordered not to fire except in self-defence. Talks are now in progress between General Menendez and our Deputy Commander, Brigadier Waters, about the surrender of the Argentine forces on East and West Falkland. I shall report further to the House tomorrow.

Thatcher must have savoured the contrast between her icy reception in April and the shouts of 'Hear, hear!' Which greeted her now.

Two days later, Enoch Powell, referring back to his earlier comment, gave his verdict on the Iron Lady's mettle: 'the substance under test consisted of ferrous matter of the highest quality, that is of exceptional tensile strength, is highly resistant to wear and tear and to stress and may be used with advantage for all national purposes.'

It was a view the electorate seemed to share. Conservative ratings in the opinion polls had been reviving from their mid-term depths, even before the Falklands War; but the 'Falklands factor' and the resolute image of the Prime Minister enhanced the trend. A year later, aided by the split in the opposition vote between Labour and the Alliance, Thatcher cruised to a second term with a massive majority.

'I remember him telling me about the horrors of what went on in that camp. They are engraved forever on my mind and heart.'

Recalling her father's account of Buchenwald Concentration Camp, Llin Golding supports the War Crimes Bill: 12 December 1989

Llin Golding was the daughter of a Labour MP who visited the Buchenwald Concentration Camp. He, along with others had been sent at the request of the Allied commander and future US President Dwight Eisenhower, who wanted an authoritative group to inspect the camp while its full horrors were still apparent. A group of volunteer peers and MPs took off from London the next day, Friday, 20 April 1945. Golding's account, in a halting, emotional voice, of how an earlier generation of parliamentarians reacted to the terrible sights they saw there, stunned MPs. She spoke during the debate on the War Crimes Bill, which would allow the prosecution of people suspected of atrocities, even decades after they had been commited.

TWO WEEKS AGO, ONE of my constituents rang me up and told me, slowly and painfully, 'I have never telephoned or spoken to an MP before but I must ring you about the war crimes debate. My family – 85 of them – were killed in concentration camps. I am the only member of the family left.' Can the House imagine how the fingers of pain have reached out over the years to hold that lady so tightly that she cannot escape living with the horrors of what happened to her family?

In 1945, a parliamentary delegation was sent from this House to Buchenwald. It was less than three weeks after the allies had liberated that camp. The delegation prepared a report to the House. The final paragraph of it states:

> In preparing this report, we have endeavoured to write with restraint and objectivity, and to avoid obtruding personal reactions or emotional comments. We would conclude, however, by stating that it is our considered and unanimous opinion, on the evidence available to us, that a policy of steady starvation and inhuman brutality was carried out at Buchenwald for a very long period of time ; and that such camps as this mark the lowest point of degradation to which humanity has yet descended. The memory of what we saw and heard at Buchenwald will ineffaceably haunt us for many years.

The report was signed by Earl Stanhope, Lord Addison, Colonel Tom Wickham, Sir Archibald Southby, Mrs Mavis Tate, Mr Ness Edwards, Mr Sydney Silverman, Mr Graham White, Sir Henry Morris-Jones, and Mr Tom Driberg.

My father was a member of that delegation. His name was Ness Edwards. He was the hon. member for Caerphilly for 29 years. I remember him telling me about the horrors of what went on in that camp. They are engraved for ever on my mind and heart.

There has been much talk tonight about the passage of time. I was but a child on the day when I opened the door to my father on his return. He stood there, grey and drawn, and said, 'Do not touch me. I am covered with lice. Everyone in the camps is covered with lice. We have been deloused many times, but I am still covered with lice.' He could not sleep for many weeks, and he had nightmares for many years. It is said that Mrs Mavis Tate never got over what she saw in the camp, for she died a number of years later.

My father spoke to me and to my brothers and sisters about what he had seen in the camp. He told us of the hanging gibbets. Human beings were put on hooks and hung from under their chins until they died. He told us that the people in charge of the camp rather liked tattoos, and they skinned people and used their skins to make lampshades. They discovered that, when people die, their skin is given to shrinking too quickly, so they tried skinning them alive. My father showed me photographs of piles of bodies on carts. Three weeks later, the allies had not had time to remove them all. He showed me photographs of men in thin clothes, photographs of skeletons, and photographs of men with haunted eyes. I will always remember the look in those men's eyes – the look of utter bewilderment and incomprehension. They had been starved and beaten, yet their spirit was still there. There comes a point when something must be done. For too long the House has ignored that delegation's report. Tonight, I hope that every hon. member will pay tribute to our former colleagues for going to that camp on our behalf, for bringing back that report to the House, and for showing the suffering of so many people. I hope that all hon. members will show their respect for and commitment to doing what every member on that delegation would wish them to do, and that is to support the motion.

Mr Speaker Weatherill would not normally have called Golding, because she was an opposition whip at the time, but decided to stretch a point when told she had a compelling contribution to make. He told her afterwards that she had undoubtedly swung the debate. In the Lords, however, objections to the bill from senior lawyers and judges eventually forced the Tory government to invoke the Parliament Act to override them, so that the bill became law.

'Arabs and Muslims believe, and they are right to believe, that we do not consider their blood as valuable as our own.'

George Galloway warns against an invasion of Afghanistan in retaliation for the terrorist attacks of 11 September 2001: 14 September 2001

The terrorist attacks which destroyed the World Trade Center in New York on a clear autumn day in 2001 prompted an immediate recall of the Commons to allow MPs to condemn the outrage, and ponder future action.

But George Galloway, a Labour backbencher with a long record of support for the Palestinians and a long record of opposition to the economic sanctions imposed on Iraq after the Gulf War, offered the House and his party leadership an unwelcome analysis of the root causes of 9/11. One of the most impressive orators in the House, Galloway gave a thundering denunciation of Western policy on Iraq, Palestine and the Arab world.

I SEND MY CONDOLENCES to the great people of the United States of America, in particular to that great city, which I know and love, New York – so great they named it twice. I also send my condolences to New York's magnificent emergency services and its much maligned mayor, Rudi Giuliani, who has proved an admirable and excellent leader of that city's response. I am sure that New York will be back, as big and magnificent as ever.

I despise Osama bin Laden, the mediaeval obscurantist savage; the difference is that I have always despised him. I despised him when weapons, money, and political and diplomatic support were being stuffed down his throat faster than he could eat it. I said in this building on the eve of the victory of those whom the hon. member for New Forest East [the Conservative Dr Julian Lewis, who had supported anti-Soviet guerrillas in Afghanistan in the 1980s] used to hail as holy warriors and freedom fighters that, although I might be the last man in this place prepared to say it, we were responsible for opening the gates to the barbarians and a long dark night would descend on Afghanistan. Never did I speak truer words.

I caution against use of the word 'civilisation'. There are many civilisations in our world. Viewed from some countries, western civilisation does not always look as benign as we see it. It would be much easier if this were truly a conflict between the forces of good and a helpfully turbaned and bearded Dr Evil, and, if only we could ker-pow that mephistopholean genius in Action Man comic style, everything would be fine again – but it is not so. What we face is a hydra-headed phenomenon precisely because it arises from real conditions and has a real base of support.

Do not mistake the condemnation from Arab and Muslim Governments. It has arisen either from a dependent relationship with us and our friends or from the fear that if they do not say what is expected of them they will be attacked. Do not mistake that for the feeling of tens, if not hundreds, of millions of people in Arab and Muslim countries that we are responsible for monumental double standards and that we consider the lives of our own people and of our friends to have a fundamentally different order of value from the lives of those people.

The House may not wish to hear this, but I must say that I have walked in the ashes of cities under aerial attack. Buildings under aerial attack, people being crushed in falling masonry and steel or incinerated by fire from aerial attack look, sound and smell exactly the same whether they are in Beirut, the West Bank, Baghdad or Manhattan.

Arabs and Muslims believe, and they are right to believe, that we do not consider their blood as valuable as our own. Our policy over decades of our history makes that abundantly clear.

The question is: what is to be done? We are the friends of the Americans. It is no service to a friend to write a blank cheque, singing, in the manner of 'White Christmas,' that 'we'll follow the old man wherever he wants to go, wherever he wants to go.' That would not do a service to the world or to the United States of America.

In Korea, the Attlee Government played a decisive role in restraining the United States of America from using nuclear weapons against Korea and the People's Republic of China. We played a decisive role in removing from the theatre of operations General MacArthur, precisely because he was likely to move out of control.

I agree with my right hon. friend the member for Hartlepool [Peter Mandelson] that the only test that matters is whether action will make matters better or worse. If a devastating attack is launched on a Muslim country, killing thousands, it will make 10,000 bin Ladens rise up in the stead of the one whose head has been cut off. I do not know what could be bombed in Afghanistan, the Stone Age country that we helped to create. There is nothing there. Hardly a building stands. The only thing to hit in Afghanistan is people, and every slain Afghan will be a new banner for new bin Ladens.

Millions of Afghans – five million of them are starving today – will spill over the borders to become refugees and asylum seekers on ships that western countries will turn away at the point of guns, as the Australian navy did just a week or so ago.

I do not have time to develop all the points that I want to make, nor is this the time to raise certain subjects, although I associate myself with others who have spoken on them, at least in this regard: if 5,000 people have died in Manhattan, and even if 10,000 have died in Manhattan and Washington and Pittsburgh, that represents less than the two-monthly total of the number of children who have died in Iraq in every month of every one of eleven years. Those figures come from the United Nations, not from me or from my hon. friend the member for Linlithgow [Tam Dalyell]. The UN itself has told us that. The Muslims do not believe that we care about that. They do not believe that we care about the children being slaughtered by General Sharon, the butcher of Beirut, today as we are speaking. They do not believe that we care about them. In some respects, they are right and until this House and this country show that we care—

At this point Galloway was cut off by the Deputy Speaker because he had used his backbencher's time allocation.

This was the first of a series of powerful speeches which continued through the Western invasion of Afghanistan and the build-up to the invasion of Iraq. But they did not divert Tony Blair's government from its strong support for the US-led war on terror. Galloway's opposition to the war eventually led him to break with Labour and form the rival group Respect – under whose banner he won the Bethnal Green seat from the Labour loyalist Oona King.

'Too Manichaean for my, perhaps now jaded, taste.'

**In the House of Lords, Roy Jenkins deplores the prospect of the Iraq war:
24 September 2002.**

Like swans, the collective noun for former Cabinet ministers should be 'a lamentation'. In the long build-up to the Iraq war, the combined wisdom of former Foreign Secretaries of several parties was repeatedly deployed against Tony Blair's policy of using force against Saddam Hussein's regime. By the time of this debate, British forces were already committed in Afghanistan, and a major deployment to Iraq was clearly in prospect.

Roy Jenkins, once seen as Blair's mentor, and his most eminent collaborator in the 'Project' to reunite the divided tribes of the British centre-left, was never Foreign Secretary, but his typically elegant dissection of the foreign policy choices of the Blair government upstaged many who had been.

MY LORDS, I HAVE FOUND this issue more perplexing than almost any that I can remember in my now excessively long political life. I have a high regard for the Prime Minister. I have been repelled by attempts to portray him as a vacuous man with an artificial smile and no convictions. I am reminded of similar attempts by a frustrated right to suggest that Gladstone was mad, Asquith was corrupt and Attlee was negligible. My view is that the Prime Minister, far from lacking conviction, has almost too much, particularly when dealing with the world beyond Britain. He is a little too Manichaean for my perhaps now jaded taste, seeing matters in stark terms of good and evil, black and white, contending with each other, and with a consequent belief that if evil is cast down good will inevitably follow. I am more inclined to see the world and the regimes within it in varying shades of grey. The experience of the past year, not least in Afghanistan, has given more support to that view than to the more Utopian one that a quick 'change of regime' can make us all live happily ever after.

I can understand the desire of the Prime Minister to maintain close relations with America, and to keep open the relatively narrow window through which the present United States Administration looks out to international opinion, as opposed to contemplating its own vast preponderance of power and feeling that this gives it a right and a duty to arbitrate the world.

That preponderance is almost without precedent in world history. Whether it is healthy for the world or comfortable for America's allies, let alone its proclaimed enemies, is open to argument. In the strenuous and sometimes frightening days of the 1950s, 1960s, 1970s and 1980s, I would never have believed that one might, 20 years later, feel a twinge of nostalgia for the balances of the Cold War, for the nearly equal strain on the tug-of-war and for America's careful cultivation of its European allies that that involved.

I have long been a natural pro-American. Ever since I first went to America in 1953, I have remained half-captivated by the vitality of its life, the quality of at least some of its leaders and the fascinating complications of its political institutions. I have never seen a conflict between my European commitment and a desire to maintain a strong transatlantic link. Indeed, I think that one of the major recurring mistakes of British foreign policy since the war has been to believe that we should get on better with the Americans if we avoided too much entanglement in Europe. In fact, for a 40-year period, our unwillingness to play a full part in Europe was an exacerbating rather than a helpful factor in our relations with the United States. They were impatient with our exclusiveness.

By the same token, I have always been loath to use the term 'special relationship'. It is too unequal a relationship – the reality being that it is more special on one side than on the other – for that to be a wise label.

It is, of course, right – as my noble friend Lady Williams[11] so eloquently set out in her brilliant speech earlier – fully to involve the UN in any action that may be taken against Iraq. Mr Blair deserves full credit for the persuasiveness with which he evidently spoke to President Bush on this issue. But involving the UN does not in itself absolve us from the responsibility of exercising cool judgement about what requests we put before the UN. Here I find considerable logical inconsistencies in what appears to be the policy of the American Government, and to some extent of the British Government too.

The reason why the international agenda has greatly changed in the past twelve and a half months is that individual acts of terrorism far exceeding anything hitherto known were then inflicted on New York. But they were not acts of governmental aggression, even though a number of states, with greatly varying degrees of complicity, bear some responsibility for having harboured and even trained, knowingly or unknowingly, those who committed the atrocity. What is wholly understandable is the overwhelming desire of the US Government to reduce the likelihood of any repetition of such attacks, either on themselves or on others.

But that is different from and does not appear to me to be very closely linked with the undesirable possession – or the desire for possession – by a number of states and by one obnoxious regime in particular of what are now commonly called 'weapons of mass destruction'.

The problems are not the same, and the remedies are not necessarily the same. Indeed, it can be argued that an armed attack to take out this contingent future threat could increase the danger of scattered groups of terrorists attempting a repeat of 9/11.

Furthermore, when we have embarked on a policy of taking out undesirable regimes by external armed force, where do we stop? There are a number of regimes which either have or would like to have nuclear weapons. I, and, I guess, the majority of your Lordships, would much rather they did not have them. But it would be difficult to justify a policy of taking them out seriatim with either common sense or international law.

I raise these issues not with a desire to be negative – I recognise the immensely difficult problem facing Her Majesty's Government – but because I believe that there is an urgent need for clarity on them both from our own Government and from that of the United States. It is no answer just to brand anyone who raises them as a lily-livered appeaser who refuses to learn the lessons of history – particularly when that history is presented so crudely as to line up Winston Churchill with the gung-ho battalions, which shows a great ignorance of his words at the time of Suez as well as his caution about pre-emptive strikes at the time of the German reoccupation of the Rhineland in 1936.

I am in favour of courage – who is ever not in the abstract? – but not of treating it as a substitute for wisdom, as I fear we are currently in danger of doing.

This was a wounding verdict on Blair, delivered by a former ally. And it was the last hurrah of an extraordinary parliamentarian.

'This is not the time to falter.'

Tony Blair seeks authorisation for war on Iraq: 18 March 2003

Tony Blair created a new constitutional doctrine when he promised the House of Commons a vote on the decision to invade Iraq and depose Saddam Hussein. Until that point a Prime Minister could use the royal prerogative to take Britain to war, as Asquith did in 1914, or Chamberlain in 1939. The precedent set with this debate will have incalculable effects in future conflicts.

But Blair had little choice. His party was bitterly divided. One senior Cabinet minister, the former Foreign Secretary Robin Cook, had already resigned. Another, the International Development Secretary, Clare Short, had gone out of her way to describe his policy on Iraq as 'reckless', although for the time being, she remained a member of the government. Blair had to carry the Commons and, more to the point, his own party. Already that day he had addressed a tense meeting of the Parliamentary Labour Party, and now he would have to confront his rebels in the chamber of the Commons.

The motion he put before MPs, with its references to UN resolutions and the legal advice of the Attorney General, Lord Goldsmith, and above all its linkage of Iraq and the Israel–Palestine conflict, was calculated to appeal to his own waverers. But he faced an amendment from the Labour anti-war camp which insisted the case for war had not been made, and called for specific UN authorisation for any military action.

Tony Blair's speech that day was a parliamentary masterpiece. Anything smacking of messianic zeal or sub-Churchillian cadence had been excised. The tone was conciliatory, but firm. We know from a behind-the-scenes account of its preparation[12] that the section drawing a tentative comparison between opposition to this war and appeasement in the 1930s provoked much debate at Downing Street, before it was finally decided to 'draw a general link between then and now', in sufficiently oblique terms that doubters would not be labelled as appeasers. Even so, the lead Labour rebel, former Defence Minister, Peter Kilfoyle, was moved to remark that the only person he had ever appeased was Mrs Kilfoyle.

I BEG TO MOVE,

That this House notes its decisions of 25th November 2002 and 26th February 2003 to endorse UN Security Council Resolution 1441; recognises that Iraq's weapons of mass destruction and long range missiles, and its continuing non-compliance with Security Council Resolutions, pose a threat to international peace and security; notes that in the 130 days since Resolution 1441 was adopted Iraq has not cooperated actively, unconditionally and immediately with the weapons inspectors, and has rejected the final opportunity to comply and is in further material breach of its obligations under successive mandatory UN Security Council Resolutions; regrets that despite sustained diplomatic effort by Her Majesty's Government it has not proved possible to secure a second Resolution in the UN because one Permanent Member of the Security Council made plain in public its intention to use its veto whatever the circumstances; notes the opinion of the Attorney General that, Iraq having failed to comply and Iraq being at the time of Resolution 1441 and continuing to be in material breach, the authority to use force under Resolution 678 has revived and so continues today; believes that the United Kingdom must uphold the authority of the United Nations as set out in Resolution 1441 and many Resolutions preceding it, and therefore supports the decision of Her Majesty's Government that the United Kingdom should use all means necessary to ensure the disarmament of Iraq's weapons of mass destruction; offers wholehearted support to the men and women of Her Majesty's Armed Forces now on duty in the Middle East; in the event of military operations requires that, on an urgent basis, the United Kingdom should seek a new Security Council Resolution that would affirm Iraq's territorial integrity, ensure rapid delivery of humanitarian relief, allow for the earliest possible lifting of UN sanctions, an international reconstruction programme, and the use of all oil revenues for the benefit of the Iraqi people and endorse an appropriate post-conflict administration for Iraq, leading to a representative government which upholds human rights and the rule of law for all Iraqis; and also welcomes the imminent publication of the Quartet's roadmap as a significant step to bringing a just and lasting peace settlement between Israelis and Palestinians and for the wider Middle East region, and endorses the role of Her Majesty's Government in actively working for peace between Israel and Palestine.

At the outset, I say that it is right that the House debate this issue and pass judgment. That is the democracy that is our right, but that others struggle for in vain. Again, I say that I do not disrespect the views in opposition to mine. This is a tough choice indeed, but it is also a stark one: to stand British troops down now and turn back, or to hold firm to the course that we have set. I believe passionately that we must hold firm to that course. The question most often posed is not 'Why does it matter?' but 'Why does it matter so much?' Here we are, the Government, with their most serious test, their majority at risk, the first Cabinet resignation over an issue of policy, the main parties internally divided, people who agree on everything else—

What gave Blair wings was an interruption here by Liberal Democrat MPs; several of them shouted that they were united – against the war. The put-down that followed was brutal, and the cross-party roar of approval that greeted it is recorded in Hansard merely as an interruption. But it was an important moment. Few things unite Labour and Tory MPs more effectively than Liberal-bashing, and the Prime Minister's confidence blossomed.

Ah, yes, of course. The Liberal Democrats – unified, as ever, in opportunism and error.

The country and the Parliament reflect each other. This is a debate that, as time has gone on, has become less bitter but no less grave. So why does it matter so much? Because the outcome of this issue will now determine more than the fate of the Iraqi regime and more than the future of the Iraqi people who have been brutalised by Saddam for so long, important though those issues are. It will determine the way in which Britain and the world confront the central security threat of the twenty-first century, the development of the United Nations, the relationship between Europe and the United States, the relations within the European Union and the way in which the United States engages with the rest of the world. So it could hardly be more important. It will determine the pattern of international politics for the next generation.

First, let us recap the history of Iraq and weapons of mass destruction. In April 1991, after the Gulf war, Iraq was given fifteen days to provide a full and final declaration of all its weapons of mass destruction. Saddam had used the weapons against Iran and against his own people, causing thousands of deaths. He had had plans to use them against allied forces. It became clear, after the Gulf war, that Iraq's WMD ambitions were far more extensive than had hitherto been thought. So the issue was identified by the United Nations at that time as one for urgent remedy. UNSCOM, the weapons inspection team, was set up. It was expected to complete its task, following the declaration, at the end of April 1991.

The declaration, when it came, was false: a blanket denial of the programme, other than in a very tentative form. And so the twelve-year game began.

The inspectors probed. Finally, in March 1992, Iraq admitted that it had previously undeclared weapons of mass destruction, but it said that it had destroyed them. It gave another full and final declaration. Again the inspectors probed. In October 1994, Iraq stopped cooperating with the weapons inspectors altogether. Military action was threatened. Inspections resumed. In March 1996, in an effort to rid Iraq of the inspectors, a further full and final declaration of WMD was made. By July 1996, however, Iraq was forced to admit that declaration, too, was false.

In August, it provided yet another full and final declaration. Then, a week later, Saddam's son-in-law, Hussein Kamal, defected to Jordan. He disclosed a far more extensive biological weapons programme and, for the first time, said that Iraq had weaponised the programme – something that Saddam had always strenuously denied. All this had been happening while the inspectors were in Iraq.

Kamal also revealed Iraq's crash programme to produce a nuclear weapon in the 1990s. Iraq was then forced to release documents that showed just how extensive those programmes were. In November 1996, Jordan intercepted prohibited components for missiles that could be used for weapons of mass destruction. Then a further 'full and final declaration' was made. That, too, turned out to be false.

In June 1997, inspectors were barred from specific sites. In September 1997, lo and behold, yet another 'full and final declaration' was made – also false. Meanwhile, the inspectors discovered VX nerve agent production equipment, the existence of which had always been denied by the Iraqis.

In October 1997, the United States and the United Kingdom threatened military action if Iraq refused to comply with the inspectors. Finally, under threat of action in February 1998, Kofi Annan went to Baghdad and negotiated a memorandum with Saddam to allow inspections to continue. They did continue, for a few months. In August, cooperation was suspended.

In December, the inspectors left. Their final report is a withering indictment of Saddam's lies, deception and obstruction, with large quantities of weapons of mass destruction unaccounted for. Then, in December 1998, the US and the UK undertook Desert Fox, a targeted bombing campaign to degrade as much of the Iraqi WMD facility as we could.

In 1999, a new inspection team, UNMOVIC, was set up. Saddam refused to allow those inspectors even to enter Iraq. So there they stayed, in limbo, until, after resolution 1441 last November, they were allowed to return.

That is the history – and what is the claim of Saddam today? Why, exactly the same as before: that he has no weapons of mass destruction. Indeed, we are asked to believe that after seven years of obstruction and non-compliance, finally resulting in the inspectors' leaving in 1998 – seven years in which he hid his programme and built it up, even when the inspectors were there in Iraq – when they had left, he voluntarily decided to do what he had consistently refused to do under coercion.

When the inspectors left in 1998, they left unaccounted for 10,000 litres of anthrax; a far-reaching VX nerve agent programme; up to 6,500 chemical munitions; at least 80 tonnes of mustard gas, and possibly more than ten times that amount; unquantifiable amounts of sarin, botulinum toxin and a host of other biological poisons; and an entire Scud missile programme. We are asked now seriously to accept that in the last few years – contrary to all history, contrary to all intelligence – Saddam decided unilaterally to destroy those weapons. I say that such a claim is palpably absurd.

Resolution 1441 is very clear. It lays down a final opportunity for Saddam to disarm. It rehearses the fact that he has for years been in material breach of seventeen UN resolutions. It says that this time compliance must be full, unconditional and immediate, the first step being a full and final declaration of all weapons of mass destruction to be given on 8 December last year.

I will not go through all the events since then, as the House is familiar with them, but this much is accepted by all members of the UN Security Council: the 8 December declaration is false. That in itself, incidentally, is a material breach. Iraq has taken some steps in cooperation, but no one disputes that it is not fully cooperating. Iraq continues to deny that it has any weapons of mass destruction, although no serious intelligence service anywhere in the world believes it.

On 7 March, the inspectors published a remarkable document. It is 173 pages long, and details all the unanswered questions about Iraq's weapons of mass destruction. It lists 29 different areas in which the inspectors have been unable to obtain information. On VX, for example, it says:

> Documentation available to UNMOVIC suggests that Iraq at least had had far reaching plans to weaponise VX.

On mustard gas, it says:

> Mustard constituted an important part . . . of Iraq's CW arsenal . . . 550 mustard filled shells and up to 450 mustard filled aerial bombs unaccounted for . . . additional uncertainty

with respect to over 6,500 aerial bombs,

> corresponding to approximately 1,000 tonnes of agent, predominantly
> mustard.

On biological weapons, the inspectors' report states:

> Based on unaccounted for growth media, Iraq's potential production of
> anthrax could have been in the range of about 15,000 to 25,000 litres . . .
> Based on all the available evidence, the strong presumption is that about
> 10,000 litres of anthrax was not destroyed and may still exist.

On that basis, I simply say to the House that, had we meant what we said in resolution 1441, the Security Council should have convened and condemned Iraq as in material breach. What is perfectly clear is that Saddam is playing the same old games in the same old way. Yes, there are minor concessions, but there has been no fundamental change of heart or mind.

However, after 7 March, the inspectors said that there was at least some cooperation, and the world rightly hesitated over war. Let me now describe to the House what then took place.

We therefore approached a second resolution in this way. As I said, we could have asked for the second resolution then and there, because it was justified. Instead, we laid down an ultimatum calling upon Saddam to come into line with resolution 1441, or be in material breach. That is not an unreasonable proposition, given the history, but still countries hesitated. They asked, 'How do we judge what is full cooperation?'

So we then worked on a further compromise. We consulted the inspectors and drew up five tests, based on the document that they published on 7 March. Those tests included allowing interviews with 30 scientists to be held outside Iraq, and releasing details of the production of the anthrax, or at least of the documentation showing what had happened to it. The inspectors added another test: that Saddam should publicly call on Iraqis to cooperate with them.

So we constructed this framework: that Saddam should be given a specified time to fulfil all six tests to show full cooperation; and that, if he did so, the inspectors could then set out a forward work programme that would extend over a period of time to make sure that disarmament happened. However, if Saddam failed to meet those tests to judge compliance, action would follow.

So there were clear benchmarks, plus a clear ultimatum. Again, I defy anyone to describe that as an unreasonable proposition.

Last Monday, we were getting very close with it. We very nearly had the majority agreement. If I might, I should particularly like to thank the President of Chile for the constructive way in which he approached this issue.

Yes, there were debates about the length of the ultimatum, but the basic construct was gathering support. Then, on Monday night, France said that it would veto a second resolution, whatever the circumstances. Then France denounced the six tests. Later that day, Iraq rejected them. Still, we continued to negotiate, even at that point.

Last Friday, France said that it could not accept any resolution with an ultimatum in it. On Monday, we made final efforts to secure agreement. However, the fact is that France remains utterly opposed to anything that lays down an ultimatum authorising action in the event of non-compliance by Saddam.

Here there was a helpful intervention from Hugh Bayley, Labour MP for York, who had opposed Britain taking part in military action without a second UN resolution. He told Blair he had changed his mind because some members of the Security Council had backed away from the commitment that they gave in November to enforce resolution 1441. 'France's decision to use the veto against any further Security Council resolution has, in effect, disarmed the UN instead of disarming Iraq,' he added. The Prime Minister was suitably grateful.

Of course I agree with my hon. friend. The House should just consider the position that we were asked to adopt. Those on the Security Council opposed to us say that they want Saddam to disarm, but they will not countenance any new resolution that authorises force in the event of non-compliance. That is their position – no to any ultimatum and no to any resolution that stipulates that failure to comply will lead to military action. So we must demand that Saddam disarms, but relinquish any concept of a threat if he does not.

From December 1998 to December 2002, no UN inspector was allowed to inspect anything in Iraq. For four years, no inspection took place. What changed Saddam's mind was the threat of force. From December to January, and then from January through to February, some concessions were made. What changed his mind? It was the threat of force. What makes him now issue invitations to the inspectors, discover documents that he said he never had, produce evidence of weapons supposed to be non-existent, and destroy missiles he said he would keep? It is the imminence of force. The only persuasive power to which he responds is 250,000 allied troops on his doorstep. However, when that fact is so obvious, we are told that any resolution that authorises force in the event of non-compliance will be vetoed – not just opposed, but vetoed and blocked.

Another sceptical Labour MP, Jon Owen Jones, asked Blair why Britain and the United States had not pursued the second resolution, to demonstrate that the French were isolated. (In the event Jones did not vote against the government.)

For the very reason that I have just given. If a member of the permanent five indicates to members of the Security Council who are not permanent members that whatever the circumstances it will veto, that is the way to block any progress on the Security Council.

That provoked another shout from the backbenches.

With the greatest respect to whoever shouted out that the presence of the troops is working, I agree, but it is British and American troops who are there, not French troops.

The tragedy is that had such a resolution ensued and had the UN come together and united – and if other troops had gone there, not just British and American troops – Saddam Hussein might have complied. But the moment we proposed the benchmarks and canvassed support for an ultimatum, there was an immediate recourse to the language of the veto. The choice was not action now or postponement of action; the choice was action or no action at all.

Another anti-war backbencher, Llew Smith (who did go on to defy the government), attacked the concept of the 'unreasonable veto'. He asked whether the 30 occasions on which the UK had used the veto and the 75 occasions on which the US had used it had been reasonable or unreasonable. But this simply gave Blair another chance to make his point.

We can argue about each one of those vetoes in the past and whether they were reasonable, but I define an unreasonable veto as follows. In resolution 1441, we said that it was Saddam's final opportunity and that he had to comply. That was agreed by all members of the Security Council. What is surely unreasonable is for a country to come forward now, at the very point when we might reach agreement and when we are – not unreasonably – saying that he must comply with the UN, after all these months without full compliance, on the basis of the six tests or action will follow. For that country to say that it will veto such a resolution in all circumstances is what I would call unreasonable.

The tragedy is that the world has to learn the lesson all over again that weakness in the face of a threat from a tyrant is the surest way not to peace, but – unfortunately – to conflict. Looking back over those twelve years, the truth is that we have been victims of our own desire to placate the implacable, to persuade towards reason the utterly unreasonable, and to hope that there was some genuine intent to do good in a regime whose mind is in fact evil.

Now the very length of time counts against us. People say, 'You've waited twelve years, so why not wait a little longer?' Of course we have done so, because resolution 1441 gave a final opportunity. As I have just pointed out, the first test was on 8 December. But still we waited. We waited for the inspectors' reports. We waited as each concession was tossed to us to whet our appetite for hope and further waiting. But still no one, not even today at the Security Council, says that Saddam is cooperating fully, unconditionally or immediately.

The Liberal Democrat Simon Hughes, a senior figure in the largest party to take an anti-war position, said the threat of force against Saddam Hussein had been effective and wondered why the diplomacy could not be continued for a little longer to secure agreement on the Security Council. Force could then be backed with the authority of the UN, if necessary. Blair said the French had foreclosed that option.

We could have had more time if the compromise proposal that we put forward had been accepted. I take it from what the hon. gentleman has just said that he would accept that the compromise proposal we put forward was indeed reasonable. We set out the tests. If Saddam meets those tests, we extend the work programme of the inspectors. If he does not meet those tests, we take action. I think that the hon. gentleman would also agree that unless the threat of action was made, it was unlikely that Saddam would meet the tests.

The hon. gentleman nods his head, but the problem with the diplomacy was that it came to an end after the position of France was made public – and repeated in a private conversation – and it said that it would block, by veto, any resolution that contained an ultimatum. We could carry on discussing it for a long time, but the French were not prepared to change their position. I am not prepared to carry on waiting and delaying, with our troops in place in difficult circumstances, when that country has made it clear that it has a fixed position and will not change. I would have hoped that, rather than condemn us for not waiting even longer, the hon. gentleman would condemn those who laid down the veto.

The loyalist Labour backbencher David Winnick said the real criticism of the UN was that it had taken twelve years to reach this point, when the Security Council should had taken action much earlier. Blair agreed.

I truly believe that our fault has not been impatience. The truth is that our patience should have been exhausted weeks and months and even years ago.

To interruptions from Labour MPs, the Scottish Nationalist leader at Westminster, Alex Salmond, said that three permanent members of the UN Security Council, the French, Russians and Chinese, had always made it clear that they would oppose a second resolution that led automatically to war. It was Blair who had abandoned his earlier position that he would go to war without a second resolution unless the UN weapons inspectors ruled that there had been no more progress, which they had not. When, Salmond asked, did he change his position, and why? Blair retorted that he did not understand the nuances of resolution 1441.

First, the hon. gentleman is absolutely wrong about the position on resolution 1441. It is correct that resolution 1441 did not say that there would be another resolution authorising the use of force, but the implication of resolution 1441 – it was stated in terms – was that if Iraq continued in material breach, defined as not cooperating fully, immediately and unconditionally, serious consequences should follow. All we are asking for in the second resolution is the clear ultimatum that if Saddam continues to fail to cooperate, force should be used. The French position is that France will vote no, whatever the circumstances. Those are not my words, but those of the French President. I find it sad that at this point in time he cannot support us in the position we have set out, which is the only sure way to disarm Saddam. And what, indeed, would any tyrannical regime possessing weapons of mass destruction think when viewing the history of the world's diplomatic dance with Saddam over these twelve years? That our capacity to pass firm resolutions has only been matched by our feebleness in implementing them. That is why this indulgence has to stop – because it is dangerous: dangerous if such regimes disbelieve us; dangerous if they think they can use our weakness, our hesitation, and even the natural urges of our democracy towards peace against us; and dangerous because one day they will mistake our innate revulsion against war for permanent incapacity, when, in fact, if pushed to the limit, we will act. But when we act, after years of pretence, the action will have to be harder, bigger, more total in its impact. It is true that Iraq is not the only country with weapons of mass destruction, but I say this to the House: back away from this confrontation now, and future conflicts will be infinitely worse and more devastating in their effects.

Of course, in a sense, any fair observer does not really dispute that Iraq is in breach of resolution 1441 or that it implies action in such circumstances. The real problem is that, underneath, people dispute that Iraq is a threat, dispute the link between terrorism and weapons of mass destruction, and dispute, in other words, the whole basis of our assertion that the two together constitute a fundamental assault on our way of life.

There are glib and sometimes foolish comparisons with the 1930s. I am not suggesting for a moment that anyone here is an appeaser or does not share our revulsion at the regime of Saddam. However, there is one relevant point of analogy. It is that, with history, we know what happened. We can look back and say, 'There's the time; that was the moment; that's when we should have acted.' However, the point is that it was not clear at the time – not at that moment. In fact, at that time, many people thought such a fear fanciful or, worse, that it was put forward in bad faith by warmongers. Let me read one thing from an editorial from a paper that I am pleased to say takes a different position today. It was written in late 1938 after Munich. One would have thought from the history books that people thought the world was tumultuous in its desire to act. This is what the editorial said:

> Be glad in your hearts. Give thanks to your God. People of Britain, your children are safe. Your husbands and your sons will not march to war. Peace is a victory for all mankind . . . And now let us go back to our own affairs. We have had enough of those menaces, conjured up . . . to confuse us.

Now, of course, should Hitler again appear in the same form, we would know what to do. But the point is that history does not declare the future to us plainly. Each time is different and the present must be judged without the benefit of hindsight. So let me explain to the House why I believe that the threat that we face today is so serious and why we must tackle it. The threat today is not that of the 1930s. It is not big powers going to war with each other. The ravages that fundamentalist ideology inflicted on the twentieth century are memories. The Cold War is over. Europe is at peace, if not always diplomatically. But the world is ever more interdependent. Stock markets and economies rise and fall together, confidence is the key to prosperity, and insecurity spreads like contagion. The key today is stability and order. The threat is chaos and disorder – and there are two begetters of chaos: tyrannical regimes with weapons of mass destruction and extreme terrorist groups who profess a perverted and false view of Islam.

Let me tell the House what I know. I know that there are some countries, or groups within countries, that are proliferating and trading in weapons of mass destruction – especially nuclear weapons technology. I know that there are companies, individuals, and some former scientists on nuclear weapons programmes, who are selling their equipment or expertise. I know that there are several countries – mostly dictatorships with highly repressive regimes – that are desperately trying to acquire chemical weapons, biological weapons or, in particular, nuclear weapons capability. Some of those countries are now a short time away from having a serviceable nuclear weapon. This activity is not diminishing. It is increasing.

We all know that there are terrorist groups now operating in most major countries. Just in the past two years, around 20 different nations have suffered serious terrorist outrages. Thousands of people – quite apart from 11 September – have died in them. The purpose of that terrorism is not just in the violent act; it is in producing terror. It sets out to inflame, to divide, and to produce consequences of a calamitous nature. Round the world, it now poisons the chances of political progress – in the Middle East, in Kashmir, in Chechnya and in Africa. The removal of the Taliban – yes – dealt it a blow. But it has not gone away.

Those two threats have, of course, different motives and different origins, but they share one basic common view: they detest the freedom, democracy and tolerance that are the hallmarks of our way of life. At the moment, I accept fully that the association between the two is loose – but it is hardening. The possibility of the two coming together – of terrorist groups in possession of weapons of mass destruction or even of a so-called dirty radiological bomb – is now, in my judgment, a real and present danger to Britain and its national security.

The Father of the House, Tam Dalyell, who was utterly opposed to the war and was later to make opposition to Britain's role in Iraq the final campaign of his long Commons career, rose to warn that bombarding Iraq with hundreds of cruise missiles would attract thousands of recruits to terrorism from across the Arab and Muslim world. Blair retorted that the terrorists had needed no provocation.

Let me come to that very point. Let us recall: what was shocking about 11

September was not just the slaughter of innocent people but the knowledge that, had the terrorists been able, there would have been not 3,000 innocent dead, but 30,000 or 300,000 – and the more the suffering, the greater their rejoicing. I say to my hon. friend that America did not attack the al-Qaeda terrorist group; the al-Qaeda terrorist group attacked America. They did not need to be recruited; they were there already. Unless we take action against them, they will grow. That is why we should act.

Let me explain the dangers. Three kilograms of VX from a rocket launcher would contaminate 0.25 sq km of a city. Millions of lethal doses are contained in one litre of anthrax, and 10,000 litres are unaccounted for. What happened on 11 September has changed the psychology of America – that is clear – but it should have changed the psychology of the world.

Of course, Iraq is not the only part of this threat. I have never said that it was. But it is the test of whether we treat the threat seriously. Faced with it, the world should unite. The UN should be the focus both of diplomacy and of action. That is what 1441 said. That was the deal. And I simply say to the House that to break it now, and to will the ends but not the means, would do more damage in the long term to the UN than any other single course that we could pursue. To fall back into the lassitude of the past twelve years; to talk, to discuss, to debate but never to act; to declare our will but not to enforce it; and to continue with strong language but with weak intentions – that is the worst course imaginable. If we pursue that course, when the threat returns, from Iraq or elsewhere, who will then believe us? What price our credibility with the next tyrant? It was interesting today that some of the strongest statements of support for allied forces came from near to North Korea – from Japan and South Korea.

The Conservative veteran Sir Teddy Taylor intervened to say that the countries which supplied anthrax and toxins to Iraq should be named and condemned for their actions. Blair for once was slow to recognise a point in his favour, falling back on the neutral comment that much of the production was in Iraq itself. He corrected himself a few moments later.

Meanwhile, another leading anti-war Labour rebel, Lynne Jones, picked up on his comment that the association between Iraq and terrorists was loose to challenge a claim from President Bush that Iraq had aided, trained and haboured terrorists, including operatives of al-Qaeda. She asked whether Blair agreed.

Yes, I do support what the President said. Do not be in any doubt at all – Iraq has been supporting terrorist groups. For example, Iraq is offering money to the families of suicide bombers whose purpose is to wreck any chance of progress in the Middle East. Although I said that the associations were loose, they are hardening. I do believe that, and I believe that the two threats coming together are the dangers that we face in our world.

I also say this: there will be in any event no sound future for the United Nations – no guarantee against the repetition of these events – unless we recognise the urgent need for a political agenda that we can unite upon. What we have witnessed is indeed the consequence of Europe and the United States dividing from each other. Not all of Europe – Spain, Italy, Holland, Denmark and Portugal have strongly supported us – and not a majority of Europe if we include, as we should, Europe's new members who will accede next year, all ten of whom have been in strong support of the position of this Government. But the paralysis of the UN has been born out of the division that there is.

I want to deal with that in this way. At the heart of that division is the concept of a world in which there are rival poles of power, with the US and its allies in one corner and France, Germany, Russia and their allies in the other. I do not believe that all those nations intend such an outcome, but that is what now faces us. I believe such a vision to be misguided and profoundly dangerous for our world. I know why it arises. There is resentment of US predominance. There is fear of US unilateralism. People ask, 'Do the US listen to us and our preoccupations?' And there is perhaps a lack of full understanding of US preoccupations after 11 September. I know all this. But the way to deal with it is not rivalry, but partnership. Partners are not servants, but neither are they rivals. What Europe should have said last September to the United States is this: with one voice it should have said, 'We understand your strategic anxiety over terrorism and weapons of mass destruction and we will help you meet it. We will mean what we say in any UN resolution we pass and will back it with action if Saddam fails to disarm voluntarily. However, in return' – Europe should have said – 'we ask two things of you: that the US should indeed choose the UN path and you should recognise the fundamental overriding importance of restarting the Middle East peace process, which we will hold you to.'

That would have been the right and responsible way for Europe and America to treat each other as partners, and it is a tragedy that it has not happened. I do not believe that there is any other issue with the same power to reunite the world community than progress on the issues of Israel and Palestine. Of course, there is cynicism about recent announcements, but the United States is now committed – and, I believe genuinely – to the road map for peace designed in consultation with the UN. It will now be presented to the parties as Abu Mazen is confirmed in office, hopefully today, as Palestinian Prime Minister. All of us are now signed up to this vision: a state of Israel, recognised and accepted by all the world, and a viable Palestinian state. That is what this country should strive for, and we will.

And that should be part of a larger global agenda: on poverty and sustainable development; on democracy and human rights; and on the good governance of nations. That is why what happens after any conflict in Iraq is of such critical significance. Here again there is a chance to unify around the United Nations. There should be a new United Nations resolution following any conflict providing not only for humanitarian help, but for the administration and governance of Iraq. That must be done under proper UN authorisation.

Mike Gapes, a Labour MP with a substantial Muslim community in his Ilford constituency, intervened to emphasise the need for progress in solving the Israeli–Palestinian conflict – and to ask Blair to dispel any impression that the impending invasion was just an Anglo-American adventure.

I shall certainly do so. The UN resolution that should provide for the proper governance of Iraq should also protect totally the territorial integrity of Iraq. And this point is also important: that the oil revenues, which people falsely claim that we want to seize, should be put in a trust fund for the Iraqi people administered through the UN.

The process must begin on a democratic basis, respecting human rights, as, indeed, the fledgling democracy in northern Iraq – protected from Saddam for twelve years by British and American pilots in the no-fly zone – has done remarkably. The moment that a new Government are in place, committed to disarming Iraq of weapons of mass destruction, is the point in time when sanctions should be lifted, and can be lifted, in their entirety for the people of Iraq.

Jeremy Corbyn, another Labour rebel, was worried that the Turks might use the opportunity of an American attack from their territory on the northern border of Iraq to crush the embryonic Kurdish state that had been formed there under US protection. In the event, Turkey did not allow an invasion to be launched from its borders, but Blair was able to give him some reassurance.

Turkey has given that commitment. I have spoken to the Turkish Government, as have the President of the United States and many others. I have to say to my hon. friend that it is clear from the conversations that I have had with people in that Kurdish autonomous zone that what they really fear above all else is the prospect of Saddam remaining in power, emboldened because we have failed to remove him.

I have never put the justification for action as regime change. We have to act within the terms set out in resolution 1441 – that is our legal base. But it is the reason why I say frankly that if we do act, we should do so with a clear conscience and a strong heart. I accept fully that those who are opposed to this course of action share my detestation of Saddam. Who could not? Iraq is a potentially wealthy country which in 1979, the year before Saddam came to power, was richer than Portugal or Malaysia. Today it is impoverished, with 60 per cent. of its population dependent on food aid. Thousands of children die needlessly every year from lack of food and medicine. Four million people out of a population of just over 20 million are living in exile.

The brutality of the repression – the death and torture camps, the barbaric prisons for political opponents, the routine beatings for anyone or their families suspected of disloyalty – is well documented. Just last week, someone slandering Saddam was tied to a lamp post in a street in Baghdad, their tongue was cut out, and they were mutilated and left to bleed to death as a warning to others. I recall a few weeks ago talking to an Iraqi exile and saying to her that I understood how grim it must be under the lash of Saddam. 'But you don't', she replied. 'You cannot. You do not know what it is like to live in perpetual fear.' And she is right. We take our freedom for granted. But imagine what it must be like not to be able to speak or discuss or debate or even question the society you live in. To see friends and family taken away and never daring to complain. To suffer the humility of failing courage in face of pitiless terror. That is how the Iraqi people live. Leave Saddam in place, and the blunt truth is that that is how they will continue to be forced to live.

We must face the consequences of the actions that we advocate. For those of us who support the course that I am advocating, that means all the dangers of war. But for others who are opposed to this course, it means – let us be clear – that for the Iraqi people, whose only true hope lies in the removal of Saddam, the darkness will simply close back over. They will be left under his rule, without any possibility of liberation – not from us, not from anyone.

Glenda Jackson, one of Blair's bitterest Labour critics, tried twice to intervene – but Blair, now approaching his peroration, did not give way.

This is the choice before us. If this House now demands that at this moment, faced with this threat from this regime, British troops are pulled back, that we turn away at the point of reckoning – this is what it means – what then? What will Saddam feel? He will feel strengthened beyond measure. What will the other states that tyrannise their people, the terrorists who threaten our existence, take from that? They will take it that the will confronting them is decaying and feeble. Who will celebrate and who will weep if we take our troops back from the Gulf now?

If our plea is for America to work with others, to be good as well as powerful allies, will our retreat make it multilateralist, or will it not rather be the biggest impulse to unilateralism that we could possibly imagine? What then of the United Nations, and of the future of Iraq and the Middle East peace process, devoid of our influence and stripped of our insistence?

The House wanted this discussion before conflict. That was a legitimate demand. It has it, and these are the choices. In this dilemma, no choice is perfect, no choice is ideal, but on this decision hangs the fate of many things: of whether we summon the strength to recognise the global challenge of the twenty-first century, and meet it; of the Iraqi people, groaning under years of dictatorship; of our armed forces, brave men and women of whom we can feel proud, and whose morale is high and whose purpose is clear; of the institutions and alliances that will shape our world for years to come. To retreat now, I believe, would put at hazard all that we hold dearest. To turn the United Nations back into a talking shop; to stifle the first steps of progress in the Middle East; to leave the Iraqi people to the mercy of events over which we would have relinquished all power to influence for the better; to tell our allies that at the very moment of action, at the very moment when they need our determination, Britain faltered: I will not be party to such a course.

This is not the time to falter. This is the time not just for this Government – or, indeed, for this Prime Minister – but for this House to give a lead: to show that we will stand up for what we know to be right; to show that we will confront the tyrannies and dictatorships and terrorists who put our way of life at risk; to show, at the moment of decision, that we have the courage to do the right thing.

Blair's supporters gave him an ovation to match the one the anti-war camp had given Robin Cook for his resignation statement the day before. Even so, 139 Labour MPs voted against the government – one of the biggest rebellions in parliamentary history.

Events have demonstrated that Iraq did not have stockpiles of weapons of mass destruction. But Tony Blair remains unrepentant in his belief that the war was justified. Whatever the judgement of history, or the electorate, this was the definitive speech of his career.

'His victims were taken from dark and overcrowded cells to the execution block that had ceiling hooks and levers that catapulted them to a grizzly death in the pits below.'

Ann Clwyd reminds opponents of the invasion of Iraq of the horrors of Saddam Hussein's regime: 16 July 2003

Ann Clwyd might have been expected to oppose the invasion of Iraq in 2003. She is on the left and she sits amongst the 'usual suspect' left-wing MPs who have been the most vociferous opponents of the invasion. Instead, she supported the removal of Saddam and his Ba'athist dictatorship on human rights grounds. While others focused on the failure to find the weapons of mass destruction on which the case for the invasion had been based, she toured Iraq as Tony Blair's special human rights envoy, visiting the mass graves, the prisons and the torture chambers.

In this speech, which deserves comparison with Llin Golding's recitation of the horrors of Buchenwald, she was heard in appalled silence as she detailed crimes of the defeated dictator. She began by recounting her membership of a series of organisations which had campaigned against human rights abuses in Iraq, before moving on to the issue of the gas attack on the Kurdish town of Halabja – perhaps the most notorious of Saddam's war crimes.

I N 1988, HALABJA TOOK place. No one took any notice of what we had said in 1987. This country continued to sell arms to the Iraqi regime and to deal with members of the regime as though they were honourable people – of course they were not. In 1988, I also took a group of women from the House of Commons to visit some of the survivors of Halabja in a London hospital.

At the beginning of this year – the last time that I spoke to the House about my visits to Iraq – the Kurds took me to the area of the country between Chamchamal and the road to Kirkuk, which was the dividing area between Saddam's Iraq and the Kurdish part of Iraq. The Kurds pointed to rockets on the hillside. They believed that chemical and biological warheads were to be fired in their direction. They were so convinced of that that they asked me to ask our Prime Minister to provide them with protective suits. I made that point to the Prime Minister and in the Chamber on my return. The Kurds contacted me several times during the following weeks to ask when they would receive the protection. They were close to everything that was going on and had their own intelligence. They sincerely believed that chemical and biological warheads existed, although I do not know whether they did or not.

I did not make an argument about weapons of mass destruction. I argued that we needed to take action in Iraq for humanitarian reasons. When I spoke in March about the plastic shredder that was used to kill in one of Saddam's prisons, I never imagined that only a month ago in Baghdad – after the war – I would read in a chillingly meticulous record that one of the methods of execution in Saddam's prisons was mincing – that was the translation from the Arabic. I had finished a press conference at the British embassy in Baghdad when a person from Fox television asked me to take a dossier that the company had been given that was an account of methods of execution. I read some of the methods outlined in the 56 pages – they were horrific.

The Abu Ghraib prison is the largest in Iraq. Since the early 1980s, I have read about executions that took place there and methods used by the regime to deal with its opponents in the prison. I visited the prison in the company of the Americans. When we reached the gate, it was locked, and the people inside refused to open it until they had received instructions from a higher military commander. We stood around for some time talking to children who were playing around the prison. The prison could house up to 75,000 people. The total prison population of this country is about 75,000, so those people could be contained in that prison alone. The fifteen- and sixteen-year-old boys who were playing around the prison had been guards there. They told us that only one day before the Americans arrived at the prison, the remaining prisoners had been killed. They had been stood in trenches up their waists and shot through the head.

There are murals of Saddam Hussein on the corridors of the prison, which is gruesome beyond imagination. The murals show Saddam with a hawk on his shoulder, Saddam with a rocket launcher with a dove in its barrel and Saddam in a silk shirt with a cigar. His victims were taken from dark and overcrowded cells to the execution block that had ceiling hooks and levers that catapulted them to a grizzly death in the pits below. Some remained alive, so the guards broke their necks by standing on them. The United Nations could have continued passing resolutions for the next 50 years and sending inspectors and reporters into Iraq, but in the end, despite my reservations, there was no realistic alternative to war.

When I was in Iraq, the people on the streets to whom I talked were irritated because the debate on weapons of mass destruction was raging here at the time. When I asked them what they thought about the weapons, they were amazed that anyone was talking about them at all. They said, 'Don't they care about us? Don't they care about the mass graves? Don't they care about the torture?' I assured them that we did care about all those things but that people were nevertheless worried about weapons of mass destruction.

This brought her fellow left-winger Tam Dalyell, who opposed the invasion of Iraq, to his feet to ask why attacks on American troops in Baghdad were increasing.

It is lamentable; my hon. friend is right. But he must know some of the reasons for that. An Iraqi friend in this country, who had a brother in the Iraqi army for 35 years to whom he had spoken recently on the telephone, was told that people are being offered $600 a head for shooting at American soldiers. Of course, my hon. friend must know that there are also the remnants of the regime – the remnants of the Ba'ath party who have so much to lose because the regime has gone, and the *fedayeen* who fought for Saddam. There are also extremists. For all those reasons, there is still insecurity in the country.

For people to feel secure in Iraq now, it is imperative that they know that Saddam Hussein is either dead or arrested. They need to know that his two terrible sons are either dead or arrested. That is necessary because people feel insecure. When I spoke to people on the streets, they said, and this is no exaggeration, 'Thanks to Bush and Blair.' That was said to me many times. Sometimes I would ask a man a question and he would turn his head away. When I asked why he was doing that, I was told, 'He thinks that the Ba'athists are still watching him, and if they come back into power, he will get into trouble.' That is the level of concern that the people still feel.

I say to my hon. friend: stand at the mass grave at al-Hillah, where between 10,000 and 15,000 people are buried, hands tied behind their backs, bullets through their brains. Look at the pitiful possessions on the ground that the forensic scientists are going through – a watch, a faded ID card, a comb, a bit of cloth. Watch an old woman in her black chador, with tattoos on her hands, looking through the plastic bags on top of the unidentified bodies that have been placed back in the graves for something to help her to find her son. Stand at the mass grave near Kirkuk. Look at the skeletons now tenderly reburied in simple wooden coffins. Talk to Nasir al-Hussein, who was only twelve at the time of the 1991 mass arrests. He, his mother, uncle and cousins were piled on to buses, and then the executions started down a farm road in the middle of the country. People were thrown into a pit, machine-gunned and buried with a bulldozer. Nasir crawled out of the mass grave, leaving his dead relatives behind.

The killing fields of al-Hillah and Kirkuk are unremarkable, but here are some of the hundreds of thousands of the perhaps 1.5 million dead or missing in Iraq. Saddam's victims were the Shi'as, the Kurds and the communists – the people of Iraq. Now the secrets of that evil and despotic regime are being revealed. How much more killing might there have been? My hon. friends may carry on about weapons of mass destruction, but I think that the action that we took was the right one, and I will always defend it.

Ann Clwyd was elected Chairman of the Parliamentary Labour Party – a key link between the leadership and the Commons rank and file – after the 2005 general election.

Five
CULTURE WARS

THE BRITAIN OF the 1950s and early 1960s seems like another country to those used to the permissive liberal social mores of the twenty-first century: murderers were hanged; prisoners were birched; a Palace official, the Lord Chamberlain, pored over the scripts of plays to be performed in the London theatre, excising references to sex and homosexuality, to guard the morals of the nation. Abortion was illegal; *Lady Chatterley's Lover* was obscene. But a series of epic parliamentary campaigns transformed the moral climate of the nation.

Forty years on, the battlefield has shifted. The sight of an openly gay man serving as master of a hunt and battling against the criminalisation of hunting with hounds epitomises the shift in the cultural battlefield over the last 60 years. Once, homosexuality, if revealed, would end a political career and possibly result in criminal prosecution – the young Tory minister Ian Harvey, caught in a bush with a guardsman in 1958, resigned from Parliament within days.[1] (He was succeeded in the Foreign Office by John Profumo.) Now, the Commons includes a number of gay and lesbian MPs, and a gay MP, Alan Duncan, has sought the leadership of the Conservative Party.

Cultural issues continue to exercise Parliament. The tortuous battle to ban hunting was fought through the first two Parliaments of the Blair administration, as was the marginally less protracted struggle to equalise the age of consent for homosexual acts. There is continuing debate over the decriminalisation of cannabis; the time limits for abortion are likely to be revisited; and the huge moral issues raised by new medical and genetic technologies look certain to prompt more parliamentary heart-searching.

In the Lords and Commons these are generally not party issues: most Labour MPs favoured a ban on hunting, but several, like the former Minister for Sport Kate Hoey, argued against it, as did the Labour peer Lady Mallalieu, whose speech appears in this chapter; most Conservatives opposed the ban, but the otherwise impeccably high-Tory Ann Widdecombe delivered a rumbustious speech in favour. The Labour MP Leo Abse was one of the foremost campaigners for the legalisation of homosexual acts in the 1960s, but was vehemently opposed to the legalisation of abortion. Reactions to such

issues are often the result of deeply felt personal and religious convictions –
rather than the more usual calculations of personal and political advantage.
And those reactions do not necessarily fall into convenient ideological
packages. This chapter collects speeches by some of the major players in our
post-1945 culture clashes, including the more recent, like hunting and gay
adoption.

'Wipe this dark stain from our Statute Book for ever.'

Sydney Silverman debates the death penalty: 16 February 1956

No single MP did more to secure the abolition of capital punishment in Britain than the irascible Labour left-winger, Sydney Silverman. An MP for 35 years, he waged a decades-long parliamentary campaign, bringing endless amendments and private members' bills, before winning a proposal for a trial abolition for five years, in 1965.

Perhaps only a parliamentary loner could have campaigned with such dedication when hanging retained firm public support. Silverman was certainly that. He did not work well with others, and his explosive temper made him enemies. But he was a master of Commons procedure and delighted in tying the House into knots with a well-aimed point of order. 'Oft-times his insistence would gradually erode the confidence of the House and, as his logic dented the seemingly self-evident proposition, the whole Chamber would be thrown into a mood of self-doubt,' wrote his fellow abolitionist, Leo Abse.[2]

A tiny figure, Silverman sat on the front bench below the gangway, the traditional haunt of Labour troublemakers. His feet dangled above the floor, once leading an irritated Churchill to observe, after an intervention in one of his speeches, that 'the hon. gentleman has hopped off his perch'. The Conservative veteran Sir Peter Tapsell did not regard him as a great orator, 'but he was a very interesting speaker who made his arguments with great clarity – and he was not a bore, as some parliamentary obsessives are.'[3]

This speech came when the Conservative government was forced to revisit the whole question of capital punishment after a series of controversial cases. The previous year, Home Secretary Gwilym Lloyd George (son of David Lloyd George, who had migrated into the Conservative Party after the break-up of the Liberals between the wars), had refused to reprieve Ruth Ellis, the last woman to be hanged in Britain. There was also great public disquiet over the hanging of Timothy Evans in 1950 for the murder of his wife. Three years later John Christie, who had shared a house with Evans, was convicted of a series of murders – and it was universally assumed that he had framed Evans to protect himself.

I WOULD NOT SAY THAT the debate has been free from emotion. I hope that this subject will never be debated or discussed without some emotion. If murder is a unique crime, the death penalty is a unique penalty, and it would not be human if the House or any other assembly were able to advocate the retention of the death penalty, or to advocate its abolition, without a proper feeling for the deeply moral issues that must inevitably be involved in deciding this question one way or the other. Let it not be thought, as is sometimes thought, that all the emotion, indeed all the sentimentality, is one way.

It is just as much a sentiment, and by no means an unworthy one, to say, as some people do say, that the principal retribution demands that one who designedly takes away the life of another shall forfeit his own, as it is a sentiment to say that the sanctity of life is better served, better honoured and better furthered in refusing to do to the criminal what the criminal himself has done. Society should refuse to adapt its standards to the standards of the crime it wishes to eradicate.

I have taken part in too many of these debates to feel it possible to advance anything very new. Indeed, though I believe most sincerely what I have said about the level of today's debate, I do not think anyone would commend it in the first place for its originality, because the truth of the matter is that there are very few arguments either way on this issue, that most of us know them all, and that we have made our own individual assessments where in the end the balance of argument lies, and are unlikely at the end of this debate, after all the debates we have so far had, to be shaken by arguments now. Therefore, I propose not to deal with the abstract merits of the proposal that capital punishment should be retained, or that capital punishment should be abolished.

It is no longer a question of defining our faith; it is a question of deciding what we propose to do. It is not a problem of belief any longer; it is a problem of action. Looking as fairly as one may at the whole picture to see whether there is action on which the House could agree, I think it is fair to say that one can derive one or two propositions that would be acceptable to almost everyone who has taken part in the debate.

The first is that, so far as I know, there is no hon. member of this House who believes that the present state of the law is satisfactory. We are unanimously agreed that there should be some change. What is unsatisfactory about the law? I am not dealing now with the general principles that lead some of us to say. 'Away with it anyhow,' and lead others to say, 'No, we ought to retain it.' I am dealing with what may be thought to be common ground. The unsatisfactoriness of the present law, I think it would be unanimously accepted, is that by it we impose the same penalty – and that the ultimate penalty in our power – for everything that the law calls murder.

There is, I think, another proposition that would be almost universally accepted in this House. It is that nobody likes the death penalty any more than

anyone likes murder. There is no hon. member of this House – I venture to
think – who would not rejoice if he felt that he could honestly and
conscientiously vote for the abolition of the death penalty without doing harm
to the principle of the sanctity of human life or the ultimate purposes of
society. We unanimously agree that we must change the law. We must get rid
of the death penalty if we can do it without doing more harm than that we
cure. I think those two propositions would be accepted.

I think there is a third that is not universally accepted, but which might
commend itself to many. There are, as we all know, deep feelings engaged on
both sides. Those who accept both the propositions that I have advanced so far
divide in the end into two classes – those who say, 'Amend the law, yes, but you
cannot and ought not to abolish the death penalty altogether; there are some
murders for which you ought to keep it,' and those who say that the risks
involved, the difficulties involved, in applying any such solution as that are so
great that it is better to abolish the death penalty altogether.

Here Silverman traced 90 years of parliamentary debate on the death penalty.
He described how a Royal Commission in 1886 recommended making a
distinction between degrees of murder, so that some carried the death
penalty and others did not, and recounted how the 1948 Commons vote
calling for a five-year suspension of the death penalty, was rejected by the
House of Lords. This led to the establishment of a new Royal Commission to
find a compromise solution, acceptable to both Houses.

I take it that that is why the then Prime Minister withheld from the Royal
Commission the right to consider whether or not in principle the death
penalty should be abolished or retained. The Commission was given these
terms of reference:

'. . . We have deemed it expedient that a Commission should forthwith issue
to consider and report whether liability under the criminal law in Great Britain
to suffer capital punishment for murder should be limited or modified, and if
so, to what extent and by what means . . .'

The right hon. and learned member for Chertsey [Sir Lionel Heald, a former
Conservative Attorney General who had chaired a committee of the Inns of
Court Conservative and Unionist Society which had urged reform, but not
abolition of capital punishment] and some of his hon. friends have produced
another attempt, about which I hope to say a few words in a moment, but that
was done recently and quickly.

That brought a protest from a member of Heald's committee, William Rees-Davies, the Conservative MP for Thanet North, who said that they had studied the issue through the whole of the previous summer and autumn.

I am perfectly certain that the work was done seriously, responsibly and conscientiously and with a genuine desire to help, but I am dealing with the Royal Commission, which did not sit for one year but for four years. It was the most influential and experienced committee it was possible to get together. It took an enormous amount of evidence in this country. It went abroad to all other countries where any such experiment had been tried and took evidence on the spot in all those countries. I will not deal with all its recommendations – some 40 of them – but, with three somewhat paltry exceptions, if I may be forgiven for so describing them, the Government at the end of four years' study by the Commission and two years' study by themselves have rejected all the recommendations.

What did the Commission say about this attempt to find a compromise? It said: 'We began our inquiry with the determination to make every effort to see whether we could succeed where so many have failed, and discover some effective method of classifying murders so as to confine the death penalty to the more heinous. Where degrees of murder have been introduced, they have undoubtedly resulted in limiting the application of capital punishment, and for this reason they have commended themselves to public opinion, but in our view their advantages are far outweighed by the theoretical and practical objections which we have described. We conclude with regret that the object of our quest, that is a compromise, is chimerical and that it must be abandoned.'

In advising us still to proceed with an attempt to find an acceptable and workable compromise, the Government are inviting us to set aside, to reject, to ignore, the advice of the most powerful and influential Commission which had considered the matter with a desire to find such a compromise, if one was to be found.

I do not think that I have said anything with which any reasonable person can so far disagree. The right hon. and learned member for Chertsey and his hon. friends have made another attempt. I have read their pamphlet. One of their number was kind enough to send me a copy. I read it with great care. It is not put forward as a compromise. The Home Secretary adopted its three main proposals. The Home Secretary put that forward as a compromise in his speech today, but the right hon. and learned member for Chertsey and his hon.

friends did not offer it to us as a compromise. They said, quite frankly, candidly and honestly, 'This has nothing whatever to do with the law of capital punishment. We want the law of murder altered because the law of murder is anomalous.' That is what they say. They would equally want it altered, because it is anomalous, whether we retain the death penalty or abolish it. I am sure that I am right about that. Therefore, it has nothing whatever to do with our discussion today.

Rees-Davies intervened again to suggest that the best approach was to remove the anomalies and then consider whether the death penalty should be retained – that, he said, was the logical way forward.

That is not the logical order. From the point of view of lawyers, these anomalies are of the greatest possible interest and importance, but so far as the death penalty is concerned they are important only because the death penalty exists, and they will remain of importance only for so long as it exists.

There would be no difficulty whatever, without altering the law at all, in giving effect to the distinctions which the hon. member wishes to draw, if only the court were not hidebound from the start by the necessity to impose the death penalty wherever a verdict of guilty of murder is found by a jury. That is the trouble.

We could give administrative responsibility – provocation by words, provocation by blows, constructive malice – and the judge who was free to fit the penalty to the crime could give effect to all those without altering the law of murder. Therefore, the hon. gentleman, in my humble opinion, is wrong when he says that is the logical order. It is not the logical order. The other is the logical order. If we must have an order at all let us deal with first things first.

In the end the question which the House of Commons has to decide tonight will not be answered out of the law books and the legal precedents. It will not be answered by statistics. It will not be answered by fine distinctions, nuances of legal or penal theory. In the end, it is a great moral issue which the House of Commons has to decide tonight.

I could not follow one part of the very interesting speech made by the hon. baronet the member for Hendon South [the Tory grandee, Sir Hugh Lucas-Tooth]. The hon. gentleman said, and I agree, that if we can prove that with the death penalty there are fewer murders than without it, then the death penalty is justified. That is what he said; that I agree with. He went on to say, 'You cannot prove that with the death penalty there are fewer murders than without it.' There, too, I agree; but when he said, 'Therefore, I shall vote to retain the death penalty,' I thought that was a complete non sequitur and that he ought to have drawn exactly the opposite conclusion.

The onus surely is not on those who wish to abolish the death penalty. The onus is on those who wish to retain it. Every jury is told, 'Do not convict this man if you have a reasonable doubt of his guilt.' We are entitled to say to the House of Commons, 'Do not retain the death penalty if you have a reasonable doubt of its effectiveness.' Surely that is right. If there are those hon. or right hon. members in the House tonight who are left in doubt at the end of the argument; if they are not sure, if they feel that the argument rests, in the end, on a fine balance and cannot conscientiously decide for themselves where it comes down, I beg of them, 'Do not, by your votes, or by neglecting to vote, continue a penalty which in your hearts you know you cannot hold to on the evidence that would be necessary.'

Finally, over and above and beyond all these arguments about deterrence, about retribution, about the state of the law and about the onus of proof, there remains in all our minds, does there not, this fear that from time to time, at 8 o'clock or 9 o'clock in the morning, we take an innocent man out of a cell and break his neck?

I feel sure that many votes in 1948 were swayed by the assurances of Sir John Anderson[4] and of Sir David Maxwell Fyfe[5] that there was no reasonable practicability of an innocent man being convicted. Then, within two years, Timothy John Evans was hanged. The worst thing about the death penalty is that it can persuade a highly intelligent, responsible, conscientious, human man like the present Home Secretary, to convince himself – because he dare not believe the contrary – that Timothy John Evans was guilty, as charged, of the crime for which he was executed. Does the right hon. and gallant gentleman really believe now, in the state of the evidence, that there is no scintilla of doubt?

I conclude by saying that we have a free vote tonight and we are grateful to the Government for letting us have it, but a free vote imposes heavy responsibilities on each one of us. We cannot shelter behind party loyalties. We cannot shelter behind group opinions, behind the prestige of Governments or parties or Ministers or anyone else. We have to come to our own honest, intelligent, conscientious judgment, and vote as we believe to be right. I say to the House of Commons: let us as free men, free women, free Members of Parliament in a free society, go forward and wipe this dark stain from our Statute Book for ever.

'No innocent man has been hanged within living memory.'

Rab Butler rejects abolition of the death penalty: 16 February 1956

Rab Butler, then Leader of the Commons and Lord Privy Seal, was a classic establishment politician – a subtle, creative, stealthy public servant. He was also, as Roy Jenkins pointed out, famous for not becoming Prime Minister. He had at least three opportunities: when Churchill suffered a stroke and Eden was incapacitated and he was the acting Prime Minister for some months; when Eden fell in the wake of Suez; and when Macmillan, who seized that moment, departed in 1963. Each time his inhibitions overrode his ambitions. But he remained an indispensable servant of the state. At the time of this speech he was Leader of the Commons, and had just caused a stir with a marvellously elliptical comment that Anthony Eden was 'the best Prime Minister we have'.

He was put up to finesse this awkward debate, and made a superbly judged winding-up speech, which offered no retreat on the principle of the death penalty, although it did include what – in the light of the Evans–Christie case – even then looked to be an extraordinary assertion about the infallibility of the courts. The government sensed a tide of intellectual opinion against the death penalty, but feared getting too far ahead of wider public opinion. His objective was to open up the prospect of reform of the law on murder, without foreclosing the option of capital punishment. 'You felt there was another side to the issue which he understood very well, but he was putting the Government case and his colleagues were not all that bright,' the veteran Conservative Sir Peter Tapsell observed on Butler's style in a series of debates on 'social reform' issues.[6] On this occasion, he began by insisting that, although the government did have a definite view that hanging should not be abolished, it believed the Commons should have a free vote on the issue.

THE RECENT HISTORY was referred to by the hon. member for Nelson and Colne [Sydney Silverman], who made a very temperate and reasoned speech. The recent debates, which took place in 1948, are still probably fresh in the minds of many hon. members and the Report of the Royal Commission, which sat for four years and more, is a singularly impressive document to which all hon. members should pay the utmost attention. I do not, however, accept the gloss on the Royal Commission's Report put by the hon. member for Nelson and Colne. I believe that the Royal Commission's recommendations include certain reforms to which my right hon. and gallant

friend the Home Secretary referred. In the opening part of my remarks I wish
to make a short reference to the lines upon which the Government propose
that the law should be amended.

We believe that a chance of amending the law does lie here, although, as I
shall show, the issue tonight is whether to abolish or not to abolish the death
penalty. I do not wish to shirk that issue; I think that I should be dishonourable
if I did so. But I claim that attention should be given to some of the
amendments, because I believe that they will create improvements which will
make things a little better than they were before.

First, I should like to dispose of another argument of the hon. member for
Nelson and Colne. We are not attempting in this case to define degrees of murder,
nor are we attempting, as was done unsuccessfully by the Administration in 1948,
to define crimes. I need not tire the House with a recitation of the history of those
attempts – but they were unsuccessful, and I accept the hon. member's view that
any such attempt is impossible. I do not see that it can be done.

I think, therefore, that at this hour of night the House must face squarely up
to the position that there are certain alterations in the law which can be made,
but that the main issue is whether we do or do not retain the penalty of death.
It is in that spirit that we can look at some of the amendments proposed.

Although I am not a lawyer, I believe that I have legal antecedents, and therefore am not too simple in these matters, and I have tried to put into ordinary
simple language the forms of amendment which we have in mind. The first
respect in which we propose to amend the law is in regard to the doctrine of
constructive malice. It is called by the Americans 'felony murder,' which
explains it more simply than the rather elaborate phrase of 'constructive malice.'

In essence, this doctrine prescribes – I quote the Report of the Royal
Commission: 'that, where death is caused in the commission of a felony
involving violence, a lesser degree of violence may justify a verdict of murder
than would be necessary in other circumstances . . .'

If, as I hope, the House passes the Motion and gives us the opportunity to
amend the law in this respect, we propose to bring forward amendments in the
law of constructive malice.

I am aware that proposals have been made to do away with this doctrine
altogether. I am also aware that my right hon. and learned friend the member
for Chertsey and his friends proposed that reservations should be made in the
case where death was caused 'by a firearm, explosive (or other dangerous
weapon) and the person charged was either himself armed with the weapon . . .
or acting in concert with a person so armed . . . and was aware that the said

person was so armed.'

That is a matter upon which I can give no final Government ruling tonight. I undertake only that we shall bring forward proposals to amend the law of constructive malice in as broad and satisfactory a manner as we can effectively do, and I ask the House to await our proposals.

The second amendment which we propose to make in the law of murder relates to provocation. To put this in simple language for the benefit of hon. members, a killing which would otherwise be murder may amount only to manslaughter if done in response to such provocation as might cause a reasonable man to lose his self-control. For a good many years, however, it has been held that provocation by words alone was not sufficient to reduce murder to manslaughter. It is in this respect – while retaining the definition of the 'reasonable man', according to the Report of the Royal Commission, and taking its advice upon this technical aspect of the subject – that we propose to amend the law relating to provocation.

The third main amendment relates to suicide pacts. At present, the survivor of any pact between two people to commit suicide is guilty of murder. The Royal Commission considered that if the survivor had himself killed the other person he should remain guilty of murder, but that if had only aided, abetted or instigated the other person's suicide without actually killing him he should be guilty only of that offence and not of murder. The Government accept that recommendation, and that will be another feature of the amendments which we shall bring forward.

The last main amendment – putting it as simply and shortly as I can – relates to the Scottish doctrine and practice of diminished responsibility. The Royal Commission referred to this doctrine of diminished responsibility in the following words:

'. . . where the jury are satisfied that a person charged with murder, though not insane, suffered from mental weakness or abnormality bordering on insanity to such an extent that his responsibility was substantially diminished, the crime may be reduced from murder to culpable homicide.'

Silverman intervened to ask how these proposals would have affected three famous murder cases. Would they mean that Heath, Haigh and Christie would have been reprieved but that Ruth Ellis – the last woman to be executed in Britain, for the murder of her lover – would still have been hanged. Neville Heath was hanged in 1946 for two murders involving sexual abuse of women; John George Haigh became known as the 'acid bath murderer', because he disposed of the bodies of his victims in this way. He confessed to six murders and claimed to have drunk the blood of one victim – but his confessions were so sensational that they were considered an attempt to establish insanity; John Christie was hanged in 1953 for the Rillington Place murders – at least seven women were murdered by Christie, who secreted their bodies at 10 Rillington Place. Christie framed his neighbour Timothy Evans for two of the killings – of Evans's wife and child. Evans was hanged, but evidence later emerged that Christie was in fact the killer. This was one of the most serious miscarriages of justice in British legal history, and the case did much to strengthen the campaign against the death penalty. Butler declined to get bogged down in the detail of particular cases.

I had decided before I began to answer that I could not give *obiter dicta* on individual cases – I think that that would be most unwise – but I will take up the controversy which I read as between Professor Goodhart and my right hon. and learned friend the member for Chertsey in *The Times* newspaper. There, Professor Goodhart,[7] speaking of the consequences of our amendment, says:

> The strange result of this amendment, if it were conscientiously followed by juries, would be that such a person as Christie, who, obviously was so abnormal as to be bordering on insanity, would not be executed, while more normal persons, such as Mrs Ellis, would be hanged.

I go on to read what my right hon. and learned friend the member for Chertsey says in reply:

> One would have thought that, far from being strange, this would be exactly the result that the man in the street would expect from a sensible law.

In any case, I do not think that such an Amendment would lead to any malpractices or to any great injustice. In supporting the side of my right hon. and learned friend in that controversy I should like to say that it would be very difficult to translate this practice into English law if only for one reason: in Scotland the jury act by majority. If we can achieve it we will achieve it, and that will be one of the amendments that we shall bring forward.

The object in general will be so to amend the law as to avoid the sentence of death being passed on a man or a woman, followed by the awful agonising wait for the possibility of reprieve and the terrible procedure which we all know is associated with the passing of the death penalty. Apart from that, we are not avoiding the issue whether there should or should not be capital punishment.

I now come to this main issue. First, I must deal quite frankly with the problem only touched upon by the hon. member for Nelson and Colne, namely, the case of Timothy John Evans. I do not propose to go into any individual case, but I will take up what has been said in the debate because I believe that hon. members are inclined to base their judgment on the question whether innocent people are in fact being hanged and they are liable to decide their vote tonight on the basis that in fact innocent men and perhaps women are hanged, and that therefore the death penalty must be removed.

I know this will create controversy, but I say it quite frankly and firmly: so far as I can ascertain from consulting the Home Secretary, his predecessor, and all the authorities whom I can consult, no innocent man has been hanged within living memory. I say that with a due sense of responsibility, and hon. members can make up their own minds, but I say it after consultation, and with the purpose of enabling hon. members to have a basis on which to decide.

I further say that the Prerogative under which the Home Secretary tenders his advice exists to see whether there are any mitigating circumstances which would justify a reprieve in proper circumstances where the death sentence has been pronounced. In particular, we do not accept that there was a miscarriage of justice either in the case of Evans or in the case of Rowland. I think it right to say that, because it is our view that it may help one or two hon. members to reach a decision apart from individual cases, and on the merits of the issue.

Our judgment should not be based on the erroneous belief that innocent men have been hanged. We should reflect that we have the best judicial system, I think, of any country of the world, and when we come to decide this question of the death penalty we should decide it not in an emotional state of mind but entirely on the moral issue as it affects our own minds.

In this connection I come to the reference to public opinion which was made by the right hon. member for Lewisham South. The right hon. gentleman indicated, with a nose for smelling out what is going to happen which is unparalleled in political life, that public opinion was coming along and that we must therefore gallop ahead of it. My opinion is that that is not the way that executive Government should behave about the death penalty. I say nothing derogatory about the right hon. gentleman's nose.

There have been reforms throughout history. If Wilberforce were here with many of our predecessors in the great realm of social reform, they might say that there was a greater indication today of public interest in the abolition of the death penalty, but as I see the situation, the position is not at present ripe, in the view of authority, for an amendment in the law to abolish the death penalty.

Before I come to my concluding reasons for that, I want to examine and reject the Amendment moved by right hon. and hon. gentlemen opposite. I do not believe that an Amendment which involves a suspension is the right way to deal with this matter. I would rather come to a final decision than suspend the death penalty and have it reviewed again.

Let us come back to the question of capital punishment – retention or not. Before I give the figures and the reasons which make the Government finally conclude that we are not prepared to recommend the abolition of the death penalty, I want hon. members to examine a little more closely than has been done in this debate what is the alternative. The alternative frankly, which I do not believe many hon. members have asked themselves, is what they would do with those murderers who, though not insane, could not possibly be allowed their liberty until they were too old and enfeebled to constitute any danger to the community.

I think that what some hon. members fear is the sense of finality in the process of hanging. What is the alternative? The alternative is, not a quick death, but a slow death and a lingering execution. Instead of the fear of finality there is certainty of an excruciating uncertainty which – and I quote from one of our most prominent experts on this subject – might 'permanently impair something more precious than the life of the physical body.'

When Dr Methven, who was Deputy Chairman of the Prison Commissioners, gave evidence before the Royal Commission, he drew special attention to the fact that it was the hope of release, ever present in every prisoner's mind, which kept that prisoner going and alive. If hon. members decide to abolish the death penalty and, to use the phrase of the right hon. member for Lewisham South, the view that imprisonment is a good deterrent is accepted by the House, hon. members will have to square their consciences to accepting something which many of us feel is infinitely more cruel than capital punishment itself. I do not necessarily expect hon. members to agree with me, but I do expect them to listen to the consequences which Dr Methven and many other specialists considered would be the result of abolishing capital punishment and introducing another deterrent.

My last remarks are in relation to the prevalence of crime. The figures were given by the Home Secretary, and I must say that I support what the right hon. member for South Shields said in 1948, a copy of which I have here, when he said that in view of the offences, statistics and indications of crime at that date he could not recommend the abolition of the death penalty. I understand why he has now changed his mind, but the figures indicate now, especially in relation to sexual offences and to crimes of violence, that there is not a decline and that the position is disquieting.

Under the circumstances, the Government cannot recommend that they would be doing their duty to our citizens if they were to abolish the death penalty at the present time. The Government have a very serious responsibility. They have a responsibility for the sanctity of human personal life, and that is where the

264

Christian ethic comes in. They also have a responsibility for society. I am not going to quote the Christian ethic in support of the Government's case. I am a Christian myself, and I believe in the retention of the death penalty. I say, at the same time, that my duty to society makes me say that under present circumstances it would be unwise for this House, without waiting for the amendments the Government suggests, to abolish the penalty of death for murder.

The Commons eventually voted against hanging, by a very small majority, when, as Harold Macmillan recorded in his diaries,[8] 'about 30–40 of our chaps (mostly young) voted for abolition'. As Leader of the House, Butler provided debating time for Silverman, who put an abolition bill before the Commons. This won a third reading by a narrow majority, but was defeated in the Lords.

Butler later became Home Secretary and wrote in his memoirs[9] of the 'hideous responsibility' which fell on the holder of that office to review all capital cases and advise on whether the royal prerogative of mercy should be exercised. 'On my desk in the Home Secretary's massively dreary room, Sir John Simon had placed a grisly text reminding himself and his successors of their duty in considering a capital sentence,' he wrote. 'I had this removed immediately, even though there were several years of such decisions before me.' He gradually became convinced that the system could not continue, and in 1957 he produced the Homicide Act, a compromise measure which retained the death penalty, but incorporated many of the features he set out in this speech.

Such was the BBC's sensitivity to any appearance of comment creeping into its parliamentary reporting, that when Conrad Voss Bark, one of its political correspondents, reported that the then Home Secretary had given a 'non-committal reply' to a question about the Evans case, he was reprimanded. Voss Bark took his script to Butler, who thought it was fair comment and said he had intended to be non-committal.[10] The incident helped persuade BBC editors that they could trust their correspondents – a little.

Silverman did eventually get his way, in the process influencing young Conservative MPs like William Whitelaw and Bernard Weatherill to change their minds on the efficacy of hanging. He finally passed a private member's bill to abolish hanging (for murder, it remained on the statute book as the penalty for treason for some years) for a five-year trial period – in 1965. He died in 1968, before it was completely done away with in the following year. He had become very frail and died a few weeks after he stubbornly returned to the chamber after collapsing from an apparent stroke, while making a point of order. His seat was defended – unsuccessfully – by the future Speaker of the House Betty Boothroyd.

'To those people who are . . . irreconcilable in their opposition to this Measure, I . . . hope that they will thank God each day of their lives that they do not belong to this 5 per cent of people who are exclusively attracted to their own sex.'

Humphry Berkeley seeks to legalise homosexuality: 11 February 1966

In the climate of the early 1960s, it was an act of considerable bravery for a single male MP – especially a Conservative one – to introduce a bill to legalise homosexual acts. And in the case of Humphry Berkeley it proved politically fatal. But Berkeley probably rather enjoyed the risk, and the affront he gave to crabbed old backbenchers of vast seniority and neolithic views. His failure to show proper respect to the fathers of the party was already legendary even before he introduced his private member's bill – he once told Sir Reginald Manningham-Buller (inevitably and appropriately spoonerised into Bullying-Manner), the Attorney General under Macmillan, to seek competent legal advice, a barb still recounted with awe 40 years later. He was also one of the handful of backbench dissidents who declined to support Macmillan after the Profumo debate.

His campaign on homosexuality was quite consciously modelled on Sydney Silverman's epic battle to abolish hanging, which Berkeley enthusiastically supported. His constituency party in Lancaster was already restive about that, but when he won a high place in the 1965 ballot for the chance to introduce a private member's bill, he declared it would be cowardly of him not to pursue homosexual law reform.

'He did not lack judgement, but caution,' recalled a close contemporary, the Conservative Sir Peter Tapsell. 'He always thought he would not live long, because he had terrible asthma. That gave him a curious fatalism.' His prospects for success were much improved, however, by the arrival of Roy Jenkins at the Home Office. Jenkins supported the verdict of the Wolfenden Committee on homosexual offences and prostitution, which recommended decriminalising homosexual acts.

Jenkins persuaded the government to give more debating time to a number of private members' bills which chimed with his liberal agenda, including Berkeley's, thus protecting them against the time-wasting tactics which are normally deployed against controversial private members' bills.

Berkeley, who was himself discreetly gay, first traced the history of previous attempts to reform the law, pointing out that the main grounds for opposition to reform advanced by two Home Secretaries – Rab Butler and Henry Brooke

– was that the time was not ripe, and that Parliament should not get too far ahead of public opinion.

Lthough I am not greatly enamoured of public opinion polls, and I think that Members of Parliament of all people should not be mesmerised by them, it is worth noting that in recent months a Gallup poll and National Opinion poll have been taken on whether the public believe that a change in the law on the lines of the Wolfenden proposals is desirable.

Curiously enough, in both cases, 63 per cent of those who were polled supported a change in the law along the lines of the Wolfenden proposals, which are the lines upon which this Bill has been based. Those who object to this Bill merely on the grounds that public opinion is not yet ready for a change in the law may wish to reconsider their attitude in the light of these polls which have recently been published.

Before the Wolfenden Committee produced its Report in 1957, there was a great deal of ignorance in this country about homosexuality, both about its causes and its prevalence and nature. A great deal more knowledge has become available to the public and hon. members about this subject. Whereas ten or fifteen years ago most of us could have been properly excused for thinking that homosexuality was a practice carried on by people of unusually perverted morals who had the alternative of leading perfectly normal heterosexual lives but who deliberately chose a more vicious way of life as a matter of preference, this is now something in which it is no longer possible for us to believe in the light of the immense amount of evidence that has become available.

One of the facts which all of us should bear in mind is that, although estimates are difficult to make with precise accuracy, it is generally believed that there are something like 5 per cent of the male population who are exclusively homosexual in their desires. That is, there are approximately 5 per cent of the males of this country who have normal sexual urges who are attracted solely and exclusively towards members of their own sex.

This provides us with evidence which many of us would have lacked ten or fifteen years ago. It makes it clear that homosexuals have a choice. Anybody who suggests that they do not have a choice is wrong; but their choice is a harsh one, sterner and more brutal than many people imagine. The basic choice which they have is whether to be chaste or to commit homosexual acts. They do not have the choice, for the most part, of whether they should commit homosexual or heterosexual acts. This I believe to be absolutely fundamental in our thinking about the law on this subject.

The second point which we should consider is this. On the evidence available, the vast number of homosexuals who were subjected to interviews to prepare the material for this book passionately wanted to be heterosexual and disliked intensely their own physical condition. As far as one can see from the evidence, it seems likely that their condition was in-born rather than the result of corruption, and the degree of proselytisation about which we have heard so much appears to have been greatly over-estimated.

Those of us in the House who are practising members of the Christian faith – and I regard myself as one – are faced with something of a problem. All of us who are Christians, and probably many who are not, regard homosexual acts as morally wrong. On the other hand, all of us who are Christians, and many others, equally must have a feeling of compassion and justice for a minority of the population who find themselves in a condition for which they have no responsibility. It is important for us to recognise that it is not a crime in this country to be a homosexual. It is a crime in this country to commit homosexual acts, and nobody has suggested – and, as far as I know, none of the opponents of the Bill has suggested – that homosexuals are responsible for their condition.

Let us see what the law as it stands does. If it is accepted that, say, 5 per cent of the males in this country are in a homosexual condition for which they have no responsibility, if it is accepted that homosexuals are likely to be as highly sexed in terms of desire as heterosexuals, we are giving this 5 per cent, who, let us face it, amount to about one million people, a stark choice; either they are chaste for their entire adult life, or they commit a single indiscretion and become criminals and liable to prosecution. We should recognise that this is what the law does and says.

One of the other interesting facets of the information now available to us is that it removes what must have been a very prevalent view among most people who were ignorant about homosexuality, namely, that the average homosexual had a preference for young boys. As far as I can judge on the evidence which I have looked at, there is absolutely no evidence to show that homosexuals are more likely to be attracted by or to assault juveniles than heterosexuals. It is extremely important for us to recognise this point. I will come to the question of penalties, particularly in relation to minors, later. I believe that our sense of justice and compassion to a sizeable element in our population means a change in the law is desirable.

Here, Berkeley estimated that millions of homosexual acts took place in Britain every year, and only a tiny proportion of these resulted in prosecution, which meant the law was being enforced in an entirely arbitrary way. He did not want to see an end to prosecutions for acts which took place in public places, involved minors or constituted assault. But there were 100 or so prosecutions a year for offences which either involved consenting adults in private, or which had occurred a long time before.

It seems to me, therefore, that we have to make up our minds whether we believe it to be right and just that people should be prosecuted in private as consenting male adults. I do not believe that we can shirk this issue by simply saying that there is not much point in changing the law because very few of them are prosecuted. If that is the case, the law is bad; and if the law is bad, it must be changed. In terms of the public good, enforceability is an essential.

The second point, which is far more horrifying, is the question of blackmail. It is easy to exaggerate both the amount of blackmail that homosexual offences arouse and, secondly, the amount of mitigation in terms of blackmail that a reform in the law would bring about. I have been interested to note, in my very large correspondence since my intention to publish the Bill became known, that a sizeable number of people who have written to me, most of whom, for obvious reasons, have been anonymous, have told me that they are victims of blackmail and that they are frightened to go to the police because they are not sure, if they go to the police, whether they will be able to prefer a charge against a blackmailer or whether the police will turn upon them and prosecute them for their offence.

It can be argued – and it was argued in another place – that the great fear of somebody who is being blackmailed is social disgrace and that homosexual acts, even though they may cease to be a crime, will still be regarded by most people as being morally reprehensible. This I accept. It is true.

What a change in the law would do, however, is this. If in future after the law has been changed a man is blackmailed, he will not hesitate to go to the police and the blackmailer will immediately be apprehended. If a prosecution takes place, the man who is being blackmailed, as is always the case in blackmail charges, will appear in court as Mr X. His identity will not become known and he will not be subject to prosecution by the police because he has not committed a criminal act. Therefore, although, obviously, one cannot eliminate blackmail or even, perhaps, reduce it as substantially as we would all like to see it reduced, this is bound to have an effect in reducing the element of blackmail in homosexual cases, which I believe to be one of the most unpleasant features of the state of law in relation to homosexuality. Those, it seems to me, are the basic arguments in favour of a reform in the law.

Basically, there are two principles behind the Bill. The first is that homosexual acts between consenting adults in private should no longer be subject to criminal penalties. The second, which is, perhaps, an amplification of the first, is that the age of consent should, we believe, be fixed at the age of 21.

We also decided that if buggery remained a criminal offence when committed between consenting adults in private, the unenforceability of the law would remain and the invasion of privacy, which is basically one's objection to the Labouchere Amendment,[11] would not in any way be diminished. For these two reasons we decided to follow precisely the Wolfenden Recommendations on this point.

This matter was discussed at great length in another place. It was pointed out by both Lord Dilhorne and Lord Kilmuir[12] that, unlike other homosexual practices which have been criminal for only a short period of time – within the lifetime of many people alive today that of buggery had been a crime for hundreds of years, dating from the Middle Ages and perhaps earlier. Until Tudor times at least it was an ecclesiastical crime, and came before the ecclesiastical courts. Were we to have ecclesiastical courts in 1966 buggery would not be a crime because the Churches, every one of them, in Britain are overwhelmingly in favour of amending the law on the lines of the Wolfenden proposals. [Interruption.]

One should ponder on a state of affairs when a secular society, which is what we are, takes a harsher view in terms of morality than the Church itself. In medieval times the Church took a harsher view, and that is why buggery became an ecclesiastical crime.

Here, in response to interventions from supporters and opponents, Berkeley listed the large number of church bodies supporting either the Wolfenden recommendations or his bill. That brought the Conservative Kenneth Lewis to his feet to suggest that while the Church and the bishops in the House of Lords had come out in favour of a change in the law, they had reserved their position on the question of whether particular cases were sins, as distinct from crimes. Berkeley took the point head on.

They have not reserved their position. They have made it perfectly clear that it is not only a sin but a great sin. Nobody disputes that. Half the trouble for the position in which we find ourselves today is that at times we find sin and crime confused with each other. One of the objects of the Bill is to cease to make these offences a crime, while recognising, as all Christians must, that they are grave sins. I hope that the House will now understand why the sponsors of the Measure have decided to follow the Wolfenden recommendations in relation to buggery.

The age of 21 as the age of consent is something to which we attach a great deal of importance. If, as would appear to be the case, the homosexual condition is a form of emotional retardedness, people who are vulnerable to pressures during adolescence must be protected. It is in some ways illogical that the age of consent for girls should be sixteen and that it is perfectly legal to corrupt a young girl into female homosexual practices at the age of sixteen while for men the age of consent should be 21.

However, we feel that the age of consent for men should remain at 21, for two reasons. The first is because adolescence is a period of emotional instability and, therefore, protection should be given. The second is that whatever one may feel about the unpleasant nature of the physical acts involved, looking at the problem of homosexuality as a whole we see that it is the appalling emotional loneliness and frustration which leads to so many mental breakdowns. That is something for which we should offer all the protection society can to adolescents.

I have, I fear, spoken at great length, but this is a problem of some complexity. I have attempted to outline what I believe to be the motives of those of us who promote the Bill, and the reasons why it is socially desirable. I recognise, of course, that there are many people who are sincerely and honestly opposed to this Bill, and who believe that it would have disastrous consequences. To those people who are, as it were, irreconcilable in their opposition to this Measure, I would say that I hope that they will thank God each day of their lives that they do not belong to this 5 per cent of people who are exclusively attracted to their own sex, and who have, as far as we know, a normal sex urge.

I hope that opponents of the Bill will reflect on the fact that those who have voluntarily undertaken to lead lives of chastity – ordained priests and monks – as opposed to being compelled to do so by the present law – and I talk about celibates who may have heterosexual or homosexual inclinations; those who have taken this vow – are strongly in favour of a reform in the law. The reason why they are, perhaps, in favour of a reform in the law is that they know from their own experience as men of God that prayer, meditation, and the aid of the Sacraments to resist strong temptation are required in order to lead a life of absolute chastity from the start of the adult state until the grave. We should remember that this Measure is supported by people like that.

I should also like to say to those people who are hoping that this Measure will go through that I can well recognise that there may be people who are far more suitable than myself to promote the Bill – I wish we could have found as promoter a father of nineteen children – but I can say that I believe that the time for a change in the law is ripe, and that, having secured so favourable a position in the Ballot, it was my duty to introduce the Bill.

I was brought up by my father, who was himself a member of this House,[13] which he loved, to believe that being a Member of Parliament was one of the greatest honours one could have bestowed on one. But he also taught me that it was the duty of an MP to do what he thought was right regardless of the consequences to himself. In that mood, I commend this Bill to the House.

Berkeley secured a second reading for his bill by 164 to 107 votes. His supporter Leo Abse suspected his eloquence would get him at least that far, but questioned whether he had the diplomatic skills to negotiate it through a committee stage. He never had a chance to find out. The bill fell when Parliament was dissolved for the 1966 general election, and Berkeley lost his seat. His constituency party might have tolerated an MP who was an enthusiastic supporter of abolition of the death penalty, or of homosexual law reform – but they could not stomach someone who was both. After his defeat he found that no Conservative Constituency Party would adopt him as a parliamentary candidate.

He did, however, have a lasting impact on the Conservative Party, when, after Harold Macmillan had been succeeded by Alec Douglas-Home, he persuaded the new leader to abolish the informal 'magic circle' system of soundings under which he himself had been chosen, and replace it with election by MPs. Twenty-five years later, the detailed requirements for a majority under the Berkeley Rules played an important part in the fall of Margaret Thatcher.

Berkeley himself later drifted into the Labour Party and the SDP.

'We want to stamp out the back-street abortions, but it is not the intention of the Promoters of the Bill to leave a wide-open door for abortion on request.'

David Steel seeks to legalise abortion: 1967

David Steel's Medical Termination of Pregnancy Bill remains one of the landmark 'permissive society' reforms of the 1960s. It replaced a tangled web of case law with an act that allowed much wider access to abortion. As a relatively new member from a small party, sitting for a marginal constituency, the decision to introduce such a controversial bill was a considerable risk for Steel, but, having come third in the annual ballot for private members' bills, giving him the prospect of enough debating time to change the law, he did not want to waste the opportunity on some trivial measure. The bill encountered strong opposition from several quarters, and Steel was careful to cite the support for reform from various church reports, as well as from medical and pressure groups. He also witnessed an abortion, to see at first hand what medical termination of a pregnancy actually meant.

He began this speech, opening the second reading debate, by complaining that 'conscience' issues of this kind were not taken up by governments, but left to the vagaries of the private members' bill system. And he summarised the existing state of the law, which rested on the prohibition in the Offences Against the Person Act 1861 against the 'administering of any poison or noxious thing or the unlawful use of any instrument with intent to procure a miscarriage'.

THERE ARE FOUR DIFFERENT methods by which, at present, a woman may obtain an abortion. The first is under the present law, uncertain as it is. Each year, either under the National Health Service or through private practice, a number of women obtain terminations of their pregnancies within the terms of the present law. But even this is not satisfactory, because the likelihood of any woman, in any given situation, being able to obtain a termination of her pregnancy is to a large extent dependent on where she happens to live and upon the practice of hospitals and medical practitioners in her area.

The other three means are all illegal. The second is to obtain an abortion by some self-inflicted means. As far as we are able to discover from the investigations made into this subject, this is far and away the largest section of illegal abortions; indeed, the number of attempted abortions – so far as surveys have been able to discover – is far higher than those which are actually attained.

The other two categories comprise abortions carried out by other persons, by a friend or someone anxious to help a neighbour, perhaps – or by someone for cash without any particularly persuasive motives. These in many respects are the most dangerous. They have led to the highest number of admissions to hospital following unsatisfactory operations carried out sometimes in the most appalling circumstances.

The fourth category comprises those which are illegal but have a covering of legality, those where the patient, because of her financial circumstances, is able to find or be directed to medical practitioners or psychiatrists who will sign the necessary certificates to cover the existing law on payment of a fee of perhaps 100 or 200 guineas and have the operation carried out in adequate circumstances. This is limited, of course, to those with the means to pay the substantial fees involved. Any law which means one law for the rich and another for the poor is in itself unsatisfactory and should be examined.

Estimates of the number of illegal operations carried out each year vary tremendously. I should not like to assert any particular figure, but a recent survey carried out and published only last week by the National Opinion Polls on behalf of the Abortion Law Reform Association assessed that, at a minimum, about 40,000 abortions took place each year. Some estimates made by people who have studied this subject go as high as 200,000. I would not settle for any definite figure, but it is probably somewhere between 40,000 and 200,000 a year.

Steel traced the growing agitation for a change in the law, which was interrupted by the Second World War. He then set out a list of grounds on which abortion would be permitted: where the pregnancy posed a threat to the physical or mental health of the mother – principles already enshrined in case law – or where the child was likely to be born with a serious handicap. This brought him to the most controversial part of the bill.

Subsection (1,c) refers to the pregnant woman's capacity as a mother being severely overstrained by the care of a child or of another child. We here come to the more controversial matter contained in the Bill. This is known, for the sake of brevity, as the 'social' Clause. There is great argument as to whether we ought to try to write into the Bill a 'social' Clause, trying to define the circumstances in which doctors would be justified in carrying out a termination of pregnancy rather than leaving it to the wider interpretation of 'risk to physical or mental health.'

It is important we should dwell on this matter for a moment.

One could say that it would be better to drop subsection (1,c) altogether and leave the continued operation of the law based solely on the definition of physical or mental health which any doctor may choose to make. But to do this is to leave too great an uncertainty still in the law. It would leave open far too much the interpretation of the law by medical practitioners and would place too great a responsibility on them.

If we in Parliament decide that we want cases of severe social hardship to be considered, we ought to say so. We ought not to demand of the medical profession that they should slip these in under a general Clause relating to physical and mental health.

An alternative way of doing it, although possibly slightly dubious, would be to leave it out and to put in another interpretation of the word 'health'. An alternative which was suggested was that if one takes the definition of 'health' contained in the World Health Organisation's constitution, that is so worded as to include, as it does, social well-being, so that the cases which we have in mind could be covered. But, again, that is not as satisfactory as being absolutely clear what we mean. Paragraph (c) may not be as well worded as many hon. members would wish.

Paragraph (d) is perhaps the most difficult paragraph in legal terms. It refers to a pregnant woman being a defective or becoming pregnant while under the age of sixteen or becoming pregnant as a result of rape. I believe that all these should be put together in one category. I find it difficult to understand the distinction between, for example, the case of a girl under sixteen and a case of rape. In fact, in Scots law if one omitted the reference to a girl under sixteen, she would in any case be covered by the reference to rape, because intercourse with a girl under sixteen is rape in Scots law. I believe that both of these should go into one category and that we should look at the category closely.

Most hon. members would agree that to have a woman continue with a pregnancy which she did not wish to conceive, or in respect of which she was incapable of expressing her wish to conceive, is a practice which we deplore, but the difficulty is to find an acceptable wording which will enable termination to be carried out following sexual offences of this kind but which does not allow an open gate for the pretence of sexual offences. I have tried to cater for this in subsection (4), but it may be that it is a difficulty. I believe that the Committee dealing with the Bill must look very closely at the whole question to see whether the wording of the Bill can be improved.

The difficulty in drafting a Bill of this kind is to decide how and where to draw the line. We want to stamp out the back-street abortions, but it is not the intention of the promoters of the bill to leave a wide-open door for abortion on request.

I am reminded of one case, in particular, which shows the need for reform of this kind. It was a case outlined by Alice Jenkins in her book *Law for the Rich*. She was approached by her domestic help about a friend who was living with her husband and two very young children in two rooms of a tenement. The only medical advice she was given was that she should have the third child and then learn to practise birth control. She was in very squalid economic conditions and Alice Jenkins was unable to do anything more for her or to give her any further advice. She writes:

> Little did I foresee what she would actually do. A few days later she was taken to hospital in a high state of delirium and died the next day. Soon after, two detectives visited my home to find out what I knew of the case, and, before leaving, were kind enough to ask if I should be interested to attend the inquiry. Several days later, in the coroner's court, the widower said in the witness box that he had not known that his wife was pregnant . . . Later, the pathologist stated that he had examined the deceased, who had died from acute septicaemia brought on by the use of a kitchen utensil . . . which had pierced the wall of the uterus. And the doctor's voice continued, 'There was no pregnancy'.

The effect of bringing the matter into the open and enabling the family doctor to be consulted would, I believe, prevent tragedies of this kind.

In conclusion, I want to deal with two opposite views on the Bill. The first is the attitude of the Roman Catholic Church. I entirely respect the doctrine and beliefs of that Church in this matter, but I would point out that the doctrine of the Church is not necessarily permanent. We are seeing now the possibility of a great change in the attitude of the Catholic Church to the whole question of contraception which would have been unthinkable 20 or 30 years ago. My respect for the Catholic position on this question is occasionally dented by references to euthanasia and other matters which are in no way connected with the Bill.

There is also nothing in the Bill which compels a Catholic patient or a Catholic doctor to be in any way involved in the termination of a pregnancy, and there is also a clear statement in the Bill that nothing in the Bill affects the protection afforded by the law to the viable foetus. I would also point out to the Catholic objectors that public opinion in the Catholic Church is not necessarily behind the doctrine of their own Church and that the surveys carried out show that among Catholics some 57 to 60 per cent, depending on which survey we take, believe that the law should be reformed. Indeed, the most recent survey, to which I have referred throughout my speech, shows that of those women who had had abortions, the percentage who were Catholics was very comparable with the percentage of all those interviewed.

The devoutly Catholic Conservative MP Norman St John-Stevas intervened to suggest it would be extremely rash to draw any conclusion from such surveys without knowing how they decided what constituted a Catholic. Steel was not impressed by that argument.

The definition of 'Catholic' is, of course, open to the person answering the interview. I would not vouch for any greater accuracy than that. I would not even stand by the complete accuracy of these figures, although I have read the surveys repeatedly and believe them to be as accurate as any can be.

All I am suggesting to those who, like the hon. member, belong to the Roman Catholic Church is that they do not necessarily speak for the entire membership of that Church, although they speak for its doctrine. I have had a mountain of correspondence on this subject, including several letters from Catholics. I remember one in particular from a Catholic, who wrote to me that she was a devout and practising Catholic and that in the course of her family life she had had five natural miscarriages and simply could not accept the doctrine of her church that on each occasion some form of human soul had been destroyed. I believe that, despite the genuinely-held beliefs of the Catholic Church, Catholics would not wish to impose their own view of this matter on those who do not agree with them. That is one view at one end of the scale.

The other is the view which has been expressed, and which some hon. members have indicated will be expressed, that the Bill does not go far enough for them and that abortion should be entirely a matter for the woman concerned to decide and that it should be open to all. Again, I respect that view and it has equal force of logic with the Roman Catholic view. It has been tried in some countries. I cannot support that decision, and I do not agree with Mr Paul Ferris, who has done a great deal of valuable work on this subject, when he says in his book that he hopes that the time will come when the whole question of abortion will be regarded in the same unemotional light as a tonsillectomy. I cannot accept that. This is an entirely different gradation of subject with which we are dealing, but again I respect that point of view. As I said earlier, what we have to do is to try to find a balance of judgment between one extreme and the other in the wording of the Bill.

Finally, those who wish to oppose the Bill have to consider the effect of their opposition. If they were opposing the Bill because they could devise some other means by which abortions would stop tomorrow and by which there would be no unwanted pregnancies and none of the tide of human misery which is developed by our uncertain state of the law, then they would have a strong case. But, as the Home Office statistics show, over the last few years an average of some 25 to 30 women have died as a result of complications following illegal abortions. Many more have been cluttering up hospital beds with the treatment required following these operations. Many lives have been lost through suicide following conditions in which it was impossible to obtain an abortion, or in which abortion was in some way involved.

I will give two instances reported in the press in May this year. In one a 27-year-old house surgeon was sentenced to four years' imprisonment in Liverpool for being an accessory before the fact of the manslaughter of his 20-year-old student nurse girl friend. She had had an illegal operation which had been performed by another doctor who later committed suicide. In a case reported in the *Evening Standard,* a 24-year-old woman was found dying in a North London street, after having had an abortion:

> ' She was the victim of a classic case of back-street butchery' a coroner said today. After hearing from police that they had been unable to find out where the abortion took place, the St Pancras coroner said: 'We are up against a blank wall of unwillingness to know and unwillingness to talk.'

Hard cases, as we are always told, make bad law, but a multiplication of bad cases reveal a very bad state of the law.

The Report of the Social and Moral Welfare Board of the Church of Scotland quotes a German theologian as stating that human life in every form is sacrosanct but that we have to ask ourselves what the quantitative item of sacrosanctity may be attached to each form of life – the ovum fertilised, the moving embryo, the born child and the mother. He said:

> A paper thin wall separates us from sacrilege – all such decisions can be made only under saving grace – such dangers always go with freedom. Those who want to avoid the dangers do so only by setting up a rigid dogma . . . So there is obviously no perfect solution. The decision has to be taken in the light of God's understanding of our human frailty.

It is in that spirit that I have approached the drafting of the Bill, and I hope that the House will give it a Second Reading.

Steel won the vote, but this was merely the first skirmish in a long attritional legislative process, which lasted nearly a year. The government was officially neutral toward the bill, but eventually showed its hand by providing extra debating time. It came into force in 1968.

'I have coached patients to say to the doctor, when asking for a termination, that they are desperate and are thinking of suicide.'

Dr David Owen calls for abortion to be permitted on 'social' grounds: 22 June 1966

The central issue in David Steel's Medical Termination of Pregnancy Bill was whether abortion should be permitted on 'social' as well as strict medical grounds – for example if the woman could not stand the strain of bringing up a child. Dr David Owen, a newly arrived Labour MP, and future Health Minister, had no doubt that it should.

In this speech, during the committee stage of consideration of the bill, the point at which a group of MPs are delegated to sift through the detailed wording, he detected a possible attempt to fudge the issue by means of amendments which replaced paragraph (c) of the original bill. The crucial point was the removal of the 'well-being' of the mother as one of the grounds for an abortion. This was a vital issue for Owen because he wanted a clause which specifically allowed abortion on 'social' grounds, rather than one which left patients to rely on the judgement and conscience of a particular doctor. He preferred the defeat of a bill including such a clause to the passage of one without it. He was not convinced that the new wording was sufficient. To make his point, he outlined the kind of cases where a social clause might apply, and courted controversy by describing how, in his previous medical career, he had coached women on what they had to say to the medical authorities to get round the existing law and obtain an abortion.

The speech is notable both for its description of iniquities of the pre-reform abortion laws, and for the early foretaste it gives of the fraught relationship which later developed between the 'two Davids' – Steel and Owen – when they headed the two parties of the SDP–Liberal Alliance in the mid 1980s. Twenty years after this speech, Owen was demanding a clear and unambiguous commitment to keep Britain's nuclear deterrent and Steel was arguing for a compromise.

I THINK THIS IS A SUBJECT on which there is considerable confusion, which I believe has come from this new and major Amendment. While I would not in any way impute the motives of the hon. member for Roxburgh, Selkirk and Peebles [David Steel] I do question his judgment in putting down this major Amendment to a Bill which has passed through the House of Lords in all its stages, and which was given an overwhelming vote of confidence by the House of Commons on Second Reading.

Though I understand his motives, he must surely realise that those motives have largely been misinterpreted. I would like to give him some idea of the headlines:

'A climb-down by MPs campaigning for the reform,' said *Scottish Daily Mail.*

'The critics of Mr David Steel's Abortion Bill . . . have won the day', said the Glasgow *Herald.*

'Substantial changes,' *Birmingham Mail.*

'Out go "offending abortion clauses",' *Medical News.*

This is very important, because we are dealing with confused case law at the moment, and this Bill has to clear up the confusion that exists in doctors' minds at present.

The Liberal MP Dr Michael Winstanley[14] thought that those who saw the change as a capitulation and were misinterpreting paragraph (c). In his view, Steel was clarifying his original intent, not moving away from his principles. Owen thought further consideration was needed.

That may be his motive. I am saying the interpretation put on the Amendment was quite clear, therefore I think it has to be faced. Before I would consider voting in any way for this new and major Amendment I would want a much more clear-cut statement from the sponsor of the Bill that this was not his intention. He said in his speech today it did incorporate paragraph (c), but I would want this to be given great publicity, that he does not consider this a climb down and this is put down for the purpose of elucidating the situation. If that is so we would have to determine in this Committee whether it does elucidate it. Paragraph (a), as at present drafted, is not sufficient to make me prepared to see (c) fall.

It is interesting to compare the new Amendment with the suggested wording of the Law Society and British Academy of Forensic Sciences which is quite excellent. I would be quite happy if the clauses they suggest were in the Bill. They say:

'Likely to damage the physical or mental health of the pregnant woman or the future well-being of herself and/or the child.'

That crucial wording is not, I believe, present in the Amendment, and unless it is put in it means that paragraph (c) is not covered.

To give two examples: a psychotic mother whose own health might be affected is not covered, someone at present in mental imbalance, simple minded, just in balance, just coping with the present family and environment – we all know these cases exist and genuine medical opinion feels that adding to that family will push her off into imbalance. This is a difficult judgment, but this is the sort of case I would like to see covered explicitly.

The former Conservative Attorney General Sir John Hobson wondered why Owen thought this was not covered by the wording on mental well-being. Owen retorted that there should be specific wording to cover the risk to life or health. 'Physical or mental,' reiterated Hobson. Owen continued without missing a beat:

– or well-being. One could say her own health will not be affected, but I would like this to be much more clearly stated.

This has come out from this debate more clearly than on previous occasions. There is considerable confusion on this. In fact I think the right hon. and learned gentleman the member for Warwick and Leamington [Sir John Hobson] on Second Reading said he thought paragraph (a) just came within present case law and had his support, though he expressed reservations about paragraphs (c) and (d). I think there is need to clarify the case law, and I want a social clause.

I would like to take up some remarks made by the hon. member for Essex South-East [Bernard Braine]. He speaks often as one of the official spokesmen on health for the Opposition, but what he said today has to my mind made a complex situation even more difficult, and I am in complete confusion as to what he wants. At one stage he said he considered 'well-being' should not be in the Bill. The point of using the word 'well-being' is that this more than anything else covers the social clause.

Braine, a future Father of the House, who opposed abortion throughout his long parliamentary career (he brought in a bill in 1978 which sought to cut the abortion time limit from 28 weeks after conception to 20 weeks), intervened to argue that the word 'health' was sufficiently precise. Doctors and lawyers knew what it meant, and it covered 'well-being', an imprecise word which he thought seemed to include something more than health. Owen leaped on his point.

I am grateful to the hon. member. This is the central point at issue. I do not want to speak in this Committee too much as a doctor. I do not think this has much validity. I am speaking basically as a Member of Parliament. Only a year ago I was working as a doctor, and what the hon. gentleman is saying is an example of what is often shown in the House, a complete lack of knowledge of what is going on outside. Only a short distance away I have coached patients to say to the doctor, when asking for a termination, that they are desperate and are thinking of suicide, because I know that doctors will not terminate pregnancy on social grounds. I have seen doctors themselves encourage patients to widen their case because they do not feel that social grounds are of themselves sufficient. There is a considerable body of opinion in this country which knows this is the case. I have had letters from doctors in which they have stated they did not consider social factors lay within the purview of a doctor. Other doctors are unhappy about taking social circumstances into consideration.

I know, Mr Chairman, you have said I should not refer to the Amendment that stands in my name to clarify the definition of health. The World Health Organisation thought it necessary to clarify what health is, and this is the central problem. If everybody thought the same as I do about health I would not wish this Bill to come into being at all. Doctors interpret this Bill and the word 'health' in different circumstances.

We all understand there are hon. gentlemen in this Committee, and a great many people outside, who are against this Bill on the grounds of religious belief and I respect that view greatly, and feel they have a perfect right to hold it. This will take a part in this Clause, but there is a much more central question which faces this Committee, that lies between those people who are not sure about the social clause – whether it should exist or to what extent it should exist.

My criticism of the hon. gentleman the member for Roxburgh, Selkirk and Peebles [David Steel] is that I detect a tendency to say, 'If we get through a Bill which is not quite clear we will carry the House with us'. I want a Bill that quite clearly lays down different criteria than existed previously. It may be we would be voted down, but I would prefer to see the Bill presented to the House honestly and voted down. I think public opinion wants this reform and the majority of medical opinion wants it also. I know the B.M.A. makes these statements, but they are balanced by the vast majority of medical opinion which does not make its views felt. It will be welcomed by general practitioners who are facing the problem day after day. It is easy for the consultant in hospital to be confronted with this question of social issues and make up his mind in isolation, but the general practitioner has to go into the home during the pregnancy and after the pregnancy and will be with the family when the children grow up. We have some evidence of individual letters written in to journals, and the great majority of general practitioners feel not only that the present law should be clarified but that social factors are an integral part of medicine and of health and should be considered in any decision.

Sir John Hobson intervened again. Did Owen think a doctor should be able to terminate a pregnancy for social and not health reasons, or was he only asking that social conditions should be taken into account in assessing the impact of continuation of pregnancy on the health of a woman? Owen replied that they should be taken into account, at which the anti-abortionist Bernard Braine said, 'Then we are not in conflict.' Owen was not so sure.

We are in conflict in our definition of health. If health is to be defined in terms of disease, in terms of illness and of complete mental breakdown, we are in conflict, because I believe, it is much more. I do not wish to draw attention to this clause, but I would go again to the definition of the World Health Organisation:

> A state of complete mental, physical and social well-being and not merely the absence of disease or infirmity.

This is crucial. I would like to see the medical profession confronted with this. The medical profession is moving more and more to the fact that a doctor should make his decision in consultation with the social worker who may have visited the family and weigh all these factors and not just consider it from the narrow definition which has previously been accepted. Medical education is making great advances. Most medical schools have a department of social medicine where all these factors are assessed.

We only have to read some of the statements that come from doctors to realise how narrowly they define health. That is an undesirable state of affairs. We have had doctors lending themselves to societies such as the Society for the Protection of the Unborn Child. I consider everybody has the right to put whatever pressure he likes on this Bill. It causes very great feelings. I try to reply to all the letters I get. This is something on which we should expect many differing views, but I think it is very poor when the medical profession lends itself to a society which is putting out an emotional appeal. They are talking about such issues as pain of the foetus. They know, as I know, that we do not know whether the foetus feels pain. It may be that one day we shall know, but we do not know now. To argue the case in those terms is, I think, undesirable, and tantamount to allowing the emotions which do exist underneath all this to well out, so that the Committee consideration of this Bill and the whole discussion of the Bill takes place in an undesirable atmosphere.

Let us be quite clear, however: those doctors who lend their support to that Society, and to some of the statements that have come out, do not consider that social factors take part in a definition of health that they are meant to decide, and they believe that such factors should be ruled out. We hear psychiatrists who tell us – and I have had this happen to me on occasions – that they will send back letters say[ing] that they do not care about how many children she's got; they are not interested in the fact that five of them are having to sleep in one bed; they do not consider that this is relevant to their making their decision on this issue; the fact that the husband has just left is not a factor.

I consider that these are factors and I would like to see this Committee face up to the issue so that in any framing of the Bill it is said that this must quite clearly be taken into account and we will not have doctors saying, 'We cannot do it for this reason because social grounds are not covered by the law'. If a doctor wishes to say, 'I do not consider social grounds as part of my medical ethics', that is fair enough, he is using his conscientious right to opt out of this decision, but he should tell the patient on what grounds he is doing it, and should let the patient know that it is on these grounds and these grounds alone that he is making the decision, that is, on purely physical and mental factors.

People say there is not confusion, but there is considerable confusion at the moment in the medical profession. Some people are frightened about the present case law. I am certainly not one of those people who think that we do not need to clarify it. I think that we do need to clarify the case law and that the present paragraph (a), not amended, does that extremely well.

I would like to see the sponsor of the Bill come clean with the Committee. What does he really want? Is he trying to get a Bill through which will be interpreted by those who want to interpret it one way, or is he trying to get a Bill through that shows quite clearly what are the grounds for terminating pregnancy? If he does that, I will support him and support the Bill through all its various stages.

'If one is going to say . . . that the streets of our country might one day run with blood . . . then surely one ought to consider whether . . . one's words are more likely to make that happen, or less likely to make that happen.'

Quintin Hogg denounces Enoch Powell's 'rivers of blood' speech: 23 April 1968

Enoch Powell's speech to a group of Conservatives in Birmingham on 20 April 1968 became one of the most controversial political orations of the century. He warned against immigration in apocalyptic terms: 'We must be mad, literally mad, as a nation to be permitting the annual inflow of some 50,000 dependants . . . It is like watching a nation busily engaged in heaping up its own funeral pyre.' Drawing on his classical scholarship he quoted from Virgil's *Aeneid*: 'As I look ahead, I am filled with foreboding; like the Roman, I seem to see "the River Tiber foaming with much blood".' He predicted that the new Race Relations Bill, which was due to come before the Commons within a few days, would be like throwing a match on gunpowder.

At the time Powell sat – albeit uncomfortably – in Edward Heath's shadow Cabinet as education spokesman. The etiquette of politics should have prevented him from intruding on the territory of his colleague Quintin Hogg, the shadow Home Secretary. Infuriated, Hogg vowed to resign if the speech was not denounced by the party leadership. He did not need to worry. Heath and his senior colleagues had had quite enough of Powell's freelancing interventions into policy areas not his own and the maverick was sacked. But that still left the question of what the party policy on race and immigration was.

In a lengthy speech on the second reading of the Race Relations Bill, most of which is not reproduced here, Hogg set out two guiding principles: that Britain was not 'noticeably underpopulated' and therefore required strict immigration controls, and that the immigrant population was here to stay, and had to be treated fairly.

He struck a delicate balance between a belief in complete racial equality and deep reservations about the efficacy of the legal remedies to discrimination proposed by the government. And he also took his chance to deliver a firm put-down to Powell, rejecting his argument, attacking the intemperate words in which it was expressed and accusing him of failing in his duty to consult colleagues.

WHAT WE HAVE TO learn is how to debate these contentious matters without losing our own tempers, or causing other people legitimate offence. I have laboured that more seriously than I have laboured any other part of the things that I have been trying to do. I really have. It is as much a part of my policy, and of the Conservative Party's policy, as the two more substantive principles which I have been trying to elaborate.

I said that I would have to speak about my right hon. friend's speech over the weekend. This is where I fall foul of my right hon. friend the member for Wolverhampton South-West [Enoch Powell]. I am bound to say so, for this reason. There is nobody that I admire more in this House than I do my right hon. friend. We have so much in common. We have the same love of Greek literature. We have the same devotion to the same political party. We have the same religion, the same religious beliefs. But if one is going to say – and this was my right hon. friend's analogy, not mine – that we are living in a roomful of gunpowder, and if one is going to say – and this was his analogy, not mine – that this Bill, which in many ways I think inappropriate, and which we have said in our Amendment will, on balance, do more harm than good – is like lighting a match to the gunpowder, it might be thought a little careless to go about with a lighted cigarette in one's mouth, flicking the ash all over the place. That is the modern equivalent to the mote and the beam, and the gnat and the camel.

If one is going to say, and goodness knows many of us have thought, that the streets of our country might one day run with blood – and make no mistake, it is usually the innocent, usually the defenceless, and sometimes just the ordinarily good, who are the victims of that kind of violence – then surely one ought to consider whether, in the more immediate future, one's words are more likely to make that happen, or less likely to make that happen.

It was not as if my right hon. friend did not know what the effect of his remarks would be. He did, because he said in terms that he could imagine the outcry he would cause. He did not come to me. He did not give me a sight of what he was going to say. He did not ask my advice, though, goodness knows, that advice is fallible enough. He summoned two television networks so that I could see him saying it. He sent a hand-out to the press, by-passing the Conservative Office. He said what he said without a word to any of his colleagues that he was going to say it.

With the utmost charity in the world, I am bound to say that this is not what I mean by loyalty to colleagues, even if there is no more serious charge to be levelled against him. If my right hon. friend the Leader of the Opposition had not anticipated it, I should have gone to the Shadow Cabinet yesterday and told my colleagues that they must choose between my approach and that of my right hon. friend the member for Wolverhampton South-West, because I attach every bit as much importance in this sphere to the way things are said as to what is said in them.

In this world we have got to be ready to take knocks. We have got to be prepared to be called 'limeys' and 'pommies'. Rude remarks are constantly being levelled at us. We must learn to bear them even if they are offensive. However, there comes a point at which things are dangerous. Then it rests for public opinion in this House, not to create a false unity which does not exist, or to paper over real differences, but to create a pattern in which controversy can take place in a civilised way, remembering that the purpose of controversy is to grow together by the discussion of differences and not, by accentuating differences, to grow further apart.

Powell never returned to the Tory front bench, although there were moments during Edward Heath's premiership when it seemed as if he looked like an alternative leader-in-waiting. Quintin Hogg never became Home Secretary; instead he returned to the Lords, to serve as Lord Chancellor under both Heath and Margaret Thatcher.

'I support the measure with all my heart.'

Matthew Parris comes out in the Commons, and nobody notices: 25 October 1982

Parliament has always contained a number of discreetly gay MPs, but in 1979, when Matthew Parris entered the Commons, an MP who was outed still faced public humiliation, tabloid condemnation and probable career termination, even if their activities were entirely within the law. The case of Jeremy Thorpe, in which an alleged conspiracy to murder seemed to take second place to luridly detailed descriptions of a gay relationship, and of Maureen Colquhoun, who was outed as a lesbian, hardly suggested a new age of sexual tolerance had dawned. It was still expected that bachelor Tories seeking selection for a winnable seat should warn the worthies of their local association to 'lock up their daughters'.

So when Matthew Parris rose, 'knees shaking', as he recorded in his memoirs,[15] to make this brief contribution to a debate on an order to legalise homosexual acts in Northern Ireland – where, rather anomalously, they had remained illegal until a judgement by the European Court of Human Rights – he was taking a considerable risk. Answering the debate, the Northern Ireland Secretary, James Prior, made kindly mention of his speech. Otherwise there was no reaction. One tabloid newspaper rang the next day, seeking clarification – which Parris did not provide. MPs may have realised what he said, but no one acknowledged it.

I WISH TO SPEAK ONLY briefly, and not on those constitutional issues on which other hon. members are more competent to speak than I. The subject of the order is adult male homosexuality in the last major part of this Kingdom where it is still outlawed. Seldom does so small a measure, debated in so short a time and brought at such a late hour, touch so deeply the lives of so many thousands of people in the United Kingdom. I do not believe that homosexuality is morally wrong or necessarily harmful, although I accept the fact that many hon. members think of it as an affliction. But surely we can all agree that it is an impractical interference in the privacy of adult life to brand such people as criminals, as we still do in Northern Ireland.

Hon. members luckier than I may find that personal conviction gives wings to their argument – the more powerfully they feel about an issue, the more powerfully they can speak. Unfortunately, that is not so in my case. I can happily argue the toss, but where I feel as deeply, strongly and personally as I do on this issue, argument altogether fails me. I support the measure with all my heart.

'A gentleman . . . who had taken grandly of wine and allowed *veritas* to overcome him went up to the Prime Minister and in words which I shall not use, told her that he had always fancied her.'

Nicholas Fairbairn opposes a law to ban kerb-crawling: 25 January 1985

The splendidly louche figure of Sir Nicholas Fairbairn, 'mad and brilliant and perpetually drunk', according to the Tory whip Gyles Brandreth,[16] could be relied upon to intervene in any Commons debate on sexual matters, usually in language at or beyond the extreme limit of parliamentary acceptability.

His private life was conducted in that dangerous zone as well. There were press reports in 1981 that a former lover had tried to hang herself from a lamp-post outside his London home, and his brief career as Solicitor-General for Scotland ended when he gave his justification for not pursuing a rape case to the *Glasgow Herald* before he was due to give it to MPs in a statement to the House. After a savaging in the Commons, he resigned.

He remained, though, one of the most brilliant advocates of his generation, and in this speech he turned his legal expertise against a private member's bill promoted by his Conservative colleague Janet Fookes, who was attempting to outlaw kerb-crawlers, whose pestering of women blighted parts of her Plymouth constituency.

A S A SCOTSMAN WHOSE constituents will not be affected by the Bill, I advance with caution and modesty into the chilly waters of the law of England, but with more bravery and courage having heard some of the abominable contradictions in the law of natural justice which I could not believe were characteristics of the law of England until they were confirmed by so honourable a source as the Minister himself.

My remarks about the Bill will perhaps be strident, but I pay tribute to the motive of my hon. friend the member for Plymouth, Drake [Janet Fookes], to her crusade and to the civilised way in which she has always treated matters criminal.

I am bound to say, as a lawyer and jurisprudent, that I am horrified that in England two policemen can tell the court what someone would have said if he had been called to give evidence. I trust that that provision will be removed from the law of England. I hope it is not proposed to convict a kerb crawler on the basis of a policeman's evidence that a woman told him that the man was kerb crawling. The policeman does not even need to meet that woman. The policeman can simply say, 'Mrs White came up to me and told me that so-and-so kerb-crawled.' That seems to be a good way for a policeman to get rid of a public nuisance. He may say, 'I shall tell you what we shall do. We shall do him for kerb crawling on our say-so.'

If that is the law of England, I trust that the Government, in their new legislation to introduce the independent prosecution system which we enjoy in Scotland, will include a clause to remove that offensive provision. That evidence is not even hearsay; it is soothsay. It is mystery evidence. I was horrified to learn that the Bill will enable a person to be convicted of an offence and cause the greatest possible harm on the say-so of witnesses who are not 'witnesses' in the proper sense of the word.

The meticulousness of the language is another issue that concerns me. According to clause 3, it is an offence for a man to solicit a woman for the purpose of prostitution. It is not, however, an offence for a woman to solicit a man. It is an offence if a man solicits from a motor vehicle in a street or public place. Complicated though that is, it is possibly comprehensible. Clause 1(1)(b) refers to a man soliciting 'while in the immediate vicinity of a motor vehicle that he has just got out of or off.'

I do not know of many people who get off motor vehicles, but I suppose that one gets off a bus. So that is fair enough: if I get out of my motor vehicle and go up to speak to a prostitute I commit a criminal offence.

That is extraordinary. I have no particular desire to get out of my motor car to speak to a prostitute because that is not a habit or recreation that is particularly attractive to me. Oddly enough, if a man goes up to a girl whom he believes is anxious for someone to sleep with her and asks whether she is willing to sleep with him, he is committing a criminal offence if he has just got out of a motor car.

However, it is not a criminal offence if the individual has not got out of his motor car. It is all right if he has just dropped in by parachute, come out of a drain or walked out of his house. That is all right, but he will be branded a naughty boy if he has just got out of his motor car. My goodness me, that is a naughty thing to do! That is the absurdity of the Bill. I wish to make it clear to my hon. friend the member for Drake that I am mocking statute law as a whole and not her. It is almost impossible to make criminal offences, especially trivial ones of the sort with which we are dealing, sensible in statute.

Clause 3 leads me to thank god that I am not English. The clause makes it an offence if a man solicits a woman for sexual purposes 'in a manner likely to cause her fear.'

I must tell my hon. friend the member for Drake that I have always been attracted to her. I have never actually dared ask her whether she would go to bed with me, but after the introduction of the Bill I must ask myself how I am to put it so that it does not cause her fear.

When I was the Solicitor General for Scotland in the palace of Holyrood House, I was in charge of events, as historically the Solicitor General for Scotland is, and in attendance on the Prime Minister who was a guest of the Lord High Commissioner of the Church of Scotland, who stands in for the Queen. The Solicitor General for Scotland has to be there in his shadow because a previous Lord High Commissioner tried to close down the Church of Scotland. I can see good reason to close down the Church of England, but that is another matter.

A gentleman who for reasons of chivalry I shall not mention but who occupied grand office and who had taken grandly of wine and allowed *veritas* to overcome him went up to the Prime Minister and in words which I shall not use told her that he had always fancied her, to which the Prime Minister replied, 'Quite right. You have very good taste, but I just don't think you would make it at the moment.' Would that have been an offence under clause 3? The answer is that it would. Therefore, I regard clause 3 as obnoxious in any possible character. It makes every advance of a man towards a woman a potential criminal offence. For example, let us suppose that a man marries a girl and on the night of their honeymoon says, 'What about going up to the bedroom?' If she shrinks back and asks, 'What do you mean?', the result would be an offence under clause 3.

Similarly, to make it an offence under clause 2 persistently to solicit a woman or women 'for the purposes of prostitution' has the ring of schizophrenia. Apparently, we are allowed to have prostitutes, but we are not allowed to ask them if they would be willing to act as prostitutes. Therefore, I find clause 2 to embody a most extraordinary concept.

I hope that I shall not pass through the thin legal skin on evidential matters of my hon. friend the Under-Secretary of State for the Home Department in referring to his silence. Am I right to understand that a crime of sodomy or buggery committed with a woman or a girl is not an offence known to the law of England? If it is an offence known to the law of England, why cannot it be charged as such? Why must it be dealt with as a charge of indecent assault? In Scotland, there is a range of common law sexual offences including indecent assault, lewd and libidinous practices, attempted rape and many others. I do not believe that it can be proved that if a man were to have anal intercourse with a girl of thirteen he would not be charged with serious assault and sodomy. If that is the law in England, the Bill does nothing to relieve it. If it is not, I find it impossible to conceive what the law of England is.

I strongly oppose fixed penalties, except perhaps for parking offences and the like, or terminal penalties. If the Poisons Act, say, provides a maximum penalty of fourteen years' imprisonment, is the judge to conclude that if the case involves half a poison the offence merits seven years? It is a bad principle and in my experience has no effect on offenders. When the judge says, 'I therefore sentence you to . . .', hesitates, coughs and finally comes out with the number of years, the defendant may get a shock, but that is the end of the matter.

If my hon. friend the member for Drake believes that people who commit minor sexual offences will be deterred by terrible penalties, I remind her of the Straffen case in England. Instead of being hanged for raping little children, the defendant was found insane and sent to Broadmoor. He then escaped and thereafter was declared sane on the basis that within 20 minutes of getting out he raped the first little child that he found. There was not much deterrent effect on him and I doubt whether there would be on anyone else.

I object strongly to the idea that so-called attempted rape should suddenly become liable to a sentence of life imprisonment. In Scotland, a sentence of up to life imprisonment is possible for any common law offence. If that is what the English want, they have only to reform their law in that way. A case has come into my hands just this week. I shall not go into details as it is *sub judice* and I have yet to defend the unfortunate gentleman concerned. It concerns a prostitute who had slept regularly over the years with a citizen whose respectability would allow him to sit in the civil servants box or even in your Chair, Mr Deputy Speaker. That man, without a smut on his reputation, has been charged with attempted rape by a woman with whom he has slept on and off for years. I believe that all criminal offences should be judged and sentenced on the facts and not on the basis of imaginary concepts framed in statute.

For all those reasons, although I applaud the purpose of my hon. friend the member for Drake, I believe that the method that she has chosen is so deficient as to be not just inequitable but positively bad.

It is universally assumed that the gentleman who went unnamed for reasons of chivalry was Fairbairn himself. Despite his speech, the bill did receive an unopposed second reading.

Fairbairn died in 1995.

'We have all been bombarded with St Paul and Leviticus, and we have been accused of joining the forces of Satan.'

Edwina Currie tries to legalise gay sex for sixteen-year-olds: 21 February 1994

Libertarian on personal behaviour as well as economics, Edwina Currie's views on sex were as unpopular within her own party as her views on Europe – as the interventions in this speech from her Conservative colleagues demonstrated. She had rushed in where other Tories feared to tread, proposing to lower the age of consent for gay sex to 16 from 21, where it had been set in 1967. Her amendment to a Criminal Justice and Public Order Bill at committee stage came against a background of successive 'sleaze' stories featuring the sexual adventures of a variety of Conservative politicians. These in turn had been inspired by John Major's 'Back to Basics' speech at the 1993 Conservative Party conference, in which he called for a return to traditional family values. Currie was going against the grain of the government's rhetoric, and worse, providing an excuse for the press and gay rights campaigners to scrutinise the lives of closeted gay Tory MPs.

'There were only a couple of dozen of our side who voted for sixteen – a mixture of libertarians and liberals and (who knows?) one or two (or three or four) closet queens, encouraged by the whips to vote with us and reduce the risk of being outed by Tatchell and his merry men,' recorded the Tory whip Gyles Brandreth.[17] (Peter Tatchell, the gay former Labour candidate for Bermondsey, was now part of the radical gay rights group OutRage! It specialised in 'outing' people it claimed were closeted homosexuals.)

A reduction in the age of consent was supported by Currie's ex-lover, Prime Minister John Major. He had risked some party opprobrium by meeting a delegation of gay rights activists from the pressure group Stonewall, led by the actor Sir Ian McKellen. Currie thought she detected a change in the climate, but she was to face a barrage of hostile interventions from her own side.

THIS IS AN HISTORIC DEBATE. It is the first time in over a quarter of a century that the age of consent for homosexuals has been discussed by the House of Commons. The taboo of silence that has denied the sexuality of young gay men has been decisively broken. Tonight's free vote establishes the question as a matter of conscience – as it should be – and the huge number of hon. members who will support the new clause will demonstrate that it is not an issue for gay men alone, and no longer a minority issue, but one of human rights, which touches us all.

Homosexuality in this country is subject to enforced discrimination, which is now out of date, indefensible and way out of line with the rest of the civilised world. The age at which gay sex is permitted in Britain, at 21, is the highest in the world, other than in places like Byelorussia and Serbia, where it is still totally illegal. Most nations have the same age of consent for straight and for gay sexual activity – and have done for years, even centuries – with no problems at all. They do not bother to make any distinction, even when the age is lower than it is here.

We need only cross the channel to see that this is the case. In France, Greece, Poland, Sweden and Denmark the common age is fifteen; in Italy, it is fourteen; in Malta, Spain and Holland, it is twelve. Those are prime destinations, it should be pointed out, for the 33 million Brits who go abroad every year on holiday or business. Germany has announced that it will equalise the age of consent at sixteen; the Republic of Ireland did so last year, at seventeen. None of these nations is troubled, as we appear almost uniquely to be, by the notion that a common age of consent causes peculiar difficulties. The fact is that it does not.

The United Kingdom is likely to have to change its law before much longer, for a case has been brought before the European Court of Human Rights on equality grounds, with an excellent chance of success. The Government have already been told that they have a case to answer, and they must give their response before the end of March. The European Court of Human Rights, which we helped to set up in 1953, is likely to rule in favour of equality, as it has done in similar cases in respect of other countries, which have complied. Surely it is better for us to change our law in the House of Commons, on a free vote, than to be forced to conform, possibly in an election year.

The Conservative MP Harry Greenway intervened to say that the House ought not to take a decision on grounds of expediency or comparisons – it had a duty to 'protect the young men of the nation'.
    Currie dealt courteously with his intervention.

Of course, it is a matter of principle. If my hon. friend bears with me, I shall deal with his point in a moment. This is an all-party new clause, and other hon. members will put forward their points of view. As a lifelong Tory, I can only say that I believe that the state should be kept out of the personal lives of the men and women of this country. Everyone is entitled to his or her privacy.

What my neighbours get up to in private is their business and not mine, and it is not for the state to interfere. If we are to have a nation at ease with itself and a nation at the heart of Europe, the unpleasant homophobic nature of current legislation must be changed – and the sooner, the better.

I may be told that public opinion is not with us. If there is one thing that is very clear it is that the polls are confusing and that we should not rely on them. The poll in yesterday's *Sunday Times* showed that many people still want to ban homosexuality altogether; others want equality, but at a different, higher, age. Since the age of consent for the rest of us has been sixteen since 1885, that is somewhat unrealistic. It is interesting that once respondents know a gay man, attitudes change dramatically and bigotry disappears. We in this Chamber all know at least one gay man[18] – possibly more. In any case, we are here to lead public opinion as well as to follow it.

In a poll last year, 83 per cent of the public stated that they were in favour of capital punishment. That did not stop a huge majority of hon. members voting the other way a few moments ago. Our constituents send us here with our brains intact, and we should be using them.

The Conservative Ian Taylor, normally one of Currie's allies on European issues, did not see what the situation elsewhere in Europe had to do with the debate. And he invited her to accept that there was no equality between homosexuality and heterosexuality. A note of irritation crept into Currie's answer.

I was merely pointing out that in countries where there has been a common age of consent for a long time, none of the problems that we are told will arise if we have a common age has arisen. In this country there are also people who dislike, even abhor, homosexuality. They are entitled to campaign for those opinions. We have all been bombarded with St Paul and Leviticus, and we have been accused of joining the forces of Satan. Such views are held with passionate sincerity – of course they are – but the people who hold them are not entitled to insist that their prejudices be written into British law. Oscar Wilde pointed out that one cannot make men moral by law; that all one can do is criminalise their preferences. We have no right to do that.

We can argue long and hard about principle—

Another Conservative MP, Tim Devlin, picked up on her phrase about criminalising preferences. To shouts of derision from Currie's supporters he said that argument could surely not be extended to child abuse. Currie was clearly stung.

I think that my hon. friend's remark has been treated with the contempt it deserves.

The law is not only prejudicial and discriminatory; it is painfully effective. Hon. members on my side of the debate cannot argue that the law is ignored. On the contrary, it is widely, if erratically, employed. Between 1988 and 1991, there were more than 2,000 arrests for offences involving consensual sex with men under 21 years of age. Even in 1992, as the research of the House of Commons Library shows, men were still being committed to prison for consensual acts with other men. The fear of being arrested and questioned, and perhaps cautioned or charged, is real and ever present.

Tony Marlow, a right-wing Tory, accused Currie of seeking to 'legalise the buggery of adolescent males'. What would her constituents make of that, he wondered? Currie's reply was barbed.

I merely repeat that I do not consider the private sexual practices of other people, including the hon. gentleman, to be any business of the law. The debate in recent weeks has taught me that one person's sexual perversion is another person's preferred sexual practice. We should all be careful about pronouncing on what goes on next door.

I shall now turn to the subject of health education. It exasperates me that the moment that anyone mentions gay sex, AIDS comes up in the next breath. When we see a heterosexual couple, we do not instantly think of gonorrhoea; we see people trying to form a long-term relationship, caring about each other and falling in love. Nevertheless, as a former Health Minister, I have a particular concern. How can we advise young gay men about the dangers of AIDS, how can we talk to them straight about safer sex, when what they are doing is supposed to be strictly against the law? When the campaign against AIDS began in 1986, Ministers had to take a deep breath and tell health care workers to ignore the law, and to reach out to men at risk in whichever way they could. That was highly unsatisfactory and hostile to any type of progress.

Currie cited the World Health Organisation, the British Medical Association and the *Lancet* in support of her view that the law on homosexual acts was an obstacle to the effective prevention of sexually transmitted diseases. At this, another member of the Conservative Christian right, Julian Brazier, inter-vened, quoting figures from America, where states with the most liberal laws on homosexuality had much higher incidences of AIDS, hepatitis A, hepatitis B and gay bowel syndrome. Currie dismissed his argument.

I am after not gay rights but equal rights for everyone. If my hon. friend considers my argument for one moment, he may agree that, if we are to improve health education for young people, it is deeply unhelpful when the law makes them criminals first. We must make progress on the matter. My arguments do not apply only to sex education. According to the Government's *The Health of the Nation* White Paper, Ministers also wish to reduce the incidence of suicide and attempted suicide, which in Britain is among the highest in the world. The best way to achieve the two objectives of a fall in the rate of HIV and AIDS and in the rate of suicide is to have open, intelligent, well-trained, well-informed talk, advice and support. The worst way is to turn our young people into criminals in the way that we do. When colleagues say that changing the age of consent will give the wrong signals, I hope that they will also recognise that young men and those trying to help them receive the wrong signals from the law as it stands.

Bill Walker, a Scottish Conservative MP, insisted it was neither natural nor normal to carry out homosexual activity, and young boys needed protection.

I recognise that my hon. friend has deeply held and sincere views on the matter and I respect them, but in the past much the same thing has been said about practices such as divorce and contraception, and we do not now make laws banning them. I am not going to persuade my hon. friend and, with respect, he is probably not going to persuade me.

We are debating not physical maturity but the ability, in law, of a person to understand, and to give or withhold consent. The age at which children in this country are held to tell the difference between right and wrong is ten. Recently, children of eleven years of age were convicted of murder on the ground that they knew what they were doing. The age at which a boy can be held to be guilty of rape was recently reduced from fourteen to ten. In law, a young man is old enough at sixteen to decide to sleep with his girlfriend and even to marry her, yet, if he is the other way inclined, he is judged to be absolutely incapable of making up his own mind. Frankly, I think that that is nuts. There is no logical or biological argument for discrimination.

I wish to tackle one other chestnut that I heard on the radio today. Someone claimed that changing the law would result in rapacious, middle-aged homosexuals hanging around school gates, waiting to seduce young boys. A part of me says that that probably tells us a lot about the peculiar attitudes of middle-aged people rather than about the behaviour of the young. No one seems equally bothered about rapacious, middle-aged heterosexuals chasing young girls. This is still an extraordinarily macho society.

I wonder whether anyone ever talks to young people. Most of them are inevitably and naturally seeking relationships with people of their own age. One year is the average age gap between partners at their first sexual experience. The idea that teenagers might be hugely and secretly attracted – for preference – to some wrinkled old biddy, old enough to be a parent or grandparent, is preposterous and offensive to most people.

The serious point is this: British courts and juries have at last begun to accept that in sexual encounters consent means consent and no should mean no. Refusal then has the power to turn any unwanted act from a flirtation to a criminal offence and that should apply not only to sixteen-year-old boys and girls but to anyone, male or female, at any age. Only then can we seriously claim to be shielding the vulnerable or the uncertain, whether gay or straight, with the protection of a sensible and balanced law.

The image of gay men is at last changing. They are men whom we know, work with and whose work we admire. They are business men, civil servants, artists, actors, soldiers, judges, bishops, priests, peers and Members of Parliament. We all know someone who is gay, even if he has not yet declared himself. It is time to take the dark shadow and turn it into a human being; it is time to seize our homophobic instincts and chuck them on the scrap heap of history where they belong. In a free society the onus to prove that restricting freedom is in the nation's interests is on those who would discriminate. That is impossible to prove. Equality is the only worthwhile and sustainable position. No compromises will satisfy those people whom they affect. There is no such thing as partial equality; people are either equal or they are not.

Tonight, we have the opportunity to be proud of the House and to bring our country into the modern world. We have the chance to remove discrimination and to challenge the injustice facing our fellow citizens; we have the choice of voting for equal rights under the law and for the same law for everyone. The time has come.

It hadn't quite. Currie's amendment was defeated by 307 to 280. Among the objectors was Nicholas Fairbairn, who was admonished by the Chairman of the Conservative Party for observing that 'putting your penis into another man's arsehole, is a perverse act'. But another amendment to reduce the age of consent to eighteen was passed. This was the first of a series of attempts to equalise the age of consent, culminating in the use of the Parliament Act to override opposition in the Lords, which allowed the Sexual Offences (Amendment) Act to become law in January 2001.

'Why is it that whenever we have to make difficult decisions, they always involve cutting somebody else's standard of living?'

Ken Livingstone rebels against cuts to benefits for single parents: 10 December 1997

For many of the bright-eyed New Labour MPs who arrived in the Commons with the landslide of 1997, 12 December was the night Bambi's mother died. Any illusion that they would spend their time in office dispensing largess to grateful constituents evaporated in the face of Chancellor Gordon Brown's determination to stick to what his predecessor had called 'eye-wateringly tight' public spending targets, and build financial credibility for the Labour government. They were marched through the lobbies to support a cut in benefits to single parents, to the ironic cheers of gleeful Tories. Peter Lilley, the former Social Security Secretary, ushered them through with cries of 'This way for the cuts.' The issue provoked the first major rebellion of Tony Blair's premiership, with 47 Labour MPs defying the party whip to vote for a well-crafted Liberal Democrat amendment striking out the benefit cut.

The depth of feeling can be gauged by a letter from one of the rebels, Brian Sedgemore, to the Chief Whip, Nick Brown, warning that he would vote against 'plans to impoverish single women'. Sedgemore added: 'My father, incidentally, died in the war when I was two years old, leaving Mum, who was then six months pregnant with my sister, to bring up three small children. The idea of Harriet Harman[19] and her friend Gordon Brown telling Mum to get a job beggars belief. Did Dad lay down his life for this? As W. H. Auden put it, "I have no gun, but I can spit."'

Even for those who supported the government, the vote was traumatic. Clive Soley, then Chairman of the Parliamentary Labour Party, who made a cleverly pitched appeal for loyalty on the basis that the government would not act in this way again, is said to have warned Brown that the government should not be worrying about the rebels, but the MPs who were ashamed and miserable to have toed the line.[20]

Ken Livingstone the future Mayor of London, was not a surprise rebel, but his attack on the cuts must have at the very least reinforced Tony Blair's determination to stop him from running for Mayor in 2000, at least as a Labour candidate. And his anger at the lack of consultation with Labour MPs was a theme which reverberated through future rebellions.

I LISTENED WITH INTEREST TO the chairman of the Parliamentary Labour Party, my hon. friend the member for Ealing, Acton and Shepherd's Bush [Clive Soley] and I heard nothing to persuade me to change my mind. I shall vote against the proposal.

I have no doubt that thousands of the votes that I received were from single parents who, given the ferocity of our attacks on the previous Government's proposals, can have been in no doubt that they would be safe in voting for a Labour Government. It sounds too much like a used-car salesman drawing attention to the small print to continue making generalisations about inheriting the Tories' spending limits. Certainly none of the single parents in my constituency would have paid £5 for the Labour manifesto and read the small print and the get-out clauses.

I also have to say to the chairman of the Parliamentary Labour Party that when the new rules of conduct for Labour Members, which forbade us to vote against the Government in any circumstances, were introduced, we were told that it was part of a package deal and that we would be involved in drawing up policy and be consulted at all stages. We were told that we were turning our backs on the past when one opened the papers and read about a new policy and that we would therefore avoid the damaging splits of the past. What nonsense that has been shown to be. If the leadership are not prepared to honour their side of the deal about honest and open consultation before decisions are made, I do not have the slightest intention of honouring their rules that I should not vote against them.

No Labour member can be in favour of the policy. When I went with other hon. members to see my right hon. friend the Secretary of State, she made it absolutely clear that she was not in favour of it. We are doing it not because we think that it would be good for lone parents or because it will advance our policies, but because we are bound by the outgoing Government's spending limits. No one is absolutely in favour of it.

Rather than turning on single parents, when will the Labour Government start taking on people who are bigger and more powerful than themselves? Why is it that whenever we have to make difficult decisions, they always involve cutting somebody else's standard of living? The students are next in line. Why are we not prepared to stand up to the hard-faced men and women who have done very well out of the past eighteen years and have gone from being well off to being millionaires?

The *Guardian* poll revealed that rather than the new Labour Government being in tune with the people, they are in a small minority, and the overwhelming majority of the British people are opposed to what they propose tonight. We have the vast majority of the public with us. Most people believe that it is time that those who have done so well out of the past eighteen years should pay a bit more towards the running and rebuilding of Britain and not let that burden fall on the poorest children in the poorest families.

The argument is all about money. We are talking about £62 million or £65 million out of a Government budget of £300 billion. What nonsense it is. We should be able to cope with this. I accept that the leadership have set their face firmly against any increase in the top rate or the standard rate of tax, but that does not prevent us from asking why higher earners pay no national insurance contributions on their earnings over £50,000 a year. Changing that would enable us to find the money. Why are we putting the burden on the poorest children in the poorest families in Britain?

Many of my colleagues have been seduced by the silken fantasies that have been woven by our Chancellor – the idea that we will be restrained in the first two years, but that in the run-up to the next election when we have more money we shall start spending here, there and everywhere. I must remind the House that all the economic prognoses are now moving towards a difficult mid-term for the Government, and I am not certain that there will be a lot of money available to make life easier in the second half of this Parliament.

We can already see the signs. How are single parents to find jobs when firms throughout Britain are starting to lay off workers because the high interest rate policies that the Chancellor is following make it more and more difficult to export goods? As those policies begin to bite in a year's time, we shall face the real prospect of unemployment figures beginning to turn up again in response to the Government's high interest rate policies.

I see no basis for introducing the changes, and I cannot in any conscience vote for them.

The future Cabinet minister Patricia Hewitt intervened. Then in the brief backbench phase of her career, after having succeeded Greville Janner in Leicester West the previous May, she made a robust defence of the government , pointing out that Livingstone had voted with the government on this precise issue in the early days of the new government. Why, Hewitt asked, had he not shared his concerns with ministers then? Hewitt and Livingstone are long-standing antagonists, from the days when Livingstone was the apostle of the London Labour left, and Hewitt was the then Labour leader Neil Kinnock's press secretary. A memo by her, blaming the GLC 'loony left' for Labour's poor showing in London, was leaked after a by-election disaster in 1997. Despite the superficially courteous language, this clash had venom.

If my hon. friend is inviting me to undertake daily trench warfare against the Labour Government, I would be prepared to do it. I was working on the assumption that I would be reluctant to join Opposition parties in any Lobby. We are forced to do that tonight because, despite the fact that we were promised an open consultative Government, all the representations that we have made in private letters to members of the Cabinet, and all our private delegations, have achieved not one jot or tittle of change in the policy. We have been talking to a brick wall.

Today, the spin doctors have been running round the Lobbies and the Lobby correspondents are going on television to say that the Government realise that they have made a great mistake. We are assured that they know that they have made a mistake, but apparently they cannot be seen to give in. Is that what we have come down to? It cannot be a matter of finance, when we are talking about £62 million out of a budget of £300 billion.

I have a horrible feeling that all this is about demonstrating to the international markets that we can be as brutal to the poor as the Government we replaced. I see no other justification for the measure. There has been no convincing argument that it will advance the situation.

When my hon. friend the member for Eastwood [Jim Murphy, a government loyalist who had earlier refused to give way to Livingstone] declined to let me pop in and help him to develop his argument, he was telling us about his time on benefit and his search for a job. Is he seriously telling us that he would have found a job more quickly if his benefit had been cut by ten quid a week? I would be prepared to give way to him now if he would like to expand on that illuminating view.

I shall vote against the cut, and I am prepared to take the consequences. What worries me most is the fact that the people who will really bear the consequences are the people who voted for us in good faith. When we speak to them in the Central Lobby and the place where they are meeting in the House today, we realise that they feel betrayed by the Government. I feel ashamed of what we are doing.

'Good parents do not want their sons to be encouraged to take up homosexual relationships at such an early age.'

Janet Young opposes the reduction of the age of consent to gay sex to sixteen: 13 April 1999

When Janet Young received a letter from Edward Heath offering her a peerage, she nearly dropped her husband's breakfast egg. As Baroness Young of Farnworth she rose to lead the Upper House and then enjoyed an active post-ministerial life as a determinedly unfashionable advocate of traditional family values. For more than a decade her redoubtable campaigning mobilised the House of Lords in opposition to a succession of liberalising measures on sexual issues. She campaigned to prevent the abolition of Section 28 – the legal ban on the 'promotion' of homosexuality by local authorities; to prevent adoption by unmarried or gay couples; to ban the sale of morning-after emergency contraception and to block the Major government's proposals for 'no fault' divorce.

But perhaps her longest and hardest fought battle was over the reduction of the age of consent for homosexual sex to sixteen. She had already seen off an attempt to equalise the age of consent for straight and gay sex at sixteen in an amendment from a Labour backbencher, Ann Keen, to the 1998 Crime and Disorder Bill, and this speech was made when Tony Blair's government tried again, in its 1999 Sexual Offences (Amendment) Bill. As a former Leader of the Lords in Margaret Thatcher's early Cabinets – she was the only other female member – Young was an expert on the procedures and traditions which could be used to impede the progress of the government's proposals. And, more than that, she was closely attuned to the socially conservative majority in the Lords. She attempted to stop the bill cold at the second reading, by moving that the vote on the bill should be delayed for six months – a procedural manoeuvre which would in effect kill it. She began by explaining why peers should take the provocative step of rejecting a government bill out of hand.

I SHALL EXPLAIN WHY I am taking this unusual course of action. This is an unusual Bill. It was not part of the Labour Party's election manifesto in 1997 and therefore is not subject to the Salisbury/Addison Convention [the constitutional rule that the Lords do not strike down a bill promised by a government in its election manifesto – and therefore assumed to have the approval of the electorate]. The House is constitutionally entitled, if it so wishes, to vote against the Bill's Second Reading. I understand that since 1966, twelve Government Bills, and 86 non-Government Bills, have been opposed at Second Reading in your Lordships' House. Of those, fifteen Bills concerned issues of social policy such as the Bill before us today. But this Bill is also unusual in being a Government measure but subject to a free vote in both Houses of Parliament. It is not therefore a party political matter. Indeed, I was grateful for the support I received from all sides of the House when this issue of lowering the age for homosexual consent was debated last July. I was also particularly grateful to the right reverend Prelate the Bishop of Winchester and to the noble Lord, Lord Jakobovits [the former Chief Rabbi], for their support. I was pleased to see the letter in today's *Times* from the Cardinal Archbishop of Westminster [Basil Hume].

I have received representations on several occasions from the Muslim community in Great Britain asking me to stand firm. I make these points to show that this is an issue which crosses both party and religious lines.

I now turn to the detail to say why I hope that the House will vote against this Bill later today. If you consider, as I do, that it is wrong to lower the age for homosexual consent from eighteen to sixteen, in effect this Bill is unamendable. As regards boys, Clauses 3 and 4 on abuse of trust are not necessary unless the age of consent is lowered to sixteen in Clause 1. I have been advised that an amendment either to leave out Clause 1 or not to accept it would be regarded as a wrecking amendment.

As regards girls, Clause 1 allows for the first time anal intercourse on sixteen-year-old girls. I can only suppose that this is regarded as another equal opportunity, but of a rather curious character! It is true that the subsequent clauses would provide some safeguards, but they are strictly limited.

During the passage of the Bill in another place Members of Parliament made repeated attempts to strengthen the clauses on abuse of trust. Amendments were tabled to cover, in addition to the provisions in Clauses 3 and 4, existing relationships, part-time pupils in schools, step-families, religious organisations, youth workers and temporary teachers and carers. Individuals in all these groups of people are in positions of trust at some time or another, yet none of those amendments was acceptable to the Government. Indeed, the defence in Clause 3(3) means that if a sexual relationship existed between an adult and a young person before the new offence of abuse of trust comes into force, that sexual relationship is afterwards exempt. This opens up a large loophole in the abuse of trust clauses which can be used for some time to come.

I now turn to the issue of principle. My overwhelming concern last July and today is the protection of young people. Sixteen-year-olds are children in law. This Bill makes legal for the first time buggery for both boys and girls. Both boys and girls can be, and often are, vulnerable and lonely at that age. They are children one day and adults the next. They are frequently uncertain about themselves. Boys in particular are often less mature than girls at sixteen, and not infrequently ambivalent about their sexuality. Good parents do not want their sons to be encouraged to take up homosexual relationships at such an early age. In my view, it is the job of responsible adults in public life to support responsible parents. It is very difficult to bring up children in today's world. I agree with the noble Lord, Lord Williams,[21] that the world today is very different from the one in which I grew up. There are temptations all around, particularly for teenagers. As I say, parents do not want their sons locked into a homosexual relationship when they are only sixteen years old.

Further, lowering the age of consent will send out the wrong signal to young people. The fact is that all law influences behaviour. We would not pass laws if we did not think they would influence behaviour. This measure will be a signal that sex at sixteen is all right for either girls or boys, whether in a heterosexual or homosexual relationship. I am sorry to say that I do not share the view of the noble Lord, Lord Williams, that there is a moral equivalence as between those two kinds of relationship. I do not believe that any responsible parent would want his or her daughter to marry at sixteen, and certainly not to have an involved affair with a much older man. But in particular parents do not want older men to form relationships with their sixteen-year-old sons. Of the hundreds of letters that I have received the overwhelming majority come from parents who make this point every single time.

The former Liberal leader David Steel, now Lord Steel of Aikwood, intervened to point out that under Scottish law a sixteen-year-old boy could get married without parental consent. But if that same sixteen-year-old man went to bed with a person of the same sex, he was branded a criminal. Lady Young sidestepped that point.

My Lords, as a mere Englishwoman, I never like to comment on the situation in Scotland, with which – I shall be perfectly honest – I am not familiar. But I advise the noble Lord, Lord Steel, that Scotland will have plenty of opportunities with its new Parliament to settle what it wants to do on this issue.

To continue, a lowering of the age of consent will lead to the demand to lower it still further. In 1994 we debated, and Parliament agreed, the lowering of the age from 21 to eighteen. Five years later the demand is to lower the age to sixteen. This is the thin end of the wedge. If one looks at the programme that Stonewall has set out, it seeks the repeal of Clause 28, gay 'marriage' and the right for gay and lesbian couples to foster and adopt children.

Let me turn to the evidence of opinion polls. They show, quite consistently, that the public do not want the age lowered. A Gallup poll, taken after the vote in your Lordships' House last July, found that 59 per cent believed that the House of Lords was right to overturn the Commons' decision. The same poll found that 65 per cent. of the population thought that the age should remain at eighteen. In this way, the House of Lords has reflected public opinion much more accurately than the House of Commons.

Let me now comment on the poll which appears in *The Times* today. Perhaps at this point I should say that I have seldom been more flattered in my entire political life than I have been by the advertisement in *The Times* so helpfully put out by Stonewall. I had no idea that I enjoyed such an elevated position. It will be read with astonishment by my family. I shall certainly have the advertisement framed and hung on my wall, to be shown with great pride to every single one of my visitors.

However, let me return to the points that Stonewall makes about the poll, which I believe to be completely inaccurate. The poll was taken by NOP, and I have taken the opportunity to read its findings precisely. The first question asked was, 'Do you believe in equality in the age of consent?' Sixty-six per cent said that they wanted an equal age of consent. It was then claimed that 66 per cent of people want equality at sixteen. But that claim is not true. Question two – asked only of the 66 per cent who answered question one – revealed that only 37 per cent of the total population want the age of consent at sixteen or lower. That simply confirms what the other public opinion polls have been saying. It is quite wrong to put out this grossly misleading information.

The Liberal Democrat peer Conrad Russell invited Young to quote parts of the poll less helpful to her argument.

Yes, my Lords. As to the findings on question three, respondents were asked to say whether they accepted the new proposals with the package on abuse of trust. But, of course, the question did not set out what the package contains nor did it explain – as I shall later make clear – that the abuse of trust clauses are very weak indeed.

There are also very great health risks. Many can speak with greater authority than I on this but, like most of your Lordships, I view the matter very seriously indeed. Both teenage boys and girls will now be exposed to all the risks of anal intercourse; they will be far more likely to run the risk of AIDS. It is very interesting that, so seriously is this matter regarded, that any man who has ever engaged in homosexual activity is barred permanently from giving blood by the National Health Service.

As I am only too well aware, all the major children's charities – the NSPCC, Save the Children, Barnado's, and Childline – as well as the BMA are in favour of lowering the age of consent. I find it extraordinary that, with the notable exception of the BMA, which sent me a brief, none of these charities has been in touch with me at all. They have neither sent a brief nor have they asked to see me to discuss any of these matters in private. But perhaps I may answer some the points which have been raised in the briefings that I have seen.

First, in practice, young people under the age of sixteen can go to the doctor and receive confidential advice, and are already doing so. In fact, government research has shown that lack of advice is not an issue in this. Secondly, education about HIV is compulsory in all schools, although parents have the right to withdraw their children from such classes if they so wish. Thirdly, bullying, for whatever cause, is always wrong and is something with which good schools should deal. Fourthly, the BMA should know that when the age of consent was lowered from 21 to eighteen, HIV infections acquired through sex between men rose by 11 per cent from 1995 to 1996. I cannot think why it is therefore advocating lowering the age still further.

Let me return to the children's charities. Like many of your Lordships, I have been deeply distressed and concerned that they should support the cause of lowering the age. I do not intend to give a kind of autobiographical sketch of what I have done to help most of these charities at some stage of my life. I find it quite extraordinary that they should take this view. When the noble Lord, Lord Williams, comes to wind up at the end of the debate, I should like him to tell me the view of the Government on this matter. Let me refer to what Mr Stuart Bell[22] asked the Home Secretary on 25 January 1999 during the Second Reading of the Bill in another place. Mr Bell said:

'Does he recall' – that is, the Home Secretary – 'the letter that he wrote to me over the summer in which he gave a firm and clear statement of Government policy – that there would be no reduction in the age of consent to fourteen for homosexual acts in our country, that no legalisation of homosexual marriages would be proposed by the Government, and that there would be no legal adoption of children by homosexual couples?'

The Home Secretary replied: 'I can give my hon. friend the undertakings that he seeks in respect of each of those propositions. We have no plans whatever to introduce legislation in respect of any of them.'

That seems to me to indicate that whatever the Government may say about equality, they do not believe in equality in all matters in this case, only with regard to the age of consent. The Government should make this clear when they use equality as the central plank of the argument.

That brings me directly to the issue of equality and in particular to the position in the European Union. We have heard it said a great deal that we shall be out of step with other countries. However, the age of consent will not even be equal throughout the United Kingdom, as it will be seventeen in Ireland. Within the EU, the age of homosexual consent ranges from twelve in Spain to eighteen in Austria, Luxembourg, Portugal as well as in the UK. In Luxembourg, the heterosexual age of consent is sixteen and the homosexual age is eighteen; in Austria, the heterosexual age is fourteen and the homosexual age is eighteen. So there is a great deal of variation within the European Union.

I have thought hard and long over this matter and I have listened to a great deal of advice. I have met representatives of Stonewall, mothers of gay sons and representatives of young gays and lesbians, and I have listened carefully to their views. But at the end of the day I believe that in public life one must stand up for those things which one believes to be right and believes to be true and I would be failing in my duty if I did not do so. I believe that in voting against the Second Reading of this Bill we shall be supporting and helping young people; we shall be supporting and helping good and responsible parents; we shall be supporting the institution of marriage, which is under threat and is causing a great deal of the breakdown of society as we see it today; and, above all, we shall be reflecting what the public want.

After a seven-hour debate Lady Young won her amendment and the bill was lost – although she owed her 76-vote majority to the support of 79 hereditary peers, who would soon be excluded from their centuries-old position in Parliament. Her efforts forced the government into an attritional battle with the Upper House, before the Parliament Act was eventually invoked to override its objections, in 2001. Lady Young died in September 2002, but on her deathbed passed her campaigning mantle on to another formidable Conservative baroness, Lady O'Cathain.

'The vulnerable children in our society who are not interested in a theory or an idealisation, but in practical help, demonstrable compassion, effective assistance now.'

John Bercow quits the Tory front bench to argue that unmarried and gay couples should be allowed to adopt children: 4 November 2002

John Bercow looked like another Thatcherite young Turk when he arrived in the Commons in 1997. But his political evolution has proved unpredictable. His social liberalism sat uncomfortably with the resurgent traditionalism of Iain Duncan Smith's leadership – and when the Conservative high command decided to oppose a measure allowing unmarried and gay couples to be considered as adoptive parents, he resigned as a front-bench spokesman on International Development. He did not want to sit miserably in his office, abstaining on a vote on an issue he cared about.

His colleagues might consider Bercow ideologically erratic, but few doubt his talents as a parliamentarian. He has a rare ability to speak fluently with minimal notes and to think on his feet. In this speech in a debate on a motion to disagree with (that is to overturn) amendments to the bill made in the Lords, he explained his career-threatening decision to resign as a party spokesman.

I, TOO, BELIEVE IN MARRIAGE. I am – I hope, God willing – soon to demonstrate my commitment to marriage, when in 33 days' time, here in the House of Commons, I get married. I look forward to the joys of marriage, and I ought to have the humility to put on record my extreme gratitude that I have been lucky enough to find a gracious future wife who has, rather generously, agreed to slow down the process of my inevitable deterioration. That said, and fan of marriage though I am, I do not think that that institution is or should be the centrepiece or defining feature of the debate about adoption. It certainly should not be.

Several hon. members have referred to the key statistics that lie at the heart of today's debate. Let the point be underlined: approximately 5,000 children are adopted each year; a similar number again have been decreed suitable to be adopted, but still await willing adoptive families, and those kids are languishing principally in institutional care.

I found extremely powerful the research conducted by British Agencies for Adoption and Fostering. In particular I focused on the research relating to March this year concerning the group of 430 children who were potentially available for and suited to adoption. It was striking that although overall there were more than 1,200 – 1,255, I think – inquiries about those children, no fewer than 129 of the 430 were children in respect of whom no inquiries were made. That is a serious situation which no democratically elected politician has the right to dismiss or ignore. That is an extremely challenging state of affairs for legislators.

Alongside those bald statistics, we have to consider the obvious and, I suspect, increasing phenomenon of people coming forward who are not married, but who are cohabiting, and who have, not merely an interest in, but a passion to realise their ambition to have a child. Often, they are people who tried to have children but were unsuccessful, and they want to adopt a child.

It is in that context that the amendments tabled by the hon. member for Wakefield [David Hinchliffe, a Labour MP and former social worker, who chaired the Health Select Committee; the committee's remit includes social services issues, including adoption] have to be considered. As has been said many times, the objective of those who have tabled the amendments is to widen or extend the pool of potential adopters, and I believe that we should judge the arguments on their merits and not seek to impugn the good motives or personal integrity of those who have put their names to the amendments.

A week or two ago, in the context of making what I thought was an important argument in relation to the Bill, a senior Conservative, who is himself strongly opposed to adoption by unmarried couples, said to me, 'This issue is not about gay rights.' It so happens that, in the course of the remarks that excited that response, I had made absolutely no reference to gay rights, but there you go. On the point of fact, I agreed with that individual: this issue is not about the rights of gay people, or of heterosexual people, or of married people, or of unmarried people – frankly, it is not about the rights of adults at all. It is about the rights, welfare and futures of some of the most vulnerable children in our society today.

I think, for example, of the seven-year-old boy in Buckinghamshire who has been waiting for adoption since July 2000. He is vulnerable and he needs help now. I think of the ten-year-old boy who has been waiting for adoption since January 2000. He is vulnerable and he needs help now. I think, for example, of the brother and sister respectively aged four and six years who come from mixed parentage and who waited for adoption from January 2000 until July 2001, at which point they were taken on by an adoptive family. Sadly, despite best efforts and no doubt good intentions on both sides, that arrangement did not work. Within two months, by September 2001, that brother and sister were back in institutional care, where I am sorry to say they have languished for the succeeding fourteen months.

I think, for example, of the sisters aged eight and nine who have been waiting for adoption for the past twelve months. Those sisters are judged and described as hard to place on the ground – surprise, surprise, in common with a great many other siblings – that they want to stay together. They have not yet been placed. Those sisters are vulnerable and they need help now.

I think of the eighteen-month-old boy who has been waiting for adoption for twelve months, since he was six months old. His situation is the more serious because in addition to the institutionalised care that he has been obliged to endure, he faces threats to himself and the possible retardation of his development for the simple and sad reason that his mother was a drug addict. These are the vulnerable children in our society who are not interested in a theory or an idealisation, but in practical help, demonstrable compassion, effective assistance now.

It is generally true and acknowledged – to try to cut through some of the statistical table tennis in this debate – that there are two valid propositions. First, on the whole, there is frequently a surplus of would-be adoptive parents, but that surplus is of would-be adoptive parents who want to adopt young, healthy, female – for that read generally less difficult – and white children.

The second correct proposition is that there is in many cases a shortage of would-be adoptive parents who are willing, as many hon. members have said, to take on and give a loving home to children in a different category. Those children might – this is often true – be older; they may very well be boys. In particular, those hard-to-place children are very likely to be those with behavioural problems, who suffer from learning difficulties, or who are afflicted by mental or physical disabilities. We have a duty to address their plight and to see what we can do about their situation.

A Conservative colleague, Julian Brazier, intervened. He praised Bercow's passion and eloquence but suggested that the proposal rejected in the Lords would not open a single extra home. All it would require was that, if a child was to be taken into a home and adopted jointly rather than adopted by one adult in the home, that couple would need to get married. Bercow disagreed.

I respect my hon. friend's sincerity, but I utterly reject the point that he has made, and I am happy to tell him and the House why I do so. If the existing arrangements are manifestly discriminatory, send out a signal of hostility and purposely create categories of adopters – one category of which is made up of first-class citizens and the other of second-class citizens – it is scarcely surprising when some who might otherwise be interested in coming forward and adopting jointly on a basis of equality of esteem choose to give up the unequal struggle against such ludicrous arrangements which continue to obtain. I say in all sincerity to my hon. friend that I know that he believes in his position with conviction, but the idea that one can simply lecture people and say, 'You get married and then you'll be all right, acceptable and we'll approve of you' is simply not acceptable in the century in which I think I now live.

I must emphasise that we are talking about abused, neglected and bereft children who need to be brought up physically, emotionally and spiritually in a family, headed preferably by two parents who are jointly and legally responsible for them. That does not seem to be an unreasonable request. Very often, there is not a great choice. I find it extraordinary that people talk as though the question is simply one of finding the ideal married couple. We should not view this debate in terms of two options that are juxtaposed and rivals to each other. The option of the 'ideal' married couple on the one hand and of the 'flawed' and, by definition therefore, inferior unmarried and cohabiting couple on the other seems to be a wrong way to look at the matter.

The truth is that in a number of cases, as is demonstrably proven by the evidence of those who continue to languish either in institutional care or in serial and unstable fostering arrangements, the choice is different. The choice in many cases, and the choice in future as cohabitation grows, will be between the offer of a decent, loving, stable and committed home headed by two people who are not married, and the alternative, which, despite the best efforts of those who provide the care, is not infrequently the living hell of institutional care or serial fostering arrangements.

It may well be valid as a general proposition, as the statistical evidence adduced would appear to suggest, that married couples' relationships are longer lasting and more stable than those of unmarried couples. However, it seems a non sequitur to generalise from those statistics when we are dealing, and when we know that we are dealing, in the context of a debate about adoption, with a specific and self-selecting group of cohabiting people who have a thirst for adoption and are coming forward in the hope that that thirst will be satisfied. That is a different category. In many cases the individuals concerned are older, and they have frequently, as I mentioned earlier, tried to have children and not been successful, which is why they have come forward and taken an interest in the adoption process. Simply to smear them as unsuitable or lesser beings is unwarranted and, in terms of attracting people to adopt, extremely counterproductive.

Here Bercow described the rigorous vetting process applied to adoptive parents by social workers and ultimately a judge.

As we know, couples who are cohabiting already adopt. That is true not only of heterosexual couples, but of gay couples. However, they do not adopt jointly, so they face the peculiarly unenviable dilemma of deciding which of them is to have the status of the adoptive parent, and which of them is to accept the lesser role of second-class citizen whose fate and limitation it is, perhaps, to acquire a residence order which will lapse when the child involved reaches the age of sixteen or eighteen.

I hope that it will command general assent to say that, quite apart from the fact that such a discriminatory arrangement within the family creates injustice, inequality, instability and possibly unhappiness in the mind of the child, who will naturally view both partners as his or her parents, there are also damaging practical consequences that flow from that peculiarly anomalous legal arrangement. For example, if the adoptive parent dies, the adoptive parent's partner – that is to say, from the vantage point of the child, his or her other parent – will not have an automatic right to become the adoptive parent. He or she will have to go through the whole process, with all the attendant uncertainty and stress, and the possibility of a sad culmination of events. If, for example, the adoptive parent's partner dies, there can be many instances in which the child does not have a right to inherit the estate of his or her other parent. If the couple split up, the partner who is not the adoptive parent currently has no responsibility in law to contribute to the cost of maintaining the child.

He pointed out that there was an overwhelming consensus among the voluntary organisations involved in adoptions, and urged MPs not to dismiss their views as 'political correctness'.

I should like to conclude with reference to the parliamentary management of this issue. There has been a good deal of discussion in the past few days, as people may have noticed, about the way in which the subject has been handled, especially on the Opposition Benches. The judgment was made to impose a three-line Whip – that is to say, to instruct Conservative Members of

Parliament to vote against the amendments. I must emphasise that this is the second occasion on which that has been done. It was done last May and it has been done again.

I do not mind saying to the House that in May this year, after much soul searching, and with a heavy heart and, frankly, a guilty conscience, I did what is not customary for me and stayed away. I did not take part. If I remember rightly, I sat instead in my office. I had on this occasion to ask myself how I should react to the situation that has been presented to me and which other hon. members will have to address. Of course, there is never any shortage of well intentioned and often friendly people who will say, 'Don't go to the wall over it; it's not worth having a big fight. After all, it is only one issue, and' – wait for it – 'it's the Government's problem to get their Bill; and if they lose it, that's their tough luck.' That would be the easy way out. I think that it would be a cop-out, a get-out and a sell-out for somebody who feels as strongly as I do on this matter to take that course of action. I concluded that I was not prepared to convict myself of that abdication of responsibility.

I think that the amendments tabled by the hon. member for Wakefield and supported by others are sound. They offer hope and could make the situation better. I believe that what we need in this debate is less prejudice and more fairness. We should aspire to govern Britain as she is, not Britain as she was. We should govern on the basis of enduring principles adapted for proper application to the circumstances of the time. What we need are open minds, generosity of spirit and a readiness to understand the point of view of others. For goodness' sake, let us try to think outside the box – the way in which we, our party members or others who think or live like us, would naturally react. I am concerned about those damaged, bereft, neglected and vulnerable children, and I am not prepared to pass up any practical opportunity that might enable us to make their lives better.

It has been a privilege to serve in the shadow Cabinet over the past fourteen months under the leadership of my right hon. friend the member for Chingford and Woodford Green [Iain Duncan Smith].[23] I am grateful to him for the opportunities that he has given to me. I hope that I have made some very modest contribution, and I look forward to supporting him and my party in the Lobbies and on these Benches in the weeks, months and years ahead.

I conclude simply by thanking my hon. and right hon. friends for the courtesy and understanding that they have shown me on the occasion of the decision that I have felt compelled to make.

'I, my husband, my children, my neighbours and many of my friends would be made criminals.'

Lady Mallalieu opposes a ban on hunting with hounds: 16 September 2003

It was déjà vu all over again. From Michael Foster's private member's bill in 1997, to the final invocation of the Parliament Act in 2004, the two Houses of Parliament hashed and rehashed the arguments for a ban on hunting at great length and with penetrating consistency. Nobody seemed to change their mind during the whole gruelling marathon. The Commons, despite some distinguished voices raised against, was overwhelmingly in favour of a ban. The Lords resisted. In 2003, the government attempted to broker a compromise. Environment Minister Alun Michael won some cautious plaudits from the pro-hunting lobby for listening carefully to their case. He then produced a proposal for a licensed hunting system, building on a report by Lord Burns, the former Permanent Secretary to the Treasury. But this did not find favour with the overwhelming anti-hunting majority in the Commons during the 2001–05 Parliament. They amended the bill, turning it into a blanket ban on hunting with hounds.

When the bill reached the Lords, the smart tactical move for peers was to re-amend the bill back into its original form and send it back to MPs, thus at least forcing the government into an embarrassing choice between voting down its own original proposals, or refusing to uphold the will of the Commons and of the vast majority of its own backbenchers.

One of the key figures in the years of debate was Lady Mallalieu, the fox-hunting Labour QC who provided a powerful internal critique of the government and the anti-hunting camp which dominated Labour parliamentary opinion. This is just one example of a series of consistently eloquent and powerful arguments against her own party. In particular she made the point that hunting was not the upper-class pastime of feudal landowners imagined in Labour mythology, but an activity which engaged rural people across the social spectrum.

MY LORDS, I THANK the Minister for explaining the Bill briefly to us. I must first declare a particular interest in it. I am president of the Countryside Alliance [the main pro-hunting pressure group, which had organised a series of massive demonstrations against a ban], I hunt regularly, and if the Bill were to reach the statute book in this form, then I, my husband, my children, my neighbours and many of my friends would be made criminals. So would literally thousands of others, including doctors, nurses, vets, farmers, magistrates, children, housewives and policemen. In fact, the people whom the Bill seeks to criminalise are a selection of the most law-abiding, responsible and decent citizens in this country. The Government have let them down.

We were promised a Government Bill based on principle and evidence. Although I argued strongly with some important aspects of Mr Alun Michael's original Bill, it had the potential, in its basic structure, to establish a regulation and licensing system which, with improvement, could have resulted in fair and lasting legislation. That Bill was destroyed in the House of Commons. All the evidence collected by the noble Lord, Lord Burns, all the evidence collected by Alun Michael, has been tossed aside. Prejudice, not principle, and bigotry, not evidence, have been allowed to prevail.

The Bill is a bad one and the Government know it. Writing to the Deputy Prime Minister on 14 May this year, prior to the debate in another place, Mr Michael said this:

> Some MPs want to say they are voting for a complete ban on hunting focusing on foxes. They think this is simple and ask why we should complicate matters. But the apparently complete ban is not as simple as it seems. If they go for such an amendment at Report it would be a wrecking amendment.

Well, they did, and it was. It is hard for me to understand how the noble Lord, Lord Whitty,[24] is now required to act as an advocate for that wrecked Bill. Principle and evidence are apparently dispensable, as are promises.

This Bill is a bad one. The police say it is unworkable and unenforceable. It has been criticised by the Justices' Association. No less than 63 per cent of rural vets say it will actually increase animal suffering. All the major farming bodies – those who are most directly affected – give it a massive thumbs down, as do the people of this country as a whole. There is no Labour Party manifesto commitment to a ban. There was none at the last general election. A clear majority of the ordinary people of this country now favour the continuation of hunting under regulation.

To those who genuinely care about trying to reduce animal suffering – which includes, as I accept, people on both sides of this debate – I beg them to look at the independent evidence before they support the Bill in this form. The most recent independent research on shooting foxes published in June of this year, after Alun Michael had completed his hearing of evidence, shows, alarmingly, that for every fox shot dead with a shotgun, at least the same number are wounded and many are never found. If hunting went, snaring and shooting would increase enormously. Prolonged suffering, and for more animals, would be the direct result.

Do not take it from me – please look at the submissions of the Exmoor National Park Authority to Alun Michael in June of last year. Look at the veterinary record for April of this year. This is recent, cutting-edge research, and it is independent. That contains the most recent evidence on red deer shooting, which indicates a wounding rate in excess of 14 per cent for red deer shot with a rifle. Look, if you will, at the gloomy forecast of the Exmoor Deer Management Group for the future of those West Country herds of red deer, currently the finest in Britain, in the event of a ban. If you can find the time, look at the contrast between the healthy deer of the hunted areas of Exmoor and compare them with the sick deer which are found on the sanctuary – so-called – of the League Against Cruel Sports, near Dulverton.

In the West Country, where I have the privilege to spend part of my time, the noble Lord, Lord Burns, found that hunting, where it takes place, has the support of two thirds of the general population, who are not all hunters by any means. The general population wants it to continue.

The electorate in every area where deer hunting takes place has returned an MP who shares the view that it should continue, and they are not all Conservatives. One MP who took a different view was rejected at the ballot box on this issue, as she accepts.[25] The democratic choice of the people who actually live in areas where deer hunting takes place is overwhelmingly that it should continue. What more can they do than cast their votes as they have?

However well intentioned a ban on hare hunting and coursing may be, in reality a ban would have serious unintended consequences for the hare. Illegal hare coursing, which is a real scourge for farmers in some areas, would inevitably increase. It is virtually unpoliceable, even at present. The only strategy left for a farmer with this serious problem who currently encourages hares and their habitat is to shoot every one which moves, and many of them will.

Look, please, before you vote to support this Bill, at the independent study by the University of Kent, which was published in Nature in May of this year. Any perceived gain to the hare or the fox or the deer would be wiped out by conservation benefits lost following a ban. Alun Michael was absolutely right: this is not simple.

If the intention of Members of Parliament is to reduce animal suffering by banning cruelty to wild animals, the Bill which was introduced in this House by the noble Lord, Lord Donoughue,[26] would do more than anything proposed in this legislation.

I am sorry to say that, to some, all of this does not matter one jot because they are prepared to sacrifice not just animals but people – their homes, their jobs, their way of life, their communities, especially in places such as Exmoor, which I love – for the sake of some transient peace from a section of the parliamentary Labour Party. If that is allowed to happen, the lasting sense of injustice and resentment in those communities will dog the Government who were responsible, not just for a Parliament or two but for a generation.

The issue raised by the Bill is no longer the relatively minor one of hunting, which directly affects only a fraction of our population. It is now something which matters to us all – namely, the future of liberty and democracy itself. Democracy is the will of the people, not just members of another place. Less than half the members of the House of Commons gave this Bill a Third Reading.

We have a Government with a massive Commons majority which they can use in office either for the good of the nation or as an instrument of abuse of a minority. To use that majority to override proper debate, to dismiss the evidence, to impose repressive, criminal legislation without just cause is, I believe, an abuse of democracy. Surely true democracy does not mean that the views of the elected majority must always prevail, right or wrong. True democracy ensures fair and proper treatment of minorities and avoids misuse of a dominant position. Its hallmarks are fairness, tolerance and broad-mindedness, which are impossible to find in this vindictive little Bill.

I hope that in the very limited time that we have in this Session to consider a Bill that has spent seven months in the other place, we shall do our best without delay or any attempt at obstruction to do what the Government promise: namely, to produce a Bill based on principle and evidence. I hope that we can return to the Commons a fair and sensible regulation system based on Mr Michael's structure, which complies with the Human Rights Act 1998, as I do not believe this Bill does.

Criminal legislation in the form of the Bill before us today would be a stain on the statute book. I remind the noble Lord, Lord Whitty, of the words that appeared in the manifesto. Far from enabling Parliament to reach a conclusion on the issue, bad legislation reflects badly on the Government who allow it to happen. The Bill is unjust, and many of us in this House on all sides, and many thousands more in the country, would not rest until that injustice was corrected. I hope that we do not have to do that.

Six

MONEY

THE ERA OF *Today in Parliament* began at much the same point as the public and politicians began to believe that governments should manage the peacetime economy to promote full employment – a belief that did not survive the 1980s unscathed. This section begins with one of the greatest economists in history arguing in the House of Lords on the best way to ensure Britain's postwar recovery, and passes through the bread-and-butter issues of tax and spending to Jeff Rooker's daring rewriting of a Labour Budget, via some high-powered economic theorising from Enoch Powell, and a world-weary dismissal of over-ideological policy from Harold Macmillan, to the more familiar debate over the proper management of a modern economy.

Taxation may be the most pervasive and intrusive feature of the modern state, and the most jealously guarded power of the Commons, but it tends to produce remarkably little in the way of great oratory – the dry leaves of forgotten Budgets seldom make compulsive reading, as Roy Jenkins remarked. Naturally, *TIP* always reports extensively on the announcements made on Budget day, but the micro-detail of tax changes quickly loses its allure. But Gerald Nabarro's blistering assault on his own Chancellor, Derick Heathcoat Amory, and Jeff Rooker's sheer brass neck in pushing through an unwelcome amendment to his government's Budget both demand inclusion.

Then there are the wider issues of economic policy. It is possible to trace in these speeches the change in Britain's self-image from victorious imperial power in 1945, when Keynes and Beaverbrook debated whether the country could go it alone without American credit, to the flagging weariness of 1960, when Nabarro chided his government for its unwillingness to cut taxes, to the crisis-ridden 1970s, when Norman Tebbit denounced rescue of the Upper Clyde Shipbuilders, and Enoch Powell rejected the easy assumption that the unions were the cause of Britain's inflationary woes, to the more confident-sounding disputations of Michael Heseltine and Gordon Brown in the 1990s.

The speeches here are not chosen because they are the most significant – Geoffrey Howe's lifting of exchange controls and Gordon Brown's restoration of Bank of England independence are not included, for example – they are chosen because they catch a little of the economic mood of their times.

'I shall never so long as I live cease to regret that this is not an interest-free loan.'

John Maynard Keynes defends the terms of the American loan: 18 December 1945

The euphoria of victory in the Second World War quickly gave way to the reality of economic crisis. Britain's reserves of gold and dollars were close to exhaustion, and when, without warning, the Truman administration terminated the Lend-Lease agreement under which the Americans had supplied food and all manner of vital materials to Britain, disaster loomed. The greatest economist of the age, John Maynard Keynes, was dispatched to Washington to negotiate a new line of credit which would keep the country afloat.

He and his team set out with expectations that the Americans would simply give their ally the money needed to tide Britain over, until its exhausted economy could be revived. That expectation did not long survive contact with the political realities of Washington. Keynes performed brilliantly in putting the British case, but the Americans faced many demands for aid, and were not minded to bankroll either the British Empire or the socialist experiment on which the Attlee government had embarked. Still less was the US Congress prepared to finance the rebirth of the Empire as an independent trading area, with American commerce excluded by tariff barriers.

To a country which – not without reason – thought itself the saviour of the world, and which for centuries had been a mighty power, the status of supplicant and pensioner seeking American charity was a bitter demotion. A loan of $3.75 billion was eventually secured, not interest-free but, as Keynes explained, on very favourable terms.

But there was a catch. The Americans wanted to trade more freely with the countries of the Sterling Area – the mainly Empire and Commonwealth countries who had pegged the value of their currencies to the pound – and so demanded that they make their pounds convertible to dollars within a year. This meant ending the regulations that limited the number of pounds that could be exchanged for dollars in order to buy American goods, and which kept the pound at an unrealistically high value against the dollar. It would expose traditionally British markets to strong American competition and guaranteed a run on the pound as soon as the deadline was reached. Convertibility day, when those restrictions would go, was set for 15 July 1947, and it did indeed result in a catastrophic sterling crisis which saw Britain's meagre dollar reserves haemorrhage away, as foreign creditors raced to swap

their overvalued pounds for secure dollars. Convertibility was soon
suspended and a painful dose of austerity imposed to rebuild Britain's dollar
reserves. All this was foreseen by Keynes and others, but he believed the
alternative was an immediate collapse in Britain's international credit and
shortly afterwards, the government believed, of living standards. The spectres
of mass unemployment and even mass starvation, not to mention the collapse
of the government and possibly the Labour Party, haunted the Chancellor,
Hugh Dalton. To his dying day, Clement Attlee, the Prime Minister, believed
there was no alternative but to accept the American terms.

In Britain the reaction to the loan and its terms mixed humiliation with
feelings of betrayal. The controversy culminated in a two-day debate in the
Lords, in which, on the second day, Keynes himself, exhausted and suffering
from heart trouble, rose to defend the deal he had negotiated. In this long
and densely argued speech he gave their lordships an eloquent account of
the weeks of bargaining in Washington. And he also laid out the advantages
of the new Bretton Woods economic system which would set the exchange
rates of currencies and prevent damaging fluctuations, of which he was one
of the designers.

For some the speech marked a disastrous political and economic
misjudgement which began the final surrender of British economic
independence. They toyed with alternative plans for an economic bloc which
would include the Empire and perhaps Western Europe. Others believed the
American loan, while unpalatable, was the only salvation for a bankrupt and
exhausted nation.

From the press gallery, Harry Boardman of the *Manchester Guardian*
thought Keynes put the case for the agreement brilliantly, to a House jam-
packed with peers, and with MPs crammed into the space behind the
Woolsack to listen.

M Y LORDS, TWO DAYS in Westminster are enough to teach one what a
vast distance separates us here from the climate of Washington.
Much more than the winter waste of the North Atlantic and that
somewhat overrated affair, the Gulf Stream, though that is quite enough in
itself to fog and dampen everything in transit from one hemisphere to the
other. Yet I can well see that no one would easily accept the result of these
negotiations with sympathy and understanding unless he could, to some
extent at least, bring himself to appreciate the motives and purposes of the
other side. I think it would be worthwhile that I should devote some part of

what I have to say to that aspect. How difficult it is for nations to understand one another, even when they have the advantage of a common language. How differently things appear in Washington than in London, and how easy it is to misunderstand one another's difficulties and the real purpose which lies behind each one's way of solving them. As the Foreign Secretary [Ernest Bevin] has pointed out, everyone talks about international cooperation, but how little of pride, of temper or of habit anyone is willing to contribute to it when it comes down to brass tacks.

Let me plunge at once into the terms of the loan and the understandings about short-term policy which are associated with it. Since our transitory financial difficulties are largely due to the role we played in the war and to the costs we incurred before the United States entered the war, we here in London feel – it is a feeling which I shared and still share to the full – that it might not be asking too much of our American friends that they should agree to see us through the transition by financial aid which approximated to a grant. We felt it might be proper for us to indicate the general direction of the policies which that aid would enable us to pursue and to undertake to move along those lines, particularly in terminating the discriminatory features of the exchange arrangements of the sterling area as quickly as circumstances permit, and that, subject to those general understandings, we should be left as free as possible to work things out in our own way. Released from immediate pressing anxieties on terms which would not embarrass the future, we could then proceed cautiously in the light of experience of the postwar world as it gradually disclosed its lessons.

Clearly that would have given us the best of both worlds. How reasonable such a programme sounds in London and how natural the disappointment when the actual proposals fall seriously short of it. But what a gulf separates us from the climate of Washington; and what a depth of misunderstanding there will be as to what governs relations between even the friendliest and most like-minded nations if we imagine that so free and easy an arrangement could commend itself to the complex politics of Congress or to the immeasurably remote public opinion of the United States. Nevertheless, it was on these lines that we opened our case. For three days the heads of the American delegation heard me expound the material contained in the White Paper to which the noble and learned Viscount, Lord Simon,[1] referred. He would have done it more eloquently, but I can fairly say that I was heard not only with obvious and expressed good will and plain sympathy, but also with a keen desire on their part to understand the magnitude and the intricacies of our problem.

I must, at this point, digress for a moment to explain the American response to our claim that for good reasons, arising out of the past they owe us something more than they have yet paid, something in the nature of deferred Lend-Lease for the time when we held the fort alone, for it was here that in expounding our case we had an early and severe disappointment. It would be quite wrong to suppose that such considerations have played no part in the final results. They have played a vital part; we could never have obtained what we did obtain except against this background. Nevertheless, it was not very long before the British delegation discovered that a primary emphasis on past services and past sacrifice would not be fruitful. The American Congress and the American people have never accepted any literal principle of equal sacrifice, financial or otherwise, between all the allied participants. Indeed, have we ourselves?

It is a complete illusion to suppose that in Washington you have only to mention the principle of equal sacrifice to get all you want. The Americans – and are they wrong? – find a post-mortem on relative services and sacrifices amongst the leading allies extremely distasteful and dissatisfying. Many different countries are involved and most of them are now in Washington to plead their urgent needs and high deserts. Some have rendered more service than others to the common cause; some have experienced more anguish of mind and destruction of organised life, some have suffered, voluntarily or involuntarily, a greater sacrifice of lives and of material wealth; and some of them have escaped from a nearer, more imminent or deadlier peril than others. Not all of them have had out of Uncle Sam the same relative measure of assistance up to date.

How is all this to be added, subtracted and assessed in terms of a line of credit? It is better not to try; it is better not to think that way. I give the American point of view. Is not it more practical and more realistic – to use two favourite American expressions – to think in terms of the future and to work out what credits, of what amount and upon what terms, will do most service in reconstructing the postwar world and guiding postwar economy along those lines which, in the American view, will best conduce to the general prosperity of all and to the friendship of nations? This does not mean that the past is forgotten, even though it may be beginning to fade, but in no phase of human experience does the past operate so directly and arithmetically as we were trying to contend. Men's sympathies and less calculated impulses are drawn from their memories of comradeship, but their contemporary acts are generally directed towards influencing the future and not towards pensioning the past. At any rate I can safely assure you that that is how the American Administration and the American people think. Nor, I venture to say, would it be becoming in us to respond by showing our medals, all of them, and pleading that the old veteran deserves better than that, especially if we speak in the same breath of his forthcoming retirement from open commerce and the draughts of free competition, which most probably in his present condition would give him sore throat and drive him still further indoors.

If the noble Lord, Lord Woolton [the wartime Minister for Food and a Conservative grandee; the day before, he had denounced the loan conditions as 'degrading'], had led the mission to Washington – as I indeed wish that he had! – I would lay a hundred to one that he would not have continued in the vein in which he spoke yesterday for more than a few days. Neither pride of country nor sense of what is fitting would have allowed him, after he had sensed from every sort of information open to him how Americans responded to it, to make an open attempt to make what every American well appreciated was well enough known in men's hearts the main basis for asking for a gigantic gift. We soon discovered, therefore, that it was not our past performance or our present weakness but our future prospects of recovery and our intention to face the world boldly that we had to demonstrate. Our American friends were interested not in our wounds, though incurred in the common cause, but in our convalescence. They wanted to understand the size of our immediate financial difficulties, to be convinced that they were temporary and manageable and to be told that we intended to walk without bandages as soon as possible. In every circle in which I moved during my stay in Washington, it was when I was able to enlarge on the strength of our future competitive position, if only we were allowed a breather, that I won most sympathy. What the United States needs and desires is a strong Britain, endowed with renewed strength and facing the world on the equal or more than equal terms that we were wont to do. To help that forward interests them much more than to comfort a war victim.

But there was another aspect of the American emphasis on the future benefits which were expected as a result of financial aid to Britain. Those on the American side wanted to be able to speak definitely and in plain language to their own business world about the nature of the future arrangements in regard to commerce between the United States and the sterling area. It was the importance attached on the American side to their being able to speak definitely about future arrangements that made our task so difficult in securing a reasonable time and reasonable elasticity of action. As the

Chancellor of the Exchequer has explained in another place, we ran here into difficulties in the negotiations; and we accepted in the end more cut-and-dried arrangements in some respects than we ourselves believed to be wise or beneficial, as we explained in no uncertain terms and with all the force at our command. We warned them that precisely these criticisms which have been raised would be raised and justly raised, in Parliament. They on their side, however, were not less emphatic that we should render their task impossibly difficult in commending their proposals to their own public unless we could find ways of meeting their desire for definiteness, at least to a certain extent.

Yet I must ask your Lordships to believe that the financial outcome, though it is imperfectly satisfactory to us, does represent a compromise and is very considerably removed from what the Americans began by thinking reasonable; for at the outset the peculiar complexities of our existing arrangements were not at all understood. I am hopeful that the various qualifications which have been introduced, the full significance of which cannot be obvious except to experts, may allow in practice a workable compromise between the certainty they wanted and the measure of elasticity we wanted. Negotiations of this character, in which requirements and political appeal must both be satisfied, are immensely difficult, and could not have been brought to any conclusion except in an atmosphere of technical collaboration between the two sides, rather than of technical controversy.

I must now turn to the financial terms of the Agreement, and first of all to its amount. In my own judgment, it is cut somewhat too fine, and does not allow a margin for unforeseen contingencies. Nevertheless the sum is substantial. No comparable credit in time of peace has ever been negotiated before. It should make a great and indispensable contribution to the strength of this country, abroad as well as at home, and to the well-being of our tired and jaded people. After making some allowance for a credit from Canada, and for some minor miscellaneous resources, it represents about as large a cumulative adverse balance as we ought to allow ourselves in the interval before we can get straight. Moreover, it may not prove altogether a bad thing that there should be no sufficient margin to tempt us to relax; for, if we were to relax, we should never reach equilibrium and become fully self-supporting within a reasonable period of time. As it is, the plain fact is that we cannot afford to abate the full energy of our export drive or the strictness of our economy in any activity which involves overseas expenditure. Our task remains as difficult as it is stimulating, and as stimulating as it is difficult. On a balance of considerations, therefore, I think that under this heading we should rest reasonably content.

That the Americans should be anxious not to allow too hot a pace to be set in this, their first major postwar operation of this kind, is readily understandable. The total demands for overseas financial assistance crowding in on the United States Treasury from all quarters whilst I was in Washington were estimated to amount to between four and five times our own maximum proposals. We naturally have only our own requirements in view, but the United States Treasury cannot overlook the possible reaction of what they do for us on the expectations of others. Many members of Congress were seriously concerned about the cumulative consequences of being too easy-going towards a world unanimously clamouring for American aid, and often only with too good reason. I mention such considerations because they are a great deal more obvious when one is in Washington than when one returns here.

On the matter of interest, I shall never so long as I live cease to regret that this is not an interest-free loan. The charging of interest is out of tune with the underlying realities. It is based on a false analogy. The other conditions of the loan indicate clearly that our case has been recognised as being, with all its attendant circumstances, a special one. The Americans might have felt it an advantage, one would have thought, in relation to other transactions to emphasise this special character still further by forgoing interest. The amount of money at stake cannot be important to the United States, and what a difference it would have made to our feelings and to our response! But there it is. On no possible ground can we claim as of right a gesture so unprecedented. A point comes when in a matter of this kind one has to take No for an answer. Nor, I am utterly convinced, was it any lack of generosity of mind or purpose on the part of the American negotiators which led to their final decision. And it is not for a foreigner to weigh up the cross-currents, political forces and general sentiments which determine what is possible and what is impossible in the complex and highly charged atmosphere of that great democracy of which the daily thoughts and urgent individual preoccupations are so far removed from ours. No one who has breathed that atmosphere for many troubled weeks will underestimate the difficulties of the American statesmen, who are striving to do their practical best for their own country and for the whole world, or the fatal consequences, if the Administration were to offer us what Congress would reject.

During the whole time that I was in Washington, there was not a single Administration measure of the first importance that Congress did not either reject, remodel, or put on one side, Assuming, however, that the principle of charging interest had to be observed, then, in my judgment, almost everything possible has been done to mitigate the burden and to limit the risk of a future dangerous embarrassment. We pay no interest for six years. After that we pay no interest in any year in which our exports have not been restored to a level which may be estimated at about 60 per cent in excess of pre-war. I repeat that. We pay no interest in any year in which our exports have not been restored to a level which may be estimated at about 60 per cent in excess of what they were pre-war.

It is relevant, I think, to remind your Lordships that the maximum charge to us in respect of the early years is not much more than half of what is being charged in respect of loans which the United States is making currently to her other allies, through the Import and Export Bank or otherwise; whilst the minimum charge per cent to which we have been asked to commit ourselves in the early years is only one-fifth of the annual service charge which is being asked from the other allies. None of those loans is subject to a five-year moratorium. All the other loans which are being made are tied loans limited to payments for specific purchases from the United States. Our loan, on the other hand, is a loan of money without strings, free to be expended in any part of the world. That is an arrangement, I may add, which is entirely consistent with the desire of the United States to enable us to return as fully as possible to the conditions of multilateral trade settlements.

Your negotiators can, therefore, in my judgment, fairly claim that the case of last time's war debts has not been repeated. Moreover, this is new money we are dealing with, to pay for postwar supplies for civilian purposes and is not – as was mainly the case on the previous occasion – a consolidation of a war debt. On the contrary, this new loan has been associated with a complete wiping off the slate of any residual obligations from the operation of Lend-Lease. Under the original Lend-Lease Agreement, the President of the United States has been free to ask for future 'consideration' of an undetermined character. This uncomfortable and uncertain obligation has been finally removed from us. The satisfactory character of the Lend-Lease settlement has not, I think, received as much emphasis as it deserves.

Is it not putting our claim and legitimate expectations a little too high to regard these proposals, on top of Lend-Lease, as anything but an act of unprecedented liberality? Has any country ever treated another country like this, in time of peace, for the purpose of rebuilding the other's strength and restoring its competitive position? If the Americans have tried to meet criticism at home by making the terms look a little less liberal than they really are, so as to preserve the principle of interest, is it necessary for us to be mistaken? The balm and sweet simplicity of no per cent is not admitted, but we are not asked to pay interest except in conditions where we can reasonably well afford to do so, and the capital instalments are so spread that our minimum obligation in the early years is actually less than it would be with a loan free of interest repayable by equal instalments.

I began by saying that the American negotiators had laid stress on future mutual advantage rather than on past history. But let no one suppose that such a settlement could have been conceivably made except by those who had measured and valued what this country has endured and accomplished. I have heard the suggestion made that we should have recourse to a commercial loan without strings. I wonder if those who put this forward have any knowledge of the facts. The body which makes such loans on the most favourable terms is the Export Import Bank. Most of the European Allies, are, in fact borrowing, or trying to borrow, from this institution.

What about the conditions associated with the loans? The noble and learned Viscount, Lord Simon, as have also several other critics, laid stress on our having agreed to release the current earnings of the sterling area after the spring of 1947. I wonder how much we are giving away there. It does not relate to the balances accumulated before the spring of 1947. We are left quite free to settle this to the best of our ability. What we undertake to do is not to restrict the use of balances we have not yet got and which have not yet been entrusted to us. It will be very satisfactory if we can maintain the voluntary war-time system into 1947. But what hope is there of the countries concerned continuing such an arrangement much longer than that? Indeed, the danger is that these countries which have a dollar or gold surplus, such as India and South Africa, would prefer to make their own arrangements, leaving us with a dollar pool which is a deficit pool, responsible for the dollar expenditure not only of ourselves but of the other members of the area having a dollar deficit.

This arrangements is only of secondary use to us, save in the exceptional wartime conditions when those countries were, very abnormally, in a position to lend to us. We cannot force these countries to buy only from us, especially when we are physically unable to supply a large quantity of what they require. It seems to me a crazy idea that we can go on living after 1947 by borrowing on completely vague terms from India and the Crown Colonies. They will be wanting us to repay them. Two-thirds of what we owe to the sterling area is owed to India, Palestine, Egypt and Eire. Is it really wise to base our financial policy on the loyalty and good will of those countries to lend us money and leave out of our arrangements Canada and the United States? And Canada, let me add, is not less insistent than the United States – if anything she is more insistent on our liberating the current earnings of the sterling area.

I hope I shall convince the noble and learned Viscount, for I have not yet finished. This was, anyhow, a condition very difficult to resist, for the main purpose of a loan of this magnitude was for the precise object of liberating the future earnings of the sterling area, not for repaying their past accumulations. Some have been misled by the fact that that has been expressly emphasised. Our direct adverse balance with the United States is not likely to exceed during the period more than about half the loan. The rest of our adverse balance is with the rest of the world—

Lord Simon intervened to ask if Britain's team had done their best to resist the American terms. Keynes said they had, but added that the surrender was not nearly as great a defeat as his critics thought. He did not believe the alternative strategy of squeezing subsidies out of the Empire and Commonwealth countries to which Britain was already in considerable debt was feasible.

The way to remain an international banker is to allow cheques to be drawn upon you; the way to destroy the sterling area is to prey on it and to try to live on it. The way to retain it is to restore its privileges and opportunities as soon as possible to what they were before the war. It would have been more comfortable to know that we could have a little more than fifteen months to handle the situation, but, nevertheless, the underlying situation is as I have described. I do not regard this particular condition as a serious blot on the loan, although I agree with the noble and learned Viscount that I would have preferred it less precise, as I would have preferred many other points to be less precise. Such a view can only be based on a complete misapprehension of the realities of the position, for apart from the question of debt, do the critics really grasp the nature of the alternative? The alternative is to build up a separate economic *bloc* which excludes Canada and consists of countries to which we already owe more than we can pay, on the basis of their agreeing to lend us money they have not got and buy only from us and one another goods we are unable to supply. Frankly this is not such a caricature of these proposals as it may sound at first.

In conclusion, I must turn briefly to what is, in the long run, of major importance – namely, the blue-prints for long-term commercial and currency policy, although I fear I must not enlarge on that. In working out the Commercial Policy Paper, to which, of course, this country is not committed, unless a considerable part of the world is prepared to come into it and not merely the United States, and in the Final Act of Bretton Woods, I believe that your representatives have been successful in maintaining the principles and objects which are best suited to the predicaments of this country. The plans do not wander from the international terrain and they are consistent with widely different conceptions of domestic policy. Proposals which the authors hope to see accepted both by the United States of America and by Soviet Russia must clearly conform to this condition. It is not true, for example, to say that state trading and bulk purchasing are interfered with. Nor is it true to say that the planning of the volume of our exports and imports, so as to preserve equilibrium in the international balance of payments, is prejudiced. Exactly the contrary is the case. Both the currency and the commercial proposals are devised to favour the maintenance of equilibrium by expressly permitting various protective devices when they are required to maintain equilibrium and by forbidding them when they are not so required. They are of the utmost importance in our relationship with the United States and, indeed, the outstanding characteristic of the plans is that they represent the first elaborate and comprehensive attempt to combine the advantages of freedom of commerce with safeguards against the disastrous consequences of a *laissez-faire* system which pays no direct regard to the preservation of equilibrium and merely relies on the eventual working out of blind forces.

Here is an attempt to use what we have learnt from modern experience and modern analysis, not to defeat, but to implement the wisdom of Adam Smith. It is a unique accomplishment, I venture to say, in the field of international discussion to have proceeded so far by common agreement along a newly-trod path, not yet pioneered, I agree, to a definite final destination, but a newly-trod path which points the right way. We are attempting a great step forward towards the goal of international economic order amidst national diversities of policies. It is not easy to have patience with those who pretend that some of us, who were very early in the field to attack and denounce the false premises and false conclusions of unrestricted *laissez-faire* and its particular manifestations in the former gold standard and other currency and commercial doctrines which mistake private licence for public liberty, are now spending their later years in the service of the state to walk backwards and resurrect and re-erect the idols which they had played some part in throwing out of the market place. Not so. Fresh tasks now invite. Opinions have been successfully changed. The work of destruction has been accomplished, and the site has been cleared for a new structure.

Therefore, much of these policies seem to me to be in the prime interest of our country, little though we may like some parts of them. They are calculated to help us regain a full measure of prosperity and prestige in the world's commerce. They aim, above all, at the restoration of multilateral trade which is a system upon which British commerce essentially depends. You can draw your supplies from any source that suits you and sell your goods in any market where they can be sold to advantage. The bias of the policies before you is against bilateral barter and every kind of discriminatory practice. The separate economic blocs and all the friction and loss of friendship they must bring with them are expedients to which one may be driven in a hostile world, where trade has ceased over wide areas to be cooperative and peaceful and where are forgotten the healthy rules of mutual advantage and equal treatment. But it is surely crazy to prefer that. Above all, this determination to make trade truly international and to avoid the establishment of economic blocs which limit and restrict commercial intercourse outside them, is plainly an essential condition of the world's best hope, an Anglo-American understanding, which brings us and others together in international institutions which may be in the long run the first step towards something more comprehensive. Some of us, in the tasks of war and more lately in those of peace, have learnt by experience that our two countries can work together. Yet it would be only too easy for us to walk apart. I beg those who look askance at these plans to ponder deeply and responsibly where it is they think they want to go.

'Eliminate Imperial preference, and we throw away this Empire.'

Lord Beaverbrook makes a last stand on behalf of Empire free trade: 18 December 1945

Some did not believe it was necessary to don sackcloth and ashes and accept the American terms. Max Aitken, Lord Beaverbrook, thought the decision to accept the Bretton Woods agreement, which set up the IMF, the World Bank and a system fixing the values of currencies against one another, was deeply damaging to British interests. But his greatest objection was to the conditions attached to the loan, including the dismantling of currency restrictions which limited trade with the US, which he thought signalled the end of British economic independence.

Beaverbrook had entered politics as a supporter of 'imperial preference,' the system proposed by Joseph Chamberlain in the early years of the century, under which the countries of the British Empire would be formed into a single trading bloc and imports from outside would be penalised by tariffs. That vision split the Tories and drove free traders like Winston Churchill into the Liberal Party. But it was eventually implemented, decades after Joseph Chamberlain's death, as a response to the Great Depression. The system of imperial tariffs introduced at an imperial conference in Ottawa in 1932 drastically reduced US trade with the Empire countries. Preventing its resurrection after the Second World War was a key aim of American policy. In this speech, which was a rejoinder to Lord Keynes in the debate on the American loan, Beaverbrook argued that Keynes and the government seriously overestimated the difficulties facing Britain, and that it was possible to recreate an imperial trading system which would maintain the country's status as a great economic power.

In the earlier part of the speech, not reproduced here, he laid out the statistics underlying his case that Britain could survive its economic crisis, without the American loan. He clashed sharply with Keynes, who intervened to say that 'in a long and rugged life spent in the statistical jungle, I have never heard statistics so funny.' Beaverbrook dismissed that. The *Manchester Guardian*'s sketch-writer Harry Boardman described how 'with superb aplomb and a smile, he turned to Lord Keynes to tell him he was guilty of a serious lapse if he could not grasp that the figures meant what Lord Beaverbrook said they meant.'[2]

Keynes was opposed to a return to a world of unfriendly, competing economic blocs – an option he derided as 'taking in each other's washing' –

even at the price of accepting American economic leadership. Beaverbrook remained devoted to his Chamberlainite beliefs.

This speech has a place in the genealogy of the European debates which haunt British economic policy in the twenty-first century; the tensions between free trade and membership of a protectionist trading area take a very different form, but there is a similar ring to many of the arguments. ·

EVEN MORE SERIOUS is the attack on Imperial preference. Here let me say how deeply I was moved by the speech today of my noble friend Lord Bennett [the Canadian Prime Minister at the time of the Ottawa Conference]. It was a most moving speech in defence of the principles which brought into being our great Empire, for it was in 1932 at the Ottawa Conference that the foundations of the Empire were laid. The Government say there will be elimination of imperial preference in exchange for the reduction of tariffs. That is the attack we say they make on imperial preference. For my part, I do not deny their definition of their policy; I think that is the meaning of the document. My complaint is that they have put imperial preference on the counter, they have offered it for sale and have named their price. Their price is not the elimination of tariffs but the reduction of tariffs.

Beaverbrook predicted the deal would yield Britain little more than a modest increase in whisky exports.

And in return for this, what do we give the United States? We give them our Empire market. We give them freedom to take from us the trade that we had before the war, on which we rebuilt our position from 1932 until the outbreak of war. Some people pretend that imperial preference will not be damaged, but we know what will happen. The noble Viscount, Lord Samuel,[3] whose speeches I admire very much – he is a magnificent speaker; I wish he could think as well as he speaks – told you that the purpose and desire is world free trade, and that the only reason for our tariffs is that other countries have them as well. I have heard that proposition getting a considerable measure of assent in this House.

But not from me. I am a protectionist. I believe in protection. I believe in protection for Britain. I am convinced that if you do not sustain a system of protection in the immediate future, your walls will fall to the underpaid labour of Europe, and you will scatter unemployment up and down all over this land. Even the Socialist Party dare not deal with that situation.

Lord Keynes said that he worked for three months in Washington. He has worked hard, I know. He has brought back a good Loan Agreement, I know. He worked for three months. Some of us in this House – Lord Croft and others – worked for 40 years. We worked hard and we laboured long to try to build up imperial preference. I have been at it for 35 years all told. At last the Ottawa Conference was called by my noble friend Lord Bennett, and out of that Conference emerged something which we thought at last was the economic Empire. It was not enough; it was only one pillar. The sterling *bloc* came from the disasters of the gold standard and of the American debt settlement [the debt from the First World War], but none the less that was another pillar of the Empire. Then came to us through the war the chance of a third pillar, the dollar pool. [The Commonwealth and Empire countries' reserves of dollars were centrally managed during the war, as an emergency measure.]

Here at last was a united Empire, bound together by Imperial preference, the sterling *bloc* and the dollar pool. The sterling *bloc* supplied us with our resources during the war. Little has been said on the subject. Much has been said in praise of Lease-Lend and Mutual Aid, and in praise of President Roosevelt's vision, with which I agree heartily, and in praise of the generosity of America, which I acknowledge. But let it be said and repeated with emphasis over and over again that the sterling *bloc* contributed more – a greater measure of financial help – to Britain than did the United States, including Lease-Lend and Mutual Aid. Contemplate that with wonder and admiration! To the resources with which we fought the war the United States of America contributed £4,000,000,000 but the sterling *bloc* contributed over £4,000,000,000. You owe your gratitude to the sterling *bloc* as well as to the United States of America. The sterling *bloc* carried you in the dark days of adversity as well as the United States of America.

Destroy the sterling *bloc*, disperse that dollar pool, eliminate imperial preference, and we throw away this Empire. I came here 35 years ago with this vision of the Empire as an economic unit. That vision came very close to realisation. The Empire structure grew in strength and purpose. Now it is being needlessly and wantonly and wickedly thrown away. One last stand is possible to preserve the opportunity for the future that Empire unity gives. One last lonely hope remains. The verdict of this House of Lords has yet to be given; after that must come the fateful and final decision.

Beaverbrook failed to convince the Upper House and Keynes won the debate; but the great economist was utterly exhausted by his efforts. He died four months later.

'The worst Budget brought in by a Conservative Chancellor since we returned in 1951 . . . It is an act of political turpitude.'

Sir Gerald Nabarro voices Tory disquiet at an unpopular Budget: 5 April 1960

Moustachioed, flaunting his two Rolls-Royces with their personalised number plates, often sporting a top hat and addressing the House with a bellowing sergeant major's delivery, Gerald Nabarro seemed to invite ridicule. But the flamboyant image, which made him the cartoonists' delight and the most recognisable backbencher in the Commons, was just one component of a formidable parliamentary persona.

He was both a highly effective speaker and a shrewd strategist, and his long campaign to highlight the absurdities of purchase tax – the forerunner to VAT – left generations of Treasury ministers floundering to explain why one type of goods was taxed at 10 per cent and another, invariably similar, at the 'luxury' rate of 15 per cent. He had made himself into an expert on tax issues, and could quote detailed figures from memory – always a major asset in debating in the Commons.

One of his particular targets was the Chancellor, Derick Heathcoat Amory, a rather uncharismatic technocrat, who never quite got the hang of Nabarro. When Heathcoat Amory raised taxes in a 'standstill' Budget, Nabarro waded in. This speech, delivered at the committee stage of the Budget process, when MPs can put down detailed amendments, was a brutal denunciation before the House not just of the financial package , but of the Chancellor himself.

The *Daily Express* described how Heathcoat Amory at first appeared amused, before his smile 'grew sicklier as the sizzling 50-minute attack continued'.[4] The speech was effective because it gave voice to the considerable backbench disquiet with the Budget, and gave notice that some determined backbenchers wanted changes made. But it was also notable for Nabarro's proto-Thatcherite language and approach. This could have been Nicholas Ridley or Norman Tebbit excoriating one of Denis Healey's Budgets in the mid 1970s. The difference is that this was a Tory backwoodsman denouncing a Tory Chancellor both for socialist tendencies and for breach of promise.

I AM PLEASED TO BE called quite late in this debate, for the Chancellor of the Exchequer has now returned to his place, having appropriately fortified himself for the rigours of the next 20 to 25 minutes. The Chancellor was in a position to take appropriate stimulant yesterday. [By tradition, the

Chancellor can sip from the drink of his choice while delivering a Budget speech.] My speech will not be so lengthy, and I shall not attempt anything of a stimulating character.

Here Nabarro welcomed a few technical changes made in the Budget.

There I part company from the Chancellor of the Exchequer. I say it literally that the sector of agreement between the Chancellor and myself on this occasion is very small and limited. I disagree with many of the fundamentals upon which his Budget propositions are based. I particularly feel queasy.

'Hear, hear!' Shouted Nabarro's supporters and a few Labour MPs who were already beginning to enjoy themselves.

Nabarro was happy to play to the gallery.

My stomach is in poor order as a result of the Chancellor's behaviour in a strictly party political sense.

I make this analogy between 1960 and 1955. In 1955, the Conservative Party, led by Sir Anthony Eden, was returned to the House with a majority of nearly 60. We came back from the hustings, in the full flush of victory, early in June of that year, largely re-elected on a ticket of continuing reductions of taxation. Within four months, an autumn Budget which slapped up taxes was introduced.

This produced some ironic 'hear hears' from Labour MPs.

The cacophony from the benches opposite will not be unusual in the ears of my right hon. friend the Chancellor. He suffered the same thing yesterday when he resumed his seat – stony silence from the Tory benches and a cacophony from the benches opposite.

In October 1959, the Conservative Party was returned to this House with a substantially larger majority – a majority of more than 100. Although many factors contributed to the large Conservative victory at that time, my assessment of the position – and I believe that it was the assessment of professional psephologists – was that the principal contributory factor was the Prime Minister's assurance that there would be continuing reductions in taxation. In this Budget the Chancellor has seen fit to raise taxes very considerably. I thought that once, in 1955, was bad politically; I think that twice in five years is disgraceful politically.

I am sorry that I have amused the Chancellor. He is laughing so loudly that I must be amusing him. I wrote before the Budget, I said on television before the Budget and I said on radio before the Budget, that if, after the assurances given last October, the Chancellor of the Exchequer chose deliberately to flaunt public opinion and raise taxes in this Budget, it would be an act of political turpitude, and I repeat that charge this evening. It is an act of political turpitude.

In April, 1959, the Chancellor of the Exchequer reduced taxes by, so far as I am aware, the largest single measure of tax reduction in any Budget in peace time.

A sum of £360 million came off taxes and three things have resulted. The first was an increase in production of 10 per cent. The second was an increase in the volume of exports of 14 per cent. The third was an increase in personal savings of 15 per cent, and in that 15 per cent is included an increase in National Savings of no less than 20 per cent. I do not wish to over-use the word 'records', but I hope that the Financial Secretary to the Treasury will note these facts and have careful regard to them.

Never before in the history of this nation have we increased production in a single year by 10 per cent. Never before in the history of the nation have we increased the volume of exports in a single year by 14 per cent. Never before in the history of the nation have we increased personal savings by 15 per cent. I believe passionately that all of these desirable results have flowed from the policy last April of reducing drastically the incidence and the level of taxation. I believe that they are most largely a direct result of that policy, but what are the budgetary considerations? I hope that my right hon. friend the Chancellor of the Exchequer, who is drawing such an elaborate doodle on his knees in front of me – he is now drawing that addled egg laid on his window sill—

'It is not an egg; it is a moustachio,' shouted a Conservative MP, presumably with a view over the Chancellor's shoulder. Nabarro ploughed on.

I think that having regard to the position as it exists today, there is room in the economy for very substantial tax reliefs this year. I do not accept the view that tax reliefs would be inflationary. I take the view that as a result of our experiences in 1959–60, and even discounting the wild inaccuracies of the Chancellor in his Budget statement last year, a relief in taxation would have two important effects. The first is that it would continue to stimulate the level of personal savings. The second is that it would provide those incentives so necessary for a continuing rise in the level of production and productivity. Putting on extra taxation has exactly the opposite effect.

I hope that the Chancellor is not going to quarrel with those principles, for they are the same principles as he himself used to enunciate from the benches opposite when he was a private member in Opposition. He used to say then that the way to get bigger production and bigger productivity – attacking the Socialist Government on this side – was to provide the incentives springing from reduced taxation. Now that he is on these benches he says the opposite.

I strongly disapprove of the increases in taxation. I believe that the interests of our economy, without strain to the balance of payments – for reasons I am prepared to explain in a moment – would have been best served by a modest but widespread reduction of taxation under five heads.

The first would have been 3d, off the standard rate of Income Tax. The second would have been the total abolition of Schedule A tax on owner-occupied houses. The third should have been further progress towards consolidation of the Purchase Tax. Here I draw the attention of the Chancellor of the Exchequer to his statement last November, when he used these words: 'I have recommended to Parliament, and Parliament has approved, a reduction of something like £120 million in Purchase Tax . . .'

If I were an American comic I should say 'Oh, yeah?'

All the Chancellor has done has been progressively to increase Purchase Tax, yet claim mendaciously to the House and the country that he has reduced it.

This produced some theatrical gasps; the word 'mendacious' is not considered parliamentary language. Nabarro was instructed to withdraw the word by Sir William Anstruther-Gray, who was chairing the committee stage deliberations.

I unreservedly withdraw the word and accept your rebuke, Sir William. I apologise for having used the word, and I substitute the words 'gross inaccuracy.' In fact, the Chancellor's claim, or boast, to have reduced Purchase Tax by £120 million is only as wildly inaccurate as his budgeting last year, the margins of error being not dissimilar in character. That is why I have little confidence in his Budget proposals and his taxation increases at the present time.

The fourth proposal should have been that the commencement level of Surtax be raised from £2,000 to £3,000, a bonus for brains.

This proposal provoked shouts from the Labour benches.

If the hon. member for Brixton thinks that is funny, may I point out to him that if he looks up the number of scientists, technicians, teachers, and doctors who left Britain in 1958 to seek their living in the Commonwealth and foreign countries, he will not find the figure very amusing. These men very largely – not entirely – leave this country because of the less onerous burden of taxation in the countries of their destination. I hope that next year the Chancellor will accept that advice, which obviously is so warmly supported by many of my hon. friends.

Fifth and last, I make to him a proposition in connection with Profits Tax. Profits Tax is highly inflationary. The addition of 2½ per cent to the Profits Tax will simply mean that a large number of companies with a steady record of profits will recoup the increase in Profits Tax by an approximately commensurate rise in the prices of their products.

'Oh!' gasped Labour MPs.

Oh, yes. I am in no doubt about that. That is why Profits Tax is inflationary.

Here Nabarro complained of the lack of control over state subsidies to the nationalised industries, and intensified his assault of Heathcoat Amory, to the noisy delight of the Labour benches.

The Chancellor of the Exchequer has deliberately flaunted the views of my hon. friends and myself, and we will endeavour to repair matters during the Committee stage of the Finance Bill. I proclaim my intentions clearly this evening. I intend to continue the struggle for annual accountability of capital investment sums in all the state boards before the money is spent and not in retrospect. I want to drive the present Chancellor of the Exchequer to a position whereby—

'Drive him out,' Labour MPs yelled.

No, I do not want to drive him out; he is a decent chap. I want to drive him to a position whereby he will take this Clause for financing nationalised industries out of the Finance Bill and have instead an annual Bill called—

'The Nabarro Bill,' someone suggested.

'Nationalised Industries (Capital Investment) Bill', with a separate Clause for the annual investment required for each of these state boards. By that means, we can devote appropriate scrutiny to it.

'Will the hon. member vote?' a voice enquired. Nabarro played along.

Yes. I will vote, if necessary.

I remind my right hon. friend the Chancellor of the Exchequer of quite the most outrageous comment made by any Conservative Minister during the last few months, namely, my hon. friend the Parliamentary Secretary to the Ministry of Power – I am sorry he is not in his place this evening – who told my hon. and gallant friend the member for Knutsford and myself that we had no statutory right whatever to challenge any item of capital investment by a state board.

What my hon. friend the Parliamentary Secretary to the Ministry of Power, with the full force of the Government and the Cabinet behind him, is saying is that a Member of the House of Commons may not challenge expenditure in nationalised industries, even when the sum of money concerned is directly raised by iniquitous imposts upon the taxpayer.

I hope that my right hon. friend the Chancellor of the Exchequer will reply to that this evening, if he can. Of course, he cannot.

'He will,' cried the Labour MP Marcus Lipton.

Of course, he cannot. I am being serious about this. He cannot reply to it. The case is unanswerable. It will have to be remedied if there is to be appropriate accountability to Parliament and proper control over the expenditure of taxpayers' money.

For all those reasons, I refrained from voting yesterday. I abstained on the first of the Budget Resolutions. It was a token abstention on my part, along with twelve of my colleagues, as a protest against what we consider to be an appallingly bad Budget, the worst Budget brought in by a Conservative Chancellor since we returned in 1951. It is anathema to me. It runs counter to many things I have ever advocated in the House of Commons or in the country.

In Committee, I shall reserve my position to vote against my party on several matters, not on Thursday evening next because I could not vote then against the entire Budget without voting against, for example, the modest relief given in the repayment of postwar credits or the other modest reliefs. On the specific issues in Committee, however, I shall suggest to my group of hon. friends—

'Your group? Nabarro boys,' Labour MPs jeered happily – but Nabarro did not indulge them.

Yes, our group, if that is what hon. members wish. We are the unofficial Opposition in the House of Commons. I claim that we are much more effective than the official Opposition, who have characterised their every action in the last few months by flatulence and by indecision on every major issue. I shall reserve my position, and many of my hon. friends will reserve their position, until the Committee, although we will not vote against the Government on Thursday evening.

I say without sorrow to my right hon. friend that it has been painful for me to make my speech tonight. I grieve that my criticism has been so severe. I believe in the philosophy of lowering taxes and not increasing them and I do not believe that the Chancellor has been correctly advised on this occasion. Long after we have departed from the Budget debates and the Finance Bill this year my right hon. friend will constantly be in trouble unless he pays heed to the careful advice given to him by my group of hon. friends and myself. There must be much more powerful control over Government expenditure. Otherwise, we shall face a series of Budgets from a Conservative Chancellor practising a Socialist philosophy and a dismal return to what I consider the drabbest and dreariest period in the fiscal history of the postwar years, characterised by the name, 'Butskellism'.

Heathcoat Amory's Budget more or less survived, but Heathcoat Amory did not. That summer he was removed. In a note to the Queen, Harold Macmillan explained that he 'has lost his buoyancy and resilience and entered into a permanent quietism more suitable to a monastery than to the busy life of every day. I do not say he was defeatist, he just seemed overwhelmed . . .'[5]

Having been MP for Kidderminster since 1950, Nabarro retired at the 1964 election, due to ill health. He returned to the House in 1966, as MP for Worcestershire South, and remained in the Commons till his death in 1973. He never achieved office, partly because some in the party leadership considered him too vulgar and *arriviste*, and partly because no Cabinet minister would want such an outspoken and independent deputy.

'I sometimes find it difficult when looking across at the right hon. gentleman not to be reminded of Peter Pan who believed in fairies and pirates and would not grow up.'

Norman Tebbit savages Tony Benn: 15 June 1971

In June 1971 Upper Clyde Shipbuilders (UCS) – a consortium of five ship-building firms put together under the Wilson government by Tony Benn – went into liquidation. Edward Heath's Conservative government came under enormous pressure to bail the company out, despite its election pledge not to pour public money into industrial lame ducks.

When the future of UCS was discussed in the House, in a debate opened by the Technology Secretary John Davies,[6] Norman Tebbit, then a back-bencher with a developing reputation for vitriol, delivered a blistering assault on Benn for first creating an unviable company and then encouraging its workers to occupy it.

IT HAS BEEN A FASCINATING day. I have found, as so often when Scottish affairs are being discussed, that England might just as well not be part of the United Kingdom. It seems that we are not supposed to be privy to the hopes, the fears or the prospects, good or bad, whatever they be, of Scotland. I happen to believe in a United Kingdom, and I fail to see why it should call for very much comment that English men dare to intrude on this debate.

We have heard some fascinating fables today, of the sort that one imagines progressive cooperative folk frighten the Woodcraft Folk with around the camp fire at night – that there is a Government in existence who think it fun to go around bankrupting prosperous companies, or that there is a sort of witches' coven of bankers who meet sometimes in the City of London and sometimes down at Cirencester,[7] with no other object than to dismember profitable companies, or that bankers go around the place looking, out of spite, for a company which would be prosperous to which they can deny funds.

These are just fables. If Upper Clyde Shipbuilders was a profitable concern, it would not find this difficulty in raising money. But only today we read in the *Evening Standard* of the hopes which have been fulfilled, of which the hon. member for Glasgow Springburn [Richard Buchanan][8] spoke – a £28 million deficit. Was that the hope that he had in mind?

An interesting point was made by the right hon. member for Bristol South-East [Tony Benn] – that other countries subsidise their shipbuilding. That was not the argument with which he came when he was restructuring UCS. Then, it was that the structure was wrong and that if it was put right the company would be viable. Now, the story is different – and what is needed is an overall subsidy.

I sometimes find it difficult when looking across at the right hon. gentleman not to be reminded of Peter Pan who believed in fairies and pirates and would not grow up. J. M. Barrie dealt with his Peter Pan very much better than the Leader of the Opposition has dealt with his. Barrie exiled his to Never Never Land, while the Leader of the Opposition brought his back from another place to try to bring Never Never Land here.

A pantomime on the stage is all very well, but pantomime as played by the right hon. gentleman yesterday goes too far. A Privy Councillor, an ex-Minister of the Crown, hot-footed it up to the Clyde, and, if the *Daily Mirror* reported him rightly, delivered himself of some interesting views. He was asked whether he agreed with the decision of Clyde workers to take over any yard threatened with closure. He said – at least, this is what the *Daily Mirror* said he said: 'It is for you as workers to decide. In my own view, in the light of what has been said, you should regard it as your yard, and it is absolutely justified in the circumstances in which you find yourselves.'

I hope that the Leader of the Opposition will take his impetuous right hon. friend on one side and have a chat with him. When he says that they should regard it as their yard, I should have thought that the right hon. gentleman, above anyone, would have known that 49 per cent of it belongs, through Her Majesty's Government, to the public.

'To them,' shouted Labour MPs, meaning to the workforce.

And not just to those 7,500, but to the other 50 million, too. We have had threats of confiscation of property by the state without any compensation – for example, British United and the Carlisle breweries. But never before have we had a Privy Councillor encouraging criminal industrial anarchy of this kind.

So we come to the prospects for this shipyard. Yesterday, the right hon. gentleman prattled on gaily about £90 million-worth of orders on the books. He should tell us whether they are like the RBA 211 orders, every one at a loss.

This was a reference to a advanced aero-engine which Rolls-Royce had been developing. It was intended to be much quieter than existing engines, to address environmental objections to the expansion of air travel. But the development costs overran and brought Rolls-Royce to the point of bankruptcy. The company was nationalised by Heath, who cited defence policy reasons for saving it.

He crowed about the £100 million-worth more orders in the pipeline. Are these new ships designed, are they priced, are they costed, are they sold? If the orders were taken, would they be delivered on time? These are the points which the right hon. gentleman knows about.

Does the right hon. gentleman still have the confidence that he used to have in a management which gives 48 hours' notice of its inability to pay its wages?

'What did Rolls-Royce do?' asked the Labour MP William Hamilton.[9] The question did not derail Tebbit's argument.

I have no confidence in that Rolls-Royce management which the right hon. gentleman set up anyway.

This is a management that, in January, knowing that its guarantees were being withheld, said that all was well and that the future was bright, and then in June is struck by bankruptcy out of a clear blue sky at 48 hours' notice. When those deals were done UCS was given £20 million by the right hon. gentleman. He knew that they were financial boozers, and he turned them into financial alcoholics – as he did Rolls-Royce.

What is more, now, when they say, 'Another little £5 million or £6 million drink will not do us any harm; we will give it up before long,' he has the audacity to suggest that we should keep feeding them with the stuff. It is another of the right hon. gentleman's white-hot technological marvels that has cooled down from white heat into the red of the account books, and he knows it. His petulant, ill-natured, ill-considered call to the workers to commit the sort of industrial anarchy that he eggs them on to ill becomes any man who has ambitions to sit on a front bench on either side of the House.

The Heath government eventually decided to close two of the four yards in UCS, triggering a 'work-in' by staff. Under intense political pressure to protect jobs in an unemployment black spot, it later agreed to put more money into the company, convincing Tebbit that Heath would soon resile on his free-market manifesto pledges.

'Both impracticable and futile.'

Enoch Powell prophesies the failure of the Heath government's attempt to control inflation: 29 January 1973

'Has my right hon. friend taken leave of his senses?' hissed Enoch Powell when Edward Heath announced stage one of his counter-inflation policy, a wage freeze. It was intended to deal with sharp price increases in Britain, set off by a surge in world commodity prices and the effects of his 'dash for growth' policy of tax cuts and investment incentives which had been funded by higher government borrowing. Together these had resulted in an alarmingly high and increasing rate of inflation.

Powell thought the policy misconceived and doomed to failure and he said so. Heath can hardly have been surprised. Powell had once questioned his 'mental and emotional stability', and likened his approach to industrial relations to Mussolini's. But seldom can a government have faced such magisterial condemnation from its own benches, as in this speech, delivered when Heath and his Chancellor, Anthony Barber, introduced the Counter-Inflation Bill to move from a total wage freeze to stage two of their incomes policy, which would allow some controlled wage increases.

'People listen to him, fascinated by his intellect and clarity,' wrote Tony Benn in his *Diaries*.[10] 'He mesmerises Labour MPs, like rabbits caught in a headlamp.'

Powell had previously abstained in a division on the White Paper which had preceded the bill, and before the debate he had made a series of speeches outside the Commons attacking the whole counter-inflation strategy. He was, Benn recorded the future Leader of the House John Biffen claiming, 'waiting for the call'. This was the culmination of his criticism. Labour MPs might have welcomed his absolution of militant trade unionists from being the drivers of inflation, but they baulked at his solutions.

Even with inflation in the high teens, Powell simply could not understand how a Tory government could repeat the kind of prices and incomes policies it had denounced in opposition. But the cycle of policy he described was to be re-enacted at least once more in the 1970s, before Margaret Thatcher introduced a counter-inflation policy based on his analysis.

WITH THIS BILL MY right hon. friends continue their pursuit of one of the hoariest futilities in the recorded history of politics, the attempt to use coercion in some form or other to prevent the laws of supply and demand from expressing themselves in terms of prices. Sometimes in the past it has been the merchants who were supposed to be to blame for rising prices; today more commonly it is the trade unions who are the butt of condemnation. The fallacy consists in supposing that if prices rise they do so because there is some malevolent or foolish group of people, large or small, somewhere who can be coerced into not doing it, after which we shall all live happily ever after.

The scheme which lies behind the Bill and for which the Bill is intended to provide the framework is, like all its predecessors in the same line, both impracticable and futile, and can be shown to be such on theoretical grounds and by empirical experience.

I will deal very briefly with the theoretical reasons why inherently this type of policy cannot succeed. Its object is to prevent the general rise in prices by prescribing individually what ought to be the price of various goods and services. That is the nature of all prices and incomes policy, whether it is statutory or voluntary, and the difficulties apply equally, if not more severely, to a voluntary scheme, if one can be imagined, as they do to a statutory scheme.

The thought behind it is that if individual prices, including the price of labour and the price of services, could be fixed, then by that means a general rise in prices could be prevented. But, alas, it is not possible to know, certainly not to know in advance, what prices ought to be. It is easy to say that they should be such that there is no inflation. It is easy to say that individual price changes ought to be consistent with general stability or with whatever decline of the value of money is regarded as acceptable. But that will not do for the implementation of this policy. For this, it is also necessary to know in regard to individual prices how over time they ought to change in relation to one another which, after all, is the basic significance of price and of change of price.

That is the reason why this drama, of which we have now arrived at Act II Scene I, always tends to run a perfectly uniform course. It starts out with a freeze – it always does, and there is good reason why: given a freeze, there is no need to attempt to find an answer to the unanswerable question 'How are individual price changes in relation to one another to be rightly determined?' because one starts by saying 'Let us all agree that there is to be no increase at all.' But, everyone knows that that cannot go on for long.

'It did not go on at all: it is a pretence,' chimed in Labour's Dennis Skinner.

Even the pretence cannot go on for long. That is the reason why Act I is invariably the briefest act in the entire drama.

Act I drawing to a close, the authors of the scheme are faced more insistently with the same question. 'How are we to find out', ask the public, the unions, the manufacturers, the retailers, 'what is the right change in our prices or wages, in relation to other prices and wages?' The Government have not quite thought that one out yet; and so we have Act II Scene I, which is still a freeze but, instead of being a freeze at 0 per cent, is a freeze at £1 plus 4 per cent. But that, of course, also dodges the basic but unanswerable question.

When, as must be admitted, prices and wages must over a period of time vary, and probably vary substantially, in relation to one another, how are we to know, how is any human being or group of human beings, even the wisest, to know, what is the right figure for this article, service or wage and what is the right one for that? It is a question impossible to answer. Hence follows another feature of the drama; for at that stage the Government, of whichever party it may be, hands the hot potato hastily to somebody else.

Here I must congratulate my right hon. friends on having introduced an element of variety into the drama. It is highly desirable, for otherwise the monotony would be almost killing. I had been waiting, I confess, with some anticipation to know whether, when they handed the hot potato over, the recipient would be described as a board or commission. I compliment my right hon. friends; they have done better still: there is a board; there is a commission; and – oh innovation! – agencies. I believe that this is the first time, at any rate in the English versions of the drama, that the term 'agency' has been introduced into the play. It certainly represents a welcome widening and enrichment of our vocabulary, and we should all be grateful.

However, the agency is liable to ask, and it is not thought that it will be more than six months before it does start asking, 'How are we to determine what individual prices should be and what individual wages should be and how they should vary in relation to one another? There is no human possibility of determining prices in this way and thus knowing what prices ought to be imposed.

Now, if one embarks upon a policy of controlling inflation by determining prices and is obliged to confess at the outset that one does not know how prices ought to be determined, it is likely that one is on a loser. That is why it is inherently impracticable by defining individual prices – other than over a short period and even then, as hon. members have interjected, with considerable absurdities and anomalies on the way – to control the general movement of prices.

Then, too, there is the element of futility in the attempt. If there is inflation, which means that prices generally are rising and the value of money generally is diminishing, this, however one defines the terms, can only reflect a tilt in the balance of supply and demand as between money and real things. Although it is difficult and controversial to define the supply of money on the one hand and to define the supply of goods and services on the other, still the basic proposition remains irrefragably true, that inflation can occur only when the supply of money, the total of monetary demand, is rising faster than the supply of good and services. Whatever may be the nicety, that remains the basic cause and condition precedent of inflation.

It follows that if monetary demand, the total demand or the money supply, is increasing too fast, no policy, whether within the terms of this or any other Bill, no compulsion brought to bear on the subject, whether that compulsion be exercised by machine guns or by firing CBEs, OBEs and MBEs, no form of duress which may be brought to bear, will prevent inflation from going on at whatever rate is represented by the gap between the flow of money and the flow of goods and services. Conversely, if that relationship is rectified or comes right, then, whether there is or is not such legislation as this upon the Statute Book, sure enough inflation will slow down and cease.

So in any case, even if it were practicable, which it is not, such legislation as this is foredoomed to futility.

I recognise that both public and politicians are rightly suspicious of theoretical demonstration, but this has also been proved *ad nauseam* by empirical experience. I remember the years when travellers' tales used to be brought from lands afar of how there were prices and incomes policies and how they were working in some distant parts of the globe, sometimes in Holland, sometimes in Sweden. 'They have a prices and incomes policy', we were told, 'Why cannot we have one here when it is working so beautifully there?' Yet at the end of the day, when a sufficient period had elapsed and the facts began to trickle through, it was discovered that the inflationary experiences of those countries had been exactly on a par with experience in other countries totally innocent of any prices and incomes policy.

However, why need we go abroad when we ourselves, on both sides of the House, have played this all through before? We have been through this from beginning to end, through two complete cycles, under a Conservative administration, from 1961 to 1964, and under a Labour administration, from 1966 to 1969. The stages have succeeded one another, the logical impossibilities have been demonstrated and in many cases fought out on the Floor of the House. In the end, the futility of the whole operation has had to be recognised by its own authors.

So it may well be asked: how can my right hon. friends, many of whom have themselves actually acted parts in the previous showings of this drama, either as actors or as critics, seized as they must be of the inherent logic which foredooms such a policy to failure, support it again with such freshness, such enthusiasm, such appearance of hope?

It has been the policy of my right hon. friend the Chancellor for the past eighteen months or more to reflate. Now, if inflation is proceeding, as it was when he initiated this policy, at the rate of 5 per cent to 6 per cent per annum, then reflation can have only one natural meaning – more, and faster inflation. In pursuit of his policy my right hon. friend has done the classic things to produce reflation or inflation. He has budgeted for a huge uncovered surplus on his Budget; he has increased expenditure and reduced taxation. He has done all the right things to achieve what he said was his objective – reflation – which in a period of going inflation equals continued or faster inflation.

Never – and perhaps this ought to be a subject for congratulation – have results more punctually matched the intentions of a Chancellor than the rise of inflation which has duly followed from my right hon. friend taking the very steps which he needed to bring about his promised reflation.

But inflation is unpopular, inflation is an evil; it is something from which, and with justice, the people of this country demand to be freed. So they point to my right hon. friends, as being in responsibility, and say 'When are you going to do something about inflation?' This places the Government in an insoluble dilemma, because they have to have a policy, at one and the same time of inflating and of stopping inflation. They must be promoting inflation and fighting inflation simultaneously in order to fulfil their policies and meet the demands placed upon them. If a man is confronted by two equally compelling but mutually contradictory requirements there is only one recourse for him—

'Resign!' and 'Suicide!' shouted Labour MPs.

I am inviting the House to follow this, if not on a political, at any on a logical plane. The recourse open to him is the recourse which not only my right hon. friends but politicians throughout the ages – else how should we have survived as a caste or profession? – have been able to adopt. That is, to do the one thing and pretend to do the other.

This is exactly what has happened. This fight against inflation is a sham fight. It is intended to be so, it has to be so. It would be fearful to its authors if it were not so. The one thing my right hon. friends are most terrified of is that they might actually succeed in slowing down and stopping inflation; for that would annul their policy of reflation. The Bill, contradictory though it is in its objectives to all experience and reason, nevertheless is a means of resolving, at any rate for the time being, an otherwise intolerable dilemma between the necessity to inflate and the necessity to be seen to be doing something about inflation.

That brings me to the vote tonight. An amendment has been moved by the right hon. member for East Ham North.

This was Reg Prentice. Later a Labour Cabinet minister under James Callaghan, he was to defect to the Conservatives after being dropped as a candidate by his left-dominated local party. He became a Conservative MP and served as a junior minister under Margaret Thatcher.

I am entirely with him and his colleagues in the last clause of the amendment. In contemplating the Bill one is struck by how fast the European disease is spreading. This is a Bill very much on European lines, if I may misuse that word for once. For the rest, hon. and right hon. gentlemen opposite have no special ideological quarrel with a prices and incomes policy, and it follows from what I have said that I do not believe the amendments to my right hon. friends' policy, which are mentioned in the motion, could or would in any way make it more practicable or effective. What is more, right hon. gentlemen opposite have featured in their policy for many years the idea of control of prices. It did not always include quite explicitly the price of labour; but at any rate control of prices has been part of their orthodoxy, though admittedly not so much with the object of avoiding inflation as of producing specific economic and social effects. So they suffer to some extent from the same crux in which my right hon. friends find themselves. I have to say that I shall not be able for that reason to help them in their attempt to improve the Bill through their reasoned amendment.

But then comes the question 'That the Bill be read a Second time.' No hon. member out of office may speak for any of his fellows. It is not for any of us to judge what appears to another to be consistency, to be proper political conduct. We can only decide for ourselves. We must judge ourselves, but we may not judge others, even though I find it difficult to understand how those who argued, as we did in the last Parliament, against something essentially indistinguishable from this Bill, who denounced it in principle and who forswore anything of the sort when they presented themselves to the electorate, can support it now. Still, we must all answer ourselves. Therefore, I answer the question now, as I shall in the Lobby tonight by saying that for myself I can not.

'The low paid are paying for the Welfare State as they have never paid for it before.'

Jeff Rooker explains why he forced through changes to his own government's Budget: 17 June 1977

Budget day is one of the great rituals of the Commons, when the Chancellor hands out – or hands back – money to a grateful populace. Whatever changes are made to tax allowances, duties on cigarettes or alcohol, on house sales and air travel and all the hundreds of ways in which the government dips into its citizens' pockets are enacted through a finance bill. It is not at all unusual for such bills to be amended – some technical problem may crop up, or some small change may avert the wrath of an angry lobby group. But it is almost unheard of for a finance bill to be amended over the objections of the government.

But that is precisely what was achieved by Jeff Rooker and Audrey Wise – then newly arrived backbenchers. Rooker had become deeply concerned about the tax burden falling on his low-paid constituents, and traced the problem to what economists call fiscal drag. This is where more people are brought into the tax system if tax allowances are not raised in line with inflation. For example, if everyone in Britain received a 5 per cent pay increase, but tax allowances rose by less than 5 per cent, more people at the lower end of the income scale would find themselves paying tax.

In the economic climate of the mid 1970s, with inflation and pay increases sometimes touching 20 per cent, more and more low-paid workers were being brought into the tax system, even if their earnings were not keeping pace with rising prices. 'I was getting loads of complaints and casework about this from my constituents,' Rooker said.[11] 'But I didn't understand how the system worked or how Denis Healey was doing it – and when I started reading about how the income tax system worked it was like the road to Damascus; I could see how we were pulling millions into income tax through fiscal drag.'

Rooker was already developing something of a reputation for fearlessness in the Parliamentary Labour Party (PLP). He had, for example, openly denounced Harold Wilson's resignation honours list, which showered peerages on individuals who were not noted as Labour supporters. Now he contemplated something rather more audacious than the odd disobliging speech. He approached the whips to say that he would like to sit on the committee considering the 1977 Finance Bill, a request they were happy to grant. He then persuaded a near parliamentary neighbour, Julius Silverman, to stand down from the committee, warning him that it would mean a lot of late-night sittings. That created an opening for Audrey Wise, who agreed with Rooker that something had to be done to raise tax allowances to help the low paid.

The whips were more suspicious of her; Wise had a reputation as a hard-line left-winger. But she was allowed on the committee after assuring them of her support for party policy – a standard get-out clause.

The two were then in a powerful position. Because the Callaghan government had a very narrow majority, the committee was finely balanced between government and opposition and if Rooker and Wise abstained, the opposition could win amendments. (The Liberal member of the committee, John Pardoe, agreed with their proposal, but was bound to support the government under the terms of the Lib–Lab Pact, which was then in operation.) They cooked up a deal under which they abstained on Tory amendments which raised the income tax threshold, while the Tories supported their amendment to require the government to continue to raise thresholds to keep pace with inflation in future Budgets. As part of the package, they also had to accept an amendment to their amendment from Nigel Lawson, who led for the Conservatives on the committee. This required Governments to seek the permission of the Commons if they wished to depart from the principle.

'It has created great panic and it looks as if the Government is falling apart at the seams,' wrote Tony Benn in his *Diaries*.[12]

The success of the amendment 'owed more to plotting and conniving than to oratory,' Rooker admitted. Certainly the speeches made during the committee debates were too technical to be worth reproducing here, but Rooker took the opportunity of a debate on poverty, later that week, to set out his case in the Commons.

T HIS DEBATE IS A TIMELY one for the Government, the House and my hon. friend the member for Coventry South-West [Audrey Wise] and myself. It has very important social and political overtones. I appreciate that we cannot refer to what happened upstairs in the Finance Bill Committee this week, but this debate is most relevant to the central issue discussed in that Committee on Tuesday.

It relates solely, as the motion does, to the tax thresholds. The motion does not go into a great deal of detail but we are talking basically about the poverty trap, which has been brought about by the operation or the non-operation of the tax threshold system. The social issue is important. The hon. member for

Norfolk North [Ralph Howell, a Conservative member of the Commons
Treasury and Civil Service Committee], along with a few of his hon. friends,
has an honourable record on this issue. The Low Pay Unit has published the
hon. member's paper drawing attention to the problem of the poverty trap
and its growth during the last few years.

It is a tragedy that we must spend £4 billion in order to keep one million
people unemployed. However, that is not the issue. The issue is that the
benefits that they receive and the price they have to pay for living in our
economic system should be safeguarded in terms of the cost of living. We are
committed to this, and I know that the Minister will make clear what the
Government have done since 1974 by way of benefits for pensioners and
increased benefits for the unemployed.

However, that is only one side of the equation. The other side is the effect of
the policies that we have pursued on the great majority of people who must
provide the income for those benefits, particularly people at the lower end of
the earnings scale. Low-paid people who wish to support a Labour
Government and those who expect the Labour Government to solve the
problem are, to use the Chancellor of the Exchequer's expression, at the sharp
end of the problem. They are on relatively low earnings and many receive less
than £50 a week, which is below the average.

They also know that because they are paying tax their net take-home pay is
far less than they would receive if they were unemployed. It is to their great
credit that people do not wish to be unemployed. They know that they are
worse off when working but they look to a Labour Government to try to
redress and solve that problem. They do not want the Government to do it
immediately by reflating the economy in such a way that everybody's living
standards will drop and there will be 50 to 60 per cent inflation, as in a banana
republic. However, they expect the Government to solve the problem or else,
in the end, they will draw the obvious conclusion – that in order to protect
their own families and living standards they must not seek opportunities for
employment as they arise. They will not deliberately chuck up a job or become
unemployed, but, when the opportunity arises, they will seek to swell the
queues for voluntary redundancy, or they will not try to prevent a firm from
closing down and moving – for example, from a once prosperous area like the
Midlands to a development area. They will not fight to save their jobs, because
they will know that if they lose their jobs, their families will be better off.

I want my Government to receive the credit for putting right a social
problem in a socialist manner. I have not examined all the submissions that

have been made to the Chancellor of the Exchequer and to the Secretary of State for Social Services by the TUC, but in each of the past two years the TUC has drawn attention to the poverty trap and put forward Socialist conclusions that it expected the Chancellor to put into operation. In 1976 the TUC pointed out to the Chancellor that a married man with two children started to pay tax at the rate of 35 per cent at the starting point of £26.60 a week, whereas even the short-term supplementary benefit rate for the same family – which would automatically include rent and rate help – would be more than £30 a week. At that time the family income supplement level was £35 a week, yet such a family started to pay income tax at the rate of 35 per cent at the starting point of £26.60 a week.

The tax threshold, as a percentage of average earnings, for the married man with two children in 1964–65 was 46 per cent. It is now 31 per cent. One does not need to be a super mathematician to calculate that the low paid and those on less than average earnings are now paying for the Welfare State, in its widest sense, in a manner in which they have never paid for it before.

They are paying for hospitals and pensions. They do not object to paying for the Welfare State, because they all know that their children must be looked after in hospital and that their elderly parents will use the social services and doctors. However, they rightly object to paying a totally disproportionate share of the cost of the Welfare State, bearing in mind that they are caught in the poverty trap. That is a quite legitimate point and it is legitimate for the poor to make it as they have repeatedly.

I have not sought to expend any more money within the Finance Bill than was anticipated by the Chancellor that he had to spend. I cannot be charged with irresponsibility. The Chancellor said that tax cuts of £2.1 billion were to be made and that the sum of £1 billion was conditional. We know that the 2 per cent which is conditional on the pay policy is there. We now know after the Budget, which we did not know before, how much the Chancellor has to play with without necessarily cutting services or raising other taxes.

A few weeks ago we gave massive tax handouts to the real rich – those earning over £140 or £150 a week. The popular press has not painted that in its reality for the working population. The Chancellor has taken 800,000 ordinary working people out of income tax altogether in his Budget. That is 800,000 out of 20 million. He also took 800,000 out of the band paying the higher rate of tax. There are only 1.8 million in there anyway. Therefore, he took 50 per cent of those paying the higher rate out of that tax band and took less than 5 per cent of all other workers paying ordinary rates of tax out of tax altogether. That is disproportionate. That is why we have only 4 per cent of the working population paying over 35 per cent.

It follows from what I have said that, because of the decrease in the threshold as a percentage of average earnings, the low paid are paying for the Welfare State as they have never paid for it before relative to the rich. That cannot be denied.

'That is socialism,' declared the future Conservative minister Peter Bottomley. Rooker disagreed.

That is not socialism. I am not prepared to say that is socialism. The position has been deteriorating every year under both Tory and Labour Governments. They have each been as bad as the other in that respect.

Bottomley tried again. The poor were paying more tax under Labour, to fund the welfare state – how could Rooker argue that wasn't socialism? Rooker was unmoved.

The hon. gentleman defines what a Labour Government do as equalling socialism. I do not define what a Labour Government do as automatically being socialism: far from it. The Government would not admit that. They are confined by the constraints of the international economic order and other problems. I am not making excuses for them. They have given thousands of millions of pounds in tax handouts to industry.

We are debating poverty surtax. Because of the loss of benefits which the low-paid lose, the marginal rate of tax that they pay is much higher than the highest rate of tax.

Who pays the highest rate of tax – the rich or the poor? Obviously, the answer for most people is that the rich pay the highest rate of tax – 75 per cent of the total. But that is not so. *The Economist* – no friend of this Government, but a friend of reality when it goes into issues in depth, as it did on 24 July last year on a brief 'Tax and poverty' – asked the question: 'Who pays the highest rate of tax on every extra pound he earns? Not, under Britain's crazy tax and welfare system, the millionaire, but the family man earning between £30 and £44 a week.' *The Economist* makes the point that that man will be paying a marginal rate of tax of 110 per cent. No one can dispute that. That was last July, and the position has not changed because of the pay policy, although the figures may be slightly different.

Last July a married man with two children under eleven and earning £30 a week entered the poverty trap. Once he got over £30 a week, he began to lose his welfare benefits, such as school milk, school uniform allowance, rent allowance and rate rebate. It was not until he earned £48 a week that he came out of the trap and started to have more money for his family.

Who got an increase of £18 a week last year at that level of earnings? Perhaps company chairmen – people who work fiddles because they are in a position to do so – but not the average wage earner on £30 to £48 a week. He was lucky if he got £6. Many of those in industries which come under wages councils did not get an increase of £6 a week. For every extra pound in wages over £30, a married man with two children lost more than £1 when he took into account the increased tax and the loss of benefits. He needed an increase of £18 a week before the situation was redressed.

It will require a massive increase in public expenditure to resolve the matter. That is why two days ago my hon. friend the member for Coventry South-West [Audrey Wise] and I attempted to go some way towards closing the gap. The hon. member for Caernarvon [Dafydd Wigley, a Plaid Cymru MP], to his credit, was the only member who joined us. We make no apology for the action that we took. We had to take the crumbs which were left under the table, because the Opposition had run away and Labour members deserted us.

There is no Labour backbencher here today to defend the Government. I defend the Government against hypocrites on the Opposition benches for the good things that they are doing and have done. However, no Labour members have come to defend the Government today. Just like Tuesday, there is abject silence.

I do not wish to detain the House too long, but the debate should not pass without the Chancellor's words in defence of the Government. My right hon. friend's words of only a few weeks ago in his Budget Statement are significant. My right hon. friend said:

'So far as those on low incomes are concerned, the highest priority for the future must be to raise the tax threshold so as to maintain the real value of personal allowances as far as possible and, if circumstances permit, to increase their level to the point where they stand clear about the levels of the main social security benefits.'

I merely sought to put the Chancellor's words into practice.

It is bad enough for the Government to run the economy in the way that they do and pay £4 billion of workers' money to keep one million workers unemployed. It is much worse that they do not pay a penny to the unemployed who are in the situation that I have outlined. The benefits that they have been provided by the Government have helped, but there is a massive poverty trap. One cannot put a percentage figure on not receiving any money at all. The percentage is so much of a minus quantity that the mind boggles.

It is a disgrace that that situation has arisen. I know that my hon. friend will tell us what the Government have done to help in the past three years. All that is to the Government's credit, but my hon. friend the member for Coventry South-West and I wish the Government to do more. We wish them to change their priorities. That is all. The answer is to change the priorities.

When the history of this debate and this week comes to be written, credit will be given to the Government for the 1977 Budget because we were in power. Because of that, we stand more chance of remaining in power. However, people outside who want to vote Labour are assailed by various problems and doubts.

They say to themselves 'I am caught in the poverty trap. Who is to blame for this? Why should I go to work? Why am I paying increased taxes? Why has this happened under a Labour Government? I shall abstain and not vote.' What we are trying to do is the sort of thing that will convince these people that hope for the future lies in the Labour Party. It may lie with only a few, but it is enough at the moment.

Audrey Wise intervened to complain that some of her Labour colleagues, who had either opposed or failed to support the Rooker–Wise amendment, were now writing to their local papers to share in the credit. Rooker was amused.

I am aware of that. I did not see the letters but I was gratified. I have been even more gratified by the letters I have been receiving from ordinary working people, Labour supporters, who were thinking of abstaining in the next election but who now say that they will vote Labour. We are helping the Government. I hope it will not be long before they wake up to that fact.

My hon. friend the member for Coventry South-West and I have tried this week, not misguidedly but in full knowledge of what we were doing, to solve the matter to help the Government on behalf of the low paid. That is what it is all about.

Rooker and Wise fought off criticism in the PLP, and – as Rooker mentioned above – they began to enjoy a certain amount of retrospective support as Labour MPs started receiving approving letters from constituents. The government decided against seeking to reverse the changes at the third reading of the Finance Bill, and so the amendment became law. Rooker claims to have dined out on the experience for 20 years, often lecturing to trainee civil servants about what can happen to legislation at committee stage. When he was made appointed Minister of State at the Northern Ireland Office after the 2005 general election, the amendment came up in conversation at his first official engagement in the Province.

Having narrowly survived the 1979 general election – he won his Birmingham Perry Bar seat by fewer than 500 votes – Rooker was promoted to the front bench, and he became a minister when Tony Blair formed his government in 1997. He entered the Lords in 2001, where he was greeted by Joel Barnett and Robert Sheldon, who had been the Treasury ministers on the Finance Bill Committee back in 1977. They were backbenchers and he was a minister. They promised to introduce a Barnett–Sheldon amendment to one of his bills at the earliest opportunity.

'It breaks my heart to see what is happening in our country today.'

Harold Macmillan demonstrates that One Nation Toryism is not quite dead: 13 November 1984

Harold Macmillan had been out of Parliament for 20 years, before accepting a peerage as Earl of Stockton. He had openly said that 'the House of Lords was not worth belonging to.' But at the age of 90 he changed his mind and accepted the earldom. His maiden speech was a triumph, charming nostalgic peers with an unfashionable blend of anecdote, dry humour and droll analysis.

He stretched convention – just as in the Commons, new arrivals are expected to avoid controversy – but delighted his audience, which included his old adversary, Harold Wilson. He reminisced about how he had been regarded with distaste, even dislike, by the leaders of his party, but dealt with the matter by assuming the leadership himself. And he took head on the emerging Thatcherite analysis that the postwar governments of which he had been a major member had preferred soggy consensus to a more robust attack on Britain's economic problems.

But the main part of his speech was a restatement – with wonderful touches of weary cynicism – of his brand of One Nation Conservatism. The old-world parable about nannies treating colds brought the House down when he reached the punchline, identifying the sterner nanny as a monetarist. And there were several more swipes at Mrs Thatcher's government and its programme – the Lords were debating the new Queen's Speech.

The most emotional section came when he talked about the miners' strike, the seemingly interminable dispute over the government's plan to close uneconomic pits. Macmillan, who had fought in the First World War and been seriously wounded, never lost the convictions about national unity he acquired in the trenches. His later speeches in the Lords included some sharp attacks on Mrs Thatcher.

MY LORDS, AS I rise to make a maiden speech in your Lordships' House I ask for the forbearance and sympathy which is traditionally extended to someone in that position. I cannot help recording that it is just 60 years since I underwent the same ordeal in another place.

Having disposed of the courtesies, he delivered a gentle rebuke to the Leader of the Lords, William Whitelaw, who had fired a warning shot at peers who opposed plans to abolish Ken Livingstone's Greater London Council and the other metropolitan counties as unnecessary tiers of local government, invoking the ghosts of two doughty defenders of the Upper House in the constitutional struggles of the Edwardian era.

My noble friend the Leader of the House made a speech which quite took my breath away; the terms of it were radical, Jacobin – 'I warn the Lords not to interfere with the elected representatives of the people.' I do not know how he slept that night. Were his dreams haunted by the shades of Lord Lansdowne and Lord Curzon? Of course, the reason is that your Lordships, I admit perhaps in a small field to start with, have been regarded as doing something to protect the individual, the small local group, the small local authority, against the ever-growing and engrossing powers of a centralised Government and an ambitious bureaucracy.

Macmillan then analysed economic history from the end of the war to the 1980s, noting in particular that the two sharp increases in the price of oil during the 1970s had created enormous economic problems for the Labour government which had preceded Mrs Thatcher, which was forced to take out an emergency loan from the IMF.

We tried to go to the IMF, where we borrowed a certain amount of money and got a great deal of rather pedantic advice. I do not know who are these people – self-appointed, I suppose – on these international bodies. They seem to lecture one a great deal. It is rather like the situation after a bad report at school – not much pocket money and a lot of pijaw.

That failed and the Government went out. Then the present Government came in. I think that most of your Lordships quite honestly will feel that, whatever else may be said in criticism – and there are criticisms, of course, to make – of the Government of the last four years, and now still the Government, they faced that terrible situation, in terms of war like the breaking of an army, with a courage, a determination and a persistence which must ever be admired by all reasonable men and women. I hold that view strongly. Of course, things were very unpleasant but they had to be done. The long boom always produces a certain amount of fat in the system, both in private and in public enterprises: too many people, over-manning on the factory floor and in the secretary's office; too many motor-cars, a bit too easy. We had to go through it. To private enterprise – and this was in the first year (do we not remember?) before the Government attacked the public sector – it came pretty hard, with interest rates of 18 per cent. Of course, all the smaller and newer firms collapsed, and those who survived were only those who could hope to borrow from the banks – and they still had losses – and who had long years of profits to show behind them. It was a great and terrible year for bankruptcy and loss.

Then the Prime Minister tried to slim the public sector, and of course it is very disagreeable. Last week I listened to some moving speeches and among the speakers were noble Lords objecting, quite rightly, to the results of the cuts in the medical, educational and other services. I see it every day as Chancellor of Oxford University. But it had to be done and it still has to be done. The question is: what do we do now? We have done this – we have got some control over the machine which was completely out of control. What do we do now? As to that, it is very difficult to answer.

As always, there are broadly two answers. There are people who are on the expansionist side – and I do not think it is really political, it is more what people feel like – who are natural expansionists. They would come along and say, like the neo-Keynesians, 'Let's spend a bit more'. The Labour Party spent, let us say, a great deal more. The Liberal Party said, 'Well, not quite that; but let's spend some more'. And the Government said, 'No. Do not spend any more'. It is the two methods: the neo-Keynesians and the monetarists, the new economists that have come into being – and nobody knows where they come from; they say that some come from America, and some from Tibet.

There are two points of view, and it goes right through. Many of your Lordships will remember that it operated in the nursery. How do you treat a cold? One nanny said, 'Feed a cold' – she was a neo-Keynesian. Another nanny said, 'Starve a cold' – she was a monetarist. It is natural. The noble Lord complained that the Government have produced in the Gracious Speech a list of things which are completely irrelevant; of course they are – they are meant to be. I do not rate the Government's intelligence so low as to think that they believe they have any importance. They are just to keep us happy.

And look what they do. As somebody said, the first affects about ten million people: the people and government of London. [Mrs Thatcher was proposing to abolish the Greater London Council.] What was the next one? That was about the fees which solicitors are to charge. Then there is one which I hope really affects only a tiny percentage – and, I am certain, none of your Lordships. As I understand it, a condemned prisoner, if he feels that the judge has been too heavy on him, can appeal, but an aggrieved prosecutor cannot appeal, and so he is going to have his chance. It is not a great contribution to either the social or the economic development of the country. The next thing,

I think, is something about the prosecutions not being by the police, but by the public prosecutor. There may be some improvement in that. Perhaps one may even cross a yellow line without being got at. But of course they are meant to be irrelevant because the policy is to go on next year as before.

But while all this is going on I think it is worthwhile to look outside Europe. First, however, we can look inside to this extent: that even France, with a president elected on a policy of reflation on a big scale, has had completely to turn round and follow the policies of Her Majesty's Government.

Let us look somewhere else – at the country of my dear mother, the United States. Ah, that is a very different thing. I rejoice at what Reagan is doing. He has broken all the rules, and all the economists are furious. He has a completely unbalanced budget. What does he do? Of course, according to the rules you have all been following and noble Lords on the front bench have been following, he ought to have increased taxation. He did not do it – not at all; he has reduced it. He even gives you special grants off your payment of income tax if you can show that you have invested in industry. Then there is this huge deficit in the balance of payments, but they have not introduced any particular protectionist thoughts. When they want a thing and they like it, they buy it, like the Jaguar motorcar.

But what has happened? What has happened has been that unemployment has fallen from one in ten to one in seventeen, whereas here it is one in eight and next year will be one in seven. Five million new jobs – the noble Lord spoke of this – have been created in the new industries, and at the same time inflation has been kept quite low. It is a miracle; the House should know how it has been done. I think I know how it has been done: it is because they have had the sense to make somebody else pay for it. By keeping the bank rate at 1 per cent above everybody else they have attracted all the money from the old world to the new. It has been flowing in – not only the quick money, but also serious investment, because everybody believes in it. It is not only the quick money that moves about. If you ask any investment banker, the trustees of funds, and even, I expect, the trade union pension funds, you will see that they are all making long-term investments in the United States. In a word, Reagan (to reverse Keynes) has called in the resources of the old world in order to finance the expansion of the new.

But of course it is something more than that, too. It is because the United States, whose scientists, inventors and technologists have been the first to see the coming of the new industrial revolution, have been the first to exploit it. Curiously enough, we fear that if it is applied, it will create more unemployment, and perhaps it will temporarily. After all, wherever you substitute a capital-intensive plant for a labour-intensive plant it must produce temporary unemployment. But the experience in California, where the new revolution has been most used, is that it has created enough wealth to make a new demand for goods and services which has reduced unemployment and made their figure the lowest in the United States. So that may appear to be the way out. At any rate they have seen it; and, my Lords, if you will allow me just a few more minutes, I shall say what, in my view, we should be looking at, and we are not – not the Government, nor the trade unions, nor the manager – not enough.

There is a new industrial revolution, or a new phase in it. The first phase was based on coal and steel and the substitution of the hand-loom and the warp-loom of the cottage for that of the factory. There were great troubles and great hardships in introducing that phase: that is because people would have theories. *Laissez-faire* was just as bad as collectivism. Good men, good Christian men, like Mr Cobden and Mr Bright [two nineteenth-century Liberal reformers], closed their eyes to factories working appalling hours, employing children under twelve – and not only hours in the factory, but underground, too. No, the Government could not interfere; it was against the doctrine of *laissez-faire*. Once you get a doctrine that is the end of you. Pragmatic politics are the only good ones. But anyway this is bound to happen.

The second phase came when I was a child, when the internal combustion engine was invented and the new fuel oil came into being. The motorcar and the aeroplane broke the monopoly of the railways, and the aeroplane completely destroyed that of the steamships.

And now the third phase has come, based upon the computer, silicon chips, automation, and all the incredible, skilful things which are being done by the scientists and technologists in America and a great deal in England, where there is more going on than we know. But I am sure we cannot say 'Oh, well, just let it come, like the others'. Then we should get into great trouble. We have got from now to think out what this means in human terms. We cannot just say, 'It would be rather nice to have a bit of it', as the Government seemed to suggest. It is a complete revolution in thought.

If really capital-intensive plants are going to take the place of all labour-intensive ones, surely we shall reach the conclusion that the capital plant might as well work. After all, today, except in the metal industries, where out of necessity the plant works for 24 hours a day, the plant which is costing this enormous sum, with interest charges and sinking funds, and the rapid replacements that are made with modem techniques, probably costs 16 or 17 per cent. For how long does it work? – 220 days a year, seven and a half hours a day? Why, if it worked all day and all night, that would save two-thirds of the interest. The answer surely should be that the machine should work and the man should have leisure. What we want is to have four six-hour shifts and the machine to work all day long and all night long. It is that kind of thing we have to face: a completely new concept.

I foresee that in ten or fifteen years' time we shall never use the word 'unemployment'. We shall refer to the proper use of leisure, and how to deploy it. We shall wish to ensure that this new leisure which man at last will be able to enjoy is properly used for his mind and education, for sport and other leisure purposes. All kinds of old beliefs on all sides will have to go by the board. Many old speeches will have to be torn up, and many old attitudes will have to be changed. We must approach the problem with an open mind. But if we are to achieve the intellectual revolution which is involved, we need also a kind of moral and spiritual revolution. Although at my age I cannot interfere or do anything about it, it breaks my heart to see what is happening in our country today. A terrible strike is being carried on by the best men in the world. They beat the Kaiser's army and they beat Hitler's army. They never gave in. The strike is pointless and endless. We cannot afford action of this kind.

Then there is the growing division, which the noble Lord who has just spoken mentioned, in our comparatively prosperous society between the South and the North and Midlands, which are ailing. This cannot be allowed to continue. There is a general sense of tension. The old English way might be to quarrel and have battles – my noble colleagues know that there were plenty of rows and battles in the past – but they were friendly. I can only describe as wicked the hatred that has been introduced and which is to be found among different types of people. That must go. Not merely an intellectual but a moral effort is required to get rid of it. I can only hope, because I am so old, to see the first gleams that precede the dawn, but I know that, if that effort is made, generations to come will see the bright sunlight of day. If some of the dreadful, wicked systems which have crept into our lives are replaced, if we abandon cynicism, criticism and hatred for each other, and if we take up the great theme which St Paul gave to us – to rely more upon faith, hope and charity, but above all upon charity – then I foresee the young men and women from every home in England setting out with confidence on a new phase along the long road which we call Man's pilgrimage here on earth.

Appreciative murmurs greeted Macmillan's words. He became quite a thorn in the side of the Thatcher government – memorably dismissing its privatisation policy as 'selling the family silver', in a later speech.

'Save the prawns.'

Michael Heseltine mocks John Smith's charm offensive in the City of London: 19 February 1992

With a general election just weeks away, and with Britain in the grip of a painful recession and high interest rates, the economic credibility of the government and the Labour opposition was the central issue in British politics. Labour was seeking to dispel its image as a high tax party, incompetent to manage the economy – with the impressively respectable figure of the shadow Chancellor, John Smith, meeting City tycoons over lunch to reassure them, in what the press dubbed 'the prawn cocktail offensive'.

  In this debate on a Labour motion pinning the blame for the recession on the government, Michael Heseltine responded to a speech by Smith with a wonderfully theatrical demolition of Labour's economic and taxation policies. Heseltine did not at the time hold an economics portfolio – although the Prime Minister, John Major, had implied he could expect to go to the Department of Trade and Industry after the impending election – but with the Chancellor due to present a Budget and an election in the offing, he was the ideal man to deliver not just a rebuttal, but a clarion call, which was to echo through the 1992 campaign.

I FEAR THAT THIS morning's newspapers reveal another casualty of the recession. Labour's campaign, as the *Guardian* reveals, has quite failed to convince the British people that the British Government are to blame. Only 9 per cent of the British people believe that the recession here is the fault of the British Government.

  If the right hon. and learned member for Monklands East [John Smith] has scanned this morning's newspapers, what he will have found interesting is not the uncritical columns of the *Daily Mail* or the *Daily Express*, but what he might have found in the uncritical columns of the *Guardian*. The Labour Party, dismayed by the right hon. and learned gentleman's failure to pin the blame on the Tory Government, is looking for a scapegoat.

  I read with some surprise that, despite the onslaught from the Labour Party, its members have already lost faith in the man at the front end of the attack. No Conservative member would say such things, but I understand that the right hon. and learned gentleman's colleagues, loyal to a man, are concerned that he is 'not radical enough on the economy'. I gather that it is felt – dare I say it – that he is 'less clever than he thinks,' and 'less busy than he should be'. There is even a suspicion growing – only on the Labour side, of course – that he has 'left Labour boxed in' and that his policies are deflationary and offer little 'comfort for the unemployed or for debt-laden firms'.

'Is that the *Guardian*?' asked a helpful Conservative.

Yes, that was the *Guardian*. The tumbrils are rolling. This evening's *Evening Standard* carries the headline 'Labour's knives out for Smith'.

The debate began as a vote of confidence in the Government's economic policies; it has rapidly become a vote of confidence in the Shadow Chancellor. I find no difficulty in agreeing with some of the anxieties that flow from the whispers on the Labour benches, although I totally reject the implication that what is needed is not less but more of them.

Here Heseltine deployed a series of statistics and quotations to demonstrate that the recession was an international problem, rather than one made in Britain.

The right hon. and learned member for Monklands East said that we were doing nothing. All that reveals is that he does not understand what must be done. During the past sixteen months, interest rates have been cut eight times and inflation has fallen from 10.9 per cent to 4.1 per cent. The contradiction in everything that the right hon. and learned gentlemen says is displayed no more eloquently than in the words of the man who is something of a hero figure to the right hon. and learned gentleman – Jacques Delors. He said that Britain is fast becoming a paradise for foreign investment. That is why, in spite of the world downturn, we have seen in recent months Toyota's announcement of further investment in Derbyshire bringing 3,000 more jobs, Nissan's additional £150 million in Sunderland and other inward investment projects from Kimberley Clarke on Humberside to Toshiba in Plymouth.

The objectives are clear. The question that we must debate today is how we are to achieve those objectives. To be fair to the right hon. and learned gentleman, I do not think that he would have too much difficulty in accepting many of the priorities that I have listed. Nobody should be especially surprised about that. He is one of the few Labour members who has served in a Government with a basic rate of 35p in the pound, a top rate of 98p in the pound, inflation running out of control at 27 per cent and more days lost in strikes in just one month in the winter of discontent than were lost in the whole of last year. I understand that he is not leaping up and down to restore the record of a Government among whom he was prepared to serve without complaint.

The right hon. and learned gentleman's problem is that most of his right hon. and hon. friends are positively enthusiastic to restore, piece by piece, the regime that Labour left behind in 1979. What is at issue this afternoon is not the debate across the Floor of the House; it is in reality the debate within the Labour Party and, even worse, the debate within the Shadow Cabinet. On the one hand, we have the much vaunted prudence of the Shadow Chancellor and on the other, the irresponsible extravagance of his Shadow Cabinet colleagues.

I hear wherever I go that the right hon. and learned gentleman has become a star attraction in the City. Lunch after lunch, dinner after dinner, the assurances flow. The prawns are consumed. Soft shells, soft words and soft lights. Not a discordant crumb falls on to the thick pile. 'All will be well,' is the message that the right hon. and learned gentleman conveys. 'The Shadow Cabinet? Don't you worry, I've stitched them up.'

The words are no sooner uttered than up pops the hon. member for Oldham West [Michael Meacher] the shadow Secretary of State for Social Security, who said:

'If you took a poll on Labour's public expenditure commitments in the City, you would find it almost 100 per cent against'. Think of the tragedy, Mr Deputy Speaker. All those prawn cocktails for nothing. Never have so many crustaceans died in vain. With all the authority that I can command as Secretary of State for the Environment, let me say to the right hon. and learned member for Monklands East, 'Save the prawns.'

John Smith was goaded into counter-attacking: did Heseltine stick by a statement he made in November 1989 that Britain should sign the European Social Charter, an anathema to Euro-sceptic Conservatives? Heseltine evaded the charge.

The right hon. and learned gentleman knows full well that the matter was then negotiated brilliantly by my right hon. friend the Prime Minister. The Labour Party has been duped on the social charter. Labour members all know that the Germans want to export their high costs, that the French cannot resist the social charter because they have a socialist Government, and that other countries will not take any notice of it. The Labour Party has been duped into signing up to that extravagant impost on our industrial economy.

Each Labour spokesman has his own variant of a crash programme. That is exactly what it would be – the biggest crash programme in British economic history.

Let us look at the heart of the matter. Only two weeks ago, Labour's housing spokesman, the hon. member for Hammersmith [Clive Soley] tried to cook the books by redefining public borrowing. He promised – his phrase was eloquent – a phased release of up to £8 billion of capital receipts,[13] without, of course, increasing the public sector borrowing requirement. Consternation in the Opposition camp. Urgent telephone calls. But they were all abroad somewhere out there across the continent. Dramatic disruption of the grand tour. Then, before we knew where we were, the climbdown.

Predicatably, Soley rose to the bait and tried to intervene.

No. I am not giving way. In order that the hon. gentleman does not get the quotation wrong, it might be helpful to provide the House with the quotation from *The Times* of 6 February this year in which he continued his saga of this phased release. He said:

'There is no plan to revise the PSBR. I was wrong. I withdraw it.' This is not really about the phased release of capital receipts. We have witnessed the phased release of the Opposition spokesman on housing. The whole House will wish to join me in saying, 'Good luck, good fortune and goodbye.'

Soley and George Howarth, the Labour MP for Knowsley North, continued to dispute with Heseltine the accuracy of the quotation for some minutes.

If I may leave the junior spokesman for the environment, I should like to come to the hon. member for Dagenham [Bryan Gould, the shadow Environment Secretary] – no slouch he, when it comes to egging up the public expenditure ante. Within the past few months, by his team alone we have been asked to support: local authority bids for an extra £2 billion a year; the full release of all those capital receipts; the unfettered discretion of local authorities to clobber the business rate payer.

That is just part of the hon. gentleman's programme. Then there is the problem of renationalising the water industry. In the past few weeks – this is why there has been so much muttering on the Labour backbenches – we have heard about the £1 billion so-called recovery package, about the £800 million that Labour wants to spend on training and the £50 million that it wants to spend on the National Health Service by cancelling private health insurance.

But hold on: not to be outdone, the hon. member for Dagenham says that renationalising the water industry is a 'priority' for Labour. What will all that cost – about £4 billion, just to get control of it. That will cost about four times the size of Labour's recovery package; five times the amount that it proposes to spend on training; and 80 times what it deems to be essential for the National Health Service. All for one purpose – to buy off the hard left of the Labour Party. The consequence would be a return to the regime when Labour cut water investment. That was Labour's contribution to the environmental enhancement of that vital industry.

Before the day is out, the hon. member for Dagenham will be back on his feet, defending the higher tax rate plans of the Labour Party, which overnight would do more to destroy the housing market than any other single thing one could do.

Now Gould rose to intervene. He was a little more wary, noting that Heseltine could hardly wait for him to get to his feet. He simply signalled his intent to attack the government's record on the recession – a subject he said Heseltine had failed to address.

My colleagues and I tremble on our feet. I promise the hon. gentleman that we shall all be here waiting for the great hour when the hon. member for Dagenham flattens us. I confess that I had intended to go out to dinner tonight, but I shall not do so now. I do not want to be unfair to the hon. member for Dagenham. Why should he respect the Shadow Chancellor's edict, when the leader of the Labour Party designs policies over Luigi's pasta, late at night – economics bolognaise?[14]

There was the leader of the Labour Party – wrestling with the twin complexities of national insurance on the one hand, and how to carve up the Shadow Chancellor on the other. Picture the scene. The Leader of the Opposition, fighting to prevent long strings of spaghetti from slipping through the prongs of his fork, while the minutiae of national insurance were slipping through the caverns of his mind. So, there we were, it was the politics of Bedlam – fork-twisting, head-spinning, mind-boggling – the right hon. member for Islwyn [Neil Kinnock] firmly in charge. He would have been better employed wrestling with the damaging consequences of his tax policies on the national economy.

The right hon. and learned member for Monklands East is not that far apart from his leader on putting up tax rates. In a recent interview, David Frost put it to him that *The Economist* had pointed out that, under his proposals, Britain would have the highest tax rates for middle managers anywhere in the world. Quick as a flash, the right hon. and learned Member for Monklands East said, 'Ah.' – [Hon. Members: – 'Ah!'] – I paused because it is so awful that I had to check it before I read it. He said, by way of excuse, 'Ah, what they took was not all the countries in the world; what they took were the G7 industrial countries.'

So, there it is, on the record, staring us in the face. Put the right hon. and learned member for Monklands East in the Treasury and, as long as he can find some clapped-out, down-at-heel, fly-blown socialist economy with higher tax rates than we have in this country, he will be content to point his lawyer's finger and say that someone, somewhere is suffering more than we are.

The Labour Party does not understand that there is a whole generation of young people out there – the skilled, the talented and the enterprising – who need to believe that there is a future for them here, in Britain, where energy and initiative will be rewarded. We want to see young teachers seek the initiative to assume responsibilities as head teachers. We want young engineers to believe that it is worth their while to be promoted to production managers. We want young doctors to stay and practice in Britain and aim for the privilege and reward of running our hospitals. We want young scientists to relish the opportunities to explore tomorrow's frontiers in our laboratories and research establishments.

Noting that Heseltine was turning his back on the opposition benches and aiming his words at Conservative MPs, Labour's Giles Radice raised a point of order. Was such conduct in order? Was it a leadership bid? But that simply led Heseltine on to his punchline.

Why should I not speak to my own benches? We are the governing party and we will stay that way because the Labour Party is out of date, out of touch and out of office. We will keep them there.

'More, more,' cheered ecstatic Conservative MPs. The themes trailed in this speech hit home on an electorate which remained wary of Labour's tax and spend image. Weeks later, the Conservatives won the general election on a campaign based around warnings of 'Labour's tax bombshell'. The lesson from Heseltine's exploitation of Labour's splits and confusion was not lost on some Labour MPs. Under Tony Blair and Gordon Brown, policy statements, particularly on tax and the economy, were ruthlessly controlled and going 'off message' became a career-shortening sin.

The interventionist tiger of the rubber chicken circuit.'

Gordon Brown lampoons Michael Heseltine: 6 July 1992

In the aftermath of the 1992 general election, which Labour had expected to win but which instead delivered a fourth term in office for the Conservatives, Gordon Brown had emerged as one of his party's most effective debaters. In the post-election interregnum before John Smith took over the party leadership, and Brown succeeded him as shadow Chancellor, a promising target presented itself.

Brown was still shadowing the Department of Trade and Industry, which was now headed by Michael Heseltine – a flamboyant interventionist in a rather grey Cabinet still dominated by laissez-faire Thatcherite orthodoxy. Heseltine had spent much of his exile from government in the late 1980s compiling an agenda for an activist industrial policy, to take British industry by the scruff of the neck and make it internationally competitive. This, in Brown's analysis, was bound to lead to tensions with Heseltine's Cabinet colleagues, providing a promising opening for invective. And to add a little spice, Heseltine had decided to revive the old title of his office, styling himself President of the Board of Trade. No mere Secretary of State, he.

John Major had been amused by the title, Heseltine recorded in his memoirs.[15] He himself thought the transatlantic overtones would stir up the press and add a little spice to his job. It certainly stirred up Brown, who directed a memorable and extended burst of mockery at Heseltine's inability to deliver his agenda in office. He began by pointing to the painful fact that the long recession, which the Conservatives had promised would lift once they were safely re-elected, was still destroying jobs and companies. The DTI's insolvency service was the only part of the department to expand its activities, he noted with gallows humour. There was the familiar Brown blizzard of statistics, illustrating deepening economic woe, before he turned his fire on Heseltine. This was a dangerous gambit. He was seeking the scalp of a formidable parliamentarian.

FACED WITH ALL these problems – a recession, a trade deficit and Britain bottom of the league – what has been happening in Government since 9 April? [the date of the general election] What has been achieved by the Trade Minister? His first action at the Department of Trade and Industry was not the much-needed change of policy, but the wholly unnecessary change of title – calling himself President. What has been achieved as the President approaches the end of his first 100 days? The President should have known the difficulties that he might have from the right of his party when he heard of the election night party of Baroness Thatcher and her right-wing friends. Although much of the media attention was focused on Mr Patten, now the member for the comparatively safe seat of Hong Kong, East, even then it was the right hon. member for Henley [Michael Heseltine] who was being targeted by the right. Here is the first-hand account of the *Daily Telegraph* correspondent. He was at the party and later wrote:

'It is not true to say the right wing cheered when the left-wing chairman of the Tory Party was defeated. I was there.'

Chris Patten was Chairman of the Conservative Party during the 1992 general election. He masterminded a successful campaign, and could have expected one of the top jobs in the Cabinet, but for his defeat in Bath by the Liberal Democrat Don Foster. Instead, he became the governor of Hong Kong, and presided over its return to China. A leading figure on the One Nation Europhile wing of the party, his defeat was greeted with shouts of 'Tory gain' at the election-night party referred to by Brown refers.

'In fact, Mrs. Thatcher was quick to express her sympathy for Mr Patten when Mr Heseltine made an appearance on the TV she did though put her hand over the screen.'

That gesture is at once symbolic and, as it turns out, prophetic. He has become President – but President of what? President of a Board of Trade which never meets, which has no active members, which must somehow spearhead a bold new industrial strategy for a new century and a new millennium, but which last met on 13 December 1850. The Board of Trade was wound up years ago, and there is no one there to notice should the President decide, on impulse and no doubt on a matter of principle, to walk out. The right hon. gentleman is not so much the emperor with no clothes as the President with no board and far too little trade.

What of the right hon. gentleman's ministerial colleagues, who are all on the Treasury Bench, all the President's men – or are they? The Under-Secretary of State for Technology [Edward Leigh] is from the No Turning Back Group [a Thatcherite ginger group] and, unlike the President, he believes that regional policy is a phoney activity of Government. Perhaps he is there to keep a watchful eye on the President. The new Minister responsible for competition

[Neil Hamilton] is also from the No Turning Back Group and, unlike the President, he believes that Britain should not be in the exchange rate mechanism and that Britain should be the free port of Europe. Perhaps he is there to report back to the Prime Minister. This is the first time it has been thought necessary to impose on a Cabinet Minister not just one minder but two. As the President would have put it in one of his great speeches in the election campaign, 'Thatcherites to the left of him, Thatcherites to the right of him, Thatcherites everywhere.'

This was a parody of Heseltine's stump speech. During the election he had appropriated Tennyson to attack Labour's tax proposals: 'Taxes to the left of them, taxes to the right of them, into the valley of taxes rode the Labour Party.'

Let us stand back and look at the right hon. gentleman's plans for the Department of Trade and Industry and at his books, *Where There's a Will* and *The Challenge of Europe*. Calling himself President was not the limit of his ambitions. As President he would create not only an English development agency, introduce a public test for takeovers in a new law, and a new European company statute, transform research and development with a tax credit, but formulate an industrial strategy that would sweep across Whitehall, encompassing every Minister.

The right hon. gentleman also had ambitions for his colleagues. The Secretary of State for Employment would be told to introduce a new training law, a tax or levy; the Secretary of State for Education would be told to have a new skills investment programme; the Secretary of State for Transport would have to have a new transport review; and in the book the Foreign Secretary was told: 'Some of the work of the Foreign Office is unsatisfactory . . .' and changes would have to be made. Of course, the Prime Minister would have to sign the social charter. The whole of Government was to be reshaped in the image of the right hon. gentleman's presidency. There were policies for every Department and roles for the President, not just as chairman of the National Economic Development Council in place of the Chancellor, because through the new industrial policy committee of the Cabinet,

> the president should have the power base of a new Cabinet committee on which he would take the chair and on which other Cabinet Ministers would sit.

One of the 'inevitable roles' of the committee would be to decide for or against major projects, such as the channel tunnel and power stations, and it would control education and even taxation policy, which sounds a bit like the Chancellor's job.

What would be the Chancellor's role in this great new strategy? The book says:

> If the DTI is to increase its influence the Treasury will see this as a threat and so it should. Somehow we have to shift the balance. We must oppose the Treasury's never ending round of book keeping.

I am sorry that there is no one here from the Treasury to hear this while the Chancellor is away. The book continues:

> How often the Treasury can fail to see the big defect in its conduct. The weakness in Government is that there is not sufficient challenge to Treasury judgments which may frustrate the strategic objectives of the Government and the work of the DTI.

What has happened to this great design, this ground plan, this master strategy? The 100 days of the President started with his determination to expand the National Economic Development Council with him in control. But they have ended, not with the President taking the chair from the Chancellor, but with the straightforward abolition of the NEDC by the Chancellor himself. In those 100 days the President's big achievement has been to make even the Chancellor look decisive and powerful. The 100 days began with his plan for the power base of a new industry committee. What has happened? The committee that started as the President's base from which to control the rest of the Government is to be chaired by Lord Wakeham, whose remit is undoubtedly to keep a close eye on the President. What started as the President's plan for an expansion of his power has become a means by which the President is kept under control. What of the Foreign Office? The 100 days were preceded by the statement:

> The present role of the Foreign and Commonwealth Office is unsatisfactory. A changed role would naturally require considerable changes in the training of diplomats.

The 100 days have now ended with him saying exactly the opposite. I quote from his speech on 1 June:

> Let me say it here, the Foreign Office has developed an experience and a sophistication in the promotion of our national enterprise that is now world class.

It is not so much a case of the 100 days that changed the Foreign Office as the 100 days that changed the views of the President. The same is true of training. The 100 days which were preceded by the demand for compulsory action, with a levy or tax on training, have ended with him praising the voluntary approach. The 100 days were preceded by the demand for action, with research tax credit, the English development agency, and investment in seed corn research. Undoubtedly, the need for new money has ended with the President in retreat, saying that he needs no more money – the first time that a spending Minister has conceded his case even before the spending round has begun.

How do we sum up the President's first 100 days? After seven years of Kennedy-style build up and campaigning for the presidency and three months of Camelot hype, I can tell him what has happened. As President Kennedy would have put it, 'Ask not what you can do for the Cabinet; ask what the Cabinet has done to you.' The City responsibilities of the DTI have gone to the Chancellor [Norman Lamont], who is almost ten years younger. The film responsibilities for the DTI have gone to the rising star, the Secretary of State for National Heritage [David Mellor]. Public spending directions are now at the behest of the youngest Cabinet Minister, the Chief Secretary to the Treasury [Stephen Dorrell]. As President Kennedy would have put it, 'The torch has passed to a new generation.'

The President is able to call himself what he wants, talk to whoever he chooses, hire any advertising agency he fancies. He has full powers and unlimited responsibilities to reorganise the desks within his Department, but he cannot begin to contemplate the implementation of a genuine industrial strategy for Britain. Perhaps next week there will be an announcement on the dramatic reshuffle of the office furniture, and the week after that, sweeping new recommendations on the colour of the curtains. But when there are no new measures on research, manufacturing, technology and exports, his is absolute power over a Department that is unfortunately becoming absolutely powerless.

The Minister – the President – who spent years in exile working out his plans, who promised so much, who stormed the country with his new ideas for an industrial strategy, who was the darling of the Conservative associations, the hero of a thousand Conservative Party lunches, the interventionist tiger of the rubber chicken circuit has been brought low, reduced to trophy status. The tiger that was once the king of the jungle is now just the fireside rug – decorative and ostentatious, but essentially there to be walked all over. My concern is not so much for the personal fate of the President, but for the fate of industrial policy. We face massive technological, demographic, industrial, training and environmental challenges in an increasingly global economy. There is an urgent need for our industrial strategy to have the backing not just of the President but of the Government. It must, first, encourage long-term investment to bridge what the President has called the investment gap. Secondly, it must boost training and technology to reverse the deterioration and erosion of our position. Thirdly, it must back exports to end the position where, as the President has said, our attitude to the trade deficit has been simplistic. Fourthly, it must ensure that our regional economies play a full part in balanced, sustainable growth in this country.

We are faced with huge regional imbalances and growth rates in our regions which, over the next few years, are predicted to be a third or less than half those of the most prosperous regions of Europe. The Secretary of State has promised action, but there was nothing in the manifesto and nothing since, and cuts are taking place in the Government's regional investment budget. Regional selective assistance is to fall by 6 per cent this year. Is it not vital that the Prime Minister and the Government listen to the views coming from the regions? Is it not vital that they do not use the review of regional aid maps to cut regional support? Also vital is detailed consideration of the creation of the long-sought English development agencies, and of work to strengthen those that already exist in Scotland and Wales. The President himself admitted a crisis in research and development funding, that the gap between ourselves and our competitors is widening, and that he proposed measures that have not yet been implemented. At the same time, support for technology has been cut this year, and nothing in the Queen's Speech reverses that.

I want from this debate a guarantee that the Government will carefully consider the reports from the House of Lords and from their own scientific advisers that specifically make the case for information technology, and the creation of a new research tax credit and country-wide technology transfer network to ensure that we do not move out of the current recession with an even weaker technology base.

Training also is recognised to be in crisis. The President spoke of Britain's lamentable training record and patchy part-time education, one of the poorest performances in science up to the age of fourteen, and alarming weaknesses in mathematics among teenagers. He said also that the youth training scheme is not an adequate building block. The right hon. gentleman proposes changes in training legislation. Will he use his influence to bring training cuts to a halt so that our country will cease to be the only one in Europe whose training budgets are being cut? Will he promise to push for a new training policy so that skill levels can be improved? We know from the British Exporters Association that United Kingdom jobs are being exported because of lack of assistance, and that workplace redundancies are occurring because of the Government's cuts in export support. In Opposition, the right hon. gentleman spoke of the importance of tackling the trade deficit. He said that it was not of incidental importance, self-correcting, or easily financed. I want the Government to outline measures to support British exports, end privatisation, and support regionally based export services that will lead to Britain winning new markets in Europe and elsewhere. I want a Government strategy for manufacturing, investment, training, technology, and our regions that measures up to the challenges of the future.

We need a Government who will act in the public interest to end the recession, tackle the trade deficit and secure lasting recovery, preside over an investment decade for the British economy, and with the ambition to make our work force the best trained and educated in Europe. We need a Government who will take measures now to reduce unemployment, tackle poverty, and eliminate low pay. We need a Government who will confront the challenges that face our country in an increasingly international economy.

We have instead a Government who, three months after an election victory, have no strategy for recovery other than to talk about it, no plan for unemployment other than further to penalise the unemployed, no policy for helping industry other than cutting its budget, and who are so complacent and arrogant that they do not even pretend to care about the misery caused by bankruptcies, closures, and unemployment in every region.

We have a Government who are creating not a classless society but a heartless society.[16] It will be the job of the Labour Opposition to attack Conservative failure, to expose the broken promises, and to point the way to a better future.

Seven
EUROPE

BRITAIN'S POLITICIANS NEVER stop debating our place in Europe for long. The decades since Edward Heath finally secured membership of the then European Economic Community have been punctuated by Euro-eruptions: a referendum, a renegotiation of membership terms, the catastrophic exit from the exchange rate mechanism of the European Monetary System – still one of the most politically decisive moments in recent history – the long attritional battle to ratify the Treaty of Maastricht, the collapse of the European Constitution, and the continuing debate over whether Britain should join the single currency, the euro.

It is noticeable how opinion on these issues swings back and forth within the parties over the decades. In the 1970s Labour was the more Euro-sceptic of the main parties – to the point where Enoch Powell urged opponents of British membership to vote Labour in 1974. The beleaguered band of largely Jenkinsite pro-Europeans found themselves increasingly uncomfortable inside Labour, and many eventually decamped to the SDP. But across the political divide, the Heath government marked the high water mark of Tory Euro-enthusiasm, and the party became steadily more sceptical throughout the Thatcher and Major years, and the process has shown no sign of abating since the Conservatives lost power in 1997. The tensions between Major's Europhile-heavy Cabinet and the increasingly sceptical rank and file in Parliament eventually sent the party into convulsions. By the mid 1990s it was Labour which sounded the more Euro-enthused, but a decade later scepticism is again detectable on the Labour benches, following the defeat in several national referendums of the proposed European Constitution and a clear swing towards scepticism in public opinion – and Tony Blair's reputed ambition to take Britain into the euro appears to have been checkmated.

Perhaps because these debates go to the heart of what nationhood means, they tend to split parties. As the stories behind the speeches in this chapter demonstrate, it has often required extraordinary efforts from party whips to get a government's European policy through the Commons. It is easy to understand why. The profound implications of the – now apparently stalled – drive to political and economic union have animated maverick talents, and produced some improbable alliances of political opposites. Europe has also ended the careers of the very great, shattered governments and generated some outrageous speeches.

'Anyone who tonight, knowing that the necessary conditions to approval of these proposals have been withheld, that they do not command the full-hearted consent either of the House or of the country, nevertheless votes for them, casts his vote against the vital principle by which this House exists.'

Enoch Powell urges the Commons not to support British entry into the European Community: 28 October 1971

The great Commons debate on Britain's accession to what was then the European Economic Community lasted for six days. People queued for sixteen hours and more for places in the public gallery. Everyone seemed to sense that a fundamental decision was about to be taken. The House was being invited to approve British membership 'on the basis of the arrangements which have been negotiated'.

The new Conservative Prime Minister, Edward Heath, had succeeded where the two Harolds – Macmillan and Wilson – had failed in the 1960s, in securing French support for British membership. This had been delivered to an astonished British press corps by President Pompidou himself. A White Paper outlining the membership terms had been published in July, when a preliminary debate had merely taken note of them. But Heath postponed the substantive vote until after the summer recess.

He faced considerable difficulties in securing parliamentary approval. His modest majority was more than outweighed by the number of Conservative MPs likely to rebel against membership. Here the astute tactical advice of Heath's Chief Whip, Francis Pym, came into play. In a detailed memo three weeks before the debate, Pym set out the reasons for allowing a free vote rather than trying to coerce the rebels. He estimated that 38 Tory MPs would not support the government, but speculated that 40 to 60 pro-European Labour MPs would, and that it would be much harder for the Labour leadership to restrain them if the Tories did not impose a whip. Heath had set his face against a free vote – an odd lapse given that he had been Chief Whip himself – and was only won over three days before the debate, after intense persuasion from Pym. Labour MPs voted narrowly to impose a three line whip, requiring all their MPs to vote against membership – but the Tory decision did indeed strengthen the resolve of the Labour rebels, even if their leading figures like Roy Jenkins had to stay silent in order to remain on the front bench.

A key figure in the debate was Enoch Powell – the de facto leader of the anti-European Tories and a formidable critic of Heath's government on several policy fronts. Powell was the final backbencher to speak. He began by mocking the contortions performed by Labour, who had attempted to negotiate accession in 1967, only to meet a humiliating rebuff from General de Gaulle, the French President, and then extended the mockery to his own side with a vicious oratorical rabbit punch.

O NE OF THE MORE repetitive characteristics of the debate has been the absolute hail of ridicule and taunts which has descended upon the heads of the occupants of the Opposition front bench. The quotations of speeches made by themselves a year, two years and three years ago, which they were now verbally and textually contradicting; the exposure of argument after argument, which, if it was valid at all, must not just be valid against one set or another of transitional terms but must go to the heart of the matter – day after day there has been a fusillade of jeers and taunts pointing all this out. Yet those jeers and taunts recoil upon those who utter them.

The question has been repeatedly – addressed to right hon. gentlemen opposite, 'What has changed? What has changed in the last year since you said that, or the last two or three years, since 1968 or 1967?' I will tell the House what has changed. What has changed is that for the first time a proposition has been put to the people of this country. For the first time the people of this country have addressed themselves to the question of membership of the Community not just as something which might happen somehow, sometime, but as something on which a decision has to be taken whether it shall or shall not happen now and in these circumstances. It has been the response of the people of this country to that sudden real proposition put before them which is the change that explains all that has happened. It has imposed the most severe gymnastic contortions upon many hon. members opposite.

'Not only opposite,' someone shouted.

Nevertheless, it has the fortunate result that the majority in the country are represented and have a voice in this House as well as the minority. It would have been tragic if that were not so.

Repeatedly in this debate words of my right hon. friend the Prime Minister have been quoted – his words about the necessity for the full-hearted consent of Parliament and people; his statement – his repeated statement – that this country could not be taken into the Common Market against the majority of the people or against the wishes of the people.

These words have not been quoted textually and repeated just to pinpoint a phrase or two which the Prime Minister used. They have been quoted because they are manifestly true. They are not true because my right hon. friend said them. Rather my right hon. friend said them because they are true; and all honour to him for having said them and all honour to him for the clarity with which he expressed them.

The reason they are true – they are not true of every question which falls to be decided by the House – is the unique character of the decision proposed to the House, which involves a cession by the House – initially perhaps minor, but destined to grow – of its present sovereignty, of its present ultimate sovereignty, and requires from the people a commitment to merge themselves and their destinies with those of the countries of the adjacent Continent.

I do not think the fact that this involves a cession – and a growing cession – of Parliament's sovereignty can be disputed. Indeed, I notice that those who are the keenest proposers of British entry are the most ready to confess – not to confess, but to assert – that of course this involves by its very nature a reduction of the sovereignty of the House. Nevertheless, it is worth while reminding the House that the advice which it was given by the Lord Chancellor in Cmnd. 3301 – the highest source of legal advice which the House can receive – put the nature of that transfer of sovereignty very succinctly in paragraph 22: 'The constitutional innovation would lie in the acceptance in advance as part of the law of the United Kingdom of provisions to be made in the future by instruments issued by the Community institutions,' then follow these words, 'a situation for which there is no precedent in this country.'

It is an unprecedented act of renunciation which this House is called upon to make. No wonder, then, that it should be a condition for that that it should have our full-hearted consent.

The development of the Community which is envisaged by those who support it on the narrowest, as by those who support it on the broadest, grounds can, in the nature of things, be only a progressive one. My right hon. friends, particularly my right hon. friend the Secretary of State for Foreign and Commonwealth Affairs [Alec Douglas-Home served as Foreign Secretary in Heath's Cabinet – a rare example of a former Prime Minister accepting lesser office], are right to assert that its ambit could be extended stage by stage only with the unanimous agreement of all the parties to the Community and that, at each point in that extension we would have a veto.

But the fact of the veto does not alter the nature of the commitment which we are asked to make. First, a veto is not only a defence: it is also a weapon. The hon. member for Ebbw Vale [Michael Foot, a Labour opponent of British membership] made this point very effectively. As we can protect ourselves by our veto, so every other member can protect itself; and its very ability to do so imposes the like duress upon us as upon all the rest.

That leads to the second aspect of the veto, which is the real one. It is that we do not enter, if we enter at all, into such an undertaking as this in order to veto whatever we do not agree with. Of course not. We enter it with the object of only dissenting where we cannot avoid dissenting, and with the intention that unanimity shall prevail more and more and in the spirit that we in this House and in this country will accept the overriding voice of something larger than ourselves.

My right hon. friends on the front bench have not sought to burke this issue. My right hon. friend the Home Secretary[1] this afternoon repeatedly said that what he looked for in the Community in the future was political unity. Political unity is meaningless if it does not mean that normally one accepts here, as others accept elsewhere, not what we ourselves might have chosen for ourselves but what is decided and decreed by the whole.

It is in this fact that the irrevocability of the decision consists. My right hon. and learned friend the member for Hertfordshire East [Sir Derek Walker-Smith, a former Conservative Minister for Health] demonstrated, I thought irrefutably, that for legal purposes we ought to regard this as an irrevocable commitment. But leaving that on one side, this is a step which by its very nature makes no sense unless it is intended to be irrevocable or irreversible. This is not the kind of community, nor are these the kind of grounds, of which one can say that we will enter into it but that if we do not like it we shall be off like a shot. What we are asked for in this House and in this country is an intention, an irrevocable decision, gradually to part with the sovereignty of this House and to commit ourselves to the merger of this nation and its destinies with the rest of the Community. It is there that the validity rests of the conditions which my right hon. friend imposed upon the achievement of that aim.

Of course, one could imagine perhaps some emergency, some sudden deterioration of our position and prospects in this country, which would justify us in brushing those conditions aside, when we might say that there may or may not be full-hearted consent for this indoors or out of doors, but that the urgency is such, the manifest unacceptability of any alternative is such, that needs must, however we do it. But although I have heard that proposition at various times during this debate, that is not an argument which the

Government and, indeed, which hon. members in most quarters of the House have sought to put. On the contrary, immediately before the general election my right hon. friend who is now the Prime Minister assured the country and the world that we could live and thrive outside the Community with equal success in the future to that which this country has enjoyed in the past.

David Crouch, Conservative MP for Canterbury, as Hansard put it, 'indicated dissent'.

My right hon. friend said it. My hon. friend shakes his head, but in the manifesto on which he and I both fought at the election we told the country that if we did not like the terms which were offered we could perfectly well stand and thrive on our own. So there can be no urgent, evident, irresistible necessity, and we come back to the fact that this act which is proposed to us is an act which by its very character must require from this House and from the country manifest, full-hearted consent, active and overwhelming commitment.

The Division which takes place tonight at 10 o'clock is being awaited not only inside the Chamber but far and wide outside. The emissaries of radio, television and the press are all waiting like harpies to pounce upon us as soon as we emerge from the Lobbies and to write their deductions, their dispatches upon the outcome. And yet, Mr Speaker, that which we require to know, that which it most concerns us to know, we know already before the Question is put.

We know before the Question is put that this House is deeply and, indeed, passionately divided. We know, and this has come from speech after speech of the most fervent supporters of the proposal that we should enter, as well as from other quarters, that full-hearted consent to this step does not exist out of doors. We know, in short, before we vote that the two conditions precedent to the decision to enter do not exist: they are not available.

In the course of these discussions, there has been repeated reference to the name of perhaps the greatest of all the sons of this House. We have been reminded repeatedly of Edmund Burke's *Letter to the Electors of Bristol*; of how in 1774 he warned them that he was a free man, that he would not consider it necessary unless his judgment approved it to be the mere mouthpiece in Parliament of their interests. But we would be mistaken, and we would mistake the nature of this House, if we thought that what Edmund Burke was saying was that this House could legislate without regard to the sentiments and opinions of the people.

It so happens that in the heart of the debates over the American colonies Edmund Burke wrote another letter to Bristol – his *Letter to the Sheriffs of Bristol*, in 1777, and he there defined what he believed was the function of this House. He wrote: 'To follow, not to force, the public inclination, to give a direction, a form, a technical dress and a specific sanction to the general sense of the community is the true end of legislature.'

Anyone who tonight, knowing that the necessary conditions to approval of these proposals have been withheld, that they do not command the full-hearted consent either of the House or of the country, nevertheless votes for them, casts his vote against the vital principle by which this House exists.

Powell's statement of the constitutional case against membership remains for many the crux of the argument over Britain's place in Europe. But the final speaker in the debate was the Prime Minister.

'When this House endorses this Motion many millions of people right across the world will rejoice that we have taken our rightful place in a truly United Europe.'

Edward Heath winds up the debate on British membership: 28 October 1971

Edward Heath devoted his maiden speech, in 1950, to a plea for Britain to join the Schuman Plan – the coal and steel trading organisation which evolved into the EEC and ultimately the EU. He did not succeed, and his almost immediate promotion to the Tory Whips' Office meant that he did not make another substantive Commons speech for nine years – at which point he entered the Cabinet. Heath had been in charge of Harold Macmillan's unsuccessful attempt to join the EEC; and now, 20 years on from his first expression of Euro-enthusiasm, he was about to seize his place in history as the leader who finally took Britain into Europe.

'I had been conscious of a tremendous weight of responsibility as I stood at the Dispatch Box,' Edward Heath wrote of his speech winding up the accession debate.[2] This was not to be another episode in his long parliamentary dogfight with Harold Wilson, who had opened the debate for Labour with an equivocal speech six days before, and left James Callaghan to wind up for the opposition. Heath's speech dealt mainly with high geopolitics and international economics, rather than the detail of the terms for British membership.

I do not think that any Prime Minister has stood at this Box[3] in time of peace and asked the House to take a positive decision of such importance as I am asking it to take tonight. I am well aware of the responsibility which rests on my shoulders for so doing. After ten years of negotiation, after many years of discussion in this House and after ten years of debate, the moment of decision for Parliament has come. The other House has already taken its vote and expressed its view.

'Backwoodsmen!' several MPs shouted.

451 frontwoodsmen have voted in favour of the Motion and, for the rest, 58.

Here Heath described the changing world situation, covering such issues as the emergence of China as a third superpower, the failure of the Commonwealth to evolve into an independent trading bloc, as some had hoped after the war, and the need for Europe to play a stronger role in its own defence – all reasons why Britain should join the Community, he argued. He then began to deal with the arguments against membership put by James Callaghan, the Labour shadow Foreign Secretary, who had struck a strongly Euro-sceptic note in the run-up to this debate – including a robust rejection of the idea that French should be considered the dominant language of Europe, a proposition he dismissed with the words *'Non, merci beaucoup.'*

In the debates of the last six days, the economic arguments have figured very prominently. They are important. Again, I do not accept the argument of the right hon. member for Cardiff South-East [Callaghan] that merely to have a reduction of a 7 per cent average tariff is not of great consequence. We know that it is not entirely the average tariff which matters; it is the very high level of some individual tariffs which are important to us and to our industries.

The questions of larger firms, technology, capital investment and rate of growth are of immense importance. I agree with those who say that there can be no final proof of this. It must be a matter of qualitative judgment. I accept that, and we have offered our judgment to the House. If one needed any indication of the difficulties, it has already been said that the economists have lined up in two columns in *The Times*. I notice that one was one-quarter of an inch shorter than the other. On what basis can one make an economic judgment of one-quarter of an inch of a column in *The Times*?

But what is important is the question of being in the best possible position to influence economic decisions which are determining our future. That seems to be the real crux of the economic argument. Over these next few years, in which new patterns will be formed and new decisions will be taken, they will affect the livelihood of everyone in this country and they will be taken in practice by those who have the greatest economic power. We may not like it, and we may wish it otherwise, but we have to recognise these facts as they exist.

But this is coming about just at the moment when we have the opportunity of joining the Community and of influencing one of the major economic powers. In those circumstances, I believe that a Prime Minister who came to this Box and recommended that we should reject the opportunity now before us of taking an active part, a share in these decisions, would be taking a terrible gamble with the livelihood of the British people for many years to come. That Prime Minister would be saying to the House, in effect, that he was prepared to accept the situation in which vital decisions affecting all of us were taken in circumstances over which we had no control and little influence. This is a gamble which I, as Prime Minister, am not prepared to advise this House to take. Nor can these matters of trade and finance ever be separated entirely – as we are seeing today in the news which comes from the United States – from the security of our country or of the Community.

The right hon. gentleman raised some matters about the terms. The Government have made their recommendation on this. They have been discussed in great detail in the House. I was not proposing at this stage of the debate to go over them again. They are better than anyone thought possible when the negotiations began. This is widely recognised in Europe by the friends of this country. It is widely recognised by the friends of the Labour Party who had great influence in securing those terms. It has been widely recognised right across the Commonwealth and the world.

The Chancellor of the Exchequer in the last Administration [the very pro-European Roy Jenkins, who later that evening was to lead 69 Labour rebels into the aye lobby with Heath; a further 20 Labour MPs abstained] himself set out the position on monetary union. I am told that, if the right hon. gentleman likes to look up the article which he himself signed in *Le Monde* in 1967, he will find there his own aspirations in that direction set out very clearly.

As to whether Britain is European, I fail entirely to understand the argument which the right hon. gentleman was trying to advance about cutting off our links with the outside world, when the members of the Community itself are the great trading countries of the world; when the Community itself is the greatest trading bloc in the world; when, as the Leader of the Liberal Party [Jeremy Thorpe] pointed out this evening, when the enlarged Community is created, it will have arrangements with 80 countries. Twenty-nine of the Commonwealth countries and nineteen dependencies will be associated with the Community. What on earth does the right hon. gentleman mean by our cutting off our links with the outside world?

To sum up, the outcome of the right hon. gentleman's analysis was, quite simply, that he wished to stipulate terms on which we would enter the Community which everybody who has observed events for the last twelve years knows from the beginning would not even have allowed negotiations to start and which, if the Community had been prepared to accept them, would have meant the break-up of the Community. That is the plain fact about the remarks which the right hon. gentleman has made about the terms for going into negotiations.

I have sometimes felt that among those who have been in this debate seeking to balance up the advantages and disadvantages there was a desire for a degree of certainty which is never obtainable in human affairs. Hon. members will not ask for it in their lives, in their own businesses. As a nation we have never hitherto asked for it in a trading agreement or in international affairs, either economic or political. Anyone who studies the length of our trading agreements outside will accept that that is the case.

It may be that it is showing a lack of confidence in ourselves, but I suggest that, whatever the explanation, we are worrying about the wrong question. Surely the right question to ask ourselves is this: has the Community the necessary and appropriate means for dealing with the problems of its members, whether they arise out of these present negotiations in which we have taken part or whether they arise from any other cause in the life of the Community? That surely is the question one has to put about a living, changing, developing organisation such as the Community. That is what matters.

The answer to that question is undeniably yes, it has got those means and, what is more they have been and are being used successfully. They are proven means for dealing with the problems inside the Community – through the Treaty, through the Commission, through the Council of Ministers these matters are being handled the whole time.

Perhaps, therefore, the final statement of the Leader of the Opposition this afternoon was not quite so bloodcurdling as he meant it to be. I must say to him that the position in Europe today is that no one is sitting there waiting to have an amicable cup of tea with him. Nevertheless, should any of the apprehensions expressed by himself or by his right hon. friends materialise, then the machinery exists and is functioning to deal with them.

This leads me to a kindred and allied point. It is understandable after ten years of negotiation and frustration that many in debate and many in the country outside have fought and talked in terms of 'we' and 'they'. Some, I think, have been overwhelmed by a fear that this country in an organisation such as the Community must always be dominated by 'they.' That is certainly not how the rest of the Community sees it. But we are approaching the point where, if this House so decides tonight, it will become just as much our Community as their Community. We shall be partners, we shall be cooperating, and we shall be trying to find common solutions to common problems of all the members of an enlarged Community.

We have confidence that we can benefit as well as contribute, that we can further our own interests and the interests of the Community at one and the same time. After all, the leaders of all three parties in this House accept the principle of entry into the European Community, as the right hon. gentleman reaffirmed this afternoon. The Community is not governed by any particular party ideology. How can it be, with a Socialist Government in the Federal Republic, with a right-wing Government in France, with a coalition in Italy containing Socialists? Of course not. What is more, all the opposition parties in the member countries of the Community support membership of the Community just as much as the governing parties.

It is right that there should have been so much discussion of sovereignty. I would put it very simply. If sovereignty exists to be used and to be of value, it must be effective. We have to make a judgment whether this is the most advantageous way of using our country's sovereignty. Sovereignty belongs to all of us, and to make that judgment we must look at the way in which the Community has actually worked during these last twelve years. In joining we are making a commitment which involves our sovereignty, but we are also gaining an opportunity. We are making a commitment to the Community as it exists tonight, if the House so decides. We are gaining an opportunity to influence its decisions in the future.

The right hon. gentleman asked me questions as to how we saw this. The Community in future months will be discussing future policy in an enlarged Community. No one is committed to this at the moment – no member country, nor we as a country, nor this House. What we shall have is an opportunity, which we do not possess and will not possess unless we join, of working out schemes for the future of the major part of Europe. I put this point in a practical form to the House. It is well known that the President of France, supported by the Chancellor of Germany, has proposed a summit meeting of heads of Government in the course of next year and probably in the spring. This meeting, will, I believe, settle the European approach to the problems that we have been discussing of monetary arrangements, trading arrangements, and future political development.

If by any chance the House rejected this Motion tonight, that meeting would still go on and it would still take its decisions which will affect the greater part of Western Europe and affect us in our daily lives. But we would not be there to take a share in those decisions. That really would not be a sensible way to go about protecting our interests or our influence in Europe and the world. But to be there as a member of the Community, in my view, would be an effective use of our contribution of sovereignty.

Surely we must consider the consequences of staying out. We cannot delude ourselves that an early chance would be given us to take the decision again. We should be denying ourselves and succeeding generations the opportunities which are available to us in so many spheres; opportunities which we ourselves in this country have to seize. We should be leaving so many aspects of matters affecting our daily lives to be settled outside our own influence. That surely cannot be acceptable to us. We should be denying to Europe, also – let us look outside these shores for a moment – its full potential, its opportunities of developing economically and politically, maintaining its security, and securing for all its people a higher standard of prosperity.

All the consequences of that for many millions of people in Europe must be recognised tonight in the decision the House is taking. In addition, many projects for the future of Europe have been long delayed. There has been great uncertainty, and tonight all that can be removed.

'No,' shouted Heath's opponents. Increasingly loud objections punctuated his speech as he approached his peroration.

The right hon. gentleman the member for Cardiff South-East was very kind in the personal remarks he made about myself. Throughout my political career, if I may add one personal remark, it is well known that I have had the vision of a Britain in a united Europe; a Britain which would be united economically to Europe and which would be able to influence decisions affecting our own future, and which would enjoy a better standard of life and a fuller life. I have worked for a Europe which will play an increasing part in meeting the needs of those parts of the world which still lie in the shadow of want. I always understood that the right hon. gentleman wanted that. I want Britain as a member of a Europe which is united politically, and which will enjoy lasting peace and the greater security which would ensue.

Nor do I believe that the vision of Europe – and the right hon. gentleman raised this specific point – is an unworthy vision, or an ignoble vision or an unworthy cause for which to have worked— [Interruption.] I have always made it absolutely plain to the British people that consent to this course would be given by Parliament.

'Resign,' several MPs shouted, but Heath sailed on.

Parliament is the Parliament of all the people.

When we came to the end of the negotiations in 1963, after the veto had been imposed, the negotiator on behalf of India said: 'When you left India some people wept. And when you leave Europe tonight some will weep. And there is no other people in the world of whom these things could be said.'[4]

That was a tribute from the Indian to the British. But tonight when this House endorses this Motion many millions of people right across the world will rejoice that we have taken our rightful place in a truly United Europe.

The result of the vote was in favour of Heath, 356 votes to 244.

'An overcrowded House, great tension and an overwhelming majority of 112, the Labour Pros having held very firm and the free vote having paid off,' Heath's political secretary, the future Foreign Secretary Douglas Hurd, recorded in his diary.[5] Powell suffered a rare loss of composure, shouting, 'It won't do, it won't do,' at his front bench. Thirty-nine Conservative MPs had followed Powell into the no lobby to vote against accession to the European Community. But 69 Labour MPs supported the government.

On the white cliffs of Dover, Harold Macmillan kindled a bonfire to signal the news to Europe. Another was lit in answer on the Pas de Calais. At the Palace of Westminster, Heath celebrated with supporters at Annie's Bar for two hours, before joining the patriarch of the European ideal, Jean Monnet, and his own European negotiator, Geoffrey Rippon, for a more sedate celebration.

The battle was not over. The European Communities Bill, which gave effect to British membership, was put before the House in 1972, and only squeaked through – with the Labour Chief Whip, Bob Mellish, having to restrain his members from hurling Jeremy Thorpe, the Liberal leader, onto the government benches, after Liberal votes proved decisive in giving Heath and his government victory. The bill's committee stage also saw a series of close votes, although Pym, Kenneth Clarke, the Government Whip for Europe, and the unofficial Pro European Labour Whip John Roper[6] ensured the government survived.

The bill was finally approved with a majority of 17 votes at the third reading. Heath posed for a group photograph with his victorious, euphoric and undoubtedly exhausted team of whips.

'I am enjoying this.'

Margaret Thatcher's bravura farewell: 22 November 1990

Nearly 20 years later, the internal Conservative arguments about Europe had taken on a new form. The issue of British participation in European Monetary Union – the precursor to the euro – had divided even the praetorian guard of monetarists around Mrs Thatcher. First Nigel Lawson had resigned from the Treasury, then Geoffrey Howe, her first Chancellor, had departed with a damaging parting shot (see Chapter 8), which in turn triggered a leadership challenge by her long-term rival, Michael Heseltine. Thatcher failed to win on the first ballot and, faced with haemorrhaging support, had announced her resignation as Prime Minister. That decision – ending a long and mostly triumphant political era – was made just a few hours before she rose to speak at the Dispatch Box. (It would not take effect until her party chose a successor.) This speech, answering a motion of no confidence from the Labour leader, Neil Kinnock, would be her farewell performance. She made a stilted start. Many Conservative MPs had just voted against her, and there was an embarrassed, remorseful note to the ritual cheers and 'hear hears'.

She was warming up by the time she delivered a mocking lash at Kinnock's grasp of the issue of European Monetary Union, but it was not until Dennis Skinner's famous intervention, after the Liberal Democrat Alan Beith had asked about her position on the European Central Bank, that, quite suddenly, the old force and fire reappeared. Hansard does not record the huge sentimental cheer that rang out from choked Tory throats as the emotional voice of Michael Carttiss rasped across the chamber, but Thatcher certainly drew strength from it.

'She was brilliant. Humorous, self-deprecating, swift and deadly in her argument and in her riposte,' wrote Alan Clark.[7] Giles Radice thought it 'a gutsy, bravado final performance. Hypocritically, the Tories, having deposed her, cheer her to the echo.'[8]

This was not quite the end for the woman who ranked with Lloyd George, Churchill and Attlee in the pantheon of twentieth-century premiers. 'A tigress surrounded by hamsters', as the historian Peter Hennessy described her. In this speech she delivered her own valedictory and she would exert a continuing fascination on her party, emerging from time to time to anoint new Conservative leaders, or to bask in the cheers of the party conference faithful. But perhaps because of the drama of the moment, or because some thought she had become irrelevant, her much harder language against European

Monetary Union in this speech went mostly unnoticed. It was a sign of things to come. The poison was seeping into Tory divisions over Europe.

IT IS, OF COURSE, the right and duty of Her Majesty's Opposition to challenge the position of the Government of the day. It is also their right to test the confidence of the House in the Government if they think that the circumstances warrant it. I make no complaint about that. But when the windy rhetoric of the right hon. member for Islwyn [Neil Kinnock] has blown away, what are their real reasons for bringing this motion before the House? There were no alternative policies – just a lot of disjointed, opaque words. It cannot be a complaint about Britain's standing in the world. That is deservedly high, not least because of our contribution to ending the cold war and to the spread of democracy through Eastern Europe and the Soviet Union – achievements that were celebrated at the historic meeting in Paris from which I returned yesterday. It cannot be the nation's finances. We are repaying debts, including the debts run up by the Labour Party. It cannot be the Government's inability to carry forward their programme for the year ahead, which was announced in the Gracious Speech[9] on 7 November. We carried that debate by a majority of 108.

The Opposition's real reason is the leadership election for the Conservative Party, which is a democratic election according to rules which have been public knowledge for many years – one member, one vote. That is a far cry from the way in which the Labour Party does these things. Two in every five votes for its leader are cast by the trade union block votes, which have a bigger say than Labour members in that decision: precious little democracy there.

The real issue to be decided by my right hon. and hon. friends is how best to build on the achievements of the 1980s, how to carry Conservative policies forward through the 1990s and how to add to three general election victories a fourth, which we shall surely win.

Eleven years ago, we rescued Britain from the parlous state to which socialism had brought it. I remind the House that, under socialism, this country had come to such a pass that one of our most able and distinguished ambassadors felt compelled to write in a famous dispatch, a copy of which found its way into *The Economist*, the following words:

'We talk of ourselves without shame as being one of the less prosperous countries of Europe. The prognosis for the foreseeable future', he said in 1979, was 'discouraging'.

Conservative government has changed all that. Once again, Britain stands tall in the councils of Europe and of the world, and our policies have brought unparalleled prosperity to our citizens at home.

In the past decade, we have given power back to the people on an unprecedented scale. We have given back control to people over their own lives and over their livelihood – over the decisions that matter most to them and their families. We have done it by curbing the monopoly power of trade unions to control, even to victimise, the individual worker. Labour would return us to conflict, confrontation and government by the consent of the TUC. We have done it by enabling families to own their homes, not least through the sale of 1.25 million council houses. Labour opposes our new rents-to-mortgage initiative, which will spread the benefits of ownership wider still. We have done it by giving people choice in public services – which school is right for their children, which training course is best for the school leaver, which doctor they choose to look after their health and which hospital they want for their treatment. Labour is against spreading those freedoms and choice to all our people. It is against us giving power back to the people by privatising nationalised industries. Eleven million people now own shares, and 7.5 million people have registered an interest in buying electricity shares. Labour wants to renationalise electricity, water and British Telecom. It wants to take power back to the state and back into its own grasp – a fitful and debilitating grasp.

This was too much for the Labour MP Martin Flannery, who questioned whether the two million people who were unemployed at the time felt particularly empowered. He pointed to the 10.9 per cent inflation rate and the £100 billion-worth of North Sea oil that Mrs Thatcher's Government had benefited from.

Two million more jobs since 1979 represent a great deal more opportunity for people. Yes, 10.9 per cent inflation is much higher than it should be, but it is a lot lower than 26.9 per cent under the last Labour Government. Yes, we have benefited from North Sea oil. The Government have made great investments abroad that will give this country an income long after North Sea oil has ceased. We have provided colossal investment for future generations. Labour members ran up debts, which we have repaid. We are providing investment for the future; we do not believe in living at the expense of the future.

These are the reasons why we shall win a fourth general election. We have been down in the polls before when we have taken difficult decisions. The essence of a good Government is that they are prepared to take difficult decisions to achieve long-term prosperity. That is what we have achieved and why we shall handsomely win the next general election.

I was speaking of the Labour Party wanting to renationalise privatised industry. Four of the industries that we have privatised are in the top ten British businesses, but at the very bottom of the list of 1,000 British businesses lie four nationalised industries. Labour's industries consume the wealth that others create and give nothing back.

Here Thatcher set out her economic record: improved living standards, lower income tax, more businesses starting up, and higher tax revenues leading to more spending on social provision.

We are no longer the sick man of Europe – our output and investment grew faster during the 1980s than that of any of our major competitors. No longer a doubtful prospect, when American and Japanese companies invest in Europe, we are their first choice. Britain no longer has an overmanned, inefficient, backward manufacturing sector, but modern, dynamic industries.

The right hon. gentleman referred to the level of inflation. Yes, in 1987 and 1988, the economy did expand too fast. There was too much borrowing, and inflation rose. That is why we had to take the tough, unpopular, measures to bring the growth of money supply within target. Inflation has now peaked and will soon be coming down. Inevitably, the economy has slowed, but we firmly expect growth to resume next year. For the fundamentals are right. Our industry is now enterprising. It has been modernised and restructured. In sector after sector, it is our companies which lead the world – in pharmaceuticals, in telecommunications and in aerospace. Our companies have the freedom and talent to succeed – and the will to compete.

Jim Sillars,[10] briefly SNP MP for Glasgow Govan, intervened to deliver a swipe at Neil Kinnock, which produced jeers from the Labour benches and a call for order from the Speaker. He told Thatcher the poll tax – her unpopular attempt to replace domestic rates as the tax funding local councils – had caused her downfall because it transferred more of the burden onto the poor. The poll tax had led to riots, civil disobedience and a vast level of hostile correspondence for Conservative MPs, but that argument did not impress Thatcher.

I think that the hon. gentleman knows that I have the same contempt for his socialist policies as the people of east Europe, who have experienced them, have for theirs. I think that I must have hit the right nail on the head when I pointed out that the logic of those policies is that they would rather the poor were poorer. One does not create wealth and opportunity that way. One does not create a property-owning democracy that way.

During the past eleven years, this Government have had a clear and unwavering vision of the future of Europe and Britain's role in it. It is a vision which stems from our deep-seated attachment to parliamentary democracy and commitment to economic liberty, enterprise, competition and a free market economy. No Government in Europe have fought more resolutely against subsidies, state aids to industry and protectionism; unnecessary regulation and bureaucracy and increasing unaccountable central power at the expense of national Parliaments. No Government have fought more against that in Europe than we have.

We have fought attempts to put new burdens and constraints on industry, such as the Social Charter which would take away jobs, in particular part-time jobs. For us part of the purpose of the Community is to demolish trade barriers and eliminate unfair subsidies, so that we can all benefit from a great expansion of trade both within Europe and with the outside world.

The fact is that Britain has done more to shape the Community over the past eleven years than any other member state. Britain is leading the reform of the common agricultural policy, getting surpluses down, putting a ceiling on agricultural spending. We have been the driving force towards the single market which, when it is completed, will be the most significant advance in the Community since the treaty of Rome itself. We have done more than any other Government to resist protectionism, keep Europe's market open to trade with the rest of the world, and make a success of the GATT negotiations.

We have worked for our vision of a Europe which is free and open to the rest of the world, and above all to the countries of Eastern Europe as they emerge from the shadows of socialism. It would not help them if Europe became a tight-knit little club, tied up in regulations and restrictions. They deserve a Europe where there is room for their rediscovered sense of nationhood and a place to decide their own destiny after decades of repression.

With all this, we have never hesitated to stand up for Britain's interests. The people of Britain want a fair deal in Europe, particularly over our budget contribution. We have got back nearly £10 billion which would otherwise have been paid over to the EC under the arrangements negotiated by the Labour Party when it was in power.

Indeed, what sort of vision does the Labour Party have? None, according to the Leader of the Opposition. Labour members want a Europe of subsidies, a Europe of socialist restrictions, a Europe of protectionism. They want it because that is how they would like to run – or is it ruin? – this country.

Every time that we have stood up and fought for Britain and British interests, Labour front bench spokesmen have carped, criticised and moaned. On the central issues of Europe's future, they will not tell us where they stand. Do they want a single currency? The right hon. gentleman does not even know what it means, so how can he know?

As Tory MPs laughed at her swipe at Kinnock, the Labour leader dismissed the issue as 'a hypothetical question'.

Absolute nonsense. It is appalling. He says that it is a hypothetical question. It will not be a hypothetical question. Someone must go to Europe and argue knowing what it means.

Are Labour members prepared to defend the rights of this United Kingdom Parliament? No, for all that the right hon. gentleman said. For them, it is all compromise, 'sweep it under the carpet', 'leave it for another day', and 'it might sort itself out', in the hope that the people of Britain will not notice what is happening to them, and how the powers would gradually slip away.

The Government will continue to take a positive and constructive approach to the future of Europe. We welcome economic and monetary co-operation: indeed, no other member state has gone further than Britain in tabling proposals for the next stage, including the hard ecu. But our proposals would work with the market and give people and Governments real choice.

We want the Community to move forward as twelve: and from my talks in Paris with other European leaders over the past few days, I am convinced that that is their aim too. Europe is strongest when it grows through willing cooperation and practical measures, not compulsion or bureaucratic dreams.

The senior Liberal Democrat Alan Beith intervened to start one of the most poignant moments of the debate. He asked Thatcher if she intended to continue her personal fight against a single currency and an independent central bank when she left office. At this Dennis Skinner called out: 'No. She is going to be the governor.' A huge burst of laughter convulsed all sides of the chamber. And Thatcher pounced on the opportunity to press her objections.

What a good idea. I had not thought of that. But if I were, there would be no European central bank accountable to no one, least of all national Parliaments. The point of that kind of Europe with a central bank is no democracy, taking powers away from every single Parliament, and having a single currency, a monetary policy and interest rates which take all political power away from us. As my right hon. friend the Member for Blaby [Nigel Lawson] said in his first speech after the proposal for a single currency was made, a single currency is about the politics of Europe, it is about a federal Europe by the back door. So I shall consider the proposal of the hon. member for Bolsover [Dennis Skinner]. Now where were we? I am enjoying this.

It was all too much for the Thatcher loyalist Michael Carttiss, who, emotions overflowing, called out: 'Cancel it. You can wipe the floor with these people.'
That produced another emotional roar from the Tory benches.

Yes, indeed – I was talking about Europe and the socialist ideal of Europe. Not for us the corporatism, socialism and central control. We leave those to the Opposition. Ours is a larger vision of a Community whose member states cooperate with one another more and more closely to the benefit of all.

Thatcher attributed the tentative democratic reforms in the Soviet Union and Eastern Europe to resolute British and Nato determination to match Soviet missile deployments, and she then turned to the build-up to the first Iraq war. At the time of her resignation, coalition forces were assembling to drive Saddam Hussein's armies out of Kuwait, which he had seized during the summer. She compared the exercise to the liberation of the Falklands during her first term.

There is something else which one feels. That is a sense of this country's destiny: the centuries of history and experience which ensure that, when principles have to be defended, when good has to be upheld and when evil has to be overcome, Britain will take up arms. It is because we on this side have never flinched from difficult decisions that this House and this country can have confidence in this Government today.

'The devalued Prime Minister of a devalued Government.'

John Smith on the events of Black Wednesday: 24 September 1992

On Black – or White – Wednesday, 16 September 1992, after a summer of rising speculation against the pound, John Major's Conservative government crashed out of the European exchange rate mechanism (ERM), which fixed the parities of the various European currencies against each other. Britain had been a member for just two years – joining, however reluctantly, was Margaret Thatcher's last major economic policy decision. Her successor, John Major, saw the ERM as the mechanism by which inflation could be defeated, and even, in a moment of optimism, told journalists he foresaw sterling becoming the most important currency in Europe, supplanting the deutschmark. But within a few months of Major's general election victory in 1992, it was becoming clear that the markets viewed the pound's ERM parity at 2.95 DM as overvalued, and devaluation as inevitable. This lead to the dramatic events of that Wednesday, when £27 billion was spent to support the value of sterling and interest rates were raised, first by 2 per cent at 11 a.m., then by a further 3 per cent early in the afternoon, taking rates to the dizzy heights of 15 per cent. Eventually, the government accepted defeat and allowed sterling to float to whatever value the markets assigned it while reducing interest rates back down to 12 per cent. Kenneth Clarke, soon to become Chancellor, remarked to colleagues that this was the first time he had been a member of a government, which did not have an economic policy.

Certainly the air of panic and crisis shattered the Conservatives' reputation for effective economic management. There was no disguising the extent of the defeat. Not only had the central plank of the government's economic strategy collapsed, but for an afternoon, the voters of middle England had contemplated the sky-high interest rates, and their impact on their mortgages, and wondered how long it would be before they lost their homes. They did not forgive.

For Labour, now led by the reassuringly respectable figure of John Smith, this was the chance to transform their political position. Former Chancellor Nigel Lawson thought Smith an effective debater with 'a particular talent for mockery'. He did not rate Smith's economic analysis, which was 'always about the importance of training and manufacturing industry'. But he knew Smith was well equipped to pounce if ministers, or the government, stumbled.

This speech was made in the special debate on economic policy, for which Parliament was recalled after Black Wednesday. The Prime Minister had proposed a motion supporting the government's economic policy. Smith on his Commons debut as party leader complained at its bald simplicity.

WHY IS THAT NOT AMPLIFIED, defined or explained? For a simple reason. The Government do not know what is their economic policy. That was startlingly clear from the Prime Minister's speech. The Prime Minister explained the tragi-comic events surrounding our humiliating withdrawal from the ERM, in simple terms. He said that we were scuppered by the speculators. That is all we are to get by way of explanation from the Government. What has happened during the past week or so is not merely an upset for the Government's economic policy, but the complete destruction of what they claimed was a total political and economic strategy – a strategy to which the Prime Minister could not have been more closely committed.

Only a few weeks ago, the *Sunday Times* carried the story that the Prime Minister had a new vision of the future. It is said that he had revealed to his colleagues and party supporters that his ambition was no less than to see the pound replace the deutschmark as the most stable currency in the European Community. Under the headline, 'Major aims to make sterling the best in Europe,' Michael Jones and Andy Grice reported that the Prime Minister had 'embarked on an economic strategy designed to see the British pound replace the German mark as the hardest and most trusty currency in the EC.'

The response to the plan to topple the deutschmark was mixed. At the time, eyebrows were raised among our recession-weary public. The most generous thought that it was a case of audacity straining the bounds of credulity, while others thought that the Prime Minister had simply taken leave of his senses.

Now, of course, the Prime Minister's words read with a mockingly hollow ring.

On 10 September the right hon. gentleman took himself to Glasgow to address the Scottish CBI – picking, as usual, hostile audiences as the best place to float his ideas. There, he said that there would be no devaluation and no realignment. As we all know, that policy was wrecked by his decision on black Wednesday, less than one week after the Glasgow declaration, to withdraw from the ERM, as a result of which the pound has now been devalued by more than 13 per cent. So much for the Prime Minister's vainglorious nonsense about the pound easily replacing the deutschmark as the anchor of the ERM. Those who have studied the Prime Minister's utterances since he became involved in our economic affairs – as Chief Secretary, then as Chancellor, and now as Prime Minister – know only too well that such delusions of grandeur

are the norm, not the exception. His words were not just a wild aberration –
bad enough though that would be for a head of Government. I believe that
such delusions have been his stock in trade since he became involved in the
management of our economy.

Look at the Prime Minister's record of economic prediction. January 1988:
'Inflation is low and will remain so.' Fact: it doubled in the two years that
followed.

Prediction, December 1989: 'The recession is neither likely nor necessary.'
Fact: we have had the longest recession since the 1930s.

Prediction in June 1991 in the *Daily Telegraph*: 'Recovery coming on in
weeks.' Fact: the economy has ever since been mired in such deep recession.
Perhaps the prediction most close to public memory was in the last election:
'Vote Tory on Thursday and recovery will continue on Friday.' Fact: there has
been no recovery at all and now we have a devaluation. So much for the Prime
Minister's key promise at the election.

In the new situation, the Government propaganda machine clearly faces
new challenges. Its principal tasks are to seek to disguise the void in
Government policy by pretending that it does not exist and to divert attention
from the Government's culpability by seeking to place the blame on others. A
good example, I understand, is the note which, according to today's *Financial
Times*, appeared in Minister's boxes on Monday evening headed: 'ERM. New
line to take.'

I am, of course, not able to say whether the line that we got from the Prime
Minister today was the line advised on Monday. After all, it might have
changed since then.

But the real problem for the Government in finding a new line to take is the
speech given by the Chancellor of the Exchequer to the European Policy Forum
on 10 July entitled 'Britain and the ERM', which is helpfully reproduced in at
least two newspapers today. The Chancellor expressed his support for the then
policy in robust and uncompromising terms but, interestingly, he went on to
examine what he described as the alternatives – all the alternatives – to such a
policy and mocked every one in turn. He said 'Plenty of alternatives are
suggested. But in my view they are all illusory or destined to fail.'

I admit that it might be difficult to know which of those alternatives now is
Government policy. After all, according to some newspapers, the Chancellor
appears to be on quite a different path from his colleagues in the Government,
including the Prime Minister, but whatever that policy is, it must be one of the
alternatives that he contemptuously dismissed in his speech.

The Chancellor described the option of leaving the ERM and cutting interest rates as the 'cut and run option' – a cut in interest rates and run on the pound. He went on to say: 'Many who advocate floating exchange know full well what the consequences would be. They intend a devaluation of the pound and they will certainly achieve it.'

He finally dismissed the option in his conclusion: 'We would have given up after less than two years and we were back to our bad old ways.'

Well, are we back to our bad old ways, lurching back to the Thatcherite economics which pulverised our economy during the 1980s? The Chancellor then went on to attack a policy of leaving the exchange rate mechanism and setting interest rates according to domestic monetary targets. Here the Chancellor had what I believe was a genuine flash of insight. He told his audience: 'We have been here before. In the 1980s we fixed domestic monetary targets, and we attempted to meet them by setting interest rates accordingly. But in practice the money supply figures often provided a poor guide to interest rate policy, particularly in the wake of the financial deregulation.'

So much for all the Thatcher years – dismissed like that. Those of us of a generous spirit would be inclined to congratulate the Chancellor on an honest, if unrepentant, reassessment. It is, however, difficult to do so if the former sinner is determined to revert so quickly to the sins of those former years. After all, now, with the benefit of experience, he knows that it is wrong and, after this performance, who can ever believe him in anything he ever subsequently says? In his speech on 10 July, the Chancellor ruled out every alternative that he could envisage. How can any one of them be offered now as convincing Government policy?

In the wake of the destruction of the Government's economic policies, we must ask where we are now. The sad but unavoidable truth is that, instead of reaching the heart of Europe, the Government have succeeded in having Britain relegated to the second division. There are two reasons for that disaster. For years, the Government followed policies that have thrown our economy into a deep and damaging recession, which made it weak and vulnerable – weak and vulnerable, incidentally, to speculators. Faced with a crisis, the Government chaotic mismanagement and sheer incompetence forced them to abandon all that that they stood for in a matter of hours.

The Conservative MP John Marshall asked Smith if he proposed to take Britain back into the exchange rate mechanism. Smith was not deflected.

That question was singularly not answered by the Prime Minister in the rather curious answer that he gave. I will answer the hon. gentleman's question directly. He will not think it unfair if I point out that, when the Prime Minister was asked a roughly similar question, he did not answer it at all. He said that, if a credible exchange rate mechanism could be achieved, he might think about whether or not he would rejoin it. That, as I fairly understand it, is what the Prime Minister said. Let me say what I think. I think that there are advantages in having a system of managed exchange rates. One is that in those circumstances, one is less likely to resort to curbing public expenditure as the anchor or one's economic policy – which is one of the difficulties that we now face. The circumstances in which we would rejoin the ERM must be judged according to the state of our economy – and that is regrettably weak. The first thing that the Government should do if they are to acquire any option for Britain's economic future is to build up the strong economy that can be the only foundation for our future.

To return to the events of Black Wednesday, a bewildered British public watched those tragi-comic events unfold. First, there was a 2 per cent increase in interest rates, and then they were up by 5 per cent – all in the course of a few hours. It all ended in Britain's withdrawal from the ERM. That was not some considered choice or policy but was forced on the Government by their weakness and incompetence.

Smith traced the economic events leading to the crisis of Black Wednesday. He clashed sharply with Major when the Prime Minister chortled at his suggestion that a concerted reaction involving all the ERM member states was required – particularly after the Italian government caved into market pressures and devalued the lira, serving to redouble the pressure on other currencies, including sterling, which were seen as overvalued.

John Major's former political secretary Judith Chaplin intervened, to Labour jeers, to accuse Smith of flouting the convention that senior opposition politicians do not say anything that jeopardises sterling in the markets; he had called for a cut in interest rates three days before Britain left the ERM. Smith ridiculed her charge.

I was waiting for someone to blame me for the devaluation last week. The hon. lady has not disappointed me. Of all the charges that could have been laid against me and of all the comment that there has been in recent weeks, the argument that I have been undermining sterling is the most far-fetched that I have ever heard. It just shows that, whatever one says or does not say, some on the Conservative benches will find it unacceptable. It seems that there is a new charge: that any criticism of the Government undermines sterling, but sterling has already been undermined by those who are in charge of our affairs.

Smith criticised Major for failing, following the devaluation of the lira, to coordinate a revaluation of all the currencies within the ERM, which brought the Prime Minister to his feet to blame Black Wednesday on the size of the speculation against sterling. No one, he snarled, not even Smith, could ever have foreseen it. Again Smith pounced.

That is the defence: overwhelmed by unforeseen events, in charge of the bridge when along came a wave and overturned the vessel, the captain pleads not guilty. That is the nature of the Prime Minister's defence. There was an alternative and I should like the Prime Minister to tell us why it was not adopted. There could have been a general realignment of the currencies. The system allows for that and we know that there were requests for that to be considered. The Prime Minister was defeated but he speaks as if he won. He did not win, he lost, and there was an alternative to that humiliating failure.

In view of the debacle, one would expect at least a word of explanation or apology, but there was not a hint of that in anything said by the Government, whose most noted characteristic is that no one takes responsibility, no one resigns – at least not yet – and no one takes the blame. They are a 'not me' Government.

The most ingenious and perhaps the most ironic of the Prime Minister's new excuse were in his first comments after he emerged from his air raid shelter. He told us that the problem was that the markets were irrational. What are we to make of that one? Now that the Prime Minister is possessed of a genuinely new insight, may we invite him to refrain from insisting that these irrational market forces should determine all aspects of our national life? Given the total mismanagement that has been so vividly demonstrated, may we have no more assertions about the Conservative Party's unique and expert knowledge of the working of markets?

The conclusion that our people are reaching is that they are governed by a Government and Prime Minister fatally flawed by incredibility and incompetence. After all, who was it who dismissed the critics of Government policies as 'quack doctors'? Who was it who told the CBI in Glasgow: 'It is too easy to regard Britain's problems as unique or blame them on the ERM'?

Who was it who said that to leave the ERM would be 'the inflationary option' and a 'betrayal of our future'? Who, in that same speech, said that there was going to be 'no devaluation, no realignment'?

This is a Government whose economic policy is in tatters, whose credibility is blown, whose incompetence has been exposed. It will no longer do to blame others and it will no longer do to say that their policies will, given time, come right. They have been in power for the longest continuous period in postwar Britain—

'Hear, hear!' shouted Conservative MPs, providing another opportunity for Smith to score.

And Tories' assent to that proposition means that they must accept that they are the only architects, the sole constructors, of our present dismal situation.

In the course of a few weeks the one policy with which the Prime Minister was uniquely and personally associated, the contribution to policy of which he appears to have been most proud, has been blown apart, and with it has gone for ever any claim by the Prime Minister or the party that he leads to economic competence. He is the devalued Prime Minister of a devalued Government.

In the *Guardian*, Andrew Rawnsley described how Smith 'dwelt on the Government's humiliation in lip-smacking detail . . . Smith and Gordon Brown (his shadow Chancellor) were both crushingly good, though in the circumstances anything less would have been a failure.'

According to Gyles Brandreth, Smith was 'magnificent, dry, droll, devastating'.[11] And even John Major, the target of most of the invective, acknowledged that it was 'a brilliant debating performance'.[12]

Major added, 'Presented with an open goal, he joyfully smashed the ball into the net. I admired his oratory as much as his brass neck – this was, after all, the same John Smith who had repeatedly lambasted us for not being in the ERM, and who, when we joined, supported the conditions of entry. Now his criticism was fierce, in a riot of freewheeling hypocrisy which gave me ample evidence that here was a man of flexible opinions who would be a formidable opponent.'

Parliamentary invective can be a pretty ephemeral thing, but Major and Lamont suffered lasting damage that afternoon, as Smith mercilessly pinned the blame for the whole debacle on them. The government never recovered in the opinion polls, and Lamont did not survive for long in the Treasury.

'"Rage, rage, against the dying of the light".'

Richard Shepherd calls for a referendum to stem the loss of British sovereignty to Europe: 21 February 1992

Richard Shepherd would not have been out of place in a much earlier House of Commons, an independently minded classical liberal who made up his mind on the merits of a case. It is not hard to imagine him rallying to the cause of Pitt the Younger, but then falling out with his leader over some point of principle. Douglas Hurd thought him a 'likeable, persistent man, who did not listen much to the argument of others, but who easily worked himself up into a storm of principled rage'.[13] In 1988, having come top of the ballot for private members' bills, he proposed to reform the Official Secrets Act, to allow a 'public interest defence' for the disclosure of information, only to see a three-line whip imposed against the measure by his own party. He became the Conservative equivalent of Frank Field or Tam Dalyell, a lone pursuer of causes. But in the Major years he found himself among the Euro-sceptic rebels who opposed the Maastricht Treaty.

Alarmed by the constitutional implications of close European integration, and taking the opportunity of a high place in the annual ballot for private members' bills, he introduced a bill requiring a referendum to be held before any more British sovereignty was ceded. With a general election looming, the measure had no chance of becoming law, but it was a chance to rally support – a declaratory exercise. The bill provided the occasion for Margaret Thatcher's final vote in the Commons. She and Shepherd may not have seen eye to eye on his measure on secrecy, but in this case he enlisted her support, although only after subjecting the bill to what he called 'gimlet-eyed' scrutiny.[14] Shepherd believes her views on Europe were hardening rapidly, and that she was increasingly distrustful of the trend towards majority voting in a variety of major policy areas in European Council meetings, seeing it as a Trojan Horse for federalism, which should be opposed. He was concerned that the government whips had forced through European legislation without proper debate, and a reference to the people was the only check on them.

Private members' bills are normally debated on a Friday morning, and Shepherd moved the second reading of his a little after 9.30. To ensure his supporters were there to vote for his bill and against any procedural motions to stop it, he spoke at far greater length than he normally would, to give his sleepier supporters every chance of making it to the chamber before any divisions were held. He knew the Conservative establishment thought he was making unnecessary waves. In the event the hard-core Euro-sceptics and Europhiles both turned out for the occasion, with Shepherd enlisting support from the Democratic Unionist Dr Ian Paisley and Labour's veteran Euro-opponent Peter Shore.

T HE BILL REQUIRES A national referendum as a pre-condition of the ratification of certain treaties. The essential thrust of the Bill is contained in the 65 words of the first clause, which provides that a referendum should be called in the event that the powers of this House to regulate the affairs of this country are diminished. To calm the disquiet of some, may I make an observation about what the referendum does not do? It does not call into question legislation that has already passed the House. Therefore, the original Communities legislation is not at risk, nor is the amendment to that original legislation which we commonly know as the Single European Act. The referendum would refer and relate specifically and only to those events that take place after the passing of this Bill.

The Maastricht treaties, which are central to the concentration of our ideas on what we are discussing, signify a further significant transfer of powers from this country and the ability of members of this House to regulate the affairs of our people. It is an extraordinary treaty in as much as it contends for a new political organisation – the union of Europe – in which, on 1 January 1993, we become citizens of a new political organisation. That also applies to Her Majesty the Queen. It would effect that which the right hon. member for Chesterfield [Tony Benn], in his Bill,[15] and the Levellers themselves no less have not succeeded in effecting – it would reduce the Queen to a citizen. That is contrary to our constitutional traditions. I cite that not because of its great importance, but because it shows the extent to which the treaty is a new political organisation. My contention is that no such profound constitutional change should take place without reference to the people. Involved in that concept is the idea of where sovereignty in this country lies. I have always maintained, as do many of my right hon. and hon. friends, that sovereignty resides with the people; we are the expression of that sovereignty. When we rise and defend the House of Commons, we defend not ourselves, our privileges or our prides, but the pride, individuality and privileges of our fellow citizens. Each one of us here assembled is here only because we have been sent forth to represent our fellow electors. We are no different from them, other than that they have reposed in us confidence that we will address ourselves to the political business of our nation. I belong to a union – the

Union of the United Kingdom of Great Britain and Northern Ireland. It is a political allegiance which I gladly give. It is one of sentiment, one of passion, one which has been fashioned over the course of centuries. That is to be set aside because the Treaty of Union seeks to make me a citizen of elsewhere. I would be a citizen with a profound and essential difference: I could not control the laws, in whole areas, by which I would be governed.

I make that point because it is essential to our nation's understanding of what our rule of law is. We maintain that every citizen of this Union should obey the law – a law that, in the end, we have formed, fashioned, made and defended. If we wish to change it, we know the processes by which to do so, and we hold Governments accountable to that effect. When we repose confidence in members of the Government front bench, the laws that they suggest we make are within our call. If they get it wrong, we may change them. Where in that Treaty of Union is the mechanism by which we may change the law? If we cannot change the law, how do we expect to insist on obedience from all of us? As I have said, we are no different from anyone else; the law applies to us just as it does to our fellow electors. When each one of us was elected in 1987, we were given the trust to maintain, control, alter and fashion law. Under the Treaty of Union, we have no such powers.

Of course, it will be argued from the front benches that the process has been a while in the making and that it has been sanctioned by the Single European Act – which is true. I am sure that in a more scrupulous age we would have argued that, on such a profound constitutional change, the electorate should be consulted. The other point often made is that it would be intolerable for a Ministry to have a referendum in which the electorate flew against the Ministry's advice. Would not the Ministry be forced to introduce policies with which it did not agree? Is not that an intolerable burden to place upon Government? Much has been made of that argument. Mr Churchill threw it across the Floor at Mr Balfour and Mr Powell enunciated it in early 1969 [on Europe] although he later changed his mind.

In the great Edwardian struggles over reform of the House of Lords, the Unionists wanted referendums to be held if the Lords and Commons could not agree on a bill, while the Liberals wanted the Commons to have the power to override the Lords. The Liberals won.

The answer to that argument is that we have all been in this House when Governments have been forced to change their mind, even on a principal policy on which they were elected – or claimed to be. I need only cite the embarrassment of myself and others on the question of the poll tax. The Ministers who said that the poll tax was absolutely essential and that it was the flagship are still in their Ministries. It is tolerable to continue in government only if Ministers recognise the virtues and the duties imposed upon them as Ministers of the Crown. It is not an answer to say that it is an intolerable burden; the proof of our history has demonstrated just how tolerable it has been to sufficient numbers of Members of Parliament.

A leading article in the *Independent* today suggested that a referendum might be appropriate on a single currency. We can pursue that debate, and I do not doubt that hon. members will do so today. I want to make it clear that my simple objection is to the political union. I have tried to sketch out the way in which the people of this country will be bound by laws and rules that are made elsewhere by unelected officials and a Council of Ministers that is accountable to no one – no Europe-wide electorate, and not even us ultimately. Even if our Minister today went to argue his corner within that unelected, undemocratic forum, and even though he may say that 100 per cent of the citizens of the United Kingdom are opposed to whatever it is, if it is the view of others by qualified majority vote – on a whole range of issues set out in the Treaty of Union – it will become the law of this country. What can we do about it? That is the great break with our tradition that requires that Maastricht should be scrutinised.

Here Shepherd argued that public opinion on the Maastricht Treaty would not be tested in the forthcoming general election, because the three main parties supported it.

I hear many of my colleagues say, 'But we were elected and all that we owe to our constituents is our judgment. We cannot be bought by our constituents because we stand aside and weigh the evidence.' All that would be true but for the three-line whip and the guillotine. We do not owe our duties and allegiances in too many instances to our electorate; we owe them to the whip. If we owe them to the whip, how can we stand in front of the electorate and say, 'But your views are honourably judged'?

I refer again to the Maastricht debate. There was a three-line whip. I go back to the Single European Act. There was not only a three-line whip but a guillotine. The House knows my views on the guillotine [a time limit on the debate]. I see that the Leader of the House is moving towards the view that guillotines are a natural, inevitable and desirable consequence of the way that we do our business. The letters that I have received shout with frustration about our political process and the fact that no longer do we seem to represent the people out there and properly express their views. How can we if we truncate great debates into three hours on a guillotine? How can we turn to our constituents and say, 'I have looked at it and considered it. I have heard the arguments'? Not a bit. We have had the innovation of Baker Bills,[16] with guillotines on all stages. It is a disgrace, and the public know that it is such.

However passionate one may be about these matters, it is the duty of the House to be cautious of the consequences of legislation because it can send us to prison – the most solemn thing that it can do within our processes.

Legislation demands the old processes and procedures of the House: the First Reading to give notice, then a pause; a Second Reading to consider the principle of the Bill, as we are doing today, and a further pause; the Committee stage, where we consider the contentions and legal arrangements of the Bill; and then it comes back to the House and is further considered. In those processes, the public may get in touch with us and argue their corner. That is terribly important for giving validity to the rule of law, because then no one can say that a Bill was smuggled through in an afternoon.

I am fortunate in having one of the great begetters of the guillotine movement in my party – my right hon. friend the member for Watford [Tristan Garel-Jones, who was Minister for Europe during the Maastricht ratification] – who required 65 guillotines during his tenure of office. I have always thought that misjudged, because in the doing of small things, as we think at the time, we corrupt the greater principle – attestation, as Burke would say, that our electorates give either consent or acquiescence. If we truncate our debates and do not weigh their views, we are contemptuous of our electorates and they, in turn, are contemptuous of us.

I have never known the standing of Members of Parliament to be so low. I see people shudder almost as we pass and say, 'You are only in it for what you can get'.

This provoked an interjection – unrecorded – from the Labour MP Dennis Skinner.

The hon. member for Bolsover [Skinner] makes us shudder in other ways – with admiration, trepidation and inspiration. Nevertheless, the point is that we have broken that trust, no one else.

The insistence of the business managers is that we must be able to legislate endlessly – no self-denying ordinance there. The Baker Bill is the final nail in the coffin of a series of tendentious and difficult Bills where great principles were rushed through in a day. We are elected every four or five years; our authority is clearly fresh. People feel that they have an idea of where we stand. During the course of a Parliament, our connection and the issues change. What people thought that they may have been voting on in 1987 is not necessarily what they think they are voting on today. The coming general election will be about a variety of issues – the economy, the National Health Service or whatever – but not about Europe. If Europe is mentioned in a party's programme, it will be as an aside – some general expression by which the public can diagnose no true intent. It is believed that, in that way, we can cover over the issue if there is an argument. That is why I make the point that there should be a specific reference to the electorate.

I say as a last note to the House that our people should 'not go gentle into that good night' but should rather 'rage, rage, against the dying of the light' that requires us to live under laws that we cannot change or control.

Shepherd's speech won praise from both camps in the Conservative argument, with the Euro-friendly Anthony Nelson complaining of the difficulty of refuting his 'passion and persuasion'. This did not prevent him from egging on his colleagues to keep talking until the bill ran out of time. To no one's surprise, that is what happened.

'European monetary union was not dreamed up by M. Jean Monnet, an idealistic European; the idea was floated in July 1940 by Walther Funk, who was a drunken, homosexual Nazi.'

Sir Peter Tapsell detects a sinister ancestry to plans for European Monetary Union: 24 March 1993

The last Tory Keynesian and the heir to a long tradition of One Nation Toryism, Sir Peter Tapsell is the only MP in the Commons whose parliamentary memory extends back to the Conservative ascendancy of the 1950s. Then, he observed the House as a member of the Conservative Research Department staff, worked for Anthony Eden during his triumphant election campaign in 1955, and entered the Commons in his own right in 1959. Were it not for a two-year break in his parliamentary career, after defeat in the 1964 election, he would be Father of the House. He also managed to become a highly successful banker. He has never been a purveyor of party orthodoxies, and even his Euroscepticism, currently fashionable in Tory ranks, is reached by way of an unconventional economic analysis. His speaking style is magisterial. Every syllable is carefully enunciated, and separated from the next by a generous pause. The staff of Hansard are said to put down their Biros and pick up tablets and chisels when he rises to speak for England.

He was one of the diverse and determined band of parliamentary rebels who fought against the Maastricht Treaty and subsequent Euro-measures. In this speech directed at the treaty provisions intended to pave the way for a single currency, he suggested that the drive to European Monetary Union would lead to German domination. He began with an ironic reference to the revelation that on Black Wednesday – after seeing Britain freed from the constraints of the exchange rate mechanism – the Chancellor, Norman Lamont was 'singing in the bath'.

WE ARE TOLD THAT the Chancellor sings in his bath, but I have less operatic tendencies when I am in my bath. Sometimes I lie there and wonder how we can be prepared to hand over the control of our central bank to a group of foreigners under German domination. I wonder what King William III would have thought about that when he drew up the original charter for the Bank of England 'to promote the public good and well-being of our people'. We may be sure that the Bundesbank will never allow a European central bank to manage and issue a single currency which, whatever its name, is anything but the deutschmark in disguise. That is a political and economic fact of life. Nor do I blame it for that. If I were German I should certainly hold that view.

Would any German banker in his senses, or, for that matter, any German citizen or saver, want to have the value of his money – his savings and his wages – determined by a secret compromise with the Greek, Italian and Portuguese directors of the European central bank, whose main interest in the Community is to receive handouts from the richer countries and to protect themselves from their own politicians, for whom they have the utmost contempt? To anybody who has ever moved in the real banking world, the idea is absolutely preposterous. With the great influence of the Whips' Office, it is certain that, if the Maastricht provisions for a central bank ever come into force, they will rapidly prove to be totally unworkable.

We ought to reflect where the idea of European monetary union originated. The more idealistic souls among us seem to suppose that European monetary union was the brainchild of that nice M. Jean Monnet. In fact, it was the brainchild of the rather less nice Herr Walther Funk.

Herr Walther Funk was the president of the Reichsbank, the predecessor of the Bundesbank, from 1939 to 1945. My point is that Funk originated the whole concept of European monetary union, which is what we are debating.

European monetary union was not dreamed up by M. Jean Monnet, an idealistic European; the idea was floated in July 1940 by Walther Funk, who was a drunken, homosexual Nazi toady and was subsequently sentenced to life imprisonment by the Nuremberg tribunal. In July 1940, just after the German panzer divisions had overrun Western Europe, Funk circulated a number of documents on European monetary union. These are all set out in the recently published excellent book *The History of the Bundesbank* by the distinguished financial journalist David Marsh. I shall not quote at length, but I have to say that the wording of the Maastricht treaty in certain sections follows almost word for word the documents circulated inside the Reichsbank in 1940. The view, which Hitler strongly shared, was that Europe could not be held permanently subordinate to Germany by force of arms alone, that it was necessary to resort to economic and monetary forces to make the domination permanent.

That is the ERM. It has all happened before.

I should like now to turn to the question of who first established an independent and unaccountable central bank. It was not, as many people think, Bismarck in 1870. On the contrary, Bismarck took the view that bankers should not be entrusted with political power, that they would always produce mass unemployment. He made sure, when he set up the Reichsbank in 1870, that it was totally subject to political control – not very democratic political control, but his control.

In 1923 – just after Germany, for the first time ever, became a democracy in the shape of the Weimar republic – a gentleman called Dr Schacht decided that it would not be a good thing for the Reichsbank to be subject to democratically elected politicians. He managed to persuade the Weimar republic in 1923 to set up an independent and unaccountable Reichsbank – the predecessor of the Bundesbank. Of course, some of our fellow countrymen share Dr Schacht's distrust of elected politicians. I am afraid that there are many such people in the City of London and in the boardrooms of British industry, as the Chancellor of the Exchequer will discover when he looks for a commercial job. Many people do not admire politicians. It is worth recalling that, when Hitler was elected to power in 1933, the already independent and unaccountable Reichsbank, far from proving a bulwark against irresponsible political adventurism – one of the arguments is that unaccountability and independence provide a barrier against political adventurism – immediately became, under Dr Schacht's presidency, a slavish and most helpful tool of Nazi tyranny.

People should not be under the illusion that an unaccountable central bank will show a degree of political independence, integrity and liberalism when faced with ruthless and corrupt politicians. History does not suggest that. Far from being a source of weakness to great institutions, their accountability to democratically elected bodies elsewhere is ultimately an essential source of strength to those institutions and those who lead them. Under the Maastricht Treaty, no effective accountability will exist – or could exist – as the Financial Secretary recognised in his reply to me on 14 January, which I have already quoted.

Until now, I have made largely economic and banking comments, but I shall now draw some political conclusions. With the loss of ultimate parliamentary control over the central bank, the House will lose the rock on which it was founded and built: control over the money supply. Our constituents will effectively be disfranchised. Those hon. members who vote for article 107, and its related articles and protocols, will effectively be echoing Cromwell's words when he pointed at the Mace and said, 'Take that bauble away.'

When I first entered the House, 34 years ago, there were still a considerable number of hon. members, particularly Conservative members, who had sat in

the Chamber throughout all the debates on Neville Chamberlain's appeasement policies. I never spoke to one such member who could recall in his heart
ever having been a supporter of those policies. I sometimes used to wonder
whether the Munich agreement had been carried single-handed by Neville
Chamberlain and the Conservative Whips' Office.

Before I entered the House, when I was personal assistant to Anthony Eden,
the then Prime Minister, Walter Elliot – a distinguished member of the House
who had been here in the 1930s and who voted for the Munich agreement –
told me in a private conversation, which I feel able to repeat as he has been
dead for many years, that he voted in favour of Munich out of a sense of
personal loyalty to Neville Chamberlain. He said that he admired
Chamberlain as a man, and felt that he had done a good job domestically.
Walter Elliot said that voting for Munich had not only eventually wrecked his
own political career but, more importantly, had damaged his self-esteem. He
said that he had never ceased to reproach himself for that vote as events
unfolded.

I ask my younger hon. friends, who have not been long in the House, have
long careers ahead of them and know in their hearts that the Maastricht treaty
is not right for Britain, to remember Walter Elliot. I predict that, ten years
from now, there will be very few Tory members of Parliament who will easily
recall that they were ever supporters of the Maastricht treaty.

Eight
RESIGNATIONS

POWERFUL MINISTERS DO not lightly relinquish office. So when a major figure leaves a government, it is usually a dramatic event. By immemorial Commons tradition, the explanations and apologias of fallen ministers are heard in the Commons without interruption – but even in the absence of normal parliamentary knockabout, these are moments of telling drama, perhaps foreshadowing the fall of a government.

Sometimes the reasons are personal – but even they can have important political ramifications. David Mellor's resignation speech avoided the air of melodramatic tragedy that ex-ministers often assume, but the forcing out of one of John Major's closest Cabinet allies intensified the atmosphere of crisis and scandal around his dying government. A few years later, the departure of Tony Blair's first Welsh Secretary, Ron Davies, after a bizarre 'moment of madness' on Clapham Common, led to an enigmatic personal statement which piqued more curiosity than it satisfied and launched a leadership struggle which convulsed the Welsh Labour Party. The able, efficient father of Welsh devolution went into permanent political eclipse.

The resignations dealt with here are the very political ones. They usually result, those involved will tell us, from a great conflict of policy. But those conflicts are often the symptom of deeper personal grievances. The epic personal feuding inside the Attlee government, which eventually saw the sulky departure of Nye Bevan, was echoed decades later by the schisms on economic and European policy which ran through the Thatcher and Major years. Geoffrey Howe had been one of Mrs Thatcher's closest ideological and political allies, but after a decade in government together, it was said she could barely stand to be in the same room as Howe. Norman Lamont helped put John Major into 10 Downing Street, but was discarded when, after the humiliation of Black Wednesday, he became a liability. But he took telling revenge on his former boss.

A more measured departure was Robin Cook's. Unlike Lawson, Howe and Lamont, he merely singed his boats, leaving open the prospect of a return to government, if not under Tony Blair, then under his successor.

It is the combination of real disagreement, political calculation – whether of future survival or present destruction – and high-class venom which makes the classic resignation statement.

'Are you next year going to take a stand on the upper denture?'

Aneurin Bevan resigns in protest at the introduction of charges into the NHS: 23 April 1951

Nye Bevan resigned as Labour Secretary in Clement Attlee's government in April 1951, along with the future Prime Minister Harold Wilson, then President of the Board of Trade, and John Freeman, a junior minister at the Ministry of Supply. It was a major blow to a government which was running out of steam and riven by bitter internal quarrels. The issue was the rearmament programme introduced by Attlee and his ailing Foreign Secretary, Ernest Bevin, to confront and contain Soviet expansionism and the charges introduced into the NHS to help pay for it. Bevan had long warned that he would resign if charging was introduced into his creation. And in the build-up to his resignation, he did so again at a public meeting in Bermondsey on 3 April, telling his audience he would 'never be a member of a government that makes charges on the National Health Service for a patient'.[1] The charges were not his only complaint. He was against the geopolitical strategy that had given rise to them, fearing that Britain was sacrificing its democratic socialist experiment to pay for the arms build-up needed for a bellicose American scheme to clip Soviet wings.

When on 10 April the Chancellor, Hugh Gaitskell, came to present his Budget, which included the charges on NHS spectacles and dentures, Bevan was not in his usual seat, preferring to lurk behind the Speaker's chair, where the Tory backbencher Chips Channon records him 'red faced and breathing like an angry bull'.[2] Bevan's wife, Jennie Lee, cried 'Shame!' but there was no further public demonstration.

Much internal manoeuvring followed, to try to keep Bevan in the Cabinet. When the future Speaker George Thomas asked Lee to persuade her husband to stay, she rounded on him: 'you yellow livered cur, you're just like all the rest. You're another MacDonald or Snowden. Go away from me.'[3] Bevan continued to threaten resignation if the date for the second reading of the bill introducing the charges was announced. Challenged by Attlee to accept collective Cabinet responsibility, he quit.

By one of those little ironies that occasionally crop up in the business of the Commons, his resignation statement was preceded by a question from Thomas about the perils caused by straying sheep in South Wales. MPs did not titter for long. Bevan's biographer, Michael Foot, described the atmosphere as he rose as 'arctic'. The speech was less about the NHS than about the cost to Britain of the defence build-up (which in any case he believed was unfeasible) and the need to pursue a more independent foreign policy. The year before, Attlee had flown to the White House to beard President Truman when it was suggested that the Americans might resort to nuclear weapons in the Korean War. The incident took on a rather mythic status, but it did seem at the time to be a reassertion of Britain's status as an independent world power. Bevan – as his words about Britain's claim to moral leadership of the world suggest – seemed to want more. But his attacks on colleagues alienated possible allies and destabilised a dying government.

M R Speaker, it is one of the immemorial courtesies of the House of Commons that when a Minister has felt it necessary to resign his office, he is provided with an opportunity of stating his reasons to the House. These occasions are always exceedingly painful, especially to the individual concerned, because no member ought to accept office in a Government without a full consciousness that he ought not to resign it for frivolous reasons. He must keep in mind that his association is based upon the assumption that everybody in Government accepts the full measure of responsibility for what it does.

Bevan reminded MPs of warnings he had given about the danger of switching too much of the productive capacity of the economy – not just of Britain, but of the West – over to defence purposes, and of the danger of creating an atmosphere of hatred and hysteria against the Soviet Union. He predicted that Britain's proposed defence build-up would prove unachievable and that America's would suck scarce resources away from peaceful industry across the world, causing a wave of social unrest.

The fact is that the western world has embarked upon a campaign of arms production upon a scale, so quickly, and of such an extent that the foundations of political liberty and parliamentary democracy will not be able to sustain the shock. This is a very grave matter indeed. I have always said both in the House of Commons and in speeches in the country – and I think my ex-colleagues in the Government will at least give me credit for this – that the defence programme must always be consistent with the maintenance of the standard of life of the British people and the maintenance of the social services, and that as soon as it became clear we had engaged upon an arms programme inconsistent with those considerations, I could no longer remain a member of the Government.

I therefore do beg the House and the country, and the world, to think before it is too late. It may be that on such an occasion as this the dramatic nature of a resignation might cause even some of our American friends to think before it is too late. It has always been clear that the weapons of the totalitarian States are, first, social and economic, and only next military; and if in attempting to meet the military effect of those totalitarian machines, the economies of the western world are disrupted and the standard of living is lowered or industrial disturbances are created, then Soviet communism establishes a whole series of Trojan horses in every nation of the western economy.

It is, therefore, absolutely essential if we are to march forward properly, if we are to mobilise our resources intelligently, that the military, social and political weapons must be taken together. It is clear from the Budget that the Chancellor of the Exchequer has abandoned any hope of restraining inflation. It is quite clear that for the rest of the year and for the beginning of next year, so far as we can see, the cost of living is going to rise precipitously. As the cost of living rises, the industrial workers of Great Britain will try to adjust themselves to the rising spiral of prices, and because they will do so by a series of individual trade union demands a hundred and one battles will be fought on the industrial field, and our political enemies will take advantage of each one. It is, therefore, impossible for us to proceed with this programme in this way.

I therefore beg my colleagues, as I have begged them before, to consider before they commit themselves to these great programmes. It is obvious from what the Chancellor of the Exchequer said in his Budget speech that we have no longer any hope of restraining inflation. The cost of living has already gone up by several points since the middle of last year, and it is going up again. Therefore, it is no use pretending that the Budget is just, merely because it gives a few shillings to old age pensioners, when rising prices immediately begin to take the few shillings away from them.

'Hear, hear!' cried Tory MPs, who must have been enjoying the spectacle.

It is no use saying 'Hear, hear' on the opposite side of the House. The Opposition have no remedy for this at all. But there is a remedy here on this side of the House if it is courageously applied, and the Budget does not courageously apply it. The Budget has run away from it. The Budget was hailed with pleasure in the City. It was a remarkable Budget. It united the City, satisfied the Opposition and disunited the Labour Party – all this because we have allowed ourselves to be dragged too far behind the wheels of American diplomacy.

This great nation has a message for the world which is distinct from that of America or that of the Soviet Union. Ever since 1945 we have been engaged in this country in the most remarkable piece of social reconstruction the world has ever seen. By the end of 1950 we had, as I said in my letter to the Prime Minister, assumed the moral leadership of the world.

This provoked jeers from across the chamber.

It is no use hon. members opposite sneering, because when they come to the end of the road, it will not be a sneer which will be upon their faces. There is only one hope for mankind, and that hope still remains in this little island. It is from here that we tell the world where to go and how to go there, but we must not follow behind the anarchy of American competitive capitalism which is unable to restrain itself at all, as is seen in the stockpiling that is now going on, and which denies to the economy of Great Britain even the means of carrying on our civil production. That is the first part of what I wanted to say.

It has never been in my mind that my quarrel with my colleagues was based only upon what they have done to the National Health Service. As they know, over and over again I have said that these figures of arms production are fantastically wrong, and that if we try to spend them we shall get less arms for more money. I have not had experience in the Ministry of Health for five years for nothing. I know what it is to put too large a programme upon too narrow a base. We have to adjust our paper figures to physical realities, and that is what the Exchequer has not done.

May I be permitted, in passing, now that I enjoy comparative freedom, to give a word of advice to my colleagues in the Government? Take economic planning away from the Treasury. They know nothing about it. The great difficulty with the Treasury is that they think they move men about when they move pieces of paper about. It is what I have described over and over again as 'whistle-blowing' planning. It has been perfectly obvious on several occasions that there are too many economists advising the Treasury, and now we have the added misfortune of having an economist in the Chancellor of the Exchequer [Gaitskell] himself.

I therefore seriously suggest to the Government that they should set up a production department[4] and put the Chancellor of the Exchequer in the position where he ought to be now under modern planning, that is, with the function of making an annual statement of accounts. Then we should have some realism in the Budget. We should not be pushing out figures when the facts are going in the opposite direction.

I want to come for a short while, because I do not wish to try the patience of the House, to the narrower issue. The Chancellor of the Exchequer astonished me when he said that his Budget was coming to the rescue of the fixed income groups. Well, it has come to the rescue of the fixed income groups over 70 years of age, but not below. The fixed income groups in our modern social services are the victims of this kind of finance. Everybody possessing property gets richer. Property is appreciating all the time and it is well known that there are large numbers of British citizens living normally out of the appreciated values of their own property. The fiscal measures of the Chancellor of the Exchequer do not touch them at all.

I listened to the Chancellor of the Exchequer with very great admiration. It was one of the cleverest Budget speeches I had ever heard in my life. There was a passage towards the end in which he said that he was now coming to a complicated and technical matter and that if members wished to they could go to sleep. They did. Whilst they were sleeping he stole £100 million a year from the National Insurance Fund. Of course I know that in the same Budget speech the Chancellor of the Exchequer said that he had already taken account of it as savings. Of course he had, so that the rearmament of Great Britain is financed out of the contributions that the workers have paid into the Fund in order to protect themselves.

That produced gasps from the Labour side, and their volume increased as Bevan developed the point.

Certainly, that is the meaning of it. It is no good my hon. friends refusing to face these matters. If we look at the Chancellor's speech we see that the Chancellor himself said that he had already taken account of the contributions into the Insurance Fund as savings. He said so, and he is right. Do not deny that he is right. I am saying he is right. Do not quarrel with me when I agree with him.

The conclusion is as follows. At a time when there are still large untapped sources of wealth in Great Britain, a socialist Chancellor of the Exchequer uses the Insurance Fund contributed for the purpose of maintaining the social services, as his source of revenue, and I say that is not socialist finance. Go to that source for revenue when no other source remains, but no one can say that there are no other sources of revenue in Great Britain except the Insurance Fund.

I now come to the National Health Service side of the matter. Let me say to my hon. friends on these benches: you have been saying in the last fortnight or three weeks that I have been quarrelling about a triviality – spectacles and dentures. You may call it a triviality. I remember the triviality that started an avalanche in 1931.[5] I remember it very well, and perhaps my hon. friends would not mind me recounting it. There was a trade union group meeting upstairs. I was a member of it and went along. My good friend, 'Geordie' Buchanan, did not come along with me because he thought it was hopeless, and he proved to be a better prophet than I was. But I had more credulity in those days than I have got now. So I went along, and the first subject was an attack on the seasonal workers. That was the first order. I opposed it bitterly, and when I came out of the room my good old friend George Lansbury attacked me for attacking the order. I said, 'George, you do not realise, this is the beginning of the end. Once you start this there is no logical stopping point.'

The Chancellor of the Exchequer in this year's Budget proposes to reduce the Health expenditure by £13 million – only £13 million out of £4,000 million.

Some MPs disputed the figure. 'Four hundred million pounds' they shouted.

No, £4,000 million. He has taken £13 million out of the Budget total of £4,000 million. If he finds it necessary to mutilate, or begin to mutilate, the Health Services for £13 million out of £4,000 million, what will he do next year? Or are you next year going to take your stand on the upper denture? The lower half apparently does not matter, but the top half is sacrosanct. Is that right? If my hon. friends are asked questions at meetings about what they will do next year, what will they say?

The Chancellor of the Exchequer is putting a financial ceiling on the Health Service. With rising prices the Health Service is squeezed between that artificial figure and rising prices. What is to be squeezed out next year? Is it the upper half? When that has been squeezed out and the same principle holds good, what do you squeeze out the year after? Prescriptions? Hospital charges? Where do you stop? I have been accused of having agreed to a charge on prescriptions. That shows the danger of compromise. Because if it is pleaded against me that I agreed to the modification of the Health Service, then what will be pleaded against my right hon. friends next year, and indeed what answer will they have if the vandals opposite come in. What answer? The Health Service will be like Lavinia – all the limbs cut off and eventually her tongue cut out, too.

I should like to ask my right hon. and hon. friends, where are they going?

'Where are you going?' retorted Bevan's Labour critics.

Where am I going? I am where I always was. Those who live their lives in mountainous and rugged countries are always afraid of avalanches, and they know that avalanches start with the movement of a very small stone. First, the stone starts on a ridge between two valleys – one valley desolate and the other valley populous. The pebble starts, but nobody bothers about the pebble until it gains way, and soon the whole valley is overwhelmed. That is how the avalanche starts, that is the logic of the present situation, and that is the logic my right hon. and hon. friends cannot escape. Why, therefore, has it been done in this way?

After all, the National Health Service was something of which we were all very proud, and even the Opposition were beginning to be proud of it. It only had to last a few more years to become a part of our traditions, and then the traditionalists would have claimed the credit for all of it. Why should we throw it away? In the Chancellor's Speech there was not one word of commendation for the Health Service – not one word. What is responsible for that?

Why has the cut been made? He cannot say, with an overall surplus of over £220 million and a conventional surplus of £39 million, that he had to have the £13 million. That is the arithmetic of Bedlam. He cannot say that his arithmetic is so precise that he must have the £13 million, when last year the Treasury were £247 million out. Why? Has the A.M.A. succeeded in doing what the B.M.A. failed to do? What is the cause of it? Why has it been done?

I have also been accused – and I think I am entitled to answer it – that I had already agreed to a certain charge. I speak to my right hon. friends very frankly here. It seems to me sometimes that it is so difficult to make them see what lies ahead that you have to take them along by the hand and show them. The prescription charge I knew would never be made, because it was impracticable.

This admission of Cabinet manoeuvring produced more gasps.

Well, it was never made.

I will tell my hon. friends something else, too. There was another policy, there was a proposed reduction of 25,000 on the housing programme, was there not? It was never made. It was necessary for me at that time to use what everybody always said were bad tactics upon my part – I had to manoeuvre, and I did manoeuvre and saved the 25,000 houses and the prescription charge. I say, therefore, to my right hon. and hon. friends, there is no justification for taking this line at all. There is no justification in the arithmetic, there is less justification in the economics, and I beg my right hon. and hon. friends to change their minds about it.

I say this, in conclusion. There is only one hope for mankind – and that is democratic socialism. There is only one party in Great Britain which can do it and that is the Labour Party. But I ask them carefully to consider how far they are polluting the stream. We have gone a long way – a very long way – against great difficulties. Do not let us change direction now. Let us make it clear, quite clear, to the rest of the world that we stand where we stood, that we are not going to allow ourselves to be diverted from our path by the exigencies of the immediate situation. We shall do what is necessary to defend ourselves – defend ourselves by arms, and not only with arms but with the spiritual resources of our people.

Immediately after his speech, a Conservative backbencher rose to enquire when an election would be held. The opposition, rightly, scented blood.

The swipe at Gaitskell over the National Insurance Fund was the first open blow in a long and bitter conflict that had been brewing since the future leader had replaced Stafford Cripps in the Treasury. 'He dealt with Mr Gaitskell contemptuously and his manner towards the Government as a whole was harsh and hectoring,' wrote the *Manchester Guardian*'s parliamentary correspondent Harry Boardman.[6] 'All the well-known tricks were at his command. He would raise that quivering index finger above his head, or he would draw it, still quivering, in an imaginary line before the front opposition bench. At times he would claw the air towards him with an open palm or he would pause to pass his hand through his unruly forelock.

'He finished on a peroration about democratic socialism being the only help for mankind, and it contained an admonition to the Government not to pollute the stream. There were no cheers when he sat down.'

Bevan's antagonist Hugh Dalton thought the speech a failure: 'Nye flopped in the House today on his resignation speech. No cheer when he entered . . . Hardly any cheers when he was speaking, nor when he sat down . . . A most vicious speech, most quotable by the Tories.'[7] Bevan had referred to his stratagems to avoid a prescription charge and a cut of 25,000 in the housebuilding programme. 'His delighted confession of having tricked his colleagues by his manoeuvres was not liked,' Dalton noted. Channon thought Bevan was 'savage, vindictive, dramatic and too long-winded . . . I watched Winston while Bevan was speaking. He sat grinning and dangling his watch chain.'

Among the Labour backbenchers present was Tony Benn, who had won a by-election in Stafford Cripps's former seat the previous year. More than half a century later, he believes the speech was one of the most powerful and prophetic he has heard in his long parliamentary career. It made the argument that there was no real threat from the Soviet Union, and that the money spent on arms would have been better deployed on social services and rebuilding the economy, an argument Benn believes has been vindicated by history.

This was the beginning – in Gaitskell's phrase – of a battle for the soul of the Labour Party. While Bevan and Gaitskell fought it out, the Conservatives ran the country.

'The tip of a singularly ill-concealed iceberg, with all the destructive potential that icebergs possess.'

Nigel Lawson quits over European Monetary Union: 31 October 1989

The resignation of a Chancellor of the Exchequer, normally the second figure in a modern government, can deal a mortal blow to any Prime Minister. In Nigel Lawson's case, the effect was delayed. He and Margaret Thatcher disagreed fundamentally over a basic issue of economic policy. He wanted to bring sterling into the exchange rate mechanism of the then European Monetary System. She did not, and the increasingly visible divisions between them attracted ever more attention. Lawson, whom she had once called 'my brilliant Chancellor', became increasingly irked by criticism from the Prime Minister's personal economic adviser, Sir Alan Walters. His description of the ERM as 'half-baked' highlighted the policy rift with Thatcher, created uncertainty in the markets and ultimately provoked Lawson into insisting that either Walters went, or he did.

Labour, naturally, seized on this clear evidence of dissension at the very pinnacle of the Thatcher government. The shadow Chancellor, John Smith, moved a motion criticising 'confusion and disarray in the content and conduct of economic policy'. Lawson took the opportunity to explain why he had left the government. His departure left his close ally Sir Geoffrey Howe in an exposed position as the most important remaining advocate of the ERM in government. In retrospect it was the first spasm in the Tory convulsions over EMU and the euro which have continued ever since.

I AM OLD-FASHIONED ENOUGH to believe that my first comment on recent events should be made to this House. This is not an easy speech for me to make, and I am sure that the House will understand that. I shall do my best to be brief, and I hope that the House will assist me in this.

I am most grateful for what my right hon. friend the new Chancellor of the Exchequer [John Major, the future Prime Minister, was sent to the Treasury from the Foreign Office; he had been Lawson's deputy, the Chief Secretary to the Treasury] has said about me, and I wish to take this further opportunity to wish him every success in the task that lies ahead of him. As he reminded the House, we worked closely together for just over two years, and he has my full and unstinting support. As for my own record, I have no doubt that I have made my share of mistakes; but I am content to be judged when the passage of time has provided a greater sense of perspective than is possible today. No one, however long he has held the post, lightly gives up the great office of Chancellor of the Exchequer. Certainly I did not. As the resignation letter that I wrote to my right hon. friend the Prime Minister clearly implies, it was not the outcome I sought. But it is one that I accept without rancour – despite what might be described as the hard landing involved. I would only add that the article written by my right hon. friend's former economic adviser[8] was of significance only inasmuch as it represented the tip of a singularly ill-concealed iceberg, with all the destructive potential that icebergs possess.

The prospects for a soft, or hard landing from the economic boom of the mid 1980s was the staple of economic debate at the time. Lawson felt he was being accused of cutting and running to evade responsibility for an impending recession.[9]

I have long been convinced that the only successful basis for the conduct of economic policy is to seek the greatest practicable degree of market freedom within an over-arching framework of financial discipline to bear down on inflation. That being so, a key question is where the exchange rate fits in. Is it to be part of the maximum practicable market freedom, or is it to be part – indeed, a central part – of the necessary financial discipline?

I recognise that a case can be made for either approach. No case can be made for seeming confusion or for apparent vacillation between these two positions. Morever, for our system of Cabinet government to work effectively, the Prime Minister of the day must appoint Ministers whom he or she trusts and then leave them to carry out the policy. When differences of view emerge, as they are bound to do from time to time, they should be resolved privately and, whenever appropriate, collectively.

But to return to the exchange rate. Faced with the question that I posed a moment ago, my answer is, unhesitatingly, that it should be seen as an essential element of financial discipline, with the rider, incidentally, that exchange rate stability is itself an economic benefit.

There is nothing novel, of course, in any of this. The House will recall the classical period of the gold standard before the First World War, the Bretton Woods system after the second world war, and, of course, over the past ten years, within the European context, the EMS.

None of these systems were or are panaceas or soft options. Tough decisions still have to be made. None of them were or are without difficulties. But those difficulties, in my judgment, are very much less than the practical difficulties and disadvantages which the world has experienced during periods of freely floating exchange rates. Nor, incidentally, can there be any doubt that the less credible the exchange rate discipline is, the greater the weight that interest rates will have to bear, and the higher they need to be to maintain the necessary anti-inflationary pressure.

Full United Kingdom membership of the EMS – I was glad to hear much of what my right hon. friend the Chancellor said – to which, again, as my right hon. friend the Prime Minister made clear at Madrid, this Government are committed, would signally enhance the credibility of our anti-inflationary resolve in general and the role of the exchange rate discipline in particular, and thus underpin the medium-term financial strategy. Indeed, given the existence of the EMS, our continuing non-participation in the exchange rate mechanism cannot fail to cast practical doubt on that resolve, however ill-founded such doubt may be.

There is, I believe, one other way in which anti-inflationary credibility might be enhanced in the eyes of the market and that is why, a year ago, I proposed to my right hon. friend the Prime Minister a fully worked-out scheme for the independence of the Bank of England. But that would be a buttress; it would not be a substitute for what I was saying earlier.

But if full United Kingdom membership of the EMS, although not indispensable, would facilitate the conduct of economic policy in general and the battle against inflation in particular, as those already participating have demonstrated, there is also a vital political dimension.

As my right hon. friend the Prime Minister made clear in her Bruges speech, Britain's destiny lies in Europe as a member of the European Community – and let me be clear that I am speaking, as she speaks, of a Europe of nation states. Within that context, it is vital that we maximise Britain's influence in the Community so as to ensure that it becomes the liberal free-market Europe in which we on the Conservative benches so firmly believe. I have little doubt that we will not be able to exert that influence effectively, and successfully provide the leadership, as long as we remain largely outside the EMS. So, for economic and political reasons alike, it is important that we seek the earliest practicable time to join, rather than the latest for which a colourable case can be made.

Finally, a word about the short-term prospects for the British economy. There always has been, and there always will be, an economic cycle. During our period of office so far, we experienced a sharp downturn between 1979 and

1981, followed by a remarkably vigorous and prolonged upswing which lasted from 1981 right through to 1988. We are now once again on the downswing, and I see no need for a further policy tightening. While this downswing will not be as sharp as the previous downturn, not least given the very much lower level of inflation that we now have, a dull 1989 is bound to be followed by a difficult 1990.

But from then on, I have every confidence that, with the policies that the Government have been pursuing and will continue to pursue, as we heard from the Chancellor today, the long-term upswing will continue, based on lower inflation and on the unprecedented underlying strength that the British economy now possesses. I have every confidence, too, that this will lead at the end of the day to a fourth election victory under the leadership of my right hon. friend the Prime Minister, whose outstanding contribution to the renaissance of Britain over these past ten years I am proud to have been able to assist.

Margaret Thatcher survived as Prime Minister for little more than a year. Lawson had damaged her, and the *coup de grâce* was administered with the resignation of Sir Geoffrey Howe. Lawson left the Commons in 1992.

'The tragic conflict of loyalties with which I have myself wrestled for perhaps too long.'

Geoffrey Howe inflicts a mortal wound on Margaret Thatcher: 13 November 1990

Margaret Thatcher was later to call it 'the most powerful Commons performance of his career'. Sir Geoffrey Howe had served her as Chancellor, Foreign Secretary and Leader of the Commons. He had been among her closest colleagues for a decade. But policy differences over Europe and increasing personal irritation had, by 1990, destroyed their relationship. Howe's removal from the Foreign Office had been accompanied by an ugly and futile argument over his status as Deputy Prime Minister, offered as a sweetener to the move. The press were briefed that the title 'didn't amount to anything'.

While still Foreign Secretary, Howe and Nigel Lawson, the then Chancellor, had jointly threatened resignation – effectively bringing down the government – if Britain did not announce a firm intention to join the European exchange rate mechanism. And after Lawson's resignation on that issue, he gave a television interview predicting that Thatcher would be 'won round'. She struck back, announcing that a single currency was not the policy of the government, and predicting that Lawson's scheme for a hard ecu, a currency which would circulate through the EU alongside existing national currencies, rather than replacing them, would not become widely used. In what seems to have been the final straw for Howe, she rejected the Delors vision of a federal Europe, with the European Parliament as its house of representatives, the Commission as its executive and the Council of Ministers as its senate with the emphatic dismissal: 'No, no, no.' Howe resigned on 31 October. His personal statement, the traditional chance for a departed minister to explain his departure, came just under a fortnight later.

I FIND TO MY ASTONISHMENT that a quarter of a century has passed since I last spoke from one of the back benches. Fortunately, however, it has been my privilege to serve for the past twelve months of that time as Leader of the House of Commons, so I have been reminded quite recently of the traditional generosity and tolerance of this place. I hope that I may count on that today as I offer to the House a statement about my resignation from the Government.

It has been suggested – even, indeed, by some of my right hon. and hon. friends – that I decided to resign solely because of questions of style and not on matters of substance at all. Indeed, if some of my former colleagues are to be believed, I must be the first Minister in history who has resigned because he was in full agreement with Government policy.

Taunted by Neil Kinnock after Howe's resignation, Mrs Thatcher had told the Commons: 'If the leader of the Opposition reads my right hon. and learned friend's [resignation] letter he will be very pressed indeed to find any significant policy difference between my right hon. and learned friend and the rest of us on this side.'

The truth is that, in many aspects of politics, style and substance complement each other. Very often, they are two sides of the same coin. The Prime Minister and I have shared something like 700 meetings of Cabinet or Shadow Cabinet during the past eighteen years, and some 400 hours alongside each other, at more than 30 international summit meetings. For both of us, I suspect, it is a pretty daunting record. The House might well feel that something more than simple matters of style would be necessary to rupture such a well-tried relationship. It was a privilege to serve as my right hon. friend's first Chancellor of the Exchequer; to share in the transformation of our industrial relations scene; to help launch our free market programme, commencing with the abolition of exchange control; and, above all, to achieve such substantial success against inflation, getting it down within four years from 22 per cent to 4 per cent upon the basis of the strict monetary discipline involved in the medium-term financial strategy. Not one of our economic achievements would have been possible without the courage and leadership of my right hon. friend – and, if I may say so, they possibly derived some little benefit from the presence of a Chancellor who was not exactly a wet himself.

It was a great honour to serve for six years as Foreign and Commonwealth Secretary and to share with my right hon. friend in some notable achievements in the European Community – from Fontainebleau to the Single European Act. But it was as we moved on to consider the crucial monetary issues in the European context that I came to feel increasing concern. Some of the reasons for that anxiety were made very clear by my right hon. friend the member for Blaby [Nigel Lawson] in his resignation speech just over twelve months ago. Like him, I concluded at least five years ago that the conduct of our policy against inflation could no longer rest solely on attempts to measure and control the domestic money supply. We had no doubt that we should be helped in that battle, and, indeed, in other respects, by joining the exchange rate mechanism of the European monetary system. There was, or should have been, nothing novel about joining the ERM; it has been a long-standing commitment. For a quarter of a century after the Second World War, we found that the very similar Bretton Woods regime did serve as a useful discipline. Now, as my right hon. friend the Prime Minister acknowledged two weeks ago, our entry into the ERM can be seen as an 'extra discipline for keeping down inflation'.

However, it must be said that that practical conclusion has been achieved only at the cost of substantial damage to her Administration and, more serious still, to its inflation achievements.

As my right hon. friend the member for Blaby explained: 'The real tragedy is that we did not join the exchange rate mechanism at least five years ago.'

As he also made clear, 'That was not for want of trying.'

Indeed, the so-called Madrid conditions came into existence only after the then Chancellor and I, as Foreign Secretary, made it clear that we could not continue in office unless a specific commitment to join the ERM was made.

As the House will no doubt have observed, neither member of that particular partnership now remains in office. Our successor as Chancellor of the Exchequer [John Major became Chancellor on Lawson's resignation] has, during the past year, had to devote a great deal of his considerable talents to demonstrating exactly how those Madrid conditions have been attained, so as to make it possible to fulfil a commitment whose achievement has long been in the national interest.

It is now, alas, impossible to resist the conclusion that today's higher rates of inflation could well have been avoided had the question of ERM membership been properly considered and resolved at a much earlier stage. There are, I fear, developing grounds for similar anxiety over the handling – not just at and after the Rome summit – of the wider, much more open question of economic and monetary union. Let me first make clear certain important points on which I have no disagreement with my right hon. friend, the Prime Minister. I do not regard the Delors report as some kind of sacred text that has to be accepted, or even rejected, on the nod. But it is an important working document. As I have often made plain, it is seriously deficient in significant respects.

But it is crucially important that we should conduct those arguments upon the basis of a clear understanding of the true relationship between this country, the Community and our Community partners. And it is here, I fear, that my right hon. friend the Prime Minister increasingly risks leading herself and others astray in matters of substance as well as of style.

It was the late Lord Stockton, formerly Harold Macmillan, who first put the central point clearly. As long ago as 1962, he argued that we had to place and keep ourselves within the EC. He saw it as essential then, as it is today, not to cut ourselves off from the realities of power; not to retreat into a ghetto of sentimentality about our past and so diminish our own control over our own destiny in the future.

The pity is that the Macmillan view had not been perceived more clearly a decade before in the 1950s. It would have spared us so many of the struggles of the last 20 years had we been in the Community from the outset; had we been ready, in the much too simple phrase, to 'surrender some sovereignty' at a much earlier stage. If we had been in from the start, as almost everybody now acknowledges, we should have had more, not less, influence over the Europe in which we live today. We should never forget the lesson of that isolation, of being on the outside looking in, for the conduct of today's affairs.

We have done best when we have seen the Community not as a static entity to be resisted and contained, but as an active process which we can shape, often decisively, provided that we allow ourselves to be fully engaged in it, with confidence, with enthusiasm and in good faith.

We must at all costs avoid presenting ourselves yet again with an over-simplified choice, a false antithesis, a bogus dilemma, between one alternative, starkly labelled 'cooperation between independent sovereign states' and a second, equally crudely labelled alternative, 'centralised, federal super-state', as if there were no middle way in between.

We commit a serious error if we think always in terms of 'surrendering' sovereignty and seek to stand pat for all time on a given deal – by proclaiming, as my right hon. friend the Prime Minister did two weeks ago, that we have 'surrendered enough'.

The European enterprise is not and should not be seen like that – as some kind of zero sum game. Sir Winston Churchill put it much more positively 40 years ago, when he said:

'It is also possible and not less agreeable to regard' this sacrifice or merger of national sovereignty 'as the gradual assumption by all the nations concerned of that larger sovereignty which can alone protect their diverse and distinctive customs and characteristics and their national traditions.'

I have to say that I find Winston Churchill's perception a good deal more convincing, and more encouraging for the interests of our nation, than the nightmare image sometimes conjured up by my right hon. friend, who seems sometimes to look out upon a continent that is positively teeming with ill-intentioned people, scheming, in her words, to 'extinguish democracy', to 'dissolve our national identities' and to lead us 'through the back-door into a federal Europe'.

What kind of vision is that for our business people, who trade there each day, for our financiers, who seek to make London the money capital of Europe or for all the young people of today?

These concerns are especially important as we approach the crucial topic of economic and monetary union. We must be positively and centrally involved in this debate and not fearfully and negatively detached. The costs of disengagement here could be very serious indeed.

There is talk, of course, of a single currency for Europe. I agree that there are many difficulties about the concept – both economic and political. Of course, as I said in my letter of resignation, none of us wants the imposition of a single currency. But that is not the real risk. The eleven others cannot impose their solution on the twelfth country against its will, but they can go ahead without us. The risk is not imposition but isolation. The real threat is that of leaving ourselves with no say in the monetary arrangements that the rest of Europe chooses for itself, with Britain once again scrambling to join the club later, after the rules have been set and after the power has been distributed by others to our disadvantage. That would be the worst possible outcome.

It is to avoid just that outcome and to find a compromise both acceptable in the Government and sellable in Europe that my right hon. friend the Chancellor has put forward his hard ecu proposal. This lays careful emphasis on the possibility that the hard ecu as a common currency could, given time, evolve into a single currency. I have of course supported the hard ecu plan. But after Rome, and after the comments of my right hon. friend the Prime Minister two weeks ago, there is grave danger that the hard ecu proposal is becoming untenable, because two things have happened.

The first is that my right hon. friend the Prime Minister has appeared to rule out from the start any compromise at any stage on any of the basic components that all the 11 other countries believe to be a part of EMU – a single currency or a permanently fixed exchange rate, a central bank or common monetary policy. Asked whether we would veto any arrangement that jeopardised the pound sterling, my right hon. friend replied simply, 'Yes.' That statement means not that we can block EMU but that they can go ahead without us. Is that a position that is likely to ensure, as I put it in my resignation letter, that 'we hold, and retain, a position of influence in this vital debate'?

I fear not. Rather, to do so, we must, as I said, take care not to rule in or rule out any one solution absolutely. We must be seen to be part of the same negotiation.

The second thing that happened was, I fear, even more disturbing. Reporting to this House, my right hon. friend almost casually remarked that she did not think that many people would want to use the hard ecu anyway – even as a common currency, let alone as a single one. It was remarkable – indeed, it was tragic – to hear my right hon. friend dismissing, with such personalised incredulity, the very idea that the hard ecu proposal might find growing favour among the peoples of Europe, just as it was extraordinary to hear her assert that the whole idea of EMU might be open for consideration only by future generations. Those future generations are with us today. How on earth are the Chancellor and the Governor of the Bank of England, commending the hard ecu as they strive to, to be taken as serious participants in the debate against that kind of background noise? I believe that both the Chancellor and the Governor are cricketing enthusiasts, so I hope that there is no monopoly of cricketing metaphors.

The real target of what followed was the Prime Minister. The night before, at the Lord Mayor's Banquet at the Guildhall, she had used a cricketing metaphor to describe her position after Howe's departure: 'I am still at the crease, though the bowling has been pretty hostile of late. And in case anyone doubted it, can I assure you there will be no ducking bouncers, no stonewalling, no playing for time. The bowling's going to get hit all round the ground.'

It is rather like sending your opening batsmen to the crease only for them to find, the moment the first balls are bowled, that their bats have been broken before the game by the team captain.

The tragedy is – and it is for me personally, for my party, for our whole people and for my right hon. friend herself, a very real tragedy – that the Prime Minister's perceived attitude towards Europe is running increasingly serious risks for the future of our nation. It risks minimising our influence and maximising our chances of being once again shut out. We have paid heavily in the past for late starts and squandered opportunities in Europe. We dare not let that happen again. If we detach ourselves completely, as a party or a nation, from the middle ground of Europe, the effects will be incalculable and very hard ever to correct.

In my letter of resignation, which I tendered with the utmost sadness and dismay, I said:

> Cabinet government is all about trying to persuade one another from within.

That was my commitment to Government by persuasion – persuading colleagues and the nation. I have tried to do that as Foreign Secretary and since, but I realise now that the task has become futile: trying to stretch the meaning of words beyond what was credible, and trying to pretend that there was a common policy when every step forward risked being subverted by some casual comment or impulsive answer.

The conflict of loyalty, of loyalty to my right hon. friend the Prime Minister – and, after all, in two decades together that instinct of loyalty is still very real – and of loyalty to what I perceive to be the true interests of the nation, has become all too great. I no longer believe it possible to resolve that conflict from within this Government. That is why I have resigned. In doing so, I have done what I believe to be right for my party and my country. The time has come for others to consider their own response to the tragic conflict of loyalties with which I have myself wrestled for perhaps too long.

Two Commons diarists gave vivid accounts of Howe's speech. Alan Clark recorded: 'He was personally wounding – to a far greater extent than mere policy differences would justify.'[10] He captured the delight on the Labour benches: 'Grinning from ear to ear they "Oooh'd" and "Aaah'd" dead on cue.' Clark was particularly intrigued by the 'ominous and strange' final sentence, which appeared to invite Thatcher's lurking challenger Michael Heseltine to launch his long-anticipated leadership bid.

On the Labour benches, Giles Radice thought the speech: 'simply the most devastating I have heard since I have been in Parliament. He has used the floor of the House to destroy the authority of an existing PM.'[11] One Tory wit, referring to Elspeth Howe's celebrated dislike of Mrs Thatcher, noted: 'It took Elspeth ten minutes to write the speech; Geoffrey took ten years to make it.'

Mrs Thatcher thought the speech a 'final act of bile and treachery'.[12] The next day Michael Heseltine launched his leadership challenge, which ended her premiership.

'We give the impression of being in office but not in power.'

Norman Lamont's departing broadside: 9 June 1993.

Norman Lamont was a coiner of memorable political phrases. The trouble was that all too frequently they came back to haunt him. In the recession of the early 1990s, he discerned 'the green shoots of recovery', but the recession went on. He claimed the unemployment generated by that recession was 'a price worth paying'. He told the middle-class by-election voters of Newbury: '*Je ne regrette rien*.' The Conservatives went on to lose the seat. And after sterling crashed out of the European exchange rate mechanism on Black (or White) Wednesday on 16 September 1992, an economic humiliation to rank alongside the diplomatic debacle of Suez, he was reported to be 'singing in the bath'.

Black Wednesday was the seminal political and economic event of the 1990s. The Conservatives' credibility as economic managers has not, at the time of writing, thirteen years later, recovered. And nor, excepting a few minor blips, has the party's opinion poll rating. (Some 'blue shoots of recovery' were being discerned at the time of writing.) But Lamont's resignation was not an immediate reaction to the collapse of the government's economic policy. He remained in office for nine months, despite advice that he should resign, do public penance and then return to the Cabinet. And, meanwhile, the government stumbled through the ratification of the Maastricht Treaty. Lamont, indeed, made a much praised winding-up speech for the government on the third reading of the Maastricht Bill. But all the while his position was unravelling. He was conscious that senior Tories wanted him sacked and made the scapegoat for the government's Euro-humiliations.

In his memoirs Lamont described the process of sacking.[13] He told how John Major began the 'calm and courteous' interview that ended in his departure with the words; 'Norman, I want you to know how very much I like you.' Major told him he ought to have one of the top Cabinet posts, but that was not, for the moment, possible. He offered instead the middle-ranking post of Environment Secretary,[14] but Lamont decided to go. Having managed Major's leadership campaign in 1990, and having been asked to stay on after Black Wednesday, his hurt was considerable.

Two weeks later, Lamont took the opportunity of an opposition day economic debate to state his case, with a speech reputedly composed with the help of the ardent Thatcherite Woodrow Wyatt. Lamont said he had not attempted to damage John Major. Others saw it differently. Gyles Brandreth thought it 'fairly devastating stuff,'[15] especially the wounding final paragraphs on the Government's political competence. Giles Radice thought it 'sub Howe stuff', although with a querulous tone.[16] The leader of the opposition, John Smith, naturally seized on his complaint, mocking 'the stark reality of a discredited Government, presided over by a discredited Prime Minister'. And the Liberal Democrat leader, Paddy Ashdown, told Major, who had sat unflinching through the speech, 'if you had bothered to turn round you would have seen your fate indelibly written on the faces of Conservative members.'

T HIS IS NOT AN EASY statement for me to make today, but I am sure that the House will understand that and that I can rely on the traditional tolerance and generosity of hon. members.

To give up being Chancellor of the Exchequer in the circumstances in which I did is bound to be an uncomfortable experience, but I have also been a Treasury Minister for almost seven years, a longer continuous period than anyone else this century. Indeed, I have been the only person ever to have held the three offices of Financial Secretary, Chief Secretary and Chancellor of the Exchequer. I should like to pay tribute to the officials with whom I worked all those years. In my opinion, they are equal to the best in the world, and I am astonished how, when things go wrong, often it is the civil servants who are blamed when it is we politicians who make the decisions and it is we politicians who should carry the blame. When the Prime Minister told me two weeks ago that he wished to make changes in his Government, I of course told him that I appreciated that he had a very difficult task. He generously offered me another position in his Cabinet, but, in my opinion, it would not have been right either for him or for myself if I had accepted. If he wished to change his Chancellor, it was surely right that I should leave the Cabinet. Perhaps I can make it clear that I wish the Prime Minister well and hope that his changes will produce whatever advantage for him and the Government he intended.

It has not been easy being Chancellor of the Exchequer in this recession, continually and wrongly described as the longest and deepest since the war or, even more inaccurately, since the 1930s. It is certainly not the deepest recession since the war and, when the figures are finally revised, it may turn out not even to have been the longest. But it is a recession which has affected many areas which have not experienced such severe recession before; and that was bound to have an adverse effect on the fortunes and popularity of the Government.

This recession was not caused by Britain's membership of the exchange mechanism. The recession began before we joined the ERM – and, incidentally, before I became Chancellor – and a large part of the fall in output occurred in late 1990 and early 1991, far too soon to be influenced by our membership of the ERM. No, this recession has its origins in the boom of 1988 and 1989. That boom made the recession inevitable.

But the recession is now behind us, and so I am able with confidence to wish every success to my right hon. and learned friend the new Chancellor [Kenneth Clarke]. He inherits, I believe, a fundamentally strong position. As Mr Lloyd Bentsen, the United States Treasury Secretary, said in a generous letter to me last week, Britain is the only European country likely to experience any significant growth this year; and inflation is at a 30-year low. Since the war only two Conservative Chancellors have been responsible for bringing inflation down to below 2 per cent. Both of them were sacked. In my view, that tells us a great deal about the difficulties of reducing inflation in a democracy as lively and disputatious as ours.

I am delighted to hear from the Prime Minister that policy will not alter. My right hon. and learned friend the Chancellor will understand if I say that he thus comes to the Treasury at a most favourable time. Much of the hard work has been done and he should be able to enjoy increasingly encouraging trends for a long time to come. I am sure that my initiative in bringing the autumn statement and the Budget together into one December Budget is a reform that will last, and I wish my right hon. and learned friend well with what is a massive task.

I have been privileged to present three Budgets. All three achieved the objectives that I set for them. The first drew the sting of the poll tax; the second, by introducing the 20p income tax band, helped us to win the election; the third, unpopular though it undoubtedly was, made a significant step towards reducing our budget deficit. That, as I have frequently observed, is the greatest threat to our long-term position.

I should now like to say a word about Britain's experience of membership of the exchange rate mechanism. Although many people are either for or against membership of a fixed exchange rate system, there are many others, including, for example, Alan Greenspan, the chairman of the United States Federal Reserve Board, whose views about fixed versus floating exchange rates have never been theological. My views are not theological either. I have always believed that one could run an economy on either a fixed or a floating rate basis, although at times one might be more appropriate than the other.

I tried to persuade my noble friend Lord Lawson that it was not worth resigning over the ERM in 1988. Although I probably would not have joined in

1989, I did not believe then that a fixed-rate system was doomed to break up. Presumably those who hold that view blame my noble friend Lady Thatcher for committing us to a policy that was bound to fail. But I do not take that view now, and I did not take it then. When I accepted the office of Chancellor, I accepted the policy, believed that it could be made to work, and did all that I could to make it work. It certainly enabled us to get inflation down dramatically. Indeed, without the ERM, I doubt whether the Government would have had the courage and determination to get inflation down; that is a point to which I shall return.

The reason why our policy on the ERM ultimately broke down was that German policy developed in a way which, in my view, was mistaken and which was not anticipated – not least when German interest rates were put up last year. As members of the ERM, we were forced to respond in a way that meant that our own policy became increasingly over-tight. I became increasingly concerned last summer that our policy was too restrictive and that our membership of the ERM was impeding recovery.

I raised with the Prime Minister the idea that we might suspend our membership temporarily at some future date if recovery were being prevented. He made it clear that he did not want to do that. Probably he was right. I accepted it. In any case, it would not have made any difference. We were talking about the distant future and we would have been overtaken by the same events in September that ultimately hit us. But I would not want the country to believe that these matters were never under consideration or that we were not aware of what was happening in the economy outside.

That perhaps explains why I did not do one thing that some have argued and urged might have enabled us to remain within the exchange rate mechanism – to put up interest rates in the summer of 1992. Because of the position of the domestic economy, I did not believe that that was an option. Furthermore, I did not believe that it would have been credible, and I am sure that I was right.

People have frequently asked me why we did not devalue within the system. I did not devalue because it would have meant higher interest rates at a time when we needed lower interest rates. One solution might have been a revaluation of the mark against all other currencies in the ERM, thus making room for lower German interest rates. I was not opposed to that, but, unfortunately, my friend and colleague, the late Pierre Beregovoy, the French Finance Minister was, despite my efforts at persuasion, implacably opposed to such a move.

I do not believe that any question of rejoining the ERM should remotely be on the agenda during this Parliament. Fortunately, my right hon. and learned friend the Chancellor has already announced his policy. I am only thankful that, despite the residual doubts of some of my colleagues, I insisted on getting my own way and on keeping the ERM out of Maastricht as a treaty obligation. I need hardly remind the House how difficult our position would be today if the Maastricht Treaty obliged us to rejoin the ERM.

Some argue that the credibility of the Government was destroyed on 16 September. But once I had reconstructed our policy, that was not the view of the markets, or of the stock exchange, which touched an all-time high not so long ago, or of the foreign exchange markets, where the pound's recovery has been strong enough to worry some businessmen.

Markets and businessmen are cynical. They know that, in a fixed exchange rate system, there are certain things that Finance Ministers have to say. Credibility and confidence depend not on words but on objective conditions. I am glad to say that those objective conditions today are better than they have been for many years. On the crucial question of credibility, I want to take this opportunity to give my right hon. friend the Prime Minister and my right hon. and learned friend the Chancellor some advice. Nothing would be more effective in establishing the Government's credibility than if my right hon. friend would have the courage to establish an independent central bank in this country. The time has come to make the Bank of England independent. It is my greatest regret that, after two and a half years of trying, I failed to persuade the Prime Minister of this essential reform. [17]

Now that we are outside the ERM, the need is even more urgent. Britain is one of the few countries where monetary policy remains firmly in political hands, and the pressures on politicians to take policy decisions for political reasons can be quite irresistible. With an independent bank, we could have lower interest rates for a given exchange rate. Policy would be more credible and it would give us the necessary discipline for keeping inflation down on a permanent basis.

While my right hon. friend the Prime Minister and I have been in general agreement on interest rate policy, I do not believe that even the timing of interest rate changes should ever be affected by political considerations. Interest rate changes should never be used to offset some unfavourable political event. To do so undermines the credibility of policy and the credibility of the Chancellor. When my resignation was announced 10 days ago, the reaction of many was that it was a delayed resignation, a resignation that should have happened on 16 September. On that day, and during the subsequent days, I did of course consider my position carefully with friends and colleagues. I was anxious to do what was right for the country and for the Government. Sir Stafford Cripps,[18] who is rightly regarded as an honourable man, did not resign after devaluing the pound. On the other hand, Lord Callaghan,[19] also an honourable man, did.

There are three principal reasons why I decided to stay in office. First, the events of last September were very different from those of 1967. They affected not just this country, but most of Europe. The Finance Ministers of no fewer than nine countries were forced to eat their words and either devalue or float. Five floated; four devalued; one both devalued and floated. In none did the Finance Minister resign or, to the best of my knowledge, come under any pressure to resign. Indeed, in one country the governor of the central bank was actually promoted: he became Prime Minister.

Secondly, membership of the exchange rate mechanism was the policy of the whole Government; and as the Prime Minister said, I was implementing Government policy. Our entry was not a decision in which I myself played any part. It was, however, a decision made after a whole decade of fierce public and private argument – a decision made by the previous Prime Minister, the present Prime Minister and the present Foreign Secretary.

Thirdly, I did not resign because that was not what the Prime Minister wanted. When the Prime Minister reappointed me after the general election, I told him two things: first, that I did not wish to remain Chancellor for very long; and, secondly, that he did not owe me any debt or any obligation. On 16 September he made it clear to me in writing that he had no intention of resigning himself, and that I should not do so either.

Of course, I discussed the question further with the Prime Minister subsequently. In all those discussions he emphasised that he regarded the attacks on me as coded attacks on himself, so I decided that my duty and loyalty was to the Prime Minister and that I should remain in office.

Two and a half years ago, I did play some part in helping the Prime Minister into the position that he occupies today.[20] I have always believed, and still believe, that in supporting him then I made the right choice, and I now wish to say one thing to him; it goes to the heart of the way in which the Government conduct themselves. There is something wrong with the way in which we make our decisions. The Government listen too much to the pollsters and the party managers. The trouble is that they are not even very good at politics, and they are entering too much into policy decisions. As a result, there is too much short-termism, too much reacting to events, and not enough shaping of events. We give the impression of being in office but not in power. Far too many important decisions are made for 36 hours' publicity. Yes, we are politicians as well as policy-makers; but we are also the trustees of the nation. I believe that in politics one should decide what is right and then decide the presentation, not the other way round. Unless this approach is changed, the Government will not survive, and will not deserve to survive.

It is a great change to return to the back benches after fourteen years in government, Madam Speaker, but I have always been proud to be a member of this House and not just a Minister. Today, when I walked through Westminster Hall and up the stairs into the Lobby, I felt exactly the same pride and excitement as when I first entered this House 21 years ago. I look forward with anticipation to the great parliamentary events and battles that lie ahead.

Lamont's own verdict is that his speech changed very little and that the government limped on, much as it always had. But his own career never recovered. Furious at a put-down by Douglas Hurd in a debate on a Labour motion of no confidence in the government, he voted with the opposition, and later supported John Redwood's unsuccessful leadership challenge to Major. But when boundary changes erased his Kingston seat, he was unable to win selection in the successor constituency. He was chosen as the candidate for marginal Harrogate only to be defeated by the Liberal Democrats.

Perhaps this speech is best viewed as the final section of a triptych of resignation statements by three Conservative Chancellors or ex-Chancellors: Lawson, Howe and Lamont. Each in different ways had been forced from office by party tensions over European Monetary Union. Lawson and Howe had wanted it; Lamont, who was much more sceptical, was broken by it. His would not be the last career to be claimed by it.

'Iraq probably has no weapons of mass destruction in the commonly understood sense of the term.'

Robin Cook resigns over the Iraq war: 17 March 2003

Day in, day out, over the long years of opposition, Robin Cook was one of Labour's deadliest parliamentary performers. In the mid 1980s, the sketch-writer Edward Pearce wrote in praise of his 'contemptuous authority, [and] dry epigrammatical style'.[21]

He shone less often on the government front bench. As Foreign Secretary he created New Labour's 'ethical foreign policy' and was much mocked whenever it was thought pragmatism overrode principle. As Leader of the House in Tony Blair's second term, he presided over substantial modernisation of the working practices of the Commons, but came unstuck over House of Lords reform, when the House failed to endorse any option for reconstituting the second chamber. He remained, though, a deadly parliamentary performer, and the question time which followed his weekly statement on the forthcoming business of the House was a showcase for his trademark wit and precision. Increasingly, in his final months in office, these qualities were used to deflect questions aimed at exposing his discomfiture with Tony Blair's support for a US invasion of Iraq. In his final business questions appearance, almost his final comment was that collective Cabinet responsibility for the impending attack on Iraq would 'apply to all who are in the Cabinet at the time'. The message was unmistakable.

In this speech, his parliamentary virtues were turned against the government he had just left. 'This was a speech that had been brewing inside me for two months,' he wrote in his diaries.[22] 'I was only glad that at last I could speak honestly.'

THIS IS THE FIRST TIME for 20 years that I have addressed the House from the back benches. I must confess that I had forgotten how much better the view is from here. None of those 20 years were more enjoyable or more rewarding than the past two, in which I have had the immense privilege of serving this House as Leader of the House, which were made all the more enjoyable, Mr Speaker, by the opportunity of working closely with you.

It was frequently the necessity for me as Leader of the House to talk my way out of accusations that a statement had been preceded by a press interview. On this occasion I can say with complete confidence that no press interview has been given before this statement. I have chosen to address the House first on why I cannot support a war without international agreement or domestic support.

The present Prime Minister is the most successful leader of the Labour Party in my lifetime. I hope that he will continue to be the leader of our party, and I hope that he will continue to be successful. I have no sympathy with, and I will give no comfort to, those who want to use this crisis to displace him.

I applaud the heroic efforts that the Prime Minister has made in trying to secure a second resolution. I do not think that anybody could have done better than the Foreign Secretary in working to get support for a second resolution within the Security Council. But the very intensity of those attempts underlines how important it was to succeed. Now that those attempts have failed, we cannot pretend that getting a second resolution was of no importance.

France has been at the receiving end of bucketloads of commentary in recent days. It is not France alone that wants more time for inspections. Germany wants more time for inspections; Russia wants more time for inspections; indeed, at no time have we signed up even the minimum necessary to carry a second resolution. We delude ourselves if we think that the degree of international hostility is all the result of President Chirac. The reality is that Britain is being asked to embark on a war without agreement in any of the international bodies of which we are a leading partner – not NATO, not the European Union and, now, not the Security Council.

To end up in such diplomatic weakness is a serious reverse. Only a year ago, we and the United States were part of a coalition against terrorism that was wider and more diverse than I would ever have imagined possible. History will be astonished at the diplomatic miscalculations that led so quickly to the disintegration of that powerful coalition. The US can afford to go it alone, but Britain is not a superpower. Our interests are best protected not by unilateral action but by multilateral agreement and a world order governed by rules. Yet tonight the international partnerships most important to us are weakened: the European Union is divided; the Security Council is in stalemate. Those are heavy casualties of a war in which a shot has yet to be fired.

I have heard some parallels between military action in these circumstances and the military action that we took in Kosovo. There was no doubt about the multilateral support that we had for the action that we took in Kosovo. It was supported by NATO; it was supported by the European Union; it was supported by every single one of the seven neighbours in the region. France and Germany were our active allies. It is precisely because we have none of that support in this case that it was all the more important to get agreement in the Security Council as the last hope of demonstrating international agreement.

The legal basis for our action in Kosovo was the need to respond to an urgent and compelling humanitarian crisis. Our difficulty in getting support this time is that neither the international community nor the British public is persuaded that there is an urgent and compelling reason for this military action in Iraq.

The threshold for war should always be high. None of us can predict the death toll of civilians from the forthcoming bombardment of Iraq, but the US warning of a bombing campaign that will 'shock and awe' makes it likely that casualties will be numbered at least in the thousands. I am confident that British servicemen and women will acquit themselves with professionalism and with courage. I hope that they all come back. I hope that Saddam, even now, will quit Baghdad and avert war, but it is false to argue that only those who support war support our troops. It is entirely legitimate to support our troops while seeking an alternative to the conflict that will put those troops at risk.

Nor is it fair to accuse those of us who want longer for inspections of not having an alternative strategy. For four years as Foreign Secretary I was partly responsible for the western strategy of containment. Over the past decade that strategy destroyed more weapons than in the Gulf war, dismantled Iraq's nuclear weapons programme and halted Saddam's medium and long-range missiles programmes. Iraq's military strength is now less than half its size than at the time of the last Gulf war.

Ironically, it is only because Iraq's military forces are so weak that we can even contemplate its invasion. Some advocates of conflict claim that Saddam's forces are so weak, so demoralised and so badly equipped that the war will be over in a few days. We cannot base our military strategy on the assumption that Saddam is weak and at the same time justify pre-emptive action on the claim that he is a threat.

Iraq probably has no weapons of mass destruction in the commonly understood sense of the term – namely a credible device capable of being delivered against a strategic city target. It probably still has biological toxins and battlefield chemical munitions, but it has had them since the 1980s when US companies sold Saddam anthrax agents and the then British Government approved chemical and munitions factories. Why is it now so urgent that we should take military action to disarm a military capacity that has been there for 20 years, and which we helped to create? Why is it necessary to resort to war this week, while Saddam's ambition to complete his weapons programme is blocked by the presence of UN inspectors?

Only a couple of weeks ago, Hans Blix [the UN's chief weapons inspector, supervising, or attempting to supervise, Iraqi compliance with the UN resolutions requiring them to dismantle their nuclear, chemical and biological weapons capabilities] told the Security Council that the key remaining disarmament tasks could be completed within months. I have heard it said that Iraq has had not months but twelve years in which to complete disarmament, and that our patience is exhausted. Yet it is more than 30 years since resolution 242 called on Israel to withdraw from the occupied territories. We do not express the same impatience with the persistent refusal of Israel to comply. I welcome the strong personal commitment that the Prime Minister has given to Middle East peace, but Britain's positive role in the Middle East does not redress the strong sense of injustice throughout the Muslim world at what it sees as one rule for the allies of the US and another rule for the rest.

Nor is our credibility helped by the appearance that our partners in Washington are less interested in disarmament than they are in regime change in Iraq. That explains why any evidence that inspections may be showing progress is greeted in Washington not with satisfaction but with consternation: it reduces the case for war.

What has come to trouble me most over past weeks is the suspicion that if the hanging chads in Florida had gone the other way and Al Gore had been elected, we would not now be about to commit British troops.

The longer that I have served in this place, the greater the respect I have for the good sense and collective wisdom of the British people. On Iraq, I believe that the prevailing mood of the British people is sound. They do not doubt that Saddam is a brutal dictator, but they are not persuaded that he is a clear and present danger to Britain. They want inspections to be given a chance, and they suspect that they are being pushed too quickly into conflict by a US Administration with an agenda of its own. Above all, they are uneasy at Britain going out on a limb on a military adventure without a broader international coalition and against the hostility of many of our traditional allies.

From the start of the present crisis, I have insisted, as Leader of the House, on the right of this place to vote on whether Britain should go to war. It has been a favourite theme of commentators that this House no longer occupies a central role in British politics. Nothing could better demonstrate that they are wrong than for this House to stop the commitment of troops in a war that has neither international agreement nor domestic support. I intend to join those tomorrow night who will vote against military action now. It is for that reason, and for that reason alone, and with a heavy heart, that I resign from the Government. [Applause.]

Hansard does not record it, but Cook's supporters gave him a standing ovation, in defiance of normal parliamentary protocol.

His colleagues on the left suspect he could have said a great deal more, but Cook carefully avoided too destructive an attack. Instead, his criticism of the case for war was notable for its precision and delicacy. At a stroke he became the most important anti-war voice in the Commons, but without destroying his prospects for a return to office, if not under Tony Blair, then under another leader who had supported the war. This was not the speech of a man whose career was behind him. His death in August 2005 deprived the Commons and the country of a great parliamentarian.

NOTES

Introduction

1   For a fuller account of this incident, see 'Almost in the Field of Human Conflict', Peter Hill, *House Magazine*, 28 March 1994.
2   The script survives in the BBC archives because the former minister Leslie Hore-Belisha was annoyed at the way his words had been reported, and embarked on a lengthy correspondence which was referred, as complaints from politicians routinely were, to the board of governors.
3   The letters from Butler and Hogg, along with the exchange of internal memos discussing the response to them, can be found in the BBC's archives at Caversham.
4   See 'The Good Old Days in the Gallery', Peter Hill, *British Journalism Review*, 1996, vol. 7, no. 1.
5   Quoted in an obituary for Thompson, by Peter Hill.

Chapter 1: Scandal and Crisis

1   *A Life at the Centre*, Roy Jenkins, Macmillan, 1991.
2   *George Wigg*, George Wigg, Michael Joseph, 1972.
3   Quoted in *Iain Macleod: A Biography*, Robert Shepherd, Hutchinson, 1994
4   Yuri Gagarin, the first man in space.
5   *George Wigg*, Wigg.
6   Patronage Secretary is one of the semi-official titles of the Chief Whip, then Martin Redmayne.
7   The Lord Chancellor, the former Sir Reginald Manningham-Buller, was asked by Macmillan to investigate.
8   Martin Redmayne, the Chief Whip; the Attorney General, Sir John Hobson; the Solicitor General, Peter Rawlinson; the Minister Without Portfolio, Bill Deedes; and Macleod, met Profumo for several hours on the night of George Wigg's speech.
9   *The Backbench Diaries of Richard Crossman*, Edited by Janet Morgan, Hamish Hamilton, 1981.
10 *The Perfomers: Politics as Theatre*, Norman Shrapnel, Constable, 1978.
11 *Palace of Varieties: An Insider's View of Westminster*, Julian Critchley, John Murray, 1989.
12 Charles Stewart Parnell, the leader of the Irish Nationalists in the Commons in the 1880s, was destroyed as a result of his affair with Kitty O'Shea, the wife of one of his MPs.
13 *The Times* had published its damning leading article, 'It *is* a Moral Issue', penned by its editor, Sir William Haley, the week before. The article warned ministers that there would be 'no hiding place from the tidal wave of overthrow and disaster . . . The Prime Minister and his colleagues can cling together and still be there a year hence. They will have to do more than that to justify themselves.'
14 This is rather hard on Keeler; she wasn't, really.
15 In 1957 Wilson, then shadow Chancellor, had alleged a leak of a decision to raise interest rates, which he said had allowed some speculators to make a killing on the Stock Exchange. Wilson accused Oliver Poole, Deputy Chairman of the Conservative Party, of involvement. A tribunal of inquiry under Lord Justice Parker was convened, and completely rejected the charges. It was a considerable humiliation for Wilson.
16 Interview with the author, 2005.

17 *Out of the Wilderness: Diaries, 1963–67,* Tony Benn, Hutchinson, 1987.

18 After retiring from the Commons, Rab Butler had become Chancellor of Cambridge University. Jenkins would eventually become Chancellor of Oxford University.

19 *A Life at the Centre,* Jenkins.

20 In 1978 Roy Mason announced an inquiry into police interrogation procedures in Northern Ireland, in the wake of a critical report by Amnesty International. The Bennett Report (Cmnd. 7497) was the result.

21 A South African scandal that involved the illegal spending of public funds, agreed secretly between the then Prime Minister, John Vorster; the head of the Bureau of State Security (BOSS), General Van der Berg; and the Information Minister, Connie Mulder, to influence media coverage of apartheid South Africa.

22 Maguire remained MP for Fermanagh and South Tyrone until 1981. He was succeeded by the hunger striker Bobby Sands, who died in prison less that a month later.

23 Having been considered a future Tory leader for nearly a decade, Maudling had become enmeshed in the Poulson corruption scandal. He served briefly in Thatcher's shadow Cabinet, but was clearly out of sympathy with her brand of Conservatism.

24 A weekend policy conference of Edward Heath's shadow Cabinet in January 1970. It launched what later came to be seen as a proto-Thatcherite policy agenda for the Tories.

25 Under amendments to the Scotland Act forced through by Labour rebels, the Scottish Parliament had to be approved not just by a majority of those voting, but by 40 per cent of the total Scottish electorate. The yes vote did not quite overcome this hurdle. Foot was offering to find a way to proceed with devolution by setting the 40 per cent requirement aside.

26 Geoffrey Prime, a junior official at GCHQ, had been convicted of spying for the Soviets.

27 The Argentine leader who ordered the invasion of the Falklands.

28 A former director general of GCHQ.

29 Leader of the Amalgamated Union of Engineering Workers.

30 The Cabinet Secretary, in charge of the intelligence services.

31 *The Time of My Life,* Denis Healey, Michael Joseph, 1989.

32 Presenter of Radio Four's *Today* programme.

33 A senior political journalist.

34 Duncan Campbell, a journalist who specialised in intelligence matters, who was the main researcher for the *Secret Society* series.

35 The parliamentary bible – the handbook on Commons procedure and precedent.

36 He was also Churchill's son-in-law and later a Cabinet minister.

37 Cook, who had been at university with Campbell, was one of the Labour MPs who sought to have the programmes shown in a Commons committee room.

38 Interview with the author, 2005.

39 The official guidelines for ministerial conduct.

40 Quoted in *Robin Cook,* John Kampfner, Gollancz, 1998.

Chapter 2: Virtuosos

1 Quoted in *Aneurin Bevan: 1945–1960,* Michael Foot, Davis-Poynter, 1973.

2 See *The Glory of Parliament,* Harry Boardman, edited by Francis Boyd, Allen & Unwin, 1960.

3 See *Iain Macleod,* Robert Shepherd, Hutchinson, 1994.

4 The Committee on Classification of Proprietary Medical Products, set up in 1948 to examine whether NHS prescription of some commercial medicines and other products should be limited, or banned.

5 Sir Stafford Cripps, then Chancellor of the Exchequer.

6 *Aneurin Bevan* Foot.

7 *The Lost Leaders,* Edward Pearce, Little, Brown, 1997

8 *Chips: The Diaries of Sir Henry Channon,* edited by Robert Rhodes James, Weidenfeld &

Nicolson, 1967.

9   *The Macmillan Diaries: The Cabinet Years, 1950–1957*. edited by Peter Catterall, Macmillan, 2003.

10   *The Performers: Politics as Theatre*,Norman Shrapnel, Constable, 1978.

11   The chamber of the Commons was destroyed by Luftwaffe bombs in 1941.

12   Lord Randolph Churchill, his father.

13   *The Price of My Soul*, Bernadette Devlin, Pan Books Ltd, 1969.

14   In the Stormont Parliament. Hume became Westminster MP for Foyle in 1983.

15   A prominent journalist.

16   Cooper was one of the few Protestant civil rights campaigners. He was later one of the founders of the SDLP.

17   Quoted in *The Time of My Life*, Denis Healey, Michael Joseph, 1989.

18   Margaret Thatcher had proclaimed in her conference speech that year that 'the Lady's not for turning'.

19   Gladstone's Midlothian campaign – a series of public meetings when he returned to the Commons in a by-election for this Scottish constituency in 1879 – was directed against Turkish atrocities in the Balkans at a time when Britain, under Disraeli, was protecting Turkey from Russian armies.

20   He was bald.

21   Formerly Sir Hartley Shawcross, Attorney General in the 1945 Labour government.He was supposed to have remarked (although he did not actually quite say it): 'We are the masters now.'

22   The Queen's Speech always contains a list of expected visits by other heads of state.

23   After a mauling in the 1999 European elections, Tony Blair declared that the third year of his administration would be 'the year of delivery', in which the promised improvements in the NHS and other services would be realised.

24   Blair was frequently criticised for his infrequent appearances in the Commons.

25   A slogan coined by Tony Blair (it was actually devised by Gordon Brown) when he was shadow Home Secretary.

26   At this point Hague was packaging Tory policies under the rubric the 'common sense revolution'.

27   The government wanted to limit defendants' rights to opt for a jury trial in circumstances where they could either appear before a magistrate or a Crown Court.

28   The wife of Lord Ivor Richard, former Leader of the Lords. She had recently published a diary covering the period when her husband was in the Cabinet.

29   The archetypal male middle-class voter, a term invented by pollsters.

30   Prescott was the proud owner of two Jaguars – hence his hated tabloid nickname 'Two Jags'.

31   *Free at Last: Diaries, 1991–2001*, Tony Benn, Hutchinson, 2002.

32   The first Independent Labour MP, and, in 1906, the first leader of the Labour Party.

33   The rather nebulous approach to government sometimes invoked by Tony Blair.

34   A French-made sea-skimming anti-ship missile, it was used to sink several British vessels during the Falklands War.

35   Richard Caborn had been a surprise appointment as Minister for Sport in the Department for Culture, Media and Sport. He had been unable to answer a number of quiz questions during an interview on BBC Radio Five Live.

36   Widow of Ian Macleod.

37   Formerly Sir Keith Joseph, Education Secretary in Mrs Thatcher's first government.

38   Shirley Williams, former Labour Cabinet minister and later SDP founder. Then Liberal Democrat leader in the Lords.

39   Then a candidate for the Conservative leadership.

40   Then a minister in the Department of Social Security.

Chapter 3: The Awkward Squad

1   Quoted in *Crossman: The Pursiut of Power*, Anthony Howard, Jonathan Cape, 1990.
2   Quoted in *Like the Roman: The Life of Enoch Powell*, Simon Heffer, Weidenfeld & Nicolson, 1998.
3   *Diaries: Into Politics, 1972–1982*, Alan Clark, Weidenfeld & Nicolson, 2000.
4   This assessment appears in *The Senate of Lilliput*, Edward Pearce, Faber, 1983.
5   Interviewed on *The Week in Westminster*, BBC Radio Four, April 2005.
6   *The Time of My Life*, Denis Healey, Michael Joseph, 1989.
7   *Acts of Defiance*, Jack Ashley, Reinhardt, 1992.
8   At this stage in his career, Powell was the Ulster Unionist MP for Down South.
9   Hansard, 15 February 1985.
10 Interview with the author, January 2005.
11 Which brought William Hague into Parliament.
12 The *General Belgrano* was an Argentine warship sunk during the Falklands War – Dalyell disputed the Government's assertion that it posed a threat to British forces. Hilda Murrell was an elderly peace campaigner whose mysterious murder gave rise to a number of conspiracy theories, which were eventually put to rest when DNA evidence led to the conviction of her killer in 2005.
13 *Ann Widdecombe: Right from the Beginning*, Nicholas Kochan, Politico's Publishing, 2004.
14 Sir John Woodcock had conducted an inquiry into the Whitemoor breakout. He was highly critical of individuals and procedures and recommended a long list of changes to improve security.
15 Interview with the author, 2005.

Chapter 4: War

1   *The Glory of Parliament*, Harry Boardman, edited by Francis Boyd, Allen & Unwin, 1960.
2   *The Time of My Life*, Denis Healey, Michael Joseph, 1989.
3   *Diaries 1980–2001*, Giles Radice, Weidenfeld & Nicolson, 2004.
4   Rex Hunt, later knighted. He put on his full ceremonial uniform before leaving the Government House.
5   *Diaries: Into Politics, 1972–1982*, Alan Clark, Weidenfeld & Nicolson, 2000.
6   *The Battle for the Falklands*, Max Hastings and Simon Jenkins, Michael Joseph, 1983.
7   *Against Goliath*, David Steel, Weidenfeld & Nicolson, 1989.
8   Enoch Powell, who had spoken earlier, raised the question of whether the marines had been ordered to surrender if confronted with a force which outnumbered them. He had warned that an inquiry would be needed to establish whether the 'consequent infamy to this country' was the result of such orders.
9   The government had been proposing cuts to the Royal Navy.
10 *Diaries*, Radice.
11 Shirley Williams, Baroness Williams of Crosby. A former Labour Education Secretary, she was one of the SDP's founding 'Gang of Four' along with Jenkins, and at this point leader of the Liberal Democrat peers.
12 *30 Days: A Month at the Heart of Blair's War*, Peter Stothard, HarperCollins, 2003.

Chapter 5: Culture Wars

1   A more detailed account of Harvey's case can be found in *Great Parliamentary Scandals: Four Centuries of Calumny, Smear and Innuendo*, Matthew Parris, Robson Books, 1995.
2   *Private Member*, Leo Abse, Macdonald, 1973.

3 Interview with the author, 2005.

4 A former Home Secretary who had previously been a senior civil servant and served as Permanent Under-Secretary at the Home Office.

5 A former Solicitor-General, Attorney General and Home Secretary. Then, as Lord Kilmuir, he was Lord Chancellor.

6 Interview with the author, 2005.

7 Professor Arthur Goodhart KBE, QC, Master of University College, Oxford, and editor of the *Law Quarterly Review*. Two of his sons entered Parliament: Sir Philip Goodhart as a Conservative MP, and William Goodhart as a Liberal Democrat peer.

8 *The Macmillan Diaries: The Cabinet Years, 1950–1957*, edited by Peter Catterall, Macmillan, 2003.

9 *The Art of the Possible*, R. A. Butler, Hamish Hamilton, 1971.

10 Quoted in 'The Good Old Days in the Gallery', Peter Hill, *British Journalism Review*, 1996, vol. 7, no. 1.

11 The change in the law in 1885 that first criminalised homosexuality. It was originated by the Liberal MP Henry du Pré Labouchere.

12 Former Lord Chancellors. A similar bill to Berkeley's had been put before the Lords by Lord Arran. Kilmuir was provoked to warn their lordships of the dangers of 'sodomitic societies,' and 'buggery clubs'.

13 He was a Liberal MP in the 1940s.

14 MP for Cheadle 1966–70 and briefly for Hazel Grove between the elections of February and October 1974. Winstanley was a well-known TV personality, presenting the Granada TV consumer programme *This Is Your Right*.

15 *Chance Witness: An Outsider's Life in Politics*, Matthew Parris, Viking, 2002.

16 *Breaking the Code: Westminster Diaries 1992–97*, Gyles Brandreth, Weidenfeld & Nicolson, 1999.

17 *Breaking the Code*, Brandreth. Brandreth was a supporter of the Currie amendment.

18 The Labour MP and future Cabinet minister Chris Smith was then the only openly gay member of the Commons.

19 The Secretary of State for Social Security.

20 Quoted in *Servants of the People*, Andrew Rawnsley, Hamish Hamilton, 2000.

21 Gareth Williams, Lord Williams of Mostyn, then a Home Office minister, and later Leader of the Lords.

22 Labour MP for Middlesbrough. In the 2001–05 Parliament, he spoke for the Church commissioners in the Commons.

23 Then leader of the Conservative Party.

24 Larry Whitty, former General Secretary of the Labour Party and now a minister in Defra, the Department for Environment, Food and Rural Affairs.

25 Jackie Ballard, Liberal Democrat MP for Taunton 1997–2001, was defeated, largely on this issue, by the Conservative Adrian Flook.

26 Bernard Donoughue, former special adviser to Harold Wilson and James Callaghan in Downing Street, who served as a minister in the old Department of Agriculture during Tony Blair's first term. When he left the government, he opposed a ban on hunting.

Chapter 6: Money

1 Formerly Sir John Simon, veteran Liberal lawyer-politician and Attorney General under Asquith, he was Foreign Secretary in the Tory-dominated National Government and Lord Chancellor (outside the War Cabinet) in Churchill's wartime coalition.

2 *The Glory of Parliament*, Harry Boardman, edited by Francis Boyd, Allen & Unwin, 1960.

3 Viscount Herbert Samuel, a Liberal peer and former Cabinet minister.

4 Quoted in *NAB 1: Portrait of a Politician*, Gerald Nabarro, Robert Maxwell/Pergammon

Press, 1969.

5   Quoted in *Harold Macmillan 1957–1986*, Alistair Horne, Macmillan, 1989.

6   John Davies, a former director general of the CBI, had been promoted to the Cabinet by
     Heath after only a few weeks in the Commons, in the reshuffle which followed the death of
     Iain Macleod. The Ministry of Technology (MinTec), which he headed, was soon to morph
     into the Department of Trade and Industry.

7   Nicholas Ridley, the Conservative MP for Cirencester, had circulated a paper calling for a
     complete end to government support for UCS. It had been obtained by Benn, who leaked
     it to the *Guardian*. But it was not the policy of the Heath government.

8   Buchanan was MP for Glasgow Springburn 1964–79. His successor was the current Speaker,
     Michael Martin.

9   Noted as the Commons' leading anti-royalist. MP for Central Fife, 1950–87, he won the seat
     from the Communist Willie Gallagher.

10   *Against the Tide: Diaries, 1973–76*, Tony Benn, Hutchinson, 1989.

11   Interview with the author, 2005.

12   *Conflicts of Interest: Diaries, 1977–80*, Tony Benn, Hutchinson, 1990.

13   Money received for the sale of publicly owned assets – in particular the huge sums made by
     local authorities from the sale of council houses – which at the time the government
     required them to use to pay off debt.

14   The shadow Chancellor John Smith was proposing to fund expensive Labour promises to
     increase pensions and child benefit through income tax and National Insurance increases,
     at a dinner with journalists, Kinnock indiscreetly mentioned the option of phasing in the
     NI increases, to help blunt Conservative attacks on the policy. Smith was infuriated and
     rejected the idea, leaving Kinnock in an awkward position.

15   *Life in the Jungle*, Michael Heseltine, Hodder & Stoughton, 2000.

16   John Major made the 'classless society' one of his slogans.

Chapter 7: Europe

1   Reginald Maudling. He had been shadow Foreign Secretary in opposition, but when Heath
     formed his government in 1970, he gave the Foreign Office to his former boss Alec Douglas-
     Home, who was notably more pro-European than Maudling.

2   *The Course of My Life*, Edward Heath, Hodder & Stoughton, 1998.

3   The Dispatch Box, from which ministers and opposition spokesmen address the House.

4   An anecdote that appears in a number of Heath's speeches about Europe over several
     decades.

5   Quoted in *Memoirs*, Douglas Hurd, Little, Brown, 2003.

6   Later an SDP defector and now a Liberal Democrat peer.

7   *Diaries*, Alan Clark, Weidenfeld & Nicolson, 1993.

8   *Diaries 1980–2001*, Giles Radice, Weidenfeld & Nicolson, 2004.

9   The Queen's Speech.

10   Sillars had been a Labour MP in the 1970s, before joining the short-lived breakaway Scottish
     Labour Party, and ultimately the SNP, for whom he won Glasgow Govan in a by-election.
     He lost his seat in the 1992 general election.

11   *Breaking the Code: Westminster Diaries 1992–97*, Gyles Brandreth, Weidenfeld & Nicolson,
     1999.

12   *John Major: The Autobiography*, John Major, HarperCollins, 1999.

13   *Memoirs*, Hurd.

14   Interview with the author, 2005.

15   Tony Benn's Commonwealth of Britain Bill would have put in place a republican
     constitution for Britain.

16   Home Secretary Kenneth Baker's Dangerous Dogs Bill.

Chapter 8: Resignations

1   Quoted in *Aneurin Bevan: 1945–1960*, Michael Foot, Davis-Poynter, 1973.

2   *Chips: The Diaries of Sir Henry Channon*, edited by Robert Rhodes James, Weidenfeld & Nicolson, 1967.

3   Quoted in *Mr Speaker: The Memoirs of Viscount Tonypandy*, George Thomas, Century, 1985.

4   An idea later implemented by Harold Wilson when he set up the Department of Economic Affairs on Labour's return to power in 1964.

5   The cuts in pensions and unemployment benefits proposed by Ramsay MacDonald and his Chancellor Philip Snowden, which first split the Labour government, then led to MacDonald forming a National Government with Conservative support, shattering Labour in the process.

6   *The Glory of Parliament*, Harry Boardman, edited by Francis Boyd, Allen & Unwin, 1960.

7   *The Political Diary of Hugh Dalton*, edited by Ben Pimlott, Jonathan Cape, 1986.

8   Sir Alan Walters had resigned in response to Lawson's departure.

9   See *The View from No. 11: Memoirs of a Tory Radical*, Nigel Lawson, Bantam, 1992.

10   *Diaries*, Alan Clark, Weidenfeld & Nicolson, 1993.

11   *Diaries, 1980–2001*, Giles Radice, Weidenfeld and Nicholson, 2004.

12   *The Downing Street Years*, Margaret Thatcher, HarperCollins, 1993.

13   *In Office*, Norman Lamont, Little, Brown, 1999.

14   At the time, the Department of Environment covered housing and local government.

15   *Breaking the Code: Westminster Diaries, 1992–97*, Gyles Brandreth, Weidenfeld & Nicolson, 1999.

16   *Diaries*, Radice.

17   One politician who was convinced, however, was Gordon Brown. He made the Bank of England independent immediately after taking office in 1997.

18   Chancellor in the postwar Labour government, serving from October 1947 to October 1950. He devalued sterling from \$4.10 to \$2.80.

19   James Callaghan served as Chancellor under Harold Wilson from 1964–67 from \$2.80 to \$2.40. He offered his resignation at the time, but it was not immediately accepted. Instead he was moved to the Home Office. This was the devaluation which gave rise to Wilson's famous phrase about the value of 'the pound in your pocket'.

20   Lamont had been Major's campaign manager in the 1990 Conservative leadership election.

21   *Hummingbirds and Hyenas*, Edward Pearce, Faber and Faber, 1985.

22   *The Point of Departure: Diaries From the Front Bench*, Robin Cook, Simon & Schuster, 2003.

INDEX